Principles
of
Risk Management
and
Insurance

Volume I

Principles
of
Risk Management
and
Insurance
Volume I

C. ARTHUR WILLIAMS, JR., Ph.D.

Minnesota Insurance Industry
Professor of Economics and Insurance
University of Minnesota

GEORGE L. HEAD, Ph.D., CPCU, CLU

Director—Risk Management/Loss Control Education
American Institute for Property and Liability Underwriters

RONALD C. HORN, Ph.D., CPCU, CLU

Professor of Insurance and Professional Studies
Baylor University

G. WILLIAM GLENDENNING, Ph.D., CPCU

Professor of Insurance and Risk
Temple University

Second Edition • 1981

AMERICAN INSTITUTE FOR
PROPERTY AND LIABILITY UNDERWRITERS
Providence and Sugartown Roads, Malvern, Pennsylvania 19355

Foreword

The American Institute for Property and Liability Underwriters and the Insurance Institute of America are companion, nonprofit, educational organizations supported by the property-liability insurance industry. Their purpose is to provide quality continuing education programs for insurance personnel.

The Insurance Institute of America offers programs leading to the Certificate in General Insurance, the Associate in Claims (AIC) designation, the Associate in Management (AIM) designation, the Associate in Risk Management (ARM) designation, the Associate in Underwriting (AIU) designation, the Associate in Loss Control Management (ALCM) designation, the Associate in Premium Auditing (APA) designation, and the Accredited Adviser in Insurance (AAI) designation. The American Institute develops, maintains, and administers the educational program leading to the Chartered Property Casualty Underwriter (CPCU) professional designation.

Throughout the history of the CPCU program an annual updating of parts of the course of study took place. But as changes in the insurance industry came about at an increasingly rapid pace, and as the world in which insurance operates grew increasingly complex, it became clear that a thorough, fundamental revision of the CPCU curriculum was necessary. This text is the second edition of one of those which were written for, and published by, the American Institute for use in the revised ten-semester CPCU curriculum which was introduced in 1978.

Throughout the development of the CPCU text series, it was—and will continue to be—necessary to draw on the knowledge and skills of Institute staff members. These individuals will receive no royalties on texts sold and their writing responsibilities are seen as an integral part of their professional duties. We have proceeded in this way to avoid any possibility of conflicts of interests. All Institute textbooks have been—

and will continue to be—subjected to an extensive review process. Reviewers are drawn from both industry and academic ranks.

We welcome criticisms of our publications. Such comments should be directed to the curriculum department of the Institutes.

Edwin S. Overman, Ph.D., CPCU
President

Preface

Like its predecessor, the second edition of this text is designed for one of the four risk management and insurance courses in the revised ten-course Chartered Property Casualty Underwriter (CPCU) curriculum introduced in 1978. Although the course for which this text has been written is called CPCU 1, this course is not necessarily intended to be a prerequisite to other CPCU courses. Its purpose is to present the basic principles of risk management and insurance. Other CPCU courses apply these principles in the contexts of specific loss exposures and insurance contracts.

The text is divided into two volumes. The first volume focuses primarily on the principles of risk management. Risk management involves the identification, measurement, and treatment of the loss exposures of a business or other organization, a family, or an individual. Insurance exists because consumers use this technique, among others, to treat loss exposures. In addition to delving into the insurance mechanism, which is the major concern of the CPCU curriculum, it is also appropriate for the student to learn some fundamentals about the process of which insurance is a part. This perspective will give the student a deeper, more balanced understanding of the nature of insurance, its advantages and disadvantages as a risk management technique, its contributions and costs to society, and its possibilities for future growth.

Chapter 1 describes in some detail the major classes of loss exposures faced by an economic unit and the key steps in the risk management process. Chapters 2 and 3 explore the nature, advantages, and disadvantages of the various control and financing techniques that can be used by risk managers. Insurance is one of the financing techniques. Chapters 4 and 5 deal with measuring loss exposures and how the risk manager can select the most appropriate set of techniques for a given exposure. In Chapters 6 and 7 the emphasis changes from risk management to the insurance technique and the ways it affects and is affected by the economic, political, and social environment in which it operates.

Volume II explores several subjects that need to be thoroughly understood in order to grasp fully the significance of many provisions found in insurance contracts. For some students, this volume may serve as an effective introduction to a more detailed study of specific coverages; for others, it may help to enhance an understanding of subjects that have already been studied, by emphasizing the principles underlying practical applications.

Chapter 8 examines the subject of insurable interests. Chapter 9 describes the structure of insurance contracts and introduces a framework for coverage analysis. This framework is used throughout the remainder of Volume II, which examines insured entities (last section of Chapter 9), insured events (Chapter 10), amounts of recovery (Chapters 11, 12, and 13), and contract conditions affecting insurance coverage (Chapter 14). In Chapter 15, this same framework is applied to one specific insurance contract—the standard fire policy.

Both volumes differ from the original edition in that they have been rewritten to decrease repetition and improve readability. The sequencing of some topics has been substantially revised. In addition, nearly all of the first edition material on tort law, and some of the discussions of life and health insurance principles have been removed. Tort law will be covered in the second edition of the CPCU 6 text, *The Legal Environment of Insurance.* Life and health insurance principles will now be covered primarily in the CPCU 2 text, *Personal Risk Management and Insurance.*

No review or discussion questions appear in this text. These are included in a companion study aid—the *CPCU 1 Course Guide.* The Course Guide, which is revised annually, contains educational objectives, outlines of study material, key terms and concepts, review questions, and discussion questions. Special study suggestions are also included for many assignments.

Any attempt to distill into two volumes the complex principles and practices that are the subject of this text will necessarily result in oversimplifications. The authors also recognize that the text may contain factual errors, especially if the facts have changed since the text was written—almost a certainty in such dynamic fields as risk management and insurance. Though we have tried to minimize such problems, we invite students and other readers to send us their comments and criticisms, in order that we may improve future editions. Comments received on the first edition have greatly aided us in the preparation of the second edition. We are also deeply interested in the usefulness of this text as a learning device. Accordingly, we would also welcome constructive comments on how we may improve our presentation of the material. All comments should be directed to the curriculum department of the American Institute.

In the revision of this text, our efforts were aided by many individuals who acted as reviewers. The authors wish to thank these persons, especially Terence Atkins, Publicity and Information Department, Lloyd's of London; Carl T. Ernstrom, CPCU, CLU, ARM, President, Ernstrom Associates, Inc.; Thomas E. Green, CPCU, CLU, Director of Education, Wausau Insurance Companies; Wallace R. Hanson, CPCU, Assistant Vice President and Educational Director, Property Loss Research Bureau; John D. Horton, CPCU, ARM, Manager Forms Simplification, St. Paul Fire and Marine Insurance Co.; Harry M. Kelsey, LL.B., CPCU, ARM, AIM, AIC, ALCM, Risk Management Consultant, John A. Soderberg Co.; A. Hunter Long, CPCU, CLU, ARM, Vice President, Frank B. Hall & Company, Inc.; and Douglas M. Temple, CPCU, Professor of Business Administration, Golden Gate University.

Two current CPCU candidates provided valuable comments from a student's perspective by reviewing Chapters 4 and 5: Bruce D. Miller, AIC, AIM, Claims Examiner, Erie Insurance Exchange; and Roger H. Perrymore, Broker, Herkness, Peyton, & Bishop.

The first edition of this text benefited from the work of four contributing authors: Walter F. Berdal, Associate Professor of Insurance and Law (Retired), Georgia State University; John R. Lewis, Ph.D., CPCU, CLU, Risk Management, Insurance and Real Estate, College of Business, The Florida State University; G. D. Seidl, CPCU, CLU, AIC, Legal Counsel, United Fire & Casualty Company; and Andrew F. Whitman, Ph.D., CLU, Professor of Finance and Insurance, University of Minnesota. The text continues to benefit from the work of these contributing authors. The original edition of Volume I also benefited during the planning stages from the comments of Professor Robert I. Mehr, Professor of Finance, University of Illinois. We also wish to acknowledge the important contributions of the many authors whose writings are cited in the text.

C. Arthur Williams, Jr.
George L. Head
Ronald C. Horn
G. William Glendenning

Table of Contents

CHAPTER 1

Loss Exposures and Risk Management

INTRODUCTION

Risk management is the treatment of loss exposures. Insurance is one very important technique used to treat loss exposures, but other techniques are used as well. Much of the CPCU curriculum deals with insurance. This course begins with a study of the reason risk management and insurance exist—exposures to loss and the need to treat them.

After examining the nature of loss exposures, this chapter will discuss the effective treatment of these exposures and the importance of risk management to individuals, families, businesses or other organizations, and society. For the sake of simplicity, the term "firm" or "business" will generally be used in this text to include a business, a nonprofit organization, or a public agency. "Family" will be used to include individuals, as well as nontraditional living arrangements. "Entity" will be used, where necessary, as a broad term covering both firms and families.

This chapter will also analyze the objectives of risk management, outline the steps in the risk management process, describe where and how the risk management function is performed, and evaluate the contributions of effective risk management to families, firms, and society. The chapter will close with a brief discussion of the impact of both the process and the function of risk management on insurer activities.

LOSS EXPOSURES

A *loss exposure* is a set of circumstances that presents a possibility of loss, *whether or not a loss actually takes place.* Even a child with an ice cream cone is aware of loss exposures. The ice cream cone *could* be accidentally dropped. It *could* be grabbed by a bigger child. Or, it *could* melt before it has been consumed, in which case a portion of the cone will fail to serve its intended purpose.

The ice cream cone represents a loss exposure whether or not it is dropped, is stolen, or melts. Losses that actually occur, as well as the uncertainty about possible losses, create problems described later in this chapter. To be considered here are

- the elements of a loss exposure,
- the distinction between pure and speculative loss exposures,
- some useful terms and concepts relating to loss exposures, and
- the relationship between loss exposures and "risk."

Elements of a Loss Exposure

A loss exposure has three elements:

(1) the item subject to loss (the ice cream cone),
(2) the perils, or forces that may cause the loss (dropping the cone on the ground), and
(3) the potential financial impact of the loss (50¢, unless it was double-dipped).

Element One—The Item Subject to Loss The term "loss" implies the existence of something that may decline in value or lose value. An orderly approach to the treatment of loss exposures demands, as a starting point, rigorous and thorough identification of precisely what is subject to loss.

Items subject to loss can be listed or classified in a number of ways. One classification approach divides items subject to loss into

assets—owned things of value, and
income—what is produced by assets.

Regardless of the specific type of loss—fire damage to a home, disability of a wage earner, or a prolonged hospital stay of a school child—the result to the family bearing the loss ultimately will take the form of either a reduction in or claim against asset values, or a reduction in or claim against future income, or both.

A second approach classifies items subject to loss as:

(1) property and its use,
(2) freedom from legal obligation, or
(3) personal health or earning capacity.

Examples can logically fit under either approach. The value of a store building is a category (1) item here, involving property or its use; under the first approach, it would involve both assets and income. The potential for being legally responsible for injuries suffered by another falls into category (2) here and into either or both of the asset-income categories. The income of a family breadwinner falls into category (3) here and into the income item of the previous division.

Either approach may be helpful in identifying loss exposures. However, the second is sometimes considered to be more useful than the first in tying loss exposures to possible treatments.

Element Two—Perils The first element of a loss exposure—the item subject to loss—dealt with *what* can be adversely affected. This second element deals with what can cause or bring about the adverse result. In the jargon of risk management and insurance, the word "peril" is used to refer to possible loss causes. A *peril*, then, is a *potential cause of loss*.

Perils may be grouped according to their origin as either (1) natural, (2) human, or (3) economic.

> *Natural perils* include fire, windstorm, hail, flood, earthquake, volcanic eruption, and sickness.
>
> *Human perils* (also referred to as "man-made perils") include theft, riot, homicide, vandalism, negligence, and failure for any reason such as incompetence, misfortune, dishonesty to satisfy an expressed obligation to another. Note that these perils are *totally* human in origin.
>
> *Economic perils* (also referred to as "business perils," or "acts of men and governments") include recessions, inflation, changes in consumer tastes, technological advances, and stock market declines.

Of course, these categories may overlap. Most fires, for example, are due to human carelessness.

Later sections of this text, as well as other CPCU courses, deal with perils at length. However, a few specific points are important here: (1) perils are the second element of loss exposures; (2) perils may be of importance to a firm or family whether they are insurable or not (loss causes do not cease to threaten economic well-being merely because they fall outside the realm of insurance); and (3) perils must be identified and analyzed in a particular context. What is regarded as a peril for one purpose might be viewed differently in another context.

Collision, for example, would be a peril in the context of considering what might happen to affect adversely the value of an asset such as an auto. From the point of view of the personal earning capacity (income) of the auto owner, however, we would tend to look at death or disability as perils and not focus on ways (an auto collision, for example) in which death or disability might occur.

Element Three—Potential Financial Impact This third element of a loss exposure is quantitative and a logical sequel to the first two elements. If some item of value is exposed, and if a peril occurs adversely affecting that value, the family or firm is faced with a decline in or disappearance of value of some magnitude. What magnitude? That question, or rather the answer to it, is essential in developing a rational approach to risk management.

A fundamental point here is that it is necessary to avoid drawing conclusions based on dollar amounts of loss alone. Whether a loss "hurts" financially is not a function of absolute loss size, but of loss size relative to the financial condition of the party suffering the loss. What would constitute a "severe" financial impact varies both among families and firms and over time for the same family or firm. A $1,000 loss might be catastrophic for a recently laid off family head but would be of virtually no significance to a large firm.

It should also be noted that some loss exposures cause nonfinancial "hurt." While these are important, particularly to the individual suffering pain as the result of an accident, most risk management is directed at potential losses that can be measured in financial terms.

Pure and Speculative Loss Exposures

Loss exposures may be classified as pure or speculative. The distinction is important because risk management is confined almost entirely to treating pure loss exposures.

Definitions "Loss exposure" has already been defined as a set of circumstances that presents a possibility of loss, whether or not a loss actually takes place.

Pure Loss Exposures. A pure loss exposure is one characterized by only two types of possible outcome—(1) loss or (2) no loss. Stated differently, to the entity facing the exposure, the possible outcomes are adverse (loss) or neutral (no loss), but in no case beneficial. A pure loss exposure involves no opportunity for gain. The nonoccurrence of a loss-causing peril means only maintenance of the status quo.

Consider, for example, the owner of a building subject to damage or destruction from the peril of explosion. *Absence* of an explosion causes no change in the financial status of the owner. This maintenance of the owner's existing financial position is the most favorable financial outcome insofar as the event under consideration—possible explosion damage to the building—is concerned. (The owner, of course, could gain because of an increase in the value of the building, but any gain would be due to other factors, such as a general rise in real estate values, and not to the mere fact that an explosion did not occur.) Should a damaging explosion occur, the entire range of potential loss magnitudes represents unfavorable outcomes.

The threat of physical damage to property does not *always* produce a pure loss exposure, but the exceptions are rare. As one example, the total loss of an old building might be more than offset by the increase in the value of the land on which the building was located. This could happen if land is worth more as a vacant lot, on which a new building can be constructed, than it is with the old building on it.

Speculative Loss Exposures. A speculative loss exposure is characterized by the presence of an *additional* type of possible outcome—financial gain. In addition to the potential for adverse and neutral outcomes, speculative exposures have inherent in them the chance of bettering the financial status of a family or business. An illustration is the exposure created by the development and marketing of a new product by a business firm. The product may have no appeal to prospective buyers in the marketplace, in which case the firm will lose its investment in the product. On the other hand, the product may turn out to be extremely popular, producing large profits for the firm. A second example is the exposure to loss that is created when a business or family invests in a common stock or a corporate or municipal bond. A third is the exposure that a roulette player faces at a Las Vegas casino. The player can leave the table a winner, a loser, or economically unaffected by the activity.

As noted above, pure loss exposures are the major concern of this course. Insurers deal almost exclusively with pure loss exposures.

Other Characteristics of Pure and Speculative Loss Exposures Pure loss exposures are always distasteful for the business or family exposed to loss; the best outcome is no change. If possible, one would like to avoid pure loss exposures. Speculative loss exposures, on the other hand, offer an opportunity for gain. They are sometimes avoided because of their loss potential, but they are more often intentionally created because of this potential for gain.

Usually no one benefits from losses arising out of pure loss exposures. Generally, there are no winners and no socially beneficial results except, perhaps, in the case of stolen or misplaced property. Here, the thief or finder is a winner, and it might be argued that society gains if the property is worth more to the thief or finder than to the victim. However, this argument ignores the moral issues involved.

The situation is different with speculative loss exposures. Someone else generally benefits when a business or a family suffers a loss from a speculative exposure. The market share lost by one business may be gained by another, and if there is a loser in a poker game, there is at least one winner. Society may gain on balance if the winners' gains are more important than the losers' losses. For example, a technological change may destroy one industry, create a new one, and on balance benefit consumers.

Coexistence of Both Classes of Loss Exposures In setting up pure and speculative as a classification basis for loss exposures, there is a danger of implying that the two types of exposures are mutually exclusive. This is not the case. In the typical business setting, at least, the two categories commonly exist at the same time. To illustrate, assume that a business has built a new plant. The firm is faced with the possibilities that the new building will be damaged or destroyed by fire, flood, explosion, or some other peril. These are pure loss exposures. At the same time, the firm faces the possibility that the plant building may change in value because of inflation or changing economic conditions in the area. There is also a possible rise or fall of business profits because of the expanded production facilities. These last two exposures are speculative.

The fact that both categories may exist simultaneously does not diminish the usefulness of separating them conceptually. As explained earlier, the two categories have different characteristics, and for this reason deserve and receive separate treatment. At the same time, the relationship between the two must be recognized. Economic well-being can be adversely affected by both, the same assets and income often are subject to losses flowing from both, and success in managing or treating one type of loss exposure may be instrumental in, or essential to, an entity's ability to deal with the other.

"Risk" and Its Synonyms

The word "risk" is used sparingly in this text and throughout the CPCU curriculum. Fundamentally, in insurance literature and practice, "risk" has been used to mean so many things that for the authors of this text to choose one definition would be arbitrary, unrealistic, and presumptuous. To use the term with multiple meanings would be confusing. Further, for each of the multiple meanings there is another term available that is at least as acceptable as "risk." The term "risk management" will be used, however, because this term is widely accepted and because a risk manager is concerned with all the meanings of "risk."

This section of Chapter 1 defines the more precise terms that will be used *instead of* "risk." The following terms are also highly important in themselves. They form part of the basic vocabulary of risk management and insurance that is used throughout the CPCU program.

"Risk" is used in risk management and insurance literature and practice to mean (1) the possibility of loss, (2) the probability of loss, (3) a peril, (4) a hazard, (5) the property or person exposed to damage or loss, (6) potential losses, (7) variation in potential losses, and (8) uncertainty concerning loss.

Possibility of Loss When a family, firm, or society faces the possibility of a loss, this possibility or state of being exposed to loss is often called a "risk." According to this usage, one faces the "risk" or possibility of a fire loss, a windstorm loss, or a liability loss. People who use this definition generally claim that "risk" cannot be measured. It either exists or does not exist.

Probability of Loss A related usage defines "risk" as the probability or chance of loss. The probability of loss is the relative likelihood that a loss will occur within some stipulated time span. According to this definition, "risk" can be measured.

Probability of loss varies between 0 and 1. If the probability of loss is 0, no loss can occur. If the probability of loss is 1, a loss is certain to occur. For other values such as 1/4, 1/2, or 3/4, the probability of loss indicates how likely it is that the loss will occur. The closer the probability of loss is to 1, the more likely it is that a loss will occur.

If "risk" is defined as the probability of loss and the "risk" of an explosion during the next year is estimated to be 1/3, this would mean that, on the average, one would expect an explosion loss to occur once every three years. The probability of loss is an important element in pricing insurance, underwriting insurance, and deciding whether to recommend insurance in a particular situation. This concept and its uses will be explored in greater depth in Chapter 4.

Peril A frequent practice is to define "risk" as a peril or a cause of loss. Examples of perils are fire, explosion, being held legally liable for a loss suffered by another, or death. Persons who define "risk" as a peril would speak of fire, explosion, legal liability, or death as "risks." Perhaps the most common use of the term "risk" to mean peril is in the use of "all-risks" to describe property insurance contracts that cover loss from all causes of physical loss or damage (i.e., perils) except those that are excluded.

Hazard   A fourth definition relates "risk" to hazard—a condition that increases the probability or likely magnitude of loss arising from some peril. Hazards are commonly divided into three categories:

- A *moral hazard* is a condition that exists when a person may try intentionally to cause a loss or may exaggerate a loss that has occurred. It refers to a defect or weakness in human character that may result in a loss occurring or being enlarged beyond its true value or duration. Property insured in excess of its value to the owner may give rise to moral hazard because it presents the property owner with an incentive for "arson for profit."

- A *morale hazard* is a condition that exists when a person is less careful than he or she should be. Carelessness with property that may increase the probability of a theft loss is an example of a morale hazard. (Note that the morale hazard lies in the carelessness, not in the fact that property is physically exposed to the theft peril.)

- A *physical hazard* is a tangible characteristic of property, persons, or operations that increases the likelihood or severity of loss. Inadequate ventilation in a painting area that increases the probability of an explosion would be a physical hazard.

Although some authors refer to the above conditions or characteristics as "risks," in the CPCU program they are more precisely referred to as hazards.

The Property or Person Exposed to Damage or Loss   Insurance practitioners often refer to the property or person exposed to damage or loss as a "risk." The insurance underwriter may speak of "risk characteristics" when evaluating a building as a subject of fire insurance applied for by the building owner. Drivers who cannot secure auto insurance through normal channels are often referred to as "assigned risks." An applicant for life insurance who has a physical condition resulting in a rate surcharge might be called a "substandard risk."

Potential Losses   The potential losses to which property or persons are exposed are sometimes called "risks." Thus, some writers refer to a "property risk," an "income risk," a "liability risk," or a "health and earning capacity risk."

Variation in Potential Losses   A seventh meaning of "risk" is the variation in potential losses. In a sense, *potential* losses, which *may* occur, but have not yet occurred, cannot vary. If they have not occurred, one might argue, how can they be different from (show variation from) anything at all? This can be clarified by noting that variation, as used here, refers to a *range* of possible outcomes and the ability to predict which outcome will result.

To illustrate this concept, assume that a business may experience employee injuries during the coming year ranging from no losses up to a very large number of losses, and that all of these possibilities have about the same probability or chance of occurring. The "risk" (by this meaning) or variation in the potential number of losses is great. Under these circumstances, it is impossible to predict with any confidence whatsoever how many losses will actually occur. Assume that in a second case the number of annual employee injuries can also range from zero to a very large number but, in the past experience of the employer, the number has usually been somewhere between forty and forty-five. In this case the "risk" or variation is much smaller; it is still impossible to predict how many losses will actually occur, but it is possible to predict with considerable confidence, though not with certainty, that the number of losses will be between forty and forty-five.

A few additional observations will clarify the concept of variation in potential losses, which is important regardless of its label. First, variation in potential losses may be related to the *number or frequency of losses* during the forecast period, the *dollar amount or severity of each individual loss* during that period, or the *aggregate dollar amount of all losses* over the period. To illustrate, the possible number of accidents may range from 0 to 100. The dollar loss associated with any individual accident may vary between $0 and $10,000. If so, the possible aggregate dollar losses would vary between $0 and 100 times $10,000, or $1 million.

Second, as when "risk" means the probability of loss, "risk" (using this definition) is measurable. "Risk" also has zero as its minimum value, as when "risk" means the probability of loss. When "risk" is zero, there is no variation. There is only one outcome and consequently no prediction problem. Unlike probability of loss, however, which has a maximum value of 1, variation in potential losses has no maximum value. Furthermore, unlike the probability of loss, whose measure has an intuitive interpretation (for example, 2/5 means two losses on the average every five periods), this "risk" measure has no such simple meaning.

Third, "risk" defined as variation in potential losses is *not* the same as probability of loss. Assume that the probability of loss is 1, meaning that there will be a loss. Variation in potential losses is zero because there is only one outcome and consequently no variation.

Uncertainty Concerning Loss When potential losses vary, or are believed to vary, a person is uncertain or doubtful about his or her ability to predict the future. This eighth definition equates "risk" with a person's conscious awareness of a variation in what might happen. Because two persons may have different information concerning potential losses or may interpret information differently, their uncertainty can vary greatly—even if they are exposed to the same potential losses. This doubt concerning ability to predict the future is an extremely important concept because it influences many risk management and insurance decisions.

WHY MANAGE LOSS EXPOSURES?

The search for security existed long before insurance. Why have businesses, families, and society been so concerned about the management of exposures to loss? Basically, there are two reasons, both of which will be explained in more detail in the following pages:

(1) the costs that arise out of the losses that actually occur, and
(2) the costs that arise out of the fact that losses might occur.

For pure loss exposures, which are the major concern of the CPCU curriculum, these costs are particularly disturbing because there are no offsetting gains or possible benefits. Speculative loss exposures also involve these costs, but may also produce great benefits for businesses, families, and society.

The following analysis of these two types of cost assumes that the persons exposed to losses have taken no steps to deal with them. In other words, they bear these costs themselves. Later, the text will discuss how these exposures might be managed.

Cost of Losses That Actually Occur

For some entities facing the possibility of a loss, the possibility will become a reality. The financial impact that results will range from minor inconveniences or setbacks to losses that cause the breakup of the business or family. The impact of the loss will depend on its magnitude and the ability of the entity to absorb the loss.

For example, the loss of $1,000 may cause a family to skip some vacation plans or not to purchase a color television. A loss of $200,000 might cause that same family to sell their home, forgo college plans for the older children, and send the younger children to live with relatives. For a family with few resources prior to the loss, even the $1,000 loss could lead to severe disruptions in their lifestyle.

Businesses may suffer similar inconveniences and catastrophes.

Small losses may cause minor fluctuations in the firm's profitability or operating margin; larger losses may threaten its continued survival.

Society as a whole loses when its members suffer financial losses that are not offset by gains to other members of society. Society loses directly because society is the sum of its parts, and one or more parts are worse off than they were previously. Society loses indirectly if the affected parts pay less tax because of their losses, if prices rise because total production in society is lessened, if welfare or other special assistance costs rise, or if there is social unrest because the lives of the affected society members are disrupted.

There are other than financial effects on society when a loss occurs. Damaged property must be repaired or replaced. Material and human resources will be consumed in this repair or replacement. The loss of use of the damaged property is also a resource loss. If people become disabled or die, the loss of their services is a loss to society. At a time when society has become highly concerned about the shortage of natural resources and the value of human resources, these nonfinancial losses take on increased significance.

Cost of Losses That Might Occur

Relatively few businesses or families actually suffer severe losses arising out of pure exposures. However, all who are exposed to a particular type of loss may fear they will be among the unfortunate few to suffer a loss. This uncertainty causes physical and mental strain and leads to less than optimum use of resources.

Physical and Mental Strain Uncertainty affects how people feel. It generates fear and worry, which disturbs the peace of mind of those exposed to loss. The effect varies depending on the degree of uncertainty, the magnitude of the potential loss, the ability of the entity to bear the loss, and the personalities of the individuals facing the potential loss. The strain may harm a person's health and disrupt his or her personal and professional life.

Less Than Optimum Use of Resources This cost of uncertainty results from how the firms and families behave as a result of the fear and worry generated by exposures to loss. This cost affects both individual entities and also society as a whole.

Individual Entities. Individual firms and families may respond to uncertainty in many ways. They may avoid certain activities, shorten their planning horizons, or maintain excessive liquidity, as illustrated in the following examples.

- *Activities avoided.* Certain desirable activities may be avoided because of the possibility of loss involved. For example, a family might decide against purchasing a summer home in the mountains because of the fear of vandalism or fire, even though on all other counts the purchase might be a wise investment. Similarly, despite some obvious advantages to owning a car, a person might elect not to own one because of the loss exposures associated with the ownership, maintenance, or operation of a motor vehicle. Doctors might change their careers because of the threat of malpractice suits. A business might postpone or abandon its plans to manufacture a new product after it considers the possibility of being held legally responsible for injuries the product may cause.

- *Planning horizons shortened.* Faced with potential losses that threaten hard times or continued survival, families and businesses tend to concentrate on short-range rather than long-range planning. However, what is best in the short run often is not best in the long run. For example, in the short run it may be best to rent a building instead of owning it; in the long run, ownership may be best.

- *Excessive concern for liquidity.* To prepare themselves to meet potential losses, businesses and families may "hoard" resources in liquid or quasi-liquid form that might have been more productively employed elsewhere. For example, instead of purchasing modern machinery, expanding sales territories, or establishing training programs for employees—all of which might produce a greater rate of return—a firm might invest the equivalent amount in a lower-yielding "rainy day" bank account. Thus, capital is diverted to a "safe" use in order to have it available to meet losses that may or may not occur.

Even though a firm's or family's behavior might not be influenced greatly by the presence of loss exposures, others on whom the entity depends may be affected. Suppliers or customers may not be willing to enter into long-term relationships with a firm whose future is uncertain. Lenders may hesitate to extend credit to families or firms whose ability to repay the loan is questionable.

All of the foregoing adverse effects are compounded because of the sometimes irrational behavior patterns of businesses and families. For example, they may insure exposures involving relatively small loss potential while neglecting exposures with catastrophic potential. This irrationality occurs largely because of difficulties in evaluating loss exposures. Another contributing factor, however, is the seemingly inexplicable ways in which some people react to uncertainty. To the objective observer, some appear foolhardy, others unduly conservative.

Society as a Whole. Society is composed of a multitude of individuals, families, businesses, institutions, and government bodies. To the extent that possible losses cause these entities to make decisions that tend to allocate resources to less than optimum uses, society as a whole reflects that misallocation and is victimized by it. For example, business firms exposed to loss (and thus allocating resources inefficiently) may be able to protect themselves in part by raising prices to consumers. Prices tend to become higher and production tends to be lower than it would be in the absence of uncertainty.

Uncertainty tends to disturb the inherent tendency of the economic system to achieve optimum balance. Decision makers demand a higher rate of return on uses of their resources characterized by economic uncertainty. Too many resources tend to flow to relatively "safe" uses, and too few to uses fraught with uncertainty. The price structure is distorted, and consumers are faced with an overabundance of products and services resulting from "safe" uses of resources but not enough products and services from uses in which uncertainty is high. (The relationship among prices, output levels, and market conditions is explored in greater detail in CPCU 9.)

RISK MANAGEMENT

Effective risk management can reduce the costs of loss exposures. Risk management is a *process* that uses physical and human resources to accomplish certain objectives concerning most pure loss exposures. It can also be defined as a *function* performed by risk managers—as discussed later in this chapter.

The risk management process can be described as a series of steps:

1. identifying and analyzing loss exposures,
2. selecting the technique or combination of techniques to be used to handle each exposure,
3. implementing the techniques chosen, and
4. monitoring the decisions made and implementing appropriate changes.

Some writers subdivide one or more of these four steps. For example, the first step may be divided into two steps: identification of the loss exposures and measurement of these exposures. The number of steps is arbitrary. It is important, however, to include the complete process from loss exposure identification to making necessary modifications.

This section will explain the types of loss exposure handled by risk managers and the objectives of risk management.

Types of Loss Exposure Handled

In a broad sense, all personal and business activities in which the future is unknown involve the management of loss exposures. In this chapter, risk management has been identified with pure loss exposures, yet there is no logical reason why the term could not embrace the management of speculative loss exposures as well. The management of pure loss exposures, however, has become a function requiring specialized knowledge and skills and for which certain unique techniques such as insurance are available.

A pioneer in the development of risk management, although rarely credited as such, was a prominent French authority on general management, Henri Fayol. As early as 1916, Fayol recognized "the security activity" as one of the six basic activities of an industrial undertaking. Fayol stated that the object of the security activity

> ... is to safeguard property and persons against theft, fire and flood, to ward off strikes and felonies and broadly all social disturbances or natural disturbances liable to endanger the progress and even the life of the business. It is the master's eye, the watchdog of the one-man business, the police or the army in the case of the state. It is generally speaking all measures conferring security upon the undertaking and requisite peace of mind upon the personnel.[1]

If Fayol's terminology had been accepted, the treatment of pure loss exposures would today be called "security management." Such is not the case. Why not? Perhaps it is because Fayol's explanation emphasized the safety and prevention aspects of the security function. Or, perhaps it is because Fayol in his definition omitted any specific reference to insurance management, a major part of risk management. Perhaps it is because, to many people, "security management" suggests only guards, electronic alarm systems, and locked doors. Whatever the reason, the label did not gain widespread acceptance.

Apparently the term "risk management" first surfaced in the fifties, but it did not receive much general acceptance until the sixties. Whereas "security management" was perhaps too narrow a term, "risk management" is too broad. It suggests management of *all* loss exposures. The term, however, has appealed to those engaged in this activity, and others have not objected, at least explicitly. One now sees the term on company organization charts; in insurance company, agency, and broker advertisements; and in the relevant literature.

In 1975, the American Society of Insurance Management, Inc. (ASIM), an organization composed mainly of persons who perform the risk management function for large organizations, changed its name to the Risk and Insurance Management Society, Inc. (RIMS). The name change should accelerate the acceptance of the risk management label.

On the other hand, by including "Risk and Insurance Management" in their title instead of simply "Risk Management," the Society recognized that the latter term is far from universally accepted and that in many organizations "risk management" is still essentially "insurance management."

An educational "Program in Risk Management" originated in 1965 under the joint sponsorship of the Insurance Institute of America (IIA) and the Risk and Insurance Management Society (then ASIM). In 1978, this three-semester program became the Associate in Risk Management program, and those who successfully complete it are awarded the ARM (Associate in Risk Management) designation. By the end of 1980, approximately 3,500 people—many of them CPCUs—had earned the ARM designation. The Associate in Risk Management program and the ARM designation have been significant factors in developing professionalism in, and recognition of, "risk management."

Pure loss exposures are the major concern of risk management. But not all management of pure loss exposures is risk management. Earlier in this section, it was stated that risk management is a process concerned with *most* pure loss exposures. *Some* pure loss exposures are not within the operating scope of risk management as commonly practiced. To illustrate, protecting a manufacturer against damages to its own products as a result of faulty employee processing is usually, but not always, a function of production management, not risk management.

The management of speculative loss exposures is rarely, if ever, considered risk management. However, as noted earlier, pure and speculative loss exposures often coexist. Facts concerning one type of exposure will influence, or force the need to make, decisions on the other. For example, the choice between producing new product A and new product B should be influenced by both the pure and the speculative loss exposures associated with each alternative.

In addition to dealing with pure loss exposures of their firms, the risk management departments of some firms also deal with pure loss exposures of employees through employee benefit plans. The nature and extent of this involvement are indicated later in this chapter.

Objectives of Risk Management

Risk management has been defined in this section as a process that uses physical and human resources to accomplish certain objectives concerning most pure loss exposures. What are these objectives? The discussion that follows is based largely on suggestions made in 1974 by Professors Robert I. Mehr and Bob A. Hedges, who classified the objectives of risk management according to whether they are (1) pre-loss objectives or (2) post-loss objectives:

> In analyzing risk management objectives, it is productive to consider them in two categories: preloss and postloss. What are the organization's objectives with respect to losses which have not yet happened (and which may never happen)? What are its objectives as to losses which have [just] happened? In the great majority of cases, the preloss objectives relate to economy and to avoidance of anxiety, while postloss objectives relate to the completeness and speed of recovery. Together, they produce the predominant risk management goal; an economical preloss assurance that postloss recovery will be satisfactory. [2]

Post-Loss Objectives   There are five possible post-loss objectives primarily related to how completely and quickly the entity wishes to recover from loss. These objectives include (1) survival, (2) continuity of operations, (3) earnings stability, (4) continued growth, and (5) social responsibility.

Survival.   Survival is the most important and basic post-loss objective. The entity wants to arrange matters in such a way that it will be able to resume at least part of its operations after some reasonable time if it should choose to do so. However, a firm or family that barely survives a loss may be left with considerably fewer assets than the entity had before the loss.

Continuity of Operations.   A more ambitious objective is continuity of operations. Such continuity is sometimes mandatory, as in the case of a public utility which is obligated to provide continuous service. Some businesses reason that it is important for them to continue to serve their clients or customers who might otherwise turn to competitors for products or services and never return. Instead of seeking total continuity of operations, their goal may be operation on at least some partial scale, or resumption of operations after a period of interruption not exceeding a stated duration.

Earnings Stability.   Earnings stability may be achieved by continuing operations at no increase in cost, by providing funds to replace earnings lost because of an interruption in operations, or by some combination of these two approaches. Perfect stability is not usually the goal; instead, some variation within a specified range may be acceptable.

Earnings stability and continuity of operations are not the same. Which of the two is more difficult to attain depends upon the circumstances. Continuity of operations may be achieved at the expense of earnings. On the other hand, in some cases, earnings may be stabilized even when operations cannot be continued. Continuing operations requires human and material resources as well as money.

Continued Growth. A firm that desires to continue its growth pattern seeks to do more than continue its operations and stabilize its earnings, although these two objectives complement the goal of continued growth. Continued growth may in addition require a strong liquidity position or the ability to spend a great deal of money on research, development, and promotion.

Social Responsibility. Seldom does an accidental loss affect only the head of a family, the officers or owners of a business, or the heads of a private or public agency. Employees, customers, suppliers, taxpayers, relatives, members of the general public—all may be affected. A social consciousness or sense of moral responsibility may result in a goal that the impact on others be minimal. This same objective also may be supported by public relations considerations—the importance of maintaining a good image. To achieve the public relations image, it is not only necessary to do good but to *appear* to do good.

A firm can achieve some satisfaction of its social responsibility objectives and some favorable public reactions with a risk management program that protects customers, suppliers, employees, and the general public against losses resulting from disruptions in the firm's operations or from injuries to their persons or property caused by the activities of the firm.

Pre-Loss Objectives With respect to losses that *may* happen, the entity's risk management objectives may include: (1) economy, (2) reduction of anxiety, (3) meeting externally imposed responsibilities, and (4) social responsibility.

Economy. The firm seeks to prepare for what may happen in the most economical way that is consistent with its post-loss goals. Some costs of losses that might occur have already been discussed in a context that assumed loss exposures go untreated. Treating loss exposures generates additional costs of preparing for losses—such as safety program expenses, insurance premiums, and the time spent analyzing the potential losses and ways in which these losses might be handled.

Reduction in Anxiety. Mention has already been made of the physical and mental strain created because of uncertainty, and of the various costs associated with this anxiety. The second pre-loss goal is to reduce this anxiety or fear and worry. Mehr and Hedges call this objective "a quiet night's sleep."[3]

Peace of mind comes from knowing that the firm has undertaken to identify all of its pure loss exposures and has considered carefully what to do about them. This peace of mind not only contributes to the mental and physical health of the management, but also permits them to devote more attention to other business uncertainties.

Meeting Externally Imposed Obligations. Risk management, like other management functions, must satisfy some responsibilities imposed by others. For example, government regulations may establish safety standards that force a business to replace some old equipment or to install safety guards. Changes in an employee-benefit plan may be dictated by a collective bargaining agreement. A secured creditor may require insurance on property used as collateral.

Social Responsibility. The final pre-loss objective repeats the post-loss objective of good citizenship or social responsibility. Society as a whole is affected not only by the losses that do occur but by the threat that losses may occur. Consequently, measures taken prior to the loss contribute to the security of society. Concern for one's image, social consciousness, or both, may be the reasons for this objective.

Conflicts Among Objectives These pre-loss and post-loss objectives are interrelated. Consequently, an entity may discover that it is impossible to fully achieve all its objectives simultaneously. Sometimes the post-loss objectives are not consistent with one another. More commonly, the post-loss objectives conflict with the pre-loss objectives or the pre-loss objectives compete with one another.

To achieve any or all of the post-loss objectives costs money. The post-loss objectives, therefore, may conflict with the *economy* pre-loss objectives. The more ambitious and costly the post-loss objectives, the greater the conflict.

The *economy* objective may also conflict with the *reduction in anxiety* objective. To obtain a "quiet night's sleep," the risk manager must be confident that the post-loss objectives will be achieved. This confidence costs money—to purchase insurance, to install guards on machinery and thus prevent industrial accidents, to maintain duplicate copies of records in case the originals are destroyed, and the like.

Externally imposed obligations and *social responsibilities* may also conflict with the *economy* objective. Some externally imposed obligations (such as safety standards dictated by building codes) may be nonnegotiable; others, such as employee benefit obligations subject to collective bargaining agreements, may be negotiable. Generally, in the short run, externally imposed obligations must be accepted as a rule of the game. Meeting social responsibilities may raise costs in the short run but yield dividends in the long run.

Because of these conflicts, difficult trade-offs are always necessary. How these trade-offs are determined will be discussed in the next section in the context of how the risk manager selects the risk management techniques to use in a given situation.

THE RISK MANAGEMENT PROCESS

As stated previously, the risk management process consists of four steps:

1. identifying and analyzing loss exposures,
2. selecting the technique or combination of techniques to be used to handle each exposure,
3. implementing the techniques chosen, and
4. monitoring the decisions made and implementing appropriate changes.

Each of these four steps is analyzed in more detail in the following pages.

Identification and Analysis of Loss Exposures

Identifying and analyzing the losses to which a family or firm is exposed consists of (1) identifying things of value exposed to loss and perils that can cause loss, and (2) obtaining information on (a) how likely it is that losses will occur and (b) if they do occur, how severe they will be.

Identifying Things of Value Exposed to Loss, and Perils That Can Cause Loss Identifying these elements of loss exposures is a most important and difficult task. It is important because one can treat intelligently only the exposures one knows about. If an exposure is not treated, any losses that occur will have to be borne by the exposed entity itself. This may, or may not, have been the best way to handle the exposure. The loss may be catastrophic, and even the minimal post-loss objective of survival may not be achieved.

Identification is a difficult process because it is easy to overlook an exposure and because exposures are constantly changing. For these reasons, identification must be both a systematic and a continuing process. To systematize the process, several approaches have been suggested, including the checklist approach, the financial statement approach, the flowchart approach, and personal inspections.

Checklist Approach. A checklist is a prepared form listing many of the typical pure loss exposures that frequently exist for a family or firm. Such checklists are available from insurers, the American Management Association, the Risk and Insurance Management Society (RIMS), and commercial publishers. A portion of the RIMS checklist is shown in Exhibit 1-1.

Risk managers, however, may prefer to develop their own forms

Exhibit 1-1
Contents Schedule*

CONTENTS SCHEDULE

Schedule number: _____
Location number: _____
Building number: _____

1. Machinery, equipment, tools, and dies:
   a. Replacement cost new _____
   b. Actual cash value _____
   c. Basis for (b)—obtain appraisal if available _____

   d. Any chattel mortgage? _____
      Name _____
      Address _____

2. Furniture and fixtures, equipment, and supplies:
   a. Replacement cost new _____
   b. Actual cash value _____
   c. Basis for (b)—obtain appraisal if available _____

   d. Any chattel mortgage: _____
      Name _____
      Address _____

3. Improvements and betterments:
   a. Date installed _____
   b. Original cost _____
   c. Replacement cost _____

d. Actual cash value _____

e. Describe _____

f. Obtain appraisal if available _____

4. Stock (raw, in process, and finished):

   a. Maximum—at cost _____ at selling price _____

   b. Maximum—at cost _____ at selling price _____

   c. Average—at cost _____ at selling price _____

   d. Present—at cost _____ at selling price _____

   e. How and when inventoried _____

   f. Any fluctuations between buildings _____

5. Property of others for repair, processing, or other purpose (including goods held on consignment): _____

6. Is there any agreement covering your responsibilities for these values? _____

7. Property of concessionaires: _____ Consignors: _____

8. Employee's belongings: _____

9. Valuable papers or drawings:

   a. Value _____ Reproduction cost _____

   b. Where kept _____

   c. Description _____

10. Value of exhibits—sales office: _____

11. Describe type, size and value of signs:

   a. On premises _____

   b. At other locations _____

12. Care, custody, or control problems:

   Property in bailment _____

   Any warehouseman's legal liability? _____

   Innkeeper's legal liability? _____

13. Water damage and sprinkler leakage exposure, including flood exposure, distance from nearest mass of water and height above water, and percentage of contents value subject to loss: _____

Continued on next page

14. Earthquake exposure and amount subject to loss: _____

15. Any unusual cameras, scientific equipment or valuable instruments: _____

16. Any fine arts in office? _____ If so, secure appraisals.

17. Any data processing equipment? _____
    a. If owned, indicate value _____
       If leased, secure copy of rental agreement _____
    b. If leased, who is responsible for damage or destruction? _____

    c. Cost to replace data stored in destroyed units _____

    d. Are duplicate cards and tapes maintained? _____
       Where? _____

    e. Any potential business interruption exposure? _____
    f. Any use by other? _____ If so, qualifications of senior personnel _____

    g. Secure copy of contract form used and estimate liability exposure _____

18. Is stock subject to:
    a. Consequential loss _____
    b. Crime loss _____
    c. Damage by heat or cold _____

19. Animals, if any: _____

20. Crops, if any: _____

*This contents schedule was prepared by and is reprinted with the permission of the Risk and Insurance Management Society.

because published checklists are often limited to loss exposures that can be insured, whereas the risk manager's concern is much broader. In addition, published checklists may not organize the information in a manner that is most useful to the risk manager. For example, the risk manager may prefer to classify loss exposures according to

(1) property and its use,
(2) freedom from legal obligation, or
(3) personal health or earning capacity.

Few published checklists organize the exposures this way. Most tend to arrange them according to the types of insurance available, using categories such as transportation exposures, fire exposures, boiler and machinery exposures, and crime exposures.

After selecting or designing a checklist, it must be applied to the particular firm or family. The purpose of this step is to provide a systematic review of all property, activities, and personnel to determine which of the potential exposures in the checklist are faced by the particular entity. (The term "activities" as used here relates to exposures centering on freedom from legal obligation. Thus, in determining if a liability exposure exists, the *activities* of the family or firm deserve scrutiny.)

For a family, the checklist approach may be relatively simple because its exposures are much fewer and less complex than those of a business. Nevertheless, the property, activities, and people subject to loss should be reviewed in as orderly a manner as possible to avoid overlooking any exposures.

Financial Statement Approach. Under the financial statement approach, the risk manager asks, with respect to each item in the financial statements (for example, balance sheet, operating statement, and budget), what loss exposures it indicates and what information concerning other loss exposures it suggests might be obtained else-where within the firm.[4] For example, finished goods inventory in the balance sheet of a manufacturing firm indicates a property loss exposure. It also suggests the existence of a manufacturing process that generates income, the existence of raw materials used in the process, and the fact that a product is sold to others to whom it might be potentially injurious. Thus, a particular entry on a financial statement can serve as a key to identify exposures other than that indicated by the entry itself.

Flowchart Approach. Under the flowchart approach, charts are constructed showing in detail all operations of the business or other organization.[5] For example, a flowchart for a manufacturer may show all operations starting with purchase of the raw materials and ending with delivery of the finished product to the ultimate consumer. Both the various entries on the chart and the process(es) indicated by the sequence of entries on the chart provide the basis for the same kind of data gathering as that using financial statements. The chart will disclose what the organization does, the sequence in which it is done, and the nature and use of the resources necessary for doing it.

Personal Inspections. Whenever possible, other methods of identifying loss exposures should be supplemented by inspections or on-site visits by the risk manager. These inspections may be the initial source of information concerning certain exposures.

Other Approaches. Checklists, financial statements, flowchart analysis, and personal inspections can be supplemented with other approaches for identifying loss exposures. Some such approaches, discussed in greater detail in CPCU 3, include the exposure meter approach, the *Coverages Applicable* approach, the loss history approach, organizational chart analysis, and the use of a wide variety of published information.

To keep acquainted with newly developing loss exposures and the experience of others in this field, a business risk manager must continually survey the literature on risk management, insurance, and the firm's industry, and exchange views and experiences with the risk managers of similar firms.

Measuring Potential Frequency and Severity After a loss exposure has been identified, it must be measured, or analyzed as to potential frequency and severity. The risk manager would like to know the number of accidents that are likely to occur and how severe the dollar losses are likely to be. With respect to both the frequency and severity, he or she also would like to know whether the number of accidents and their severity tend to be about the same each year or whether they fluctuate greatly from year to year. In other words he or she would like to know the variation in the potential losses—related to number of accidents, dollar losses per accident, and total dollar losses per year.

This information helps the risk manager rank the exposures according to their importance and determine how best to handle them. For example, an exposure with the potential to bankrupt the firm is much more important than one with small loss potential. An exposure for which the loss experience tends to be the same year after year may create a budgeted operating expense, whereas an exposure subject to fluctuating experience may require some outside help. Chapters 4 and 5 will cover this subject in more detail.

Exhibit 1-2
Techniques for Treating Loss Exposures

CONTROL TECHNIQUES	FINANCING TECHNIQUES
Avoidance	Some Noninsurance Transfers
Loss Control	Insurance Transfers
Loss Prevention	Retention
Loss Reduction	
Separation	
Combination	
Some Noninsurance Transfers	

Selecting the Techniques

The techniques available can be divided into two classes as illustrated in Exhibit 1-2.

Control techniques attempt to change the exposure itself by reducing loss frequency, loss severity, or the annual variation in the potential losses. These techniques include

- avoidance
- loss control
- combination
- some transfers

Financing techniques are designed to provide funds to handle the losses that do occur. Financing techniques include

- most transfers including but not limited to insurance, and
- retention

Avoidance Avoiding the loss exposure is a control approach. The entity never acquires the exposure or, if it has the exposure, it causes the exposure to cease to exist. If the loss exposure arises out of the manufacture of some hazardous materials, the organization never enters that field or, if it is in that field, it ceases operations in that area. Avoidance focuses on either or both of the first two elements of a loss exposure—items subject to loss and forces that may cause the loss. When this control technique is used, the probability of loss remains or becomes zero.

Loss Control Like avoidance, loss control is designed to change the loss exposure itself by either reducing the frequency of occurrence of perils (loss prevention) or minimizing the adverse financial impact of such occurrences (loss reduction), or both. Because of the savings in human and material resources that may result, loss control efforts always deserve serious consideration. They may not, however, always pay off in success or in benefits that justify the costs. Unlike avoidance, loss control does *not* reduce the probability of loss to zero—some loss may still occur.

One special form of loss control is *separation*. Separation breaks up a loss exposure into more units. For example, instead of building one large warehouse exposed to fire, explosion, vandalism, and so on, a business might build many widely scattered smaller warehouses. In addition to reducing loss severity, separation makes future loss experience more predictable because it increases the number of exposure units.

Combination   Combination means the acquisition of more exposure units. Because the ability to predict depends in part on the availability of sufficient data on what has happened to independent exposure units, combination—like separation—enhances the predictability of future losses by increasing the number of exposure units. As a practical matter, combination is *not* used, except by insurers, merely to make future loss experience more predictable. Other objectives of the entity dictate the combination decision, with increased predictability of losses being simply a by-product.

Noninsurance Transfers   *Transfers* may be control techniques or financing techniques. The difference between these two types of transfer will be explained in Chapters 2 and 3. Here, the purpose is to establish the distinction between noninsurance transfers and insurance. Noninsurance transfers include:

(1) the transfer to another entity of all three elements of a specific loss exposure (item subject/perils/impact), or
(2) the transfer only of the third element of a loss exposure—potential financial impact.

Transfer of All Elements.   All elements of a loss exposure may be transferred through a gift or sale. For example, if a business that had been manufacturing hazardous materials sells its plant, equipment, process, market information, and so on, to some other business, it is employing a noninsurance transfer. Unlike avoidance, the exposure continues to exist, but it now rests with another entity. From the point of view of the transferring business, all losses involving either the property or the future manufacturing process are transferred to the other entity. Neither the remaining assets nor the income of the transferring firm are subject to such losses, and the associated perils inherent in the transferred exposure are no longer threats to the firm's economic well-being.

Transfer of Potential Financial Impact. Under the second type of noninsurance transfer, the financial consequences of the loss exposure—but not the exposure itself—are transferred to some other party. Examples would be transfers under a lease of responsibility for damage to rented premises from the landlord to the tenant, transfer under a purchase agreement of liability for defective products from a retailer to a manufacturer, or a transfer of the possibility that a borrower might not repay a loan from the lender to a guarantor who guarantees the loan. Like insurance, the noninsurance transfers deal with the financial consequences of a loss exposure. However, they differ in that noninsurance transfers do not possess the characteristics of insurance to be noted in the next section.

Insurance Insurance is a transfer technique. Insurance makes it possible to transfer the financial consequences of potential accidental losses from an insured firm or family to an insurer. Insurance is also a mechanism of sorts—a social device under which two or more persons make or promise to make contributions to a fund from which the insurer promises to make certain cash payments or render certain services to those contributors who suffer losses that are accidental from their point of view.

The special characteristic that distinguishes insurance from other transfers is that the insurer enters into similar arrangements with many other entities exposed to loss. Most, but not all, pure loss exposures can be the subject of insurance coverage. Proper use of the insurance technique is a key risk management responsibility.

Retention Retention is the last and most basic risk management technique to be discussed in this text. Retention is, simply, keeping or retaining all elements of the exposure. An entity that retains a loss exposure bears itself the financial consequences of any losses. If a business or a family does not transfer the potential financial consequences to someone else, it has retained them.

Retention may be the result of a conscious or an unconscious act. For example, failure to identify certain loss exposures means that the entity unconsciously decided to retain these loss exposures. Only by chance might this have been the best thing to do. On the other hand, the entity may have explored the various alternatives and consciously decided, for reasons to be developed in Chapter 3, that the best course of action was retention.

The term "self-insurance," which many persons consider to be a synonym for retention, has been studiously avoided in this discussion. The problems with this term will be explained in Chapter 3.

Determining Specific Objectives

Selecting among the above risk management techniques is a matter of determining which combination of techniques meets the optimum mix of post-loss and pre-loss objectives. Before beginning the selection process, it is necessary to state the entity's objectives in terms more specific than "survival," "growth," "economy," "a quiet night's sleep," and so on. The purpose here is to convert the various possible objectives from broad statements into meaningful criteria for the firm or family involved.

Specifying Post-Loss Objectives If the entity's most important objective is *survival,* what is meant by survival? In the case of a business, what minimum assets, both physical and human, must the firm have to survive? Generally, legal obligations such as debts for materials purchased or liability judgments will have to be satisfied. Assets such as premises, equipment, and inventory will be required to operate at the minimum level necessary for survival. This exact survival level must be determined in the individual case. Plans should probably be made for the continuation of some salaries in order that a nucleus of the pre-loss personnel is available during the immediate post-loss period. Finally, suppliers, creditors, customers, regulators, and the public must be convinced through extra public relations efforts following the loss that the business will in fact survive. Meeting the survival objective, therefore, can generally be restated in terms of the resources necessary to meet legal obligations, to provide some minimum productive capacity, to retain a minimum work force, and to convince outsiders that the business intends to and will be able to survive. The dollar requirements depend on the facts in the individual situation.

The *continuity of operations, earnings stability* and *continued growth* objectives can be restated similarly in terms of the resources needed to deal with the same four areas: legal obligations, productive capacity, work force, and public acceptance. Determining the necessary resources in each case requires specific statements by senior management with respect to the level at which the operations are to be continued, the permissible downward fluctuation level in monthly, quarterly, or annual earnings, or the desired rate of growth.

Specifying Pre-Loss Objectives The *economy* objective requires minimizing pre-loss costs consistent with achieving the selected post-loss objectives. These pre-loss costs must be measured. They include such items as opportunities forgone because of avoidance, the cost of applying loss control techniques, insurance premiums, and the time spent on negotiations with insurers or other transferees. The effect of taxes on these costs must be considered. For example, property insurance premiums are deductible expenses for a business but not for a family. Money set aside under a retention program to cover future property losses is not deductible by either a business or a family.

What it takes to *reduce anxiety* and obtain "a quiet night's sleep" depends largely upon the personality of the persons setting the goal. Some people seldom seem to worry even though they face substantial potential losses; others appear to worry about seemingly unimportant exposures. Some people worry in advance of a loss; others prefer a lifestyle that postpones the worry until a loss has occurred. Some people can relax as long as their risk management program compares favorably with that of others in a similar situation; others worry if their businesses or families are still exposed to some serious losses that other businesses or families seem willing to ignore.

Determining Trade-Offs Once the objectives have been re-stated in more specific terms, the risk management process requires evaluation of the trade-offs among the conflicting objectives. For example, if the cost of transferring certain serious but not catastrophic potential losses turns out to be very expensive, the risk manager may decide that survival is a more realistic objective than earnings stability.

The Selection Process

Three methods that have been suggested for selecting among risk management alternatives are (1) the insurance method, (2) the minimum expected loss method, and (3) capital budgeting.[6]

The Insurance Method Using the insurance method, the *first* step is to design an insurance program on the assumption that all loss exposures that can be insured are to be insured. The *second* step is to divide the types of insurance included in the program into three categories:

- essential
- desirable
- available

The *essential* category includes those types of insurance required by law (workers' compensation insurance, for example) or by contract (for example, property insurance required by mortgagee). It also includes insurance against those losses that would threaten the continued survival of the firm. (Liability insurance frequently falls in this class.)

Desirable insurance includes protection against losses that would cause the firm serious financial difficulties but from which it could be expected to recover. For example, some type of loss, though not potentially ruinous to the firm, might result in a reduction in earnings sufficient to interfere with the completion of new facilities already under construction.

Available insurance covers less serious losses including those that may simply inconvenience the business or family.

The *third* step is to review each type of insurance to see whether some other risk management tools—generally loss control, a noninsurance transfer, or retention—might be more appropriate than insurance or might be used in some combination with insurance.

Essential Insurance. For essential coverages that are required by law or by contract, the risk manager has no choice. For the other coverages in the essential category, retention is an unlikely alternative, because losses, if they occur, would threaten the continued existence of the business or the family. On the other hand, the risk manager may decide that, through a deductible provision in an insurance contract, it may be desirable to retain losses up to some amount consistent with the post-loss goals of the firm.

Loss control is unlikely to eliminate all possibility that such catastrophic losses will occur, but it may reduce the potential severity to such a level the insurance could be moved from the essential to the desirable category. In most instances, however, the risk manager probably will decide to purchase the insurance listed in this essential category. Even the minimum post-loss objective, that of survival, favors the purchase unless the premiums are unreasonably high. The motivation is even higher for the continuity of operations, earnings stability, growth, and "quiet night's sleep" objectives. The social responsibility objective also favors such a purchase.

Desirable Insurance. In reviewing the desirable insurance coverages, the risk manager is likely to conclude that loss control, a noninsurance transfer, or retention would be both feasible and desirable. Because premiums must be spent on the essential coverages, the premiums for the desirable coverages can create an additional burden. Because the potential losses are less serious, the worry or anxiety—though still present and perhaps still a most persuasive factor—is probably less. The survival objective has been satisfied by the essential coverages.

On the other hand—for a business or a family with important post-loss objectives relating to earnings stability, continuity of operations, or growth—much more than the essential coverages are required. Only if equally effective noninsurance transfers would be less costly, or if separate loss controls could at reasonable expense substantially reduce the impact of these potential losses, would the risk manager be likely to forgo insurance. Retention alone would be inappropriate because it would not be consistent with these demanding post-loss objectives.

As a result of this entire analysis, the risk manager may conclude that the post-loss objectives are unrealistic, that is, that the cost of achieving these objectives is too high to meet the economy objective. Also, as was true for the essential coverages, insurance may cost less or be more readily available if insurance is supplemented by the use of other risk management techniques. Through deductibles, retention can be used to handle the smaller potential losses otherwise covered by the insurance and thus reduce the premium. Through loss control, the frequency or severity of the potential losses may be reduced, which should result in a lowering of the insurance premiums.

Available Insurance. The available coverages are, or should be, least likely to be purchased. Potential losses covered by the insurance in this category do not threaten the continued existence of the firm or family. They do not, except for a very short time, cause the firm or family to interrupt its normal activities. Earnings are not likely to fluctuate greatly as a result of these losses. Even growth plans may not be disturbed by these losses. Thus, the risk manager probably could "sleep well" if these losses were simply retained.

Retention, however, may not be the most economical solution. Loss control efforts may produce less benefit than cost. Insurance premiums may be so low that insurance appears to be a bargain. The insurer may provide certain services such as safety inspections that cannot be duplicated elsewhere in quality and price. The special arrangements insurers have made for prompt replacement of broken glass are often cited as an important reason for buying glass insurance, a type of insurance usually classified as "available insurance" because of very low potential severity. Tax or social responsibility considerations also may tip the scale one way or the other in decisions on available coverages.

Some Additional Observations. In selecting between insurance and other risk management techniques, the risk manager must consider carefully the characteristics, advantages, and disadvantages of each. Chapters 2 and 3 provide much of the background knowledge needed for this analysis, but, to determine the appropriate technique or combination of techniques in a particular instance, one must assign weights to the advantages and disadvantages of each. This is a subjective process that may produce substantially different weightings for different managers. Some situations are so clear that almost all risk managers would assign approximately the same weights and arrive at the same decisions; others lend themselves to a variety of weightings.

These differences in weightings are to some extent based on objective factors such as the financial status or financial ability of the firm or family to withstand adversity; the personality of the firm or family, mainly its attitude toward uncertainty, is the major subjective variable.

The insurance method discussed above is an insurance-based approach to determining risk management priorities. As a true risk management approach, it is severely limited because whether a loss exposure is insurable has nothing to do with its possible significance as a subject taking a high risk management priority. The insurance method is biased in favor of insurance to the extent that its usefulness is limited to those exposures for which insurance is available. Although this encompasses most pure loss exposures of any significance, the limitation must be kept in mind and remedied if the method is used. Also, the use of insurance as an assumed treatment norm, with departures from the norm where appropriate, should not suggest a philosophical bias in this text.

The Minimum Expected Loss Method   One rule that has been suggested to help risk managers choose among the various risk management techniques is to select that technique or combination of techniques that will minimize the expected loss *in the long run* (that is, the long run average loss). As used here, the term "loss" includes:

(1) dollar losses borne by the entity,
(2) costs incurred by the entity, such as insurance premiums, in treating loss exposures, and
(3) the cost of the worry or anxiety associated with any uncertainty that remains concerning the losses retained by the entity.

This approach will be discussed in more detail in Chapters 4 and 5.

Minimizing long run average loss may not produce the best results in the *short* run. For example, this rule may suggest the purchase of insurance that proves in a single year to have been unnecessary because there are no losses. Conversely, the rule may suggest retention in a year when there are many losses. On the other hand, if either of these decisions was repeated year after year and the underlying conditions (for example, the probability that an accident will take place, how serious the resulting losses are likely to be, and the insurance premiums) remain unchanged, no other technique can be expected to produce a lower average loss in the long run. Also, if the same rule is used in making all risk management decisions within a given year, the average loss per decision should be minimized.

Calculating the average loss associated with each technique or combination of techniques involves some subjective decisions. For example, the importance attached to various potential losses will depend on the post-loss objectives specified by the business or family. The dollar losses must be weighted to reflect the importance of various sizes and types of loss. Moreover, dollar values must be assigned to the social responsibility aspects of each possible decision and to the worry or anxiety associated with any remaining uncertainty. The minimum expected loss method thus forces explicit assumptions about various factors that are made implicitly in less formalized approaches to selecting the appropriate techniques. Even such an informal method as playing hunches involves implicit assumptions. The advantage of explicit assumptions is that one is forced to consider carefully each assumption. Further, one can test the effect of a range of assumptions on the possible result. Often it is found that a wide range of assumptions produces the same decision. For example, the risk manager may find it extremely difficult to place a dollar value on a "quiet night's sleep," but discover that, as long as the value is at least a specified amount, the resulting decision is the same. Thus, a crude estimate may be all that is necessary to use this method to make the correct decision.

Capital Budgeting The third method suggested for selecting among risk management techniques is capital budgeting. Capital budgeting is the process financial managers use to decide whether to make long-term investments such as the construction or purchase of a new building. Financial managers, to whom risk managers often report, are likely to understand and appreciate the reasoning behind a risk management proposal based on it.

Capital budgeting is too complicated to be discussed in much detail here. CPCU 8 does cover the basic concept of capital budgeting. In general, through capital budgeting, a business attempts to select those projects that will produce the best return on the cash invested in them.[7]

Risk managers can use capital budgeting in two ways. First, some risk management decisions involve long-term investments to which capital budgeting is directly applicable. For example, in deciding whether to install an automatic sprinkler system, a risk manager can compare the installation cost to the present value of the net cash inflows (considering reduced fire losses and insurance costs, system maintenance costs, and so on) resulting from the installation of the system. Second, in making capital budgeting decisions on long-term investments such as manufacturing a new product or constructing a new building, financial managers often ignore the pure loss exposures or assume that they are handled through the purchase of insurance. In some cases, this failure to give pure loss exposures the same careful treatment as speculative loss exposures leads to the wrong decision. For example, ignoring the possibility of products liability suits could make manufacturing a product look much more attractive than it is. To assume insurance will be purchased—or even to include insurance premiums when evaluating the projected rate of return on this product—can be misleading because retention may be appropriate and less costly in some cases, thus increasing the return on those investments. Consequently, the risk manager should be involved in decisions on long-term projects. To participate, the risk manager should know the fundamentals of capital budgeting.

Implementing the Selected Techniques

After the risk manager has determined what technique or combination of techniques should be used, the next step is to implement the selected techniques. Failure to implement these techniques effectively can negate what would otherwise be a wise decision. Implementation requires action and further decisions.

For example, if loss control is the technique selected for a particular exposure, past occurrences should be analyzed—regardless of whether these occurrences caused any significant losses—to determine their causes and the best way to attack these causes. The risk manager must decide whether the firm or family will install and maintain the control program or devices, or whether outsiders should be hired to perform this service. If insiders are the choice, should it be the risk management department or some other division of the firm? If other divisions are involved, how can they be motivated to support or conduct the necessary activities?

If insurance is the recommended technique, the risk manager must choose an agent or broker and an insurer, draft a policy or choose one from among many forms prepared by the insurer, determine the most favorable pricing method, prepare for loss adjustment negotiations with the insurer, and check on whether the insurer has sent the necessary evidence of insurance to workers' compensation commissions, secured creditors, or others requiring such proof.

Monitoring the Risk Management Program

A risk management program must be monitored to determine whether it should be modified. Experience with the program may suggest that the best technique or combination of techniques was not selected originally or that the choices made were not properly implemented. Conditions may also change so much that, although the original decision and implementation were correct, a different solution is now required.

To monitor a program, the risk manager must establish performance standards, check compliance with these standards, and decide what degree of noncompliance calls for a correction. If a correction is in order, the risk manager should repeat the first three steps in the risk management process to determine the appropriate correction.

THE RISK MANAGEMENT FUNCTION

To this point the risk management *process* has been the principal item of discussion. In the sense of risk management being something to be done, it also constitutes a *function*. This section will deal with where and how this function is performed, and the scope of the function.

The risk management function tends to be more formalized in large organizations. However, it is important to understand that risk management problems exist without regard to entity type or size. In a small organization or family, risk management is less complex, perhaps, and less amenable to the full variety of treatment techniques than in a large organization, but the problems are nevertheless present.

The Risk Management Function in a Large Business

Large businesses recognize far more than most that risk management is a part of all management functions. Many large businesses have developed highly skilled specialized risk management departments. The discussion that follows describes

(1) who within a large business is primarily responsible for risk management decisions,
(2) the types of activities in which these risk managers typically engage,
(3) the role of risk management policy statements and manuals, and
(4) the many ways in which other departments in a large business perform or affect the risk management function.

Who Within the Business Is Primarily Responsible for Risk Management Decisions? The membership of the Risk and Insurance Management Society provides one clue to the importance of the risk management function and who performs this function. The 1980 membership consisted of over 3,400 corporations, institutions, and governmental bodies in the United States and Canada. About 90 percent of the *Fortune* top 500 companies are members.

In 1977 RIMS retained a consulting firm to study the role of the risk managers who were members of this society.[8] About half of the United States respondents to this RIMS survey held the title of manager. Director was the next most popular title with 4 percent being vice presidents and 4 percent treasurers. About 46 percent reported directly to a vice president.

In What Activities Are Risk Managers Engaged? What do these risk managers do? To what extent is responsibility for the risk management function shared with others?

About 70 percent of the United States respondents to the RIMS survey in 1977 said they spent at least 90 percent of their time on risk management. The findings presented below are based on the responses of these full-time risk managers.

- Almost 55 percent of the respondents were responsible only for managing property and liability exposures. About 41 percent were responsible for both property-liability exposures and employee benefit plans. Less than 2 percent managed only employee benefit plans.
- Five levels of risk management activity were identified according to (1) the number of areas for which an individual had some responsibility and (2) whether this responsibility was full, shared with someone else, or merely advisory. Type 5 risk managers, about one-third of the total, had all the functional responsibility and authority that could be associated with the risk management function. Another 40 percent of the respondents performed functions which approximated full risk management responsibility and authority. Only about 1 percent of the total were essentially insurance buyers with little authority even to select the insurer or the broker. All of the Type 5 risk managers were responsible for (1) "risk determination" (exposure identification) and evaluation, and (2) handling property and liability claims other than workers' compensation and products liability (99 percent of the Type 5 risk managers handled workers' compensation claims; 97 percent handled products claims).
- Over 80 percent also listed among their responsibilities determining how the "risks" (potential losses) were to be financed, loss control of property and liability exposures (except industrial injuries for which 69 percent were responsible) and administration of the risk management department.
- Loss control responsibilities were more likely to be shared or advisory than full. About one-third shared with others the responsibility for determining how the potential losses were to be financed.

The Role of Policy Statements   Large organizations commonly have formal risk management policy statements developed at a high management level. These policy statements describe the general risk management objectives of the firm. The involvement of high management levels, including the board of directors, in the formulation of risk management policy statements, has the following advantages:

(1) top managers become better acquainted with the risk management function,
(2) the policy statement carries more weight throughout the firm, and
(3) the policy statement sets a standard against which the risk manager's performance can be judged.

The preparation of a general risk management policy statement forces management to consider the total risk management program at one time, highlights inconsistencies that might otherwise arise, and provides a vehicle for disseminating risk management objectives throughout the firm.

Policy statements should be specific enough to provide direction but not so specific as to tie the risk manager's hands or require frequent modifications. A common format is a brief statement of the general risk management objectives followed by a statement of more specific objectives. It is also common to have different policy statements prepared by different levels of management. For example, the risk manager commonly develops a fairly specific policy statement that implements the more general policy statement prepared at higher levels.

Darwin Close and John O'Connell list six desirable characteristics of policy statements. Such statements should be:

(1) an explicit statement of the objectives and plans of both the organization as a whole and the risk management department. Risk management policy should be a function of (a) corporate goals, (b) the corporate environment, and (c) specific company attributes.
(2) consistent internally and with other policy statements.
(3) flexible enough to be adaptable to change and to provide some discretionary power for the risk manager. Too much flexibility, of course, is also to be avoided, because the statement would then provide little or no guidance.
(4) limited to goals and objectives. The procedures or steps to be taken to attain these goals and objectives should be left to the risk management department. To go further may restrict the

manager from taking effective action and destroy his or her initiative.

(5) written. Preparing a written document forces a more careful policy statement and enables the statement to meet the needs of both the organization and the risk manager stated above. On the other hand, a written policy must be reviewed and updated periodically and at times may be interpreted too literally.

(6) communicated to all affected persons. This communication should take place while the policy is being formulated and after it goes into effect.[9]

The examples in Exhibits 1-3 and 1-4 illustrate two different approaches to policy statements. The first example is the relatively broad statement used by one university. The second is a much more detailed statement prepared for a large chemical company.

The Role of Risk Management Manuals Risk managers of large firms commonly develop a risk management manual for their own use and for use by other departments. The purpose of the manual determines its content. A publication of the Risk and Insurance Management Society suggested the following sections:[10]

(1) Statement of policy signed by the chief executive officer supplemented, if necessary, by a more specific statement that describes the general responsibilities of the risk management department.

(2) A description of the property insurance contracts purchased by the firm. The master policy covering most, if not all, of the firm's property should come first, followed by other policies. Details that might be provided include the purpose of the policy, the insurer, the policy dates, the limit of liability, deductibles, the perils covered and the perils excluded, how claims are to be reported, and how the premium is to be allocated among the various divisions of the firm.

(3) A similar summary of the firm's workers' compensation policy.

(4) A similar summary of the firm's liability insurance contracts, starting with the basic liability coverages covering the majority of the firm's properties.

(5) A description of the various public insurance programs in which the firm is a participant. For example, the business may operate in a state with an exclusive state workers' compensation insurance fund.

(6) A summary of the firm's fidelity and surety bonds along the lines described above.

Exhibit 1-3
Risk Management Policy Statement—Major University*

The administration of the University recognizes its role of stewardship over the assets of the University, both human and financial. It interprets its responsibility in this area as requiring the highest possible concern for the safety of its students, employees, and the public, combined with a concern that the maximum protection be accorded University property to prevent financial loss.

The management of the University's loss exposures in terms of both human and financial resources shall be the responsibility of the Director of Risk and Insurance. It is his duty to identify loss exposures. He shall then recommend means of eliminating, abating, transferring, or retaining these loss exposures after consultation with the Vice President and Treasurer. Only when it is deemed that the University cannot eliminate or economically retain an exposure to loss shall it be transferred by purchase of insurance. The form and sufficiency of limits of liability for casualty protection of the University shall be determined by the Director of Risk and Insurance, again in consultation with the Vice President and Treasurer, who shall keep the Board of Governors informed of actions taken.

The University recognizes its ability to budget for and thereby retain limited and predictable exposures to financial loss. It shall not be the University's practice to attempt to insure such foreseeable and bearable expenses, if the alternatives can be achieved with due regard to sound business practice. The deductibles on property insurance shall be determined by the Vice President and Treasurer after recommendation from the Director of Risk and Insurance and in recognition of insurance market conditions.

The University administration will continue to purchase insurance with full consideration of the services offered by the insurer, their reliability and financial stability, as well as the price of the insurance coverage as competitively determined. The University does not recognize any other obligation to be satisfied by the selection of any particular insurance underwriters, brokers, or agents.

The University will remain alert to all opportunities for cooperative action with other institutions that promote mutual benefit in handling loss exposures that are not readily insured or safely retained. Any such cooperative activity shall be explored by the Director of Risk and Insurance and reported to the Board of Governors by the Vice President and Treasurer.

---

*Adapted with permission from John F. Adams, *Risk Management and Insurance: Guidelines for Higher Education* (Washington, DC: National Association of College and University Business Officers, 1972), p. 24.

Exhibit 1-4

Risk Management Policy Statement—Special Chemical Company*

---

1. Because of the need to protect the assets of this enterprise against catastrophic loss (or to provide financial restitution if such loss should occur) and the expense involved in such protection, risk management is a critical part of the total management of the Special Chemical Company.

2. Risk management is a specialized discipline intended to provide the decision-making management level with data pertinent to the identification, analysis, evaluation, and alternative treatment of exposures to loss through chance events, for both program review and planning new undertakings. In these management areas, the Special Chemical Company will utilize the services of qualified risk management specialists either on its own staff or through the use of outside consultants.

3. The following techniques of risk management will be employed by the Special Chemical Company.

A. *Recognition.* The recognition function will be to identify, analyze, and evaluate all exposures to loss through chance events, either in existence or subsequently created, that involve loss potentials of significant amounts either in one event or in the aggregate annually. In this company, such exposures should be recognized when loss potentials of $25,000 or more exist.

B. *Avoidance.* The anticipated financial rewards for assuming any exposures to loss should exceed or at least be approximately equal to potential loss. The Special Chemical Company will avoid incurring disproportionate exposures to loss in contractual agreements. All new undertakings shall be evaluated carefully and those already in existence shall be reevaluated periodically for the purpose of determining if any loss exposures can be avoided.

C. *Loss Prevention.* Once it is decided that a loss exposure should be retained (or transferred) and not avoided, it is the policy of this company to try to utilize loss prevention techniques wherever possible, consistent with the costs involved. It is the belief of this company that it is preferable to attempt to prevent losses before considering other techniques for handling loss exposures.

The reduction of losses depends primarily upon a careful review of all operations, equipment, and facilities to identify potential hazards and to eliminate or reduce them to their practical minimum. This review must be a constant process—in the design, construction, and operating stages on the part of all management and supervisory personnel. Periodic safety inspections should serve as an overall second look in all of the above stages. The essential part of these reviews is the corrective actions taken as a result of the recommendations enacted.

D. *Retention.* Generally, the Special Chemical Company will retain a loss exposure under the following circumstances:

(1)When the amount of annual potential loss is relatively so small that it may conveniently be treated as a normal operating expense;

(2)When

(a)the probability of loss (frequency) is so great that loss is almost certain to occur; and

(b)the rates for insurance or other transfer mechanisms are disproportionately high; and

(c)potential loss amounts are within the financial ability of the Company to retain; and

(d)no accessory insurance services are required;

(3)When the probability of occurrence is so remote that the ordinarily prudent businessman will not incur any amount of premium expense for insurance; and

(4)When insurance is not available, or only available at prohibitive cost.

E. *Noninsurance Transfer.* In all contractual relationships, the Special Chemical Company will transfer to others all exposures to loss from chance events appropriate to the transaction and relationship of the parties. This means that Special Chemical will consider before contractually transferring a loss exposure to another party, that party's ability to assume the potential loss, ability to control the loss, and the customs and traditions of the parties and the industries involved. In the absence of adequate net worth of other parties, contractual transfers shall be supported by insurance of the indemnitor and evidence thereof required. Whenever a choice exists among two or more methods of accomplishing a business purpose, the opportunity to transfer the exposure shall be given appropriate consideration.

F. *Insurance Transfer.* The Special Chemical Company will purchase insurance under the following circumstances:

(1)When required by law or contract;

(2)When the amount of potential loss is too large to be safely retained (measured against assets, operating income, earnings, and cash flow);

(3)When the probable annual cost variation is unacceptable and insurance is available on acceptable terms;

(4)When insurance can better or more economically provide accessory services required, such as inspection, claims handling, legal qualification, and loss prevention.

G.*Joint Insurance Transfer and Retention.* The Special Chemical Company will combine insurance transfer and retention through the use of deductibles, franchises, excess insurance, and retrospective rating plans where relatively low loss amount exposures can be safely retained.

---

* Adapted with permission from Jerry S. Rosenbloom, *A Case Study in Risk Management* (Englewood Cliffs, NJ: Prentice-Hall, Inc., 1972), pp. 41-42, 47-48.

(7) A statement of the purpose of the firm's property conservation (loss control) program and a listing of the responsibilities of the risk management department and other departments.

(8) A statement of the safety programs designed by the firm to protect employees, customers, and the general public against bodily injuries.

(9) A more detailed statement of the inspection services to be conducted as part of the loss control programs.

(10) A more detailed statement of the security (protection from theft, assault, etc.) programs that are to be part of the loss control programs.

(11) A brief description of the purpose of each federal and state act affecting the firm's operations and the related responsibilities of the risk management and other departments. Illustrative examples are the Occupational Safety and Health Act and the Consumer Products Safety Act.

(12) A statement of the firm's policy and procedures with respect to issuing certificates of insurance that the firm may be asked to provide in accordance with certain contractual agreements.

(13) A description of how the risk management department and other divisions should respond to legal actions against the business.

(14) A similar description of the responsibilities of the various departments toward contractual agreements entered into by the firm.

(15) A summary of the firm's employee benefit program including such items as the insurer, the policy date, the benefits provided, the departments involved and their responsibilities, and the formula for allocating the premium among the firm's divisions.

Such a risk management manual is useful to the risk manager because it requires explicit statements about many relationships that might otherwise remain poorly defined and subject to many misunderstandings. If the manual has been endorsed by top management, the risk manager's hand is strengthened in dealing with other departments.

The manual is also useful as an educational device and reference source. New personnel can learn a great deal about the department and its activities by studying the manual. Experienced personnel can conveniently update themselves and, by consulting the manual, answer more quickly and accurately many questions from outsiders. A review of the important decisions made in the past and the reason for these decisions can be extremely helpful in making today's decisions.

Risk management manuals are useful to persons in other departments because of their educational value. In addition, they spell out the risk management obligations of these other departments.

Relationship Between Risk Management and Other Management Functions   The extent to which the responsibility for risk management decisions is shared with other departments of a large business is one indication of the many relationships between risk management and other management functions. We now turn to a more systematic investigation of these relationships.

After examining how a risk manager's responsibilities overlap into other management areas, the discussion that follows will describe the risk management activities of the leading departments of a large business and how the work of these departments may create—and may help manage—exposures to loss. As the discussion unfolds, remember that the term "business" here is broad enough to include not only business firms in the narrow sense, but nonprofit institutions (e.g., some hospitals and universities) and governmental agencies and units as well.

Risk Management Activities.   What activities does the risk manager perform in addition to dealing with loss exposures? Like all managers, the risk manager must manage. He or she must

- plan the actions to be taken by the risk management department,
- organize the department's human and material resources,
- direct and coordinate the department's actions, and
- monitor the department's performance.

Similarly, like all managers, risk managers keep various accounts— insurance premiums paid, property valuations, salaries of risk management personnel, and so on. A major financial activity is the preparation of a budget for the risk management department. Risk managers may become involved in the design of a new product, quality control procedures, or the types of machines to be used in a manufacturing process. A risk manager may be asked to comment on how the firm markets its products or services because the method and messages used may create important loss exposures. Risk managers also purchase insurance and other risk management services and materials.

Other Department Activities Involving Risk Management.   The other major departments of a large business whose relationship to risk management will be considered are (1) accounting, (2) finance, (3) marketing, (4) production, and (5) personnel. In each case we will consider the risk management activities of the department and how the department may, through its other activities, create exposures to loss of which the risk manager should be informed.

- The *accounting* department performs many important risk management activities. Through various internal controls, the accounting department attempts to reduce the opportunity for employee fraud. Illustrations of this loss control technique include reconciling invoices with purchase orders, checking disbursements for proper authorizations, and comparing cash receipts with postings to customer accounts. Through asset accounts, the accounting department identifies and measures property loss exposures. Through valuation accounts such as the allowance for bad debts, the department recognizes the probable costs of retaining certain loss exposures. By allocating risk management costs among the various departments of the firm, the accounting department helps the risk manager monitor the performance of the risk management program and isolate problem areas. Decisions on the amount of loss a firm may safely retain must be based in part on an analysis of the financial statements prepared by the accounting department. Computers and other expensive equipment used by accountants may create important property loss exposures. The firm may be sued because of faulty information supplied by the accounting department that misleads investors or creditors.

- The *finance* department makes many determinations affecting risk management. First, the risk manager often reports to a financial vice president. For this reason risk management is sometimes considered a part of financial management. Second, it is the finance department that is the source of data needed to analyze the effect of disruptions in profits and cash flow. The levels beyond which such disruptions would interfere with the firm's goals are critical benchmarks for the risk manager and the risk management program. Third, in determining whether the firm should purchase some expensive equipment or a new building, the financial manager considers (or should consider) the pure loss exposures created by these actions. Fourth, if the firm borrows money using property as collateral, the lender will usually insist that its interest in the property be protected by insurance. The finance department must arrange for this protection as part of the negotiation or proposal. In this way, the finance department creates special loss exposures.

- The *marketing* department's principal involvement consists of the creation of loss exposures, identification of these exposures, and loss control efforts designed to minimize their effects. In marketing the product or service, the marketing department may use defective packaging that leads to liability claims. It may overstate the advantages or uses of the product or fail to state certain dangers associated with some uses. Through a hold harmless agreement with other businesses (manufacturers, wholesalers, or distributors), the marketing department, in its eagerness to sell, may accept some legal responsibilities that the firm would otherwise not have to bear. (Note that from the point of view of the *other* party, a loss exposure has been handled via a noninsurance transfer.) In transporting the product to customers, the marketing department exposes the firm to some important losses, such as the exposure to loading and unloading accidents. The marketing department may also handle purchasing activities, in which case it may also assume under contracts some liability exposures the firm would not otherwise have.

Marketing departments should be aware of the loss exposures they are creating and should keep the risk management department informed. By using care in the selling or distribution of the product or service, they may prevent or reduce loss exposures without diminishing marketing effectiveness. Finally, in pricing the goods or services sold, the marketing department should recognize risk management costs. Recognizing these costs gives the firm a more accurate picture of the contribution each product makes to the firm's profits, and the areas where loss control efforts are most badly needed.

● In designing and manufacturing a product or service, the *production* department typically exposes its employees to more frequent and serious injuries than most other departments. The product it manufactures or the service it provides may cause property damage or bodily injury to others. Even if a defective product does not harm others, the business may suffer a substantial loss because the product cannot be marketed or has to be replaced. The department should identify and evaluate the dangers associated with both the product or service, and the process by which it is created. Safer production lines, more careful design, and tighter quality controls illustrate loss control efforts associated with the production department.

● The *personnel* department has many risk management responsibilities. Although some firms give the risk manager full responsibility for employee-benefit programs, most firms give the personnel department full or shared responsibility for these plans. Where risk managers and the personnel department share responsibility for these plans, the personnel department usually negotiates the benefits with a union, establishes the eligibility requirements and benefits, and administers the daily operations. The risk manager selects the insurer and negotiates the coverage. The personnel department also shares responsibility for safety programs with the engineering or risk management department, seeks ways to minimize absenteeism and unemployment, and encourages prompt rehabilitation of injured workers. Some of these activities also create loss exposures. For example, the design and administration of a pension plan, if improperly handled, can result in successful suits against the firm by aggrieved employees.

These myriad relationships between the risk manager and other managers show why there must be continuous, systematic, two-way communications between them. Risk management in its broad sense is really coextensive with the general management of the firm.

The Risk Management Function in a Small or Medium-Sized Business

Large and small businesses differ significantly both in the degree to which they have specialized risk management departments and the extent to which the risk management function is performed by persons outside the firm. In small businesses, separate risk management departments are not common. Primary responsibility for risk management is often assigned to a treasurer, accountant, or personnel manager who devotes only part of his or her time to this function. In the smallest operations, a sole proprietor may make *all* management decisions. Because these part-time risk managers are less informed and experienced in risk management, they rely strongly on outsiders. More often than not, an insurance producer (agent or broker) is the chief source of risk management information. Recently there has been rapid growth in the role of consulting firms that advise on a fee basis and do not sell insurance. (This is not to imply that the services of insurance producers and consultants are useful only to small firms.)

The Risk Management Function in a Family

Though one member of a family usually assumes responsibility for risk management decisions, it is becoming more common for two or more family members to participate in the risk management process. Since families, like small businesses, are usually unfamiliar with risk management and cannot afford to donate large amounts of time or money to the risk management process, they tend to rely on the services of outsiders, particularly insurance producers.

CONTRIBUTIONS OF RISK MANAGEMENT

Risk management contributes significantly to the welfare of businesses, families, and society.

Risk Management Contributions to a Business

Risk management makes it possible for a business to achieve some preferred combination of its post-loss and pre-loss objectives.

Proper risk management may also improve profits directly and indirectly. Profits can be increased directly by reducing expenses. Economy, a pre-loss objective of risk management, is achieved by selecting the most economical techniques consistent with post-loss objectives and implementing these techniques in the most economical fashion. To illustrate, a firm may reduce its expenses because the risk manager chooses to retain a loss exposure instead of insuring it, because Insurer A is selected over Insurer B, or because the firm efficiently adjusts to a post-loss situation.

Risk management contributes indirectly to profits in various ways:

- A business that can worry less about pure loss exposures because of effective risk management is financially and psychologically better prepared to seek speculative opportunities that may increase its profits. For example, if a business feels secure in the way it has managed its present property loss exposures, it may consider more favorably a proposal to manufacture a new product or expand present sales territories.
- Proper risk management produces more profitable decisions by forcing financial managers to consider the pure loss exposures associated with speculative ventures. To illustrate, assume that a financial manager is debating whether to buy Building A or Building B. Ignoring pure loss exposures, Building A would be the better investment. Building A, however, is subject to more frequent and more severe property losses. Consequently, insurance on Building A would be much more costly, as would other risk management techniques. Recognizing these extra costs could make Building B, not Building A, the better investment.
- Proper risk management allocates pure loss exposure costs among the products or services sold or markets serviced by the business. This allocation produces a more accurate picture of the profitability of the various products, services, or markets,

thus permitting the firm to direct its activities in the most profitable directions.

- An effective risk management program improves relationships with creditors, customers, suppliers, and employees. Credit can be expected to be more readily available and at lower cost. Customers know that the business will not fail because of adverse events arising out of pure loss exposures. Customers tend to favor a business that will continue to meet their needs over a long time. Similarly, suppliers favor a long-term relationship. A firm with an effective risk management program usually attracts a more loyal, productive group of employees. Not only can they be assured that the firm will not fail or be seriously disrupted by a loss, but employee benefit plans protect the employees against losses occasioned by death, poor health, unemployment, or old age. Lower credit costs, customer loyalty, reliable suppliers, and productive employees tend to make any business more efficient and more profitable.

Risk Management Contributions to a Family

Families benefit in similar ways from effective risk management:

- Families can cope more effectively with financial disasters that might otherwise cause personal bankruptcy, family breakups, or a greatly reduced standard of living.
- Families enjoy greater peace of mind knowing that their pure loss exposures are under control. They are subject to less physical and mental strain and can become more venturesome in other activities.
- Effective risk management can increase the family's income or reduce its expenses. Risk management can reduce expenses by handling loss exposures in the most economical fashion. This economy is especially important to families because proper risk management may reduce income taxes in certain cases. Income can be stabilized by protecting the breadwinners' earnings against interruption; expenses can be stabilized by protection of various sorts.
- Proper management of pure loss exposures may permit the family financially and psychologically to take more chances on speculative ventures with high profit potential such as certain common stocks, career choices, or a part-time business. Families make better decisions on speculative ventures when they consider their associated pure loss exposures. Speculative ventures that are assumed can be pursued more aggressively

and efficiently. Long-range planning is facilitated and credit costs are lower.

● Risk management may make it possible for a family to continue its activities following an accident at or near the pre-loss level. Family inconvenience is thus minimized.

● Most families are concerned about their image in the community. Outsiders may be favorably impressed by the preparation a family makes to face adversity; they are even more likely to admire a family that successfully faces actual adversity. By caring for itself, the family also satisfies to some degree its sense of social responsibility.

Risk Management Contributions to Society

By benefiting themselves through effective risk management, businesses and families benefit the society of which they are a part.

● Society gains in that its resources are used more efficiently by the individual units. Output is higher and prices are lower than they would otherwise be.

● To the extent that businesses and families avoid financial reverses through risk management, society has more taxpayers and fewer persons depending upon society for support.

● Because families and firms practice risk management, society also avoids disruptions in the economic and social environment.

IMPACT OF RISK MANAGEMENT UPON INSURERS AND THEIR REPRESENTATIVES

Thus far, the discussion has been about and from the point of view of entities exposed to loss. The acceptance and development of the risk management process and the corresponding risk management function, particularly among large concerns, have affected significantly both insurance producers and insurance companies, in several highly significant ways. This is particularly noticeable for large business and institutional purchasers of insurance for whom the risk management function is quite formal.

In order to obtain the respect and business of risk managers, insurers and their representatives need to be familiar with the risk management approach to handling loss exposures. Insurers and their representatives must see insurance in perspective, as one technique among several for handling loss exposures. Because the risk managers of large firms are growing in sophistication and knowledge, insurers increasingly are called upon to provide products and services based as much on what risk managers want to buy as on what insurers want to sell. Insurer personnel who deal with risk managers are expected to be highly skilled, experienced, and well-educated professionals.

Insurers and their representatives are called upon increasingly to do more than sell insurance. They are asked to expand and improve other risk management services, such as exposure identification, loss control, and claims adjustment services. Risk managers seek to effectively manage their firms' loss exposures in the most economical manner. Consequently, they can be expected to seek the lowest price that is consistent with the financial stability and service they seek. Insurers are challenged to respond with products, prices, and services to meet these needs.

Chapter Notes

1. Henri Fayol, *General and Industrial Management* (New York: Pitman Publishing Corp., 1949), p. 4.
2. Robert I. Mehr and Bob A. Hedges, *Risk Management: Concepts and Applications* (Homewood, IL: Richard D. Irwin, 1974), p. 4.
3. Mehr and Hedges, p. 3.
4. This financial statement approach was originally suggested by the late A. Hawthorne Criddle, CPCU. See A. Hawthorne Criddle, "A Theory of Risk Discovery," *National Insurance Buyer*, Vol. 6, January, 1959, pp. 8, 14-18, 31, 35, 39. For a more complete development, see A. H. Criddle, "The Use of Financial Statements in Corporate Risk Analysis," *Identifying and Controlling the Risks of Accidental Loss.* The financial statement approach is discussed in greater detail in CPCU 3.
5. The flowchart method was first explained by A. J. Ingley, "Problems of Risk Analysis," *The Growing Job of Risk Management,* (New York: American Management Association, 1962), pp. 137-398. The flowchart method is discussed in greater detail in CPCU 3.
6. The application of capital budgeting to risk management is extensively treated in the study materials for the RM 54 and RM 56 parts of the Insurance Institute of America Associate in Risk Management (ARM) designation program.
7. More specifically, investments are compared based on the present value, or today's lump-sum equivalent, of the net cash inflow (future cash inflows or benefits minus future cash outflows or costs) resulting from the investments. The discount rate used to calculate the present value is the minimum acceptable rate of return, which depends in part on the possible variations in the cash flows. The greater the uncertainty, the greater the discount rate, and the lower the present value of the expected net cash inflow. With respect to any particular investment, if the present value of the net cash flow is less than the initial cash investment, the project is not acceptable. If the present value of the cash inflow exceeds the investment, the project is acceptable, but the return on this project must be compared with the return on other acceptable projects to determine their relative attractiveness.
8. *The Risk and Insurance Manager Position: A Study of Responsibilities and Compensation,* conducted for the Risk and Insurance Management Society, Inc. (Princeton: Sibson and Company, Inc., 1978).
9. D. B. Close and J. J. O'Connell, "A Guide to Formulation of Risk Management Policy Statements," *CPCU Annals* (September 1976), pp. 195-200.
10. Douglas I. Craven, *Guidelines for Developing an Insurance Manual* (New York: Risk and Insurance Management Society, 1975).

CHAPTER 2

Controlling Loss Exposures

INTRODUCTION

Risk management techniques can be divided into two major categories: (1) control techniques, and (2) financing techniques. By altering the entity's exposures, control techniques attempt to reduce the loss frequency, the loss severity, or the annual variation in the potential losses. Financing techniques provide funds to finance recovery from losses that actually occur.

This chapter will analyze the basic characteristics of four control techniques—avoidance, loss control, combination, and noninsurance transfers of the control type. It will also discuss briefly how the risk manager might decide which of these techniques would be most appropriate in a given situation, a subject that will receive additional attention in Chapter 4. Finally, it will consider how various techniques might be implemented and monitored. Chapter 3 will analyze three loss financing techniques—noninsurance transfers of the financing type, insurance, and retention—in the same fashion.

For the most part, Chapters 2 and 3 will discuss each risk management technique separately. However, the reader should not conclude that the techniques are mutually exclusive. *Except for avoidance, which eliminates the loss exposure, each of the risk management techniques to be discussed is compatible with and can be used with any other technique.*

In treating loss exposures a risk manager should always *consider* the use of at least one control technique to see if it would be appropriate. Unless that control technique is completely effective (that is, there will be no loss), he or she *must* use at least one financing technique.

With this caveat, the chapter now turns to separate discussions of four control techniques—avoidance, loss control, combination, and noninsurance transfers.

AVOIDANCE

Avoiding a loss exposure entirely is one way to treat that loss exposure. An exposure can be avoided by

(1) never having that particular exposure, even momentarily, or
(2) abandoning the exposure so that it ceases to exist.

Examples of Avoidance

The following examples illustrate the first way in which an exposure can be avoided—by never having that particular exposure, even momentarily:

(1) A firm can avoid the loss exposures associated with the manufacture of a dangerous product by electing never to manufacture that product.
(2) A firm can avoid the loss exposures connected with sponsoring an employee softball team, a Junior Achievement group, or a picnic for customers by never sponsoring such activities.
(3) A family can avoid the loss exposures associated with skiing, motorcycling, sailing, or mountain climbing by never engaging in those activities.

The second type of avoidance involves abandonment of an existing exposure, as illustrated in the following examples:

(1) A firm that manufactures a dangerous product stops the activity.
(2) A firm terminates its sponsorship of an employee bowling team, a Cub Scout group, or education seminars for customers.
(3) A family discontinues certain sports activities.

Often, when avoidance is used, only certain exposures can be completely eliminated. Some exposures continue to exist. For example, when the manufacture of a dangerous product is discontinued, liability for products manufactured in the past does not cease to exist. The only exposures that do not exist are those that might have been incurred if the product manufacture had been continued.

Noninsurance transfers will be discussed later in this chapter, at which time the distinction between avoidance and noninsurance transfers will become clearer. The key point here is that avoidance often fails to eliminate *all* potential losses connected with a certain activity or operation. When avoidance is practiced, it is necessary to identify or define carefully what exposures have been avoided and what exposures continue.

Advantages

The greatest advantage of avoidance is that it either keeps the probability of loss equal to zero (the result of the first category of applications) or eliminates the possibility of loss that would have existed had the exposure not been avoided (the result of the second category of applications). The risk manager has no doubt about the outcome. There is no need to apply any other risk management technique to exposures that have been avoided because no exposure exists or remains to be treated.

Limitations

Although extremely useful on occasion as a risk management technique, avoidance has some severe limitations:

(1) Avoidance may not be possible.
(2) Avoidance may not be feasible.
(3) Avoidance may not be desirable.
(4) Avoiding one exposure may create other exposures.

Avoidance May Not Be Possible A clear example of the first limitation is the exposure through sickness to loss of a person's health or earning capacity. There is no way in which this exposure can be completely avoided.

Avoidance May Not Be Feasible For some exposures, while avoidance is not impossible, in practice it is not feasible. The broader the loss exposure is defined, the more likely this is to be the case. For example, it may be feasible to avoid *the exposure associated with owning* a new building by electing not to buy or build that building. However, if the exposure is defined more broadly to include *the potential losses that could arise out of the occupancy* of any building, owned or nonowned, from any peril, it may be possible to avoid such an exposure, but clearly it is not feasible. Similarly, a firm can avoid the exposures arising out of business operations by not conducting any operations, but a firm without any business operations would not be feasible under normal circumstances. Finally, a family would find it difficult, or even impossible, to avoid completely exposure to loss arising out of their activities.

Avoidance May Not Be Desirable Even if it is feasible to avoid a narrowly defined exposure, to do so may cause the firm or family to give up such great advantages that avoidance clearly is not desirable. To illustrate, not building a new plant may so diminish a firm's profit potential that avoidance is not a serious alternative to dealing with the exposures inherent in a new plant. Although it is feasible for an individual to avoid the exposures created by owning or operating a car, this may not be an attractive or practical alternative.

Avoiding One Exposure May Create Other Exposures When the exposure being treated is defined narrowly, avoidance becomes easier. However, at the same time it becomes less meaningful and beneficial because it becomes more likely that avoidance of one exposure creates another. For example, not using trucks to transport products to customers will enable a firm to avoid certain narrowly defined loss exposures arising out of the use of trucks, but the firm would still have a general transportation exposure if it is to continue in business. Using some other delivery method such as private passenger cars, trains, or airplanes would create new exposures.

Removing personal property from Warehouse A to Warehouse B eliminates the specific exposure at Warehouse A but creates a new exposure at Warehouse B. Refusing to ski because of the dangers involved would avoid only a small part of the exposure to loss of personal health or earning capacity. If the person decides to trade skiing for snowshoeing, one narrowly defined loss exposure is traded for another.

When Desirable

Despite its limitations, avoidance may on occasion be the most appropriate technique for treating a loss exposure. Sometimes retention is the only possible alternative to avoidance and the potential losses are so great that it would be unwise to retain the exposure. In other cases with a high loss potential, loss control or transfer may also be possible, but the cost of applying these techniques may far exceed either the firm's or family's ability to pay or the benefits to be derived from the control or transfer.

For example, a firm may find that it cannot secure at any price insurance that will protect it against its liability for defective products as long as it chooses to manufacture a certain drug. If no other means of transfer is possible, retaining this exposure might be unwise because of its catastrophic potential, leaving avoidance as the clearly preferred alternative. Thus, the firm would not add the drug to its product line or, if the drug were already one of its products, it would abandon the product. (While avoiding the creation of any additional exposures from this product, this approach does not eliminate loss exposures already existing due to products already sold.) In the same situation, if insurance were available but at too high a price, avoidance would be the preferred technique.

Implementing

To implement the avoidance technique, the risk manager must (1) define the exposures that are to be avoided, and (2) where possible, indicate alternative measures that might be taken to achieve the objectives that are forgone because of the avoidance. The more narrowly the exposure is defined, the easier it is to suggest alternative ways to achieve forgone objectives. For example:

- A manufacturing firm cannot completely avoid the loss exposures created by manufacturing processes unless it ceases its operations. It can avoid certain loss exposures associated with the manufacture of dangerous products by instead manufacturing safer products.
- A firm may find it impossible to avoid all exposures associated with owning a building, but some exposures created by ownership can be avoided by leasing a property.
- A family might find it impossible to avoid completely an auto exposure. It would be impractical never to own, operate, or occupy any auto. The family, however, could be advised to avoid only the ownership exposure by riding taxis or buses.
- A firm that wishes to avoid the losses that may arise out of the sponsorship of employee sports teams may be willing to sponsor other employee activities that are less likely to result in injuries.

Monitoring

The avoidance technique, once implemented, should be monitored to determine (1) whether it has been properly implemented, and (2) whether it is still appropriate. If a loss occurs, it is clear that avoidance has been unsuccessful. However, the absence of losses does not necessarily indicate that avoidance has been properly implemented. Good luck may result in no losses even when the exposure is not avoided.

Avoidance may become inappropriate because the conditions that made avoidance necessary or attractive may change. Other techniques may become available, or the avoidance itself may become undesirable or less feasible.

LOSS CONTROL

Loss control embraces those *control* techniques designed to reduce the loss frequency or the loss severity associated with a loss exposure that the entity has and does not wish to abandon or transfer. This section compares loss control with avoidance. Subsequent sections discuss (1) two theories on accident causes and effects, (2) various ways in which loss controls can be classified, (3) the role of loss control specialists and need for a safety policy, and (4) the four steps in loss control. The treatment of various exposures will be used to illustrate the discussion.

Comparison with Avoidance

Loss control is sometimes confused with avoidance. Like avoidance, loss control deals with the loss exposure itself rather than with the financing of the potential losses from that exposure. Unlike avoidance, however, loss control deals with an exposure that the entity has and does not wish to abandon. The purpose of loss control is to change the characteristics of the exposure in order that it might become more acceptable to the entity. A firm or family that avoids the exposure will never assume the exposure or, if it has that exposure, it will abandon it; a firm or family that applies loss controls to the exposure will keep the exposure but hopes to reduce the number of accidents or the dollar loss per accident. Thus, some possibility of loss remains even when the entity uses loss control.

Loss control and avoidance are mutually exclusive techniques. If an exposure is avoided, there is no potential loss to control.

TWO THEORIES ON
ACCIDENT CAUSES AND EFFECTS

Loss control activities take many forms. Before describing these, two theories of "accident" (or occurrence) causes and effects will be examined because they make the subsequent analysis of loss control measures more meaningful. They also help explain why one measure might be preferred over another as well as how the measures might be implemented and monitored.

To date, no one has developed a dominant general theory of accident causes and effects. Instead there are separate theories, each of which has some explanatory and predictive value. The two theories presented here are (1) the "domino" theory developed by H. W. Heinrich, a safety engineer and a pioneer in the field of industrial safety, and (2) the "energy release" theory developed by Dr. William Haddon, Jr., President of the Insurance Institute for Highway Safety and a contemporary safety expert. The Heinrich theory, introduced decades ago, is still useful and widely quoted. The Haddon theory, developed only about ten years ago, provides some additional insights.

Heinrich's Domino Theory

According to Heinrich, an "accident" is one factor in a sequence that *may* result in an "injury."[1] The factors can be visualized as a series of dominoes standing on edge, as shown in Exhibit 2-1. Each of these factors is dependent upon the preceding factor. In Heinrich's theory:

(1) A personal injury (the final domino) occurs only as the result of an accident.
(2) An accident occurs only as the result of a personal or mechanical hazard.
(3) Personal and mechanical hazards exist only because of the faults of persons.
(4) Faults of persons are inherited or acquired as a result of their environment.[2]

The converses of these statements are not true. For example, persons with faults do not always commit unsafe acts or permit mechanical hazards to exist. A personal or mechanical hazard does not always result in an accident and an accident does not always result in an injury or property damage. Indeed, as will be explained later, Heinrich places great stress on the fact that an accident can occur without an injury.

The domino theory asserts that, if there is an injury or property damage, all five factors are involved. If the fifth domino falls, it is because the first domino fell causing the others to fall in turn. If one of the factors in the sequence leading to an accident can be removed, the loss can be prevented. For example, as illustrated in Exhibit 2-2, elimination of an unsafe act makes the action of the preceding factors ineffective.

A more complete explanation of each of the five factors is shown in Exhibit 2-3.

Heinrich held that a person responsible for loss control should be interested in all five factors but be concerned primarily with accidents and the proximate causes of those accidents. The factor preceding the accident—an unsafe act and/or a mechanical or physical hazard—

Exhibit 2-1

Heinrich's Domino Theory *

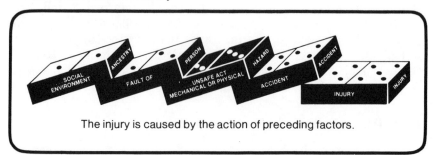

The injury is caused by the action of preceding factors.

*Reprinted with permission from H. W. Heinrich, *Industrial Accident Prevention*, 4th ed. (New York: McGraw-Hill Book Company, 1959), p. 15.

Exhibit 2-2

Loss Prevention in Heinrich's Domino Theory *

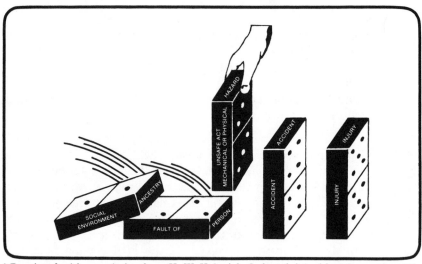

* Reprinted with permission from H. W. Heinrich, *Industrial Accident Prevention*, 4th ed. (New York: McGraw-Hill Book Company, 1959), p. 16.

should receive the most attention. If this third domino can be removed (see Exhibit 2-2), the accident sequence will be interrupted even if the first two dominoes fall.

After a study of 75,000 industrial accidents, Heinrich concluded that 98 percent of these accidents were preventable and that it should, therefore, be possible to reduce industrial accident costs with some form of loss control.[3]

What is the primary cause of accidents—unsafe acts of persons, or

Exhibit 2-3
Accident Factors *

Accident Factors	Explanation of Factors
1. Ancestry and social environment.	**Recklessness, stubbornness, avariciousness,** and other undesirable traits of character may be passed along through inheritance. Environment may develop undesirable traits of character or may interfere with education. Both inheritance and environment cause faults of person.
2. Fault of person.	Inherited or acquired faults of person; such as recklessness, violent temper, nervousness, excitability, inconsiderateness, ignorance of safe practice, etc., constitute proximate reasons for committing unsafe acts or for the existence of mechanical or physical hazards.
3. Unsafe act and/or mechanical or physical hazard.	Unsafe performance of persons, such as standing under suspended loads, starting machinery without warning, horseplay, and removal of safeguards; and mechanical or physical hazards, such as unguarded gears, unguarded point of operation, absence of rail guards, and insufficient light, result directly in accidents.
4. Accident.	Events such as falls of persons, striking of persons by flying objects, etc., are typical accidents that cause injury.
5. Injury.	Fractures, lacerations, etc., are injuries that result directly from accidents.

* Reprinted with permission from H. W. Heinrich, *Industrial Accident Prevention*, 4th ed. (New York: McGraw-Hill Book Company, 1959), p. 15.

unsafe mechanical or physical conditions? The answer is extremely important because it tells the risk manager or loss control specialist where to direct most attention. For Heinrich the answer was clear. Among the 75,000 cases he studied, Heinrich charged 88 percent to the unsafe acts of persons and 10 percent to dangerous physical or mechanical conditions. The cause of the remaining 2 percent was not determinable.

Many accidents involved both unsafe acts and unsafe conditions, in which case Heinrich assigned responsibility to the primary cause. Two cases illustrate how he made this decision:

- An employee was injured by a flying fragment from a burst grinding wheel. The grinding wheel could have been more completely guarded, but the primary cause was the fact that the employee, completely disregarding instructions, attempted to grind a heavy casting on a wheel designed for light tool work only. Heinrich, therefore, blamed this accident on an unsafe act.
- A worker operating under instructions to turn in worn tools continued to use a badly mushroomed chisel. He was injured when a piece of the burred head flew off and struck him in the cheek. Although the equipment was unsafe, *the primary cause of the accident* was an unsafe act—the use of unsafe tools.

Heinrich also emphasized that *accidents,* not injuries or property damage, *should be the point of attack.* According to Heinrich, "An accident is an unplanned and uncontrolled event in which the action or reaction of an object, substance, person, or radiation results in personal injury or property damage."[4]

Accidents, however, *need not* result in injuries. If a person slips and falls, an injury may or may not result (depending on the surface on which he or she falls, the nature of the fall, the bone structure of the victim, and other factors) but an accident, in the Heinrich framework, has taken place.

Again according to Heinrich, "An injury is merely the result of an accident. The accident itself is controllable. The severity or cost of an injury that results when an accident occurs is difficult to control."[5] Following Heinrich's logic, it would be a mistake for a risk manager to concentrate entirely on preventing accidents like those that have caused injuries in the past. Accidents that occurred in the past without causing injury may cause serious injuries the next time they occur.

Heinrich acknowledged that the exact number of no-injury accidents will never be known. Nevertheless, after a study of industrial injuries resulting from unsafe acts, he estimated that a person who suffers a disabling injury has had over 300 narrow escapes from serious injury as a result of committing the same unsafe act. Specifically, for every accident resulting in a major injury (one causing death, lost time, or a permanent injury), twenty-nine accidents of the same kind and involving the same person would result in minor injuries. Three hundred would produce no injuries.

Two illustrations indicate how Heinrich derived this ratio:[6]

- An employee injured his kneecap when he slipped and fell on a wet floor. Investigation revealed that for more than six years too great an area of floor space had been wet down at one time, wiping up was delayed unnecessarily, and one or more employees slipped daily on the wet surface. Any one of these slips might have resulted in an injury. Each, in Heinrich's framework, was an accident. The ratio of no-injury accidents to the kneecap injury accident was set at 1,800 to 1.
- A millwright was killed when he attempted to put a belt on a revolving pulley. He stood on an unsteady stepladder, wore a loose jacket with long sleeves, and did not use the correct equipment. For several years the belt had been replaced daily under approximately the same conditions. In this case the ratio of no-injury accidents to this fatal-injury accident was set at 600 to 1.

In both cases, if the risk manager had detected and corrected the unsafe acts that led to no-injury accidents, the serious injuries would have been prevented.

Heinrich's research concentrated on industrial accidents, but his theory seems well-suited to many situations in which the actions of the victim are important. Industrial injuries, products liability losses, and fire losses are in this category. The theory is less applicable to losses caused by thieves, vandals, or acts of God.

Haddon's Energy Release Theory

Instead of concentrating on human behavior, Haddon treats accidents as a physical engineering problem. Accidents result when energy that is out of control puts more stress on a structure (property or a person) than that structure can tolerate without damage. Accidents can be prevented by controlling the energy involved or by changing the structures that the energy could damage. More specifically, Haddon suggests ten strategies designed either to suppress conditions that produce accidents or to enhance conditions that retard accidents.[7] In brief, these ten strategies, with examples of each, are as follows:

(1) *To prevent the creation of the hazard in the first place.* (Examples: prevent production of plutonium, thalidomide, LSD.)

(2) *To reduce the amount of the hazard brought into being.* (Examples: reduce speed of vehicles, lead content of paint, mining of asbestos; make less beverage alcohol—a hazard itself and in its results, such as drunken driving.)

(3) *To prevent the release of the hazard that already exists.* (Examples: pasteurizing milk, bolting or timbering mine roofs, impounding nuclear wastes.)

(4) *To modify the rate or spatial distribution of release of the hazard from its source.* (Examples: brakes, shutoff valves, reactor control rods.)

(5) *To separate, in time or space, the hazard and that which is to be protected.* (Examples: isolation of persons with communicable diseases; walkways over or around hazards; evacuation; the phasing of pedestrian and vehicular traffic, whether in a work area or on a city street; the banning of vehicles carrying explosives from areas where they and their cargoes are not needed.)

(6) *To separate the hazard and that which is to be protected by interposition of a material barrier.* (Examples: surgeon's gloves, containment structures, childproof poison-container closures, vehicle air bags.)

(7) *To modify relevant basic qualities of the hazard.* (Examples: altering pharmacological agents to reduce side effects, using breakaway roadside poles, making crib slat spacing too narrow to strangle a child.)

(8) *To make what is to be protected more resistant to damage from the hazard.* (Examples: immunization, making structures more fire- and earthquake-resistant, giving salt to workers under thermal stress, making motor vehicles more crash resistant.)

(9) *To begin to counter the damage already done by the environmental hazard.* (Examples: rescuing the shipwrecked, reattaching severed limbs, extricating trapped miners.)

(10) *To stabilize, repair, and rehabilitate the object of the damage.* (Examples: posttraumatic cosmetic surgery, physical rehabilitation for amputees and others with disabling injuries—including many thousands paralyzed annually by spinal cord damage sustained in motor vehicle crashes—rebuilding after fires and earthquakes.)

Haddon emphasizes that Strategy 1 is not necessarily more important than, say, Strategy 2. To illustrate this point, he indicates that a shipper can avoid broken teacups by proper packaging (Strategy 6) even if the package is abused by the postal system. Generally speaking, however, the larger the amount of energy generated relative to the resistance level of the property or persons exposed to the energy, the earlier (lower-numbered) the strategy that must be employed to control it. In the ultimate case, the only effective approach is to prevent the creation of the hazard (Strategy 1).

The Two Theories Compared

The difference between the Heinrich and Haddon theories can be viewed as a difference in emphasis. Both the Heinrich and the Haddon theories explain a sequence that leads to damage or injury. Heinrich's sequence starts with ancestry and social environment and ends with an injury or property damage. Haddon starts with the build-up of energy and ends with an injury or property damage. Haddon's theory can be viewed primarily (Strategies 1 through 8) as an expanded analysis of *part* of the third domino in Heinrich's sequence—mechanical or physical hazards that cause accidents—and what to do about them.

Unlike Heinrich, who places most of the blame for accidents on human behavior that leads to mechanical or physical hazards, Haddon concentrates on the physical engineering aspects of the conditions that give rise to accidents. To illustrate, assume that an auto, being driven at eighty miles an hour, crashes into a rigid roadside sign causing serious bodily injuries to the occupants of the car and extensive physical damage to the car. Heinrich's approach would emphasize the unsafe act of speeding as a personal fault of the driver and the fault of the highway department in installing the rigid sign. Haddon's approach would emphasize the amount of energy created by speeding and the contact surface that increases the injury or damage that results from the impact. In other words, Haddon's analytical framework is more concerned about the physical conditions surrounding the accident than who was responsible for those conditions. He is also more optimistic about what can be done to control accidents by correcting mechanical or physical causes. Consequently, Haddon would have greater faith that more sturdily built cars would reduce injuries from auto accidents even if driving habits and attitudes remained unchanged. (On the other hand, correcting the physical conditions that led to the uncontrolled release of energy may require some change in human behavior.) Haddon does not claim, however, that his ten strategies are exhaustive or that he has detailed all the causes of accidents.

Other writings by Haddon refer to unsafe acts of persons. For example, in an article on auto accidents, Haddon suggests conditions in persons that affect the likelihood of an accident and the severity of injuries resulting from an accident. He cites the skill or sobriety of the driver, the physical condition of the driver, and the first-aid knowledge of persons present at the scene of the accident.

Although Haddon has not directed as much attention to how his strategies might be applied to unsafe acts, they can be so adapted. For example, in the auto crash analysis noted above, drunken drivers can be arrested, thus preventing them from starting and moving vehicles (Strategy 1). Driver training courses can improve the skills and attitudes of drivers by alerting them to the dangers of speeding (Strategy 2) and telling them how to handle a car under icy conditions (Strategy 3). Persons considering traveling with drivers who drink can be warned against such an exposure (Strategy 5). Physical examinations, good diet, and daily exercises strengthen the ability of crash victims to avoid or recover from injuries (Strategy 8). Finally, first aid courses would enable persons at the scene to reduce the effect of the accident (Strategy 9).

Many strategies applied to unsafe acts are difficult to fit into one of Haddon's ten categories. Consequently, valuable as it is, Haddon's framework needs to be supplemented. Together, the Heinrich and Haddon analyses provide a comprehensive view of the causes of accidents and the possible application of loss control measures.

CLASSIFICATION OF LOSS CONTROL MEASURES

Loss control measures can be classified according to various dimensions, including:

1. *Objective*—whether they are loss prevention or loss reduction measures.
2. *Approach*—whether they employ an engineering or human behavior approach.
3. *Timing*—when they are applied.

Any loss control measure can be classified according to all of these dimensions. For example, one measure may be a loss prevention method using the human behavior approach applied before the accident. Another measure may be a loss reduction method using the engineering approach applied before the accident.

By Objective: Loss Prevention or Loss Reduction

Loss control measures that seek to reduce the probability that a loss will occur are called loss *prevention* measures; loss control measures aimed at reducing loss severity are called loss *reduction* measures. Many loss control measures are designed to accomplish both objectives, making them both loss prevention and loss reduction measures.

Loss prevention is one goal of:

- building codes,
- boiler inspections,
- driver examinations,
- quality control checks on manufactured products,
- safety locks on doors,
- mopping up and drying floors,
- reviewing labels on products to determine whether any promises are made that cannot be fulfilled,
- repairing defective stairways,
- constructing guardrails on highways to separate cars moving in opposite directions,
- forbidding construction in flood-prone areas, and
- examining baggage at airports to prevent hijacking.

Most of these, even if they are not completely effective in preventing a loss, may still contribute to a reduction in the severity of losses.

Some illustrations of measures that are more specifically directed to the *reduction* of losses include:

- automatic sprinklers,
- early treatment of injuries,
- limiting the amount of cash accessible to employees,
- burglar alarms that summon a private protection service to the scene,
- fire fighting equipment,
- rehabilitation of injured workers,
- refurbishing and sale of damaged property, and
- raising a truck and its cargo from the bottom of a ravine.

One loss reduction measure, *separation*, has some special characteristics. Separation breaks an item of value subject to loss into independent units. For example:

- Instead of concentrating all its property in one warehouse, a firm might distribute the property among many warehouses across the country.
- Instead of locating all its workers in one giant manufacturing plant, a business might place the workers in smaller plants spread throughout the state.
- Instead of scheduling its shipments such that a single truck usually carries large values of these shipments, a firm might

reschedule so more frequent shipments of smaller values are made.

To the extent that separation reduces the loss arising out of a single occurrence because the potential financial impact is smaller, separation is like other loss reduction measures. However, separation has an added result that differentiates it from other loss control measures. By increasing the number of units subject to loss for the firm or family, separation improves the ability of the entity to predict future loss experience. In other words, the increase in the number of units makes it less likely that the actual experience during a particular period will differ from the average experience in the long run by more than a specified amount. The probability of a relatively large deviation between actual losses and predicted losses is lessened.

By Approach: Engineering or Human Behavior

Classified according to their objective, loss control measures may focus on loss prevention, loss reduction, or both. Classified according to the causes with which they attempt to deal, loss control measures use either of two approaches:

(1) *An engineering approach*—stressing the elimination of unsafe physical conditions by such measures as machine guards, fire-resistive construction, burglar-resistant safes, boiler inspections, railroad underpasses to reduce the number of grade crossings, and safer cars.

(2) *A human behavior approach*—stressing safety education and motivation for persons whose actions might precipitate a loss. For example, workers might be motivated and trained to prevent industrial injuries by pamphlets explaining the dangers associated with certain machinery, by safety classes and safety contests, and by rest periods.

The engineering approach might employ Haddon's ten strategies which, as already noted, emphasize the physical or mechanical causes of loss. The human behavior approach accepts Heinrich's argument that unsafe acts of persons are responsible for most accidents. The relative popularity of these two approaches has varied over time and continues to vary among types of exposures. For example, the human behavior approach may be more effective in controlling industrial accidents than in controlling fires.

Because accidents result from both unsafe acts of persons and physical or mechanical hazards, and because both often interact and reinforce each other, both the human behavior and engineering approaches are useful.

By Time of Application

Loss control measures can also be classified according to the time when they are applied. One timing classification categorizes the measures according to whether they are applied:

1. before the accident,
2. during the accident, or
3. after the accident.

Because loss prevention measures seek to reduce the likelihood that an accident will occur, they must be applied before the accident. Loss reduction measures are classified as *minimization* efforts if they are applied before or during the accident and *salvage* efforts if they are used after the accident.

Haddon's ten strategies have a time dimension. The first eight strategies must be used prior to an accident, the ninth in the same time frame as the accident, and the tenth following the accident.

Another useful timing classification distinguishes among (1) the planning phase, (2) the safety-maintenance phase, and (3) the emergency phase.[8]

Planning Phase Planning phase measures are those taken in anticipation of some major change in an entity's operations—the construction of a new building, the manufacture of a new product, merger with another business, the purchase of a barge, or the leasing of an important piece of equipment. These measures deserve special attention for at least two reasons. First, in determining whether to make a major change, the firm or family should consider the pure loss exposures associated with that change and what loss control measures can accomplish with respect to those exposures. Second, some loss control measures can be applied during the planning phase that would be impossible or much more expensive to apply at some later date. For example, a firm may be considering the construction of a new building. Whether this construction would be a good investment depends in part upon the probability that it would be damaged or destroyed in a fire. By making the walls thicker or using different construction materials than originally planned, the probability of a serious fire may be so reduced that the total investment is made more attractive than would otherwise be the case. Furthermore, these changes may not be possible after the building is completed or, if possible, they would probably be more expensive.

Safety Maintenance Phase Safety maintenance measures include all actions taken after the advance planning phase but prior to the accident. In addition to regular maintenance on the measures introduced during the planning stage, this group of loss control measures includes techniques that were not implemented during the planning phase. Fire drills, first-aid training, auto fleet maintenance checks, and monitoring of industrial emissions are examples.

Emergency Phase Emergency measures are those minimization and salvage efforts applied during or after the accident—for example, spraying water on a burning building or placing a tarp over a damaged roof.

ORGANIZATION FOR LOSS CONTROL

Loss control is a risk management function often involving loss control specialists. Loss control specialists perform the functions expressed in a loss control policy statement, as discussed in the following sections.

Loss Control Specialists

Whether or not the loss control specialist in a firm is a member of its risk management department, loss control specialists typically have staff authority, rather than line authority, with respect to loss control. Line authority implies a superior-subordinate relationship that permits one person to order another to do something. A supervisor, for example, has line authority over a number of workers. Staff specialists typically cannot command line personnel to perform. To accomplish their objectives, they must usually rely on persuasion and motivation of line managers or their subordinates. They may persuade a line manager to order his or her subordinates to behave in a certain way, or persons lower in the chain may accept the staff specialist's recommendations voluntarily. These specialists may also influence line managers or their subordinates through supporting services or through advice and counsel. Staff specialists, including those charged with loss control, can exert this power because they are experts in their field, have certain status in the firm, and have the support of the firm's top management.

To whom should loss control specialists report? Many reporting relationships are possible, depending upon the general organizational pattern of the firm and the personalities of the people involved.[9] The relationship selected must take into account that, because root causes of accidents exist everywhere throughout the firm, the loss control specialist(s) should be able to exert some influence on every line supervisor. His or her boss should be a person with influence who is committed to safety and who has a channel to upper echelons of management.

From the preceding discussion, and from the observation that risk management is to some degree a function of all levels of management, it is apparent that the loss control specialist is responsible for only part of the loss control function in the firm. Management, in consultation with the loss control specialist, should set goals for the firm and assign responsibility for achieving these goals to line managers with the advice and assistance of staff specialists.

Just as risk managers may have other responsibilities, especially in small- and medium-sized firms, so do loss control specialists. For example, they also may be personnel managers or production managers. Small firms may depend for loss control expertise on outsiders such as firms specializing in loss control, insurance agencies or brokerage firms, or insurance companies. Even large firms may rely on outsiders to provide advice and counsel in highly specialized areas or to render special services such as salvage operations, training classes, or the installation of certain safety equipment.

Loss Control Policy Statement

Like a risk management policy statement, a loss control policy statement provides a vehicle for disseminating information about loss control objectives throughout the firm. Because some action is required of all employees with respect to loss control, it is desirable that as many employees as possible be alerted to this information. Loss control policy objectives vary greatly. At the minimum, these statements should include answers to the following questions:[10]

(1) What is management's intent?
(2) Is the policy statement sufficiently broad to cover such diverse activities as on-the-job and off-the-job safety, physical damage control, and liability loss control?
(3) Who is responsible for each loss control activity?
(4) Who is authorized to carry out loss control activities, and what are the limitations on each person's authority?
(5) What is the role of the loss control specialist?
(6) What is the role of an inter-departmental safety committee, if any?
(7) What standards of performance are expected?
(8) How will compliance with these standards be measured?

The advantages of having a loss control policy statement developed at a high management level are the same as those for a risk management policy statement approved by top management:

(1) The top managers become acquainted with the nature and importance of the loss control function.
(2) Management involvement strengthens the loss control specialist's hand in persuading and motivating others to act.
(3) Management has a standard against which the loss control performance of the firm can be measured.

There are economic, legal, and social reasons why top management should be deeply concerned about loss control.[11] The economic reason is that loss control can make a firm more efficient and more profitable. The legal reason is that many laws and regulations impose fines or even prison sentences on persons who fail to introduce certain loss control measures. The social reason is that a good citizen wants to take all reasonable steps to prevent or reduce the severity of injuries or property damage.

FOUR STEPS IN LOSS CONTROL

Loss control includes four steps:

(1) loss and hazard identification and analysis,
(2) selecting the best loss control measures,
(3) implementing these measures, and
(4) monitoring their performance.[12]

Loss and Hazard Identification and Analysis

The first step is to identify and analyze (1) the losses experienced by the entity, and (2) the hazards that caused those losses or might cause losses in the future. To identify the losses that have occurred and the hazards that exist or may exist in the future, the loss control specialist should develop a comprehensive reporting system and supplement it by periodic inspections. The analysis of losses and hazards may involve a variety of quantitative and qualitative methods.

Identifying the losses experienced by the entity requires that the loss control specialist be informed as promptly and as accurately as possible about accidents and their causes. To obtain such information the loss control specialist needs to develop a network of informants and the forms they can use to submit their reports.

Data Sources The most important members of the information network are the supervisors responsible for the operations where accidents occur. These supervisors are close to the accidents and, because of their familiarity with operations, they can provide many details. Completing an accident report form should also increase their awareness of what causes accidents and how serious they can be. On the other hand, few operations personnel are loss control specialists. Most know little about accidents and their causes. They may not be highly motivated to provide information about losses. Self-interest may sometimes cause them to conceal losses or misrepresent accident causes.

Accident Report Forms   In designing forms for accident reporting by operations personnel, the risk manager or loss control specialist must keep in mind the objective—to obtain the information required for loss analysis. The forms should be relatively easy to understand and not too burdensome to complete.

Ideally, one would study not only those accidents that caused injuries or property damage, but all those unplanned events that did *or might have* caused such losses. In other words, the "near-misses" as well as accidents causing losses would ideally be reported and studied. Cost and the burden of reporting all such events place such an approach beyond feasibility in most cases.

Uses of Data   The information on losses provided through accident report forms can be used to:

(1) measure the performance of line managers,
(2) determine which operations, if any, need to be corrected,
(3) identify the hazards that have been responsible for the losses, and
(4) provide information that can be used to motivate workers and managers to pay more attention to loss control.

Analyzing Loss Data   Most firms do not have enough accidents to justify sophisticated statistical analysis. For large firms, however, statistical measures may be feasible and desirable, especially for loss exposures characterized by high loss frequency.

Industrial injuries occur frequently enough in many firms to have been the subject of numerous statistical analyses. Various measures of a firm's current performance can be compared with its past performance or the performance of comparable firms to determine whether some corrective measure is necessary. Similarly, the performance of one department can be compared with that of another department to determine which is performing more satisfactorily.

OSHA Incidence Rates.   The only accident records kept by many businesses are those required by the Occupational Safety and Health Administration (OSHA). Therefore, it is particularly important to recognize the ways in which data based on OSHA records can be used to analyze a firm's safety record. This section will examine how incidence rates are compiled and computed and the value of comparing the incidence rates for a given firm with the national incidence rates.

The Occupational Safety and Health Act requires that records of occupational injuries and illnesses be prepared and retained for five years. These records develop annual totals of:

   (1) the number of injury-related *fatalities,*
   (2) the number of *injuries* involving days away from work, days of restricted work activity, or both,
   (3) the number of *injuries* involving days away from work,
   (4) the number of *days* away from work,
   (5) the number of *days* of restricted work activity, and
   (6) the number of *injuries* without lost workdays.

Similar records also must be kept for fatal and nonfatal occupational illnesses.

The raw total figures in each category can be used to compare safety performance in one year with safety performance the previous year, but this comparison does not recognize possible differences in the degree of exposure during the two years. To adjust for differences in exposure, and to facilitate comparison of data among firms or operations of different sizes, these raw figures are converted to *rates* such as the following:

$$\text{Incidence rate for total recordable cases} = \frac{\text{No. of recorded injuries and illnesses} \times 200{,}000}{\text{Total hours worked by all employees during the period covered}}$$

In this formula, recordable cases are defined as all cases requiring more than first aid treatment. The 200,000 is a constant used to reflect incidence rates as a certain number of incidences per one hundred full-time equivalent worker years (100 workers $\times$ 40 hours $\times$ 50 weeks = 200,000 worker hours). Since the typical firm subject to OSHA has approximately 100 workers, this serves as a convenient basis.

The formula above would develop an incidence rate for all recordable cases. Similar incidence rates can be developed for any individual component of the data accumulated by OSHA reports. For example, rates can be developed for the number of lost workday *cases,* for the number of nonfatal *cases* without lost workdays, or for the number of lost *workdays.*

To illustrate, assume that Company Z recorded 500,000 hours worked in the year 19X1 and developed the illness and injury figures

Exhibit 2-4
Company Z and National Injury and Illness Report

	Company Z			National incidence rates[†]	
	1 Raw Data 19X1	2 Incidence Rates 19X1	3 Incidence Rates 19X0	4 All Industries 19X1	5 Same Industry 19X1
Recordable cases	21	8.4	7.8	8.07	13.64
Lost workday cases	8	3.2	3.3	3.33	4.24
Nonfatal cases					
without lost workdays	13	5.2	4.5	4.74	9.37
Lost workdays	89	35.6	37.2	59	72

[†]These are hypothetical rates used for illustrative purposes only.

shown in Column 1 of Exhibit 2-4. By plugging these data into the incidence rate formula, the incidence rates in Column 2 can be calculated. This information still is not particularly meaningful unless it can be *compared* with other incidence rates, such as those shown in Columns 3, 4, and 5.

Column 3 shows the incidence rate for Company Z for the previous year. Analysis of Columns 2 and 3 would lead to the observation that the frequency of illness and injury is on the rise but that severity has decreased. This would still not provide any information as to how Company Z's safety record compares with the safety record of other firms. A comparison with national incidence rates for all industries, shown in Column 4, would seem to indicate that Company Z is showing average performance, with a lost workday's rate notably below the national average. A more precise comparison can be developed based on the data in Column 5, which reflects national incidence rates *for the same industry* in the same year. Since every figure in Column 5 is higher than the figure in Column 2, this information would give even more valuable information as to Company Z's relative safety performance. From these data, it would seem that Company Z's performance is notably superior to the performance of other firms in the same industry.[13]

Because of the ways in which OSHA data are accumulated, it is possible to compute and compare information regarding the frequency of accidents involving various degrees of severity (from nonfatal cases without lost workdays to fatal cases). Likewise, incidence rates for lost workdays give an indication of relative accident severity. Comparative data are available so that a given organization's injury and illness rates can be compared with others in the same industry. Yet, there are limitations on the use of OSHA data for risk management purposes. For example, what is a recordable injury or illness for OSHA purposes is not necessarily a compensable injury under the workers' compensation system and vice versa. An even greater limitation lies in the fact that OSHA measurements do nothing to measure injuries and illnesses in terms of their dollar cost.

Petersen's Measurements. Petersen has suggested some additional measurements, a few of which are presented below:[14]

(1) A *frequency-severity indicator* can be calculated as follows:

$$\text{Indicator} = \sqrt{\frac{F \times S}{1,000}}$$

where F is the number of injuries per 100 full-time equivalent workers and S is the number of days lost per injury. To illustrate, if F = 10, and S = 25, the indicator is

$$\sqrt{\frac{10 \times 25}{1,000}} = 0.5$$

If F = 40 and S = 25, the indicator is

$$\sqrt{\frac{40 \times 25}{1,000}} = 1.0$$

If F = 4 and S = 250, the indicator is also 1.0

(2) *Costs incurred* (the disability income, death, and medical expenses paid plus the estimated amounts still to be paid for accidents that occurred during the period).

(3) *Costs incurred per 1,000 man-hours of exposure.*

(4) *Costs incurred expressed as a percentage of the workers' compensation insurance premiums paid.*

(5) To determine whether a firm's loss frequency rate is improving or getting worse, a *Safe-T-Score* may be calculated, as follows:

$$\text{Safe-T-Score} = \frac{\text{Frequency rate now} - \text{Frequency rate past}}{\sqrt{\dfrac{\text{Frequency rate past}}{\text{Number of full-time equivalent workers (in hundreds) now}}}}$$

To illustrate, assume that the current loss frequency rate per 100 full-time equivalent workers is twelve, the past rate nine, and the number of full-time equivalent workers 100. The Safe-T-Score is:

$$\frac{12-9}{\sqrt{\dfrac{9}{1}}} = \frac{3}{3} = 1.0$$

If the current and past loss frequency rates had been twelve and nine but the firm had four times as many workers, the Safe-T-Score would be:

$$\frac{12-9}{\sqrt{\dfrac{9}{4}}} = \frac{3}{1.5} = 2.0$$

"Small" Score values can reasonably be explained by chance fluctuations; the current rate does not represent either an improvement or worsening in the accident record. Petersen suggests that a Score between +2.0 and −2.0 is "small." For large firms, the probability that the Score will fall outside this range if there has been no change in the true probability of loss is about 5 percent. If the Score exceeds +2.0, a loss control specialist could reasonably conclude that the accident record had worsened and that the change from the past is not due to chance. If the Score is a negative value greater than −2.0, the accident record has probably improved significantly. The test is not foolproof, however. The true loss probability of the firm may have worsened but because of chance fluctuations the current value may be close to the past rate. True loss probability may be the same but the current rate may be much different from the past. Both such outcomes, however, are unlikely.

Similar tests can be developed to compare the firm's accident frequency rate with the rate for the industry or the accident frequency rate in one department with the rate for another department.

Other Uses of Loss Data.   In addition to alerting loss control specialists to whether the loss situation may be in need of special attention, statistical records can also be analyzed with respect to such accident characteristics as:

- peril,
- nature of the accident,
- month, day, and hour of the accident,
- supervisor or the worker involved,
- operation affected, and

- hazard or underlying cause of the accident (an unsafe condition or an unsafe act including the reason for the unsafe act).

Accident records should summarize these characteristics for accidents during the most recent period and how these characteristics have changed over time. If certain characteristics appear frequently in the accident summary, or if frequency of appearance is changing, they are worthy of special attention. The loss control specialist must remember, however, that some characteristics should normally appear more often. For example, some operations are more hazardous than others. Some perils occur more frequently than others. Primary attention should be focused on those characteristics that exceed their normal frequency.

Accidents causing serious losses are commonly investigated in much more detail than other accidents. The loss control specialist may supplement the report of the operations supervisor with an on-the-spot investigation. The special attention accorded these serious accidents is understandable, and may even be necessary for legal defense purposes, but most experts agree that the emphasis is misplaced because the severity of the accident is largely a matter of chance.

Even though the accident records of small firms are particularly likely to be affected by chance fluctuations, they are still useful as an indicator of possible hazards. For example, if several accidents are reported that mention defective ladders, the firm would be well advised to investigate its ladders and the conditions surrounding their use. Small firms, however, should be aware that they may be exposed to many hazards that, because of chance fluctuations, have not yet caused an accident. They must rely more upon hazard analysis, discussed next.

Hazard Analysis Loss analysis should reveal hazards that need to be investigated more carefully. Hazard analysis, however, cannot be limited to the hazards that have already caused accidents. Some hazards are "accidents waiting to happen." It is necessary to investigate the possible existence of other hazards that have caused losses to the firm in earlier loss analysis periods or that the experience of other firms, insurers, or government organizations suggests should be investigated. Increasingly, loss control specialists learn of new hazards that have not as yet caused a loss for anyone but have been discovered through experimentation under controlled conditions. Hazards in new products (such as newly developed pharmaceuticals) have been uncovered in this way.

Hazards that have not yet caused losses also are discovered through inspections. Line supervisors are primarily responsible for these inspections, but loss control specialists usually also become involved.

As an aid in making an inspection, the line supervisor or specialist often has a checklist that reminds the inspector of the many possible hazards and facilitates a comparison with existing conditions. The loss control specialist usually is responsible for the design of these checklists and the forms used to report the results of the inspection. These inspection forms vary. For example, one form asks only for (1) an evaluation of the general conditions regarding housekeeping, equipment, hand tools, and so on, and (2) recommendations for improving these conditions. A more comprehensive form asks for (1) the unsafe conditions or acts noted, (2) whether each of these "symptoms" was discussed with the supervisor, (3) the causes found for each of these symptoms, and (4) suggestions as to future actions with respect to these causes.[15]

One method that has proved increasingly useful in analyzing the causes of accidents is *fault tree analysis*. This technique may be used in loss analysis to determine the causes of actual losses, or in hazard analysis to determine the causes and effects of hazardous situations. It shows the multiple causes of accidents and whether all or only some of these causes must be present to precipitate an accident. It thus provides a basis for preventing such accidents.

An example is presented in Exhibit 2-5. This diagram analyzes accidents in which persons slip on floors left wet following a cleanup. For the accident to occur, not only must the floor be wet, but also the floor must have a surface that becomes slick when wet and someone must walk across the floor. That person may be the cleanup person or someone else. The cleanup person may walk across the floor because of items left behind or because of having to cross the floor to get to the next work location. Someone else may walk across the floor because the floor was cleaned at a time when others had to use it, or the floor might be used in defiance or ignorance of orders to the contrary. The fault tree shows these multiple causes and their interconnections. It shows that the accident can be prevented by not leaving the floor wet following a cleanup, by changing the floor surface, or by keeping persons off the floor. Merely keeping others off the floor may not prevent the accident because the cleanup person may fall.[16]

Selection of Loss Control Measures

In order to select the appropriate loss control measures, the person making the decision must first know what measures might be taken to reduce the likelihood or severity of the accident and then decide which measures would be best in a specific situation. Selection of a particular loss control measure, such as the proper guard on a machine or the type of safe to be used, is a matter for specialists in the areas affected. The loss control specialist should know enough about the available mea-

Exhibit 2-5
A Simple Fault Tree Diagram*

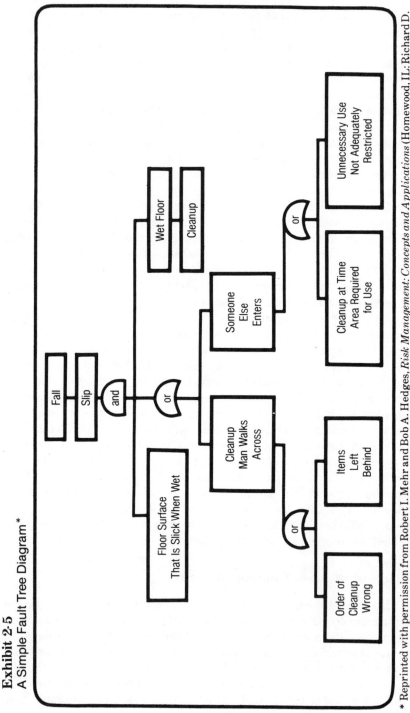

* Reprinted with permission from Robert I. Mehr and Bob A. Hedges, *Risk Management: Concepts and Applications* (Homewood, IL: Richard D. Irwin, 1974), p. 433.

sures and the decision process to assist those specialists and to evaluate their decisions.

In estimating the benefits to be derived from a particular risk management technique, or from loss control efforts generally, it is important to recognize *all* of the accident costs that might be incurred in the absence of control. Recognizing all of these losses strengthens the case for loss control and aids the loss control specialist trying to motivate top management. For example, if damaged shipments lead to customer dissatisfaction, the losses should include this additional cost.

Heinrich's Method for Determining Accident Costs   According- ing to Heinrich, the cost of industrial accidents is usually stated only in terms of compensation paid the injured employee for lost time and medical expenses. The actual costs, however, are much greater because the "incidental" or "hidden" costs have been found to be four times as great as the compensation benefits.[17] Workers' compensation insurance usually covers the compensation benefits, but most of the hidden costs must be retained by the insured. If Heinrich's argument is accepted, the case for loss control, with or without insurance, is considerably strengthened. The factors that Heinrich included among these hidden accident costs were as follows:

(1) Cost of lost time of injured employee.
(2) Cost of time lost by other employees who stop work:
    (a) out of curiosity.
    (b) out of sympathy.
    (c) to assist injured employee.
    (d) for other reasons.
(3) Cost of time lost by foremen, supervisors, or other executives as follows:
    (a) assisting injured employee.
    (b) investigating the cause of the accident.
    (c) arranging for the injured employee's production to be continued by some other employee.
    (d) selecting, training, or breaking in a new employee to replace the injured employee.
    (e) preparing state accident reports, or attending hearings before state officials.
(4) Cost of time spent on the case by first-aid attendant and hospital department staff, when not paid for by the insurance carrier.
(5) Cost due to damage to the machine, tools, or other property or to the spoilage of material.

(6) Incidental cost due to interference with production, failure to fill orders on time, loss of bonuses, payment of forfeits, and other similar causes.

(7) Cost to employee under employee welfare and benefit systems.

(8) Cost to employer in continuing the wages of the injured employee in full, after his return—even though the services of the employee (who is not yet fully recovered) may for a time be worth only about half of their normal value.

(9) Cost due to the loss of profit on the injured employee's productivity, and on the idle machines.

(10) Cost that occurs in consequence of the excitement or weakened morale due to the accident.

(11) Overhead cost per injured employee—the expense of light, heat, rent, and other such items, which continues while the injured employee is a nonproducer.[18]

Heinrich did not contend that his 4 to 1 (indirect cost to direct cost) proportion applied to every accident or to every plant. He also acknowledged that the ratio may vary in nationwide application.

Heinrich's major point—that the "indirect" costs are substantial—holds true, but many writers have challenged the 4 to 1 ratio. Grimaldi and Simonds, using the terms "insured" and "uninsured" to correspond to Heinrich's "direct" and "indirect," believe that (1) the ratio of uninsured costs to insured costs in industrial accidents is probably less than 4 to 1 because some of the uninsured costs included by Heinrich are not valid, and (2) because there is no direct correlation between uninsured costs and insured costs, applying a single ratio to total direct costs to determine the indirect costs produces inaccurate results.[19]

Grimaldi and Simonds' Method for Determining Accident Costs According to Grimaldi and Simonds, the following are valid uninsured costs:

(1) Cost of wages paid for working time lost by workers who were not injured.

(2) Net cost to repair, replace, or straighten up material or equipment that was damaged in an accident.

(3) Cost of wages paid for working time lost by injured workers, other than workers' compensation payments.

(4) Extra cost due to overtime work necessitated by an accident.

(5) Cost of wages paid supervisors while their time is required for activities necessitated by the accident.

(6) Wage cost due to decreased output of injured worker after return to work.

(7) Cost of learning period of new worker.

(8) Uninsured medical cost borne by the company.

(9) Cost of time spent by higher supervisors and clerical workers on investigations or in the processing of compensation application forms.

(10) Miscellaneous unusual costs such as public liability claims, lost profits on orders lost, and cost of hiring new employees if the additional hiring expense is significant.[20]

Grimaldi and Simonds exclude certain items (suggested by various writers such as Heinrich) which they deem generally invalid, valid only under special circumstances, or duplicate costs already included in other items.

As an alternative to expressing uninsured costs as a single multiple of insured costs, Grimaldi and Simonds suggest the following formula for the ordinary run of accidents:[21]

$$
\begin{aligned}
\text{Total cost} = \ & \text{Insurance cost} \\
& + A \times \text{The number of lost-time cases} \\
& + B \times \text{The number of doctor's cases} \\
& + C \times \text{The number of first-aid cases} \\
& + D \times \text{The number of no-injury accidents}
\end{aligned}
$$

where A, B, C, and D are the average uninsured costs for each category of cases, and the number of cases refers to the actual count of each type during the period. Lost-time cases include those causing permanent partial disabilities and temporary total disabilities. Death and permanent total disability cases are excluded because they are unusual and merit separate individual investigation. Doctor's cases include those accidents not included in the lost-time category but which necessitate a doctor's attention. First-aid cases are medical treatment cases requiring only first aid which cause the worker to lose less than eight hours of working time and property damage less than some specified amount. No-injury accidents either cause no injury or require only first-aid treatment, but cause property damage in excess of some specified amount.

This four-way classification does not include all accidents but it does extend beyond bodily injury accidents. Excluded are property-damage-only accidents causing losses below a specified amount. Grimaldi and Simonds say it would be unduly burdensome to collect cost data on such accidents. Indeed they recognize that most firms in their study of industrial accidents do not include any no-injury accidents. If the firm has no such records, they suggest, on the basis of a national study, that the number be set at the number of lost-time cases.

The values of A, B, C, and D should be based where possible on the experience of the individual firm, but a national study by Simonds

Exhibit 2-6
Total Measurable Cost*

Insurance cost		$33,500.00
Uninsured cost:		
14 lost-time cases	@ $270.00 =	3,780.00
45 doctor's cases	@ 68.00 =	3,060.00
1,390 first-aid cases	@ 14.90 =	20,711.00
14 no-injury cases	@ 500.00 =	7,000.00
Total uninsured cost		$34,551.00
Total measurable cost		$68,051.00

* Adapted with permission from J.W. Grimaldi and R.H. Simonds, *Safety Management*, 3rd. ed. (Homewood, IL: Richard D. Irwin, 1975), p. 416.

indicated the following values at 1974 cost levels:[22]

$$A = \$220$$
$$B = 55$$
$$C = 12$$
$$D = 400$$

To illustrate the application of the method, they presented the example shown in Exhibit 2-6 for a firm using the values above adjusted to an assumed 1975 cost level. In this case the uninsured cost exceeds slightly the insured cost, a result they apparently believe is more representative than Heinrich's 4 to 1 ratio.[23]

Bird and Germain's Method for Determining Accident Costs Bird and Germain claim, however, that this revised concept also has proved to be ineffective in safety motivation. Obtaining and updating the necessary information, they believe, is a difficult, time-consuming task. Allocating uninsured costs among departments poses technical problems and is even more likely to be opposed than the allocation of insured costs. They suggest instead a *ledger costs concept*, so-named because it involves only costs that appear on department ledgers.[24] Government agencies call it the "elements of production-accident cost" concept. This method of accident cost accounting does not include all accident costs but it does add some accurate, noninsured costs that could be many times the insured costs. The factors considered in this accounting are the following:

- Manpower:
  - Total workers' compensation benefits
  - Wages and medical costs paid during disability in addition to workers' compensation benefits

- Time lost on day of injury and on subsequent days
- Time spent on light work or reduced output
● Machinery, Material, Equipment:
  - Cost of repairing damage, or cost of replacement
  - Lost production time

The method is applicable to all accidents, not only those that cause bodily injuries or which might have caused bodily injuries.

Conclusions Regarding Accident Costs Despite their differences, Heinrich, Grimaldi and Simonds, and Bird and Germain all emphasize that accident costs tend to be underestimated. Whether a firm decides to retain or insure an exposure to loss, it should seriously consider loss control. In comparing the benefits with the costs, it is important to consider *all* the costs that might be reduced, not just the direct costs or the insured costs.

Once all accident costs have been recognized, it is possible to measure how loss control measures might reduce accident costs. The most appropriate loss control measures are those for which the expected benefits bear the most favorable relationship to the expected costs. The minimum expected loss method, introduced in Chapter 1, provides one approach for making these decisions. When a loss control measure involves a long-term investment, the capital budgeting method, briefly introduced in Chapter 1, should prove particularly useful.

Capital Budgeting Loss control often involves a capital expenditure that will produce benefits for many years. Automatic sprinkler systems, fire-resistive construction, burglar-resistive safes, and machine guards illustrate this kind of loss control. In order to determine whether a loss control-related expenditure is worthwhile, one must determine whether the stream of benefits to be derived from the loss control measure is worth the capital expenditure and maintenance costs.

For example, consider an automatic sprinkler system, ignoring the effects of inflation and taxes. Assume that it would cost $10,000 to install an automatic sprinkler system with a life expectancy of ten years. Annual maintenance costs would be $400. The sprinklers would reduce annual insurance premiums by $1,900 and "expected" (or average) annual uninsured costs by another $500. In other words, a $10,000 expenditure would reduce annual expenditures for the next ten years by the reduction in the insurance premiums and expected annual uninsured costs less the maintenance cost. The *net* annual expenditures, therefore, would be reduced by $1,900 + $500 − $400, or $2,000. Deciding whether $2,000 annual savings for ten years is worth a

$10,000 capital expenditure *now*, is a capital budgeting decision.[25] Capital budgeting has already been introduced in Chapter 1 and is discussed at length in CPCU 8. All that is presented here is the basic concept.

The $10,000 expenditure is worth serious consideration if the present value of the annual benefits (in this case the net reduction in expenditures), discounted at the firm's required rate of return on investment, exceeds the capital expenditure. Assume for illustrative purposes that the $2,000 reduction in expenses occurs at the beginning of each year for the next ten years. Because the first $2,000 is saved immediately, there is no discount. The second $2,000, however, will not be saved until one year from now. Its *present value* is the amount we could invest for one year at the firm's required rate of return and have $2,000 at the end of that year. In other words, if the minimum acceptable rate of return is 10 percent, the present value of $2,000 saved at the beginning of the second year is calculated as follows:

$$(\text{Present value}) \times (1.00 + 10\%) = \$2,000 \text{ one year from now.}$$

Or:

$$(\text{Present value}) \times (1.10) = \$2,000$$

Therefore, dividing both sides of the equation by 1.10:

$$\text{Present value} = \$2,000\left(\frac{1}{1.10}\right) = \$2,000\ (.9091) = \$1,818$$

Similarly, the present value of the third $2,000 saved two years from now is

$$\text{Present value} = \$2,000\left(\frac{1}{1.10}\right)^2 = \$2,000\ (.8264) = \$1,653$$

For the ten years of $2,000 annual savings, the present values would be $13,518, calculated as shown in Exhibit 2-7. The expenditure deserves serious consideration because the $13,518 present value of the benefits exceeds the $10,000 expenditure.

This description of the capital budgeting procedure has assigned no value to the fact, in addition to the benefits noted, the automatic sprinkler system may increase the predictability of losses and reduce the probability that the more serious losses will occur. Assigning a value to these advantages is not easy, but it would be a serious mistake to ignore them.

Most loss control decisions are not made as formally or as

Exhibit 2-7
Capital Expenditure Calculations

$2,000		=	$2,000	=	$ 2,000
2,000	$\left(\dfrac{1}{1.10}\right)^{1}$	=	2,000 (0.9091)	=	1,818
2,000	$\left(\dfrac{1}{1.10}\right)^{2}$	=	2,000 (0.8264)	=	1,653
2,000	$\left(\dfrac{1}{1.10}\right)^{3}$	=	2,000 (0.7513)	=	1,503
2,000	$\left(\dfrac{1}{1.10}\right)^{4}$	=	2,000 (0.6830)	=	1,366
2,000	$\left(\dfrac{1}{1.10}\right)^{5}$	=	2,000 (0.6209)	=	1,242
2,000	$\left(\dfrac{1}{1.10}\right)^{6}$	=	2,000 (0.5645)	=	1,129
2,000	$\left(\dfrac{1}{1.10}\right)^{7}$	=	2,000 (0.5132)	=	1,026
2,000	$\left(\dfrac{1}{1.10}\right)^{8}$	=	2,000 (0.4665)	=	933
2,000	$\left(\dfrac{1}{1.10}\right)^{9}$	=	2,000 (0.4241)	=	848
					$13,518

quantitatively as the preceding discussion would suggest. Although many such decisions might be improved if they did incorporate some of this reasoning, and although the trend is in this direction, the data and effort required for such careful analysis often are not available. Further, the results may not justify so much effort or time. Instead, decisions are commonly made on the basis of a qualitative assessment of how the loss control measure will affect the future. A limited data base may be considered in this assessment. For example, the loss control specialist may not be able to estimate with any degree of confidence how a given measure will affect the total dollar losses per year from industrial accidents or fires, but he or she may have some feeling for the present loss frequency rate and whether the loss control measure will substantially reduce that rate. The loss control expenditure will be especially attractive if the present loss rate is unusually high by historical or industry standards and the loss control is expected to return it to an acceptable range.

Sometimes the loss control specialist has no choice in introducing some loss control measure. Government laws or regulations may require certain controls. For example, fire codes may specify the materials to be used in constructing a new building, the Occupational Safety and Health Act requires compliance with numerous safety standards designed to reduce industrial accidents, and the Consumer Product Safety Act establishes similar standards for the manufacturers of consumer products. Businesses usually comply voluntarily with consensus standards developed by private industry groups without carefully considering the benefit-cost implications for their particular firms. Finally, as a condition of transferring the loss exposure to someone else such as an insurer or a landlord, the firm may be obliged to engage in some loss control measure(s).

In addition to these externally imposed obligations, businesses or families may see the need for some loss control primarily because of the pre-loss and post-loss social responsibility objective. This objective is especially potent when human lives or health are at stake.

Implementation of Loss Control Measures

Implementation of a particular loss control measure in the most economical, effective manner presents special challenges. A loss control specialist must be acquainted with the various ways a measure can be implemented and the advantages and disadvantages of each different way. For example, automatic sprinklers can be purchased from various manufacturers. The features and costs of the various systems must be compared. Similar reasoning might apply to machine guards, locks on doors, fire doors, safety literature, or various equipment. Similarly, loss control services such as security guards, fire fighters, safety instructors, and rehabilitation specialists may be available from several sources. Instead of obtaining these services from outsiders, the firm may decide to use its own staff because it would cost less or because familiarity with the firm's property and personnel may be more important than the outsider's safety expertise. Equipment may also be fabricated internally instead of being purchased.

Implementing a loss control measure, like the decision to use that measure, is most often the direct responsibility of line managers. The loss control specialist must (1) motivate these line managers to do their safety job well, (2) assist these managers where appropriate, and (3) implement the aspects of the measures for which he or she is directly responsible.

To motivate line managers, loss control specialists can use such techniques as:

- publication of accident and loss summaries,
- allocation of accident costs among departments,
- distribution of literature,
- conducting classes that demonstrate why safety pays,
- assisting line managers by alerting them to new loss control devices and activities,
- helping line managers seek out the information they need to implement a decision, and
- instructing supervisors on how to motivate workers.

Loss control specialists must themselves implement such activities as training classes and the development or obtaining of safety literature. Sometimes they also manage such things as fire brigades, plant guards, and other direct loss control activities that are not otherwise assigned.

Monitoring Loss Control Measures

Loss control measures must be constantly monitored to determine (1) whether they are being implemented correctly, and (2) whether they are achieving the desired results. They may not be producing the desired results because the initial decision to use those measures was not correct or because conditions have changed.

To check on the implementation of loss control measures, loss control specialists can request activity reports from line managers which tell what the line managers are doing on such matters as hazard analysis, safety meetings, and orientation of new employees. Points can be assigned for each activity as a measure of how each supervisor and the firm as a whole is performing. A disadvantage of this approach is that it relies on the supervisor to report activities accurately and does not reveal the effect these activities have had upon how workers perform or upon the physical environment.

Loss control specialists can visit each department to inspect the premises and observe worker adherence to job safety rules. Using statistical sampling theory, the specialist can obtain a reasonably accurate picture of a department's performance through a limited number of observations on the site. [26] The inspections themselves are believed to motivate supervisors and workers to perform more safely.

The results of these inspections must be interpreted with care. It may be unfair and unwise to judge the performance of a department or a department head on the basis of a single inspection.

Determining whether loss control methods are producing the desired results in terms of accidents and dollar losses is closely related to the first step in loss control—loss analysis. One difference is that the monitoring process may emphasize performance in areas that have been recently subjected to some special loss controls. Another is that the monitoring process may be a continuing review designed to alert the loss specialist only when the number of accidents or the losses exceed certain tolerance levels. The monitoring process may suggest a quite different loss control technique from the present measure, a modification of the present measure or how it is to be implemented, or no change.

COMBINATION

In the introduction of this chapter, it was stated that control techniques attempt to reduce the loss frequency, loss severity, or variation in potential losses. Thus far, most discussion has centered on measures used primarily to lower loss frequency (loss prevention measures) and loss severity (loss reduction measures). Separation has also been mentioned as a special type of loss control measure that reduces the loss arising out of a single occurrence and also improves the ability of the entity to predict future loss experience. Before studying the control technique of combination, it will be helpful to examine more closely how separation improves predictability.

How Separation Improves Predictability

Separation breaks an item of value subject to loss into smaller, independent units. For example, a firm that formerly made shipments on a single truck might use separation and split a large shipment into twenty smaller shipments, each traveling on a different truck. This is a loss reduction measure to the extent that the maximum value that can be lost if one truck's cargo is destroyed is reduced by 95 percent when the value on each truck is reduced to 5 percent of the original value. Often, this is the primary goal of separation—to limit the size of the probable maximum loss in any one occurrence.

Note that the expected number of cargo losses will actually

increase twenty times if twenty times as many trucks are carrying cargo. Everything else being equal, the increase in number of expected losses will offset the decrease in expected loss severity, and aggregate expected losses on the average in the long run will be unchanged. In the short run, however, predictability is increased because there will be less variation in total dollar losses from one year to the next. With improved predictability, the risk manager is better able to finance those losses that occur. The law of large numbers provides the scientific basis for analyzing predictability, and will be examined in greater detail in Chapter 5.

How Combination Improves Predictability

The third *control* technique to be discussed in this chapter is combination. Combination is not a *loss control* measure; it does not reduce either the probability of loss or loss severity. However, combination does improve the ability of the risk manager to predict future loss experience by increasing the number of units subject to loss.

In contrast to separation, combination does not divide one or a few existing exposure units into many exposure units; instead, it seeks to increase the number of exposure units through the acquisition of additional units. For example, a firm making shipments may:

- use *separation* by making a larger number of smaller shipments, or
- use *combination* by merging with another similar firm so that it is able to make a larger number of shipments.

Combination is seldom, if ever, practiced merely because it gives more predictability to pure loss exposures. Instead, combination usually results as a byproduct of action taken to achieve some other objective. For example, a taxicab company may purchase new cabs or merge with another taxicab company for various business reasons. Regardless of the motivation, the result is a greater number of taxicabs (more exposure units). One result of this greater number is greater predictability of future loss experience.

The effectiveness of separation or combination in making loss experience more predictable should not be overstated. The discussion of "How Large Is Large?" in Chapter 5 will show that (1) the number of exposure units required to satisfy even modest forecasting criteria is rather large, and (2) for most entities and exposures the number of exposure units would have to be increased substantially to improve the accuracy of loss predictions significantly.

NONINSURANCE TRANSFERS

Insurance was described in Chapter 1 as a technique that permits insureds to transfer the financial consequence of loss exposures to an insurer. Not all loss exposure transfers involve insurance. This section deals entirely with *noninsurance* transfers.

Some noninsurance transfers are *control* measures. Like avoidance, loss control, and combination, these control-type noninsurance transfers alter the entity's exposures in an attempt to reduce the loss frequency, the loss severity, or the variation in potential losses. Noninsurance transfers that are control devices would include such transfers as:

- the sale of a building,
- subcontracting a part of a construction project,
- the sale of a product line to another firm, or
- an exculpatory agreement.

Other noninsurance transfers are *loss financing* techniques. These financing-type noninsurance transfers resemble insurance in that the financial consequences of certain loss exposures are transferred to another entity. Financing-type noninsurance transfers differ from insurance in that the entity to which the financial consequences of the loss exposures are transferred (the transferee) is not an insurance company.

Examples of financing-type noninsurance transfers include:

- provisions in leases under which the landlord promises to finance losses that may occur and that otherwise would have to be financed by the tenant or vice versa,
- similar agreements between manufacturers and retailers,
- incorporation of a business, and
- contracts of suretyship.

Financing-type noninsurance transfers will be analyzed in detail in Chapter 3. What follows deals with noninsurance transfers of the control type.

Control-Type Noninsurance Transfers

When noninsurance transfers are used as a control technique, the intention is to alter the loss exposures. As a result of an effective noninsurance transfer of this type, certain specific loss exposures should be affected in at least one of the following ways:

(1) losses should have a lower potential frequency,

(2) losses should have a lower potential severity, or

(3) losses should be more predictable.

It is important to remember that noninsurance transfers do not eliminate all exposures connected with the transferred property or activity. As a result, the risk manager needs to recognize those specific exposures that have been transferred and those specific exposures that remain.

These principles can be illustrated by elaboration on the examples previously introduced:

(1) *The sale of a building.* This transfer of property shifts to the new owner most of the property and liability exposures associated with that property. The ownership exposures now exist for the new owner. Despite the sale, the seller may be faced with a loss due to an activity that took place on the property before it was sold, or due to a defect in the property sold. If the seller remains an occupant of the property (tenant), many exposures are unchanged. However, the probability of any loss connected with the property is lower (for the seller) after the sale.

(2) *Subcontracting part of a construction project.* When a contractor hires a subcontractor to do work that the contractor could have handled, the contractor has greatly reduced its chance of loss connected with that particular work.

(3) *The sale of a product line to another firm.* When a manufacturing activity is transferred to a different firm, the chance of injury to workers engaged in the manufacturing activity usually is transferred also.

(4) *Exculpatory agreements.* With an exculpatory contract, a transferee agrees not to hold the transferor responsible for losses to the property or person of the transferee that might otherwise be the responsibility of the transferor. Before performing surgery, a surgeon frequently requires the patient to sign an agreement absolving the surgeon of any liability should the operation prove unsuccessful. The patient (transferee) agrees not to hold the doctor (transferor) responsible for losses to the patient's person. From the perspective of the surgeon, this exculpatory agreement is a control-type transfer because it alters the loss exposure. The chance of being sued by the patient is greatly reduced. The exposure is not entirely eliminated, however, because the exculpatory agreement may not be upheld.

Comparison with Avoidance, Loss Control, and Combination Control-type noninsurance transfers—like avoidance, loss control, and combination—are control techniques dealing with the exposure itself. It is sometimes difficult to distinguish a noninsurance transfer from avoidance achieved through the abandonment of an existing exposure. However, when an exposure is abandoned, it ceases to exist for anyone. Under a noninsurance transfer, the exposure continues to exist but it is someone else's concern.

Loss control and combination seek to reduce the frequency and/or severity of a loss exposure, or to improve the predictability of an exposure by modifying some characteristic(s) of the exposure itself. Control-type noninsurance transfers do not modify the exposure—that is, the property or the activity itself is not changed; instead, the exposure is shifted to another entity.

Chapter Notes

1. Herbert W. Heinrich, *Industrial Accident Prevention*, 4th ed. (New York: McGraw-Hill Book Co., 1959), pp.14-16. In 1980, a fifth edition of *Industrial Accident Prevention* was published, containing revisions by Dan Petersen and Nester Roos. The fifth edition includes a discussion of recent "updates" of Heinrich's domino theory by a variety of safety experts.
2. Heinrich, p. 17.
3. Heinrich, p. 20.
4. Heinrich, p. 16.
5. Heinrich, p. 29.
6. Heinrich, pp. 32-33.
7. The Energy Release Theory first appeared in William Haddon, Jr., "On the Escape of Tigers: An Ecologic Note, "*Technology Review*, May, 1970. The version here appeared in "Strategies to Reduce Damage from Environmental Hazards, "*Status Report*, Vol. 15, No. 17, Nov. 21, 1980, Insurance Institute for Highway Safety. *Status Report*, in turn, summarized an article by Haddon, "The Basic Strategies for Reducing Damage from Hazards of all kinds, "*Hazard Prevention*, September/October, 1980, pp. 8-12.
8. W. T. Brightman, Jr., "What the Underwriting Company Can Offer, "*Insurance Costs and Controls: A Reappraisal*, AMA Management Report No. 19, pp. 36-37.
9. Dan Petersen, *Techniques of Safety Management*, 2nd ed. (New York: McGraw-Hill, 1978), pp. 37-40.
10. Petersen, p. 35.
11. Robert I. Mehr and Bob A. Hedges, *Risk Management: Concepts and Applications* (Homewood, IL: Richard D. Irwin, 1974), p. 669.
12. Mehr and Hedges, pp. 102-111.
13. Information of the type used for this illustration can be obtained from data published by the National Safety Council in its annual booklet, *Accident Facts* and from other sources.
14. Petersen, *Techniques of Safety Management*, pp. 116-117. Petersen calculates the frequency and severity rates as follows:

$$\text{Frequency} = \frac{\text{Number of disabling injuries} \times 1{,}000{,}000}{\text{Number of person-hours worked}}$$

$$\text{Severity} = \frac{\text{Total days charged} \times 1{,}000{,}000}{\text{Number of person-hours worked}}$$

The examples in this text use the frequency and severity measures used by the Bureau of Labor Statistics in its reports on industrial injuries.
15. Petersen, pp. 107-108.
16. Mehr and Hedges, pp. 431-433.

17. Heinrich, p. 50.
18. Heinrich, pp. 51-52.
19. R. H. Simonds and J. W. Grimaldi, *Safety Management,* rev. ed. (Homewood, IL: Richard D. Irwin, 1965), pp. 106-112. (This work has been superseded by a third edition. The revised edition is cited here because its successor, cited below, does not explain the authors' case in questioning the 4 to 1 ratio.)
20. J. W. Grimaldi and R. H. Simonds, *Safety Management,* 3rd ed. (Homewood, IL: Richard D. Irwin, 1975), pp. 397-402.
21. Grimaldi and Simonds, p. 404.
22. Grimaldi and Simonds, p. 415.
23. Grimaldi and Simonds, p. 416. These authors use this example in the context of justifying the costs of a safety program.
24. F. E. Bird and G. L. Germain, *Damage Control,* pp. 67-69. A ledger is a group of accounts. In this case, the accounts involved would be records of the various types of costs of operating a department, division, or other subunit of an entity.
25. The person interested in capital budgeting and risk management decisions should refer to C. A. Williams, Jr., and R. M. Heins, *Risk Management and Insurance,* 4th ed. (New York: McGraw-Hill, 1981), pp. 254-262.
26. Petersen, *Techniques of Safety Management,* pp. 84-90.

CHAPTER 3

Financing Loss Exposures

INTRODUCTION

Once identified, loss exposures need to be treated. When the control technique of avoidance is successfully used to treat a loss exposure, that specific exposure no longer exists; the probability that it will cause a loss becomes zero. Loss exposures that have not been avoided may lead to a loss or losses. If a loss occurs, it must be paid for, or "financed," internally or externally. It is necessary to plan in advance how losses will be financed if they happen. Thus, financing loss exposures deals with planning for losses that might occur, as well as actually paying for losses that do occur.

Three techniques for financing loss exposures have been briefly introduced. Noninsurance transfers are one such technique. Some noninsurance transfers are control techniques, and these have been discussed in Chapter 2. Other noninsurance transfers are used to finance loss exposures. Financing-type noninsurance transfers are the first subject of discussion in Chapter 3.

Insurance, one of the most important tools of risk management, is the next major subject of discussion. This chapter discusses insurance as a risk management technique, rather than analyzing the insurance business or insurance coverages. Those topics will be discussed later in this text and are also discussed in other CPCU courses. As a risk management technique, insurance is defined as a special transfer technique having important differences from noninsurance transfers.

If potential financial losses are not avoided or transferred, the risk manager has retained the exposure. Inevitably, losses will be borne internally should they occur. The discussion on retention will examine the relationship of retention to other risk management techniques, the distinction between planned and unplanned retention, the conditions requiring or favoring the use of retention, and the advantages and disadvantages of retention. Also discussed will be some guidelines for making decisions on retention and ways in which an entity can arrange to obtain the dollars to handle retained losses that actually occur.

Although retention is the last item that will be discussed in this text's description of risk management techniques, it would be a serious mistake to dismiss it as less important than other techniques for financing loss exposures. Retention is treated last because retention is a *residual technique.* Unless a loss exposure is handled completely through one or more of the other risk management techniques, the remaining exposure is retained. Unless the risk manager avoids all loss exposures—an impossibility—some losses may occur. Unless the financial consequences of these losses are transferred via insurance or noninsurance transfers, they must be borne internally.

Retention is not a method of last resort to be considered only after all other methods have been attempted. Retention is often the best way to handle all or part of an exposure. There are reasons to suggest that an exposure should always be retained unless a strong case can be made for transferring the potential losses to another entity.

Most of the discussion in this chapter deals with alternative ways of financing loss exposures. Advantages and disadvantages of the various financing methods are discussed, and guidelines for deciding among the various techniques are introduced. However, it is not enough to decide which method to use. The decision must be effectively implemented and monitored. For each risk management technique discussed in this chapter, some factors involved in implementing the technique will be discussed, as well as the ways in which the use of the technique can be monitored.

FINANCING-TYPE NONINSURANCE TRANSFERS

Noninsurance transfers that transfer only the responsibility for financing the potential losses arising out of an exposure resemble insurance. Both are financing techniques. Noninsurance transfers differ from insurance in that:

(1) they are not legally considered insurance,
(2) they are not sold by insurers,
(3) they are usually accomplished in a contract that deals mainly with other matters, and
(4) there is no significant pooling of exposure units.

These differences will be explained in detail later in this chapter.

Under a typical noninsurance transfer, one party to the contract, known as the *indemnitee*, secures a promise from the other party, known as the *indemnitor*. The indemnitor promises to bear some or all of the potential financial consequences from some loss exposure that otherwise would be borne by the indemnitee. Through this promise, the indemnitee has transferred these potential financial losses to the indemnitor.

Illustrations of Financing-Type Noninsurance Transfers

Noninsurance transfers that shift only the financial consequences of a loss, not the exposure itself, take many forms. Some, such as the exculpatory contracts discussed in Chapter 2, are control transfers. Attention here, however, is focused on transfers that provide funds to finance losses. The same contract may contain both a control technique and a financing technique. Those provisions that relieve the indemnitee of responsibility for losses to the person or property of the indemnitor which, except for the contract, would be the responsibility of the indemnitee, are control transfers. Those provisions that would, except for the contract, be the responsibility of the indemnitee are financing transfers. The indemnitee remains responsible for these payments to third parties if the indemnitor does not satisfy his or her obligation. Provisions that make the indemnitor responsible for losses to the person or property of the indemnitee for which, except for the contract, the indemnitor would not be responsible, would also be financing transfers. The form of business organization may be a means of loss transfer. However, most financial-type loss transfers involve contracts such as:

- leases,
- construction contracts,
- bailment contracts,
- contracts of sale, supply, and service, and
- surety contracts.

Form of Business Organization The corporation provides many opportunities for loss transfer. The liability of the stockholders is generally limited to their investment. Creditors, not the owners, take the chance that the firm's debts will exceed its assets. Firms suffering such reverses normally do so because of speculative losses, but they also may be caused by serious property or liability losses.

Incorporating a previously unincorporated business also permits the persons who owned the unincorporated business to share some loss exposures of the firm with new stockholders, if any. Individual stockholders can transfer their ownership exposure by selling their shares of stock.

Leases   A lease spells out the relationships between a landlord and a tenant. The lease may change responsibilities that would otherwise exist under common law or a state statute.

At common law, the landlord is the entity exposed to loss caused by damage to the premises. However, a tenant is responsible for damage caused by negligent acts of the tenant or his or her agents.

Under a lease, the landlord may assume responsibility for some physical damage caused by the negligent acts of the tenant. In such cases, the tenant has transferred some potential financial losses to the landlord. As noted earlier, however, this transfer is a control transfer, not a financing-type transfer. The tenant is excused from paying a loss for which he or she would otherwise be responsible. More commonly, however, the landlord transfers additional responsibility to the tenant. Under a common provision, the tenant agrees to return the premises at the end of the lease in as good condition as it was received, loss by fair wear and tear excepted. It makes no difference if the damage is caused intentionally, by negligence, by a third party, or by an act of God. This transfer is a financing-type transfer because the tenant agrees to finance the landlord's losses.

At common law, if the premises become uninhabitable due to accidental physical damage, the tenant must continue to pay the rent. Most states, however, have statutes that excuse residential tenants from this obligation. This shifts the potential loss to the landlord. Such statutes are control transfers because they excuse tenants from a payment they would have to make under common law. Leases usually contain provisions that specify whether or not the tenant must continue the rent. Whether the potential loss is thus transferred from the landlord to the tenant or vice versa depends on the condition in the lease and whether the situation would otherwise be governed by common law or a special statute. Whether the transfer is a control or financing-type transfer depends on whether the transfer merely excuses one party from making a payment it would otherwise have to make or requires one party to pay the other party some money it would not otherwise have to pay.

Liability for bodily injury or property damage to another party is at common law the financial responsibility of whoever was negligent—the landlord or the tenant. Under a lease, however, the tenant may agree to "indemnify and hold harmless" the landlord for injury to persons or damage to property arising out of the leased premises. Such transfers are always financing-type transfers. If enforceable by the landlord, the tenant bears the financial consequences of liability imposed on the landlord. While, in a legal sense, the "liability" would still be the landlord's, the tenant has agreed to make the landlord financially "whole" if the landlord suffers loss because of that liability. The most far-reaching version of this promise would make the tenant responsible regardless of whether the tenant, the landlord, or some third party was negligent. However, some state laws forbid such a broad transfer of responsibility. Sometimes the tenant has the stronger bargaining position and thus is able to shift part of his or her own liability exposures to the landlord.

Construction Contracts Construction contracts between a property owner and a contractor often deal with such questions as:

- who will be responsible for damage to the building while it is being constructed, and
- who will be responsible for liability suits arising out of the construction process.

Construction contracts are usually financing-type transfers. They usually make the contractor responsible for damage to the property being constructed. At common law, the contractor would probably be responsible anyway, but the construction contract clarifies the situation. In some cases, it also transfers potential losses that would otherwise be borne by the property owner.

The trend in tort law is to increase the number and types of situations in which the property owner is held responsible for the negligent acts of independent contractors and their employees and subcontractors. The contract between the property owner and the contractor may transfer some of the owner's potential liability to the contractor or, alternatively, shift to the owner some of the contractor's potential liability.

Bailment Contracts. A *bailee* is a person who has property of another, called a *bailor*, in his or her custody on a temporary basis. The bailee may have borrowed the property, or may be storing, cleaning, repairing, or transporting the property.

The relative responsibilities of the bailee and the bailor for damage to the property while in the bailee's custody depend on the nature of the bailment. If the temporary transfer of the property benefits only the bailor (for example, a person keeps and maintains a neighbor's pet, at no charge, while the neighbor goes on vacation), courts require the bailee to exercise only slight care. If, on the other hand, the bailment benefits only the bailee, the bailee must be extraordinarily careful with the property to avoid responsibility for any damage. In the typical commercial bailment (such as those illustrated in the next paragraph), both parties benefit. The bailee is responsible for damage to the bailed property caused by his or her failure to exercise the same degree of care that average businesses would use relative to their own property.

A bailment contract may change the degree of care required. For example:

- A parking lot may disclaim any responsibility for theft of personal property from inside the customer's vehicle.
- A manufacturer whose product requires final processing by another firm may be willing to release that firm from any responsibility for damage to the product except that caused by poor workmanship. If the product is destroyed by fire while on the processor's premises, the manufacturer will bear the loss even if the fire was caused by the processor's negligence.
- Bailees such as laundries, dry cleaners, and cold-storage companies, to improve customer relations, often extend their responsibility under the bailment contract to cover any damage to the customers' goods—regardless of liability under the common law.

In the first two examples, potential property losses were transferred from the bailee to the bailor; the third example shifts potential losses from the bailor to the bailee. The first two transfers are control transfers; the third is a financing-type transfer.

Contracts to Supply Goods and Services Contracts relating to the distribution of goods and services may shift responsibilities for replacement or repair of the goods or services and for liability arising out of defective products or services. The responsibility may be shifted by contract from the seller to the buyer, or vice versa; or from the manufacturer or processor to the distributor, or vice versa. Whether they are control or financing-type transfers depends upon whether one party simply excuses the other party for damage to the first party's property or whether one party agrees to pay some money to the other party or to some third party.

Sellers often issue maintenance agreements under which the seller agrees to perform maintenance services. The agreement may be extended to include replacement of the product if the product develops defects within a stated period. The buyer is thus protected against some potential losses. Car warranties illustrate such an extension.

One of the most common transfer agreements is the railroad sidetrack agreement. If a business wants a sidetrack leading to its property from the main railroad track, the railroad will almost always require that the firm hold the railroad harmless for certain injuries or damage caused by the use or existence of the sidetrack.

Surety Contracts Whenever one person promises to do something for someone else and the promisee asks the promisor to have a third party guarantee the promise, the situation could conceivably lead to a surety contract. Under a surety contract, one person—called the *surety*—guarantees that a second person—called the principal or the *obligor*—will perform his or her expressed obligation to a third person—called the creditor, *obligee*, or beneficiary. Through a surety contract, the obligee transfers to the surety the potential loss from nonperformance of the principal. Surety contracts are always financing-type transfers.

Advantages and Disadvantages of Noninsurance Transfers

From the viewpoint of the risk manager, noninsurance transfers have four potential advantages:

(1) Noninsurance transfers may permit the risk manager to transfer some potential losses that cannot be transferred through insurance.
(2) Noninsurance transfers may be less expensive than insurance.
(3) Noninsurance transfers can be tailor-made to specific situations.
(4) The loss may be shifted to a transferee who is in a better position than the transferor to exercise loss control.

Noninsurance transfers also have some serious limitations:

(1) The transfer may not be as complete as the risk manager had intended. The contract language may be incomplete. If the contract is ambiguous, courts tend to interpret the provisions in favor of the transferee. Even if the language is clear, courts sometimes hold broad transfers to be invalid because they violate public policy or specific statutes prohibiting such transfers.
(2) If the transfer is tailor-made to specific situations, one has no (or few) precedents to determine how the courts will interpret the contract language.
(3) The indemnitor (transferee) may be unable to pay the loss, in which case the indemnitee (transferor) will remain responsible. Because there is no significant pooling of exposure units under most noninsurance transfers, the indemnitor is subject to substantial fluctuations in loss experience. (This disadvantage does not apply to exculpatory agreements because the indemnitor is the one who suffers if he or she is unable to finance his or

her own loss. The indemnitee would be relieved of any responsibility.)

(4) Despite the shifting of some responsibility for insurable losses, noninsurance transfers may not reduce insurance costs. Insurers sometimes fail to give any credit for such transfers because they question the efficacy of the language or the financial soundness of the transferee. On the other hand, the indemnitor may be charged more for his or her insurance because of the additional responsibility assumed under the contract.

(5) The responsibility may be shifted to an indemnitor or transferee who is unable to exert much, if any, loss control.

Criteria for Noninsurance Transfers

Mehr and Hedges list the following "ideal conditions" for the use of noninsurance transfers:

(1) The allocation of losses as between transferors and transferees is clear and unambiguous.

(2) The loss transferees are able and willing to meet their financial obligations promptly.

(3) Each transferee has significant authority for reduction and control of the losses he bears.

(4) The losses are transferred on a basis at least as efficient (i.e., as inexpensive or as profitable) as other equally safe methods of risk bearing.

(5) The losses are transferred at a price attractive to both the transferor and transferee.[1]

Aggressive and Defensive Noninsurance Transfers

Noninsurance transfers can be applied aggressively or defensively. A firm that transfers potential losses to others by inserting hold harmless clauses into its contracts or by insisting on a surety bond is using this technique aggressively. A transferee that convinces others to remove clauses in existing contracts is using the technique defensively. It has shifted back to others the potential loss it assumed. (A firm that stops others from even inserting hold harmless clauses in contracts making that firm the transferee is using the avoidance technique, because it never has the exposure.)

Implementation

Once a decision is made to implement a noninsurance transfer aggressively, the terms of the transfer must be developed. Legal expertise must be secured to accomplish this. Contract drafting skill is only part of the problem. The terms must also be negotiated with the transferee. The contract that results depends mainly on the parties' relative bargaining power and negotiating skills.

Defensive use of noninsurance transfers also requires negotiating skills and bargaining power. If the business proposes to keep a hold harmless clause but to limit or clarify its scope, contract drafting skills are also required.

The risk manager for the most part must rely on others to implement this technique. The risk manager's major involvement is education and motivation. A communications system must be devised that will alert other personnel to opportunities for using noninsurance transfers in a way that will benefit the firm. Many such transfers simply increase costs for all parties combined, without reducing cost significantly for anyone. For example, the indemnitor may pay increased insurance premiums to cover the liability assumed in the transfer but the indemnitee's premiums may not be reduced at all. Thus, the risk manager should not encourage unconstrained aggressive use of this technique.

With respect to defensive transfers, company personnel also need to know the many ways in which the business may become the indemnitor under a hold harmless agreement and the potential consequences. This information should also encourage avoidance of such transfers in new contracts. With respect to nonroutine contracts, the risk manager should be actively involved in order to explore the special problems that such contracts might entail.

The communications network should also provide for continuous reporting to the risk manager of (1) ways in which the firm has successfully transferred potential losses to others through noninsurance transfers, and (2) similar transfers in which the firm has become the indemnitor. In the first instance the risk manager needs to know how these transfers affect the use of other techniques. For example,

- Can the business now expect the indemnitor to provide loss control services?
- Is insurance on this exposure still necessary?
- Should the indemnitor be required to purchase insurance or a bond to strengthen his or her promise?
- If insurance is still advisable, can a reduction in premium be negotiated because of the transfer?

In the second instance—involving the firm as an indemnitor—the risk manager needs to know whether the firm's present risk management program covers these new exposures. For example,

- Should the firm introduce some new loss control measures?
- Do present insurance contracts cover these exposures?
- If not, should these exposures be retained or insured?

In reviewing these contracts, the risk manager may also become aware of ambiguities in the contract language that should be brought to the attention of the person most directly involved. Removing these ambiguities may benefit the indemnitee as well as the indemnitor.

Monitoring

Noninsurance transfers should be monitored with respect to (1) whether they are being implemented correctly, and (2) whether the decision to use this technique still appears to be correct. The initial decision to use a noninsurance transfer may later prove to have been incorrect, or changing conditions may suggest a different decision.

Periodically the risk manager should review transfers to others of which he or she is aware to determine:

- how closely they meet the conditions stated earlier,
- what money or services the firm has actually received under these contracts,
- whether the firm has met its obligations before and after any losses, and
- whether the conditions that gave rise to these contracts have changed. The nature of the exposure may have changed or the relative bargaining powers of the two parties may have changed.

A similar analysis should be made of contracts in which the firm has become the indemnitor rather than the indemnitee. Analyzing these contracts is a matter of uncovering loss exposures and perhaps revealing opportunities for defensive use of noninsurance transfers.

The communications process should also be evaluated to determine whether it is providing effective two-way communications. Is the educational material and other information disseminated by the risk manager clearly written? Does it motivate people to investigate proper uses of noninsurance transfers? Is the risk manager made aware of all routine transfers and actively involved in nonroutine transfers? A sampling of contracts made by the various divisions within the firm and regular personal interviews with individuals in key positions is one way to check on the effectiveness of the communications.

The results of this monitoring may suggest changes in the communications system, discontinuing noninsurance transfers in some instances and introducing them in others, and renegotiating the terms of certain existing transfers.

INSURANCE

This section begins by defining "insurance." Unfortunately, there is no single, generally accepted conceptual definition of insurance. Any definition advanced in this text, therefore, must be arbitrary. However, an attempt has been made to include elements that are rather widely accepted.

Insurance Defined as a Concept

From the viewpoint of a risk manager, insurance is a risk management technique that makes it possible to transfer the financial consequences of potential accidental losses from the insured entity to an insurer. The term is also used to mean the protection provided under an insurance contract.

Neither of these definitions indicates what distinguishes insurance from noninsurance transfers. It is the mechanism of insurance that makes the difference.

Insurance Defined as a Mechanism

As a mechanism, insurance is a social device under which two or more entities (generally many more than two) make or promise to make contributions to a fund from which the insurer promises to make certain cash payments or render certain services to those contributors who suffer accidental losses. As a mechanism, insurance differs from most noninsurance transfers in the following ways:

(1) The insurer pools or combines many loss exposures.
(2) The insureds contribute to a fund out of which cash payments or services are provided.
(3) The insurance contract deals solely with the transfer.

Pooled Loss Exposures The characteristic that best distinguishes insurance from noninsurance transfer devices is that the insurer accepts similar transfers from at least two entities and generally many more. The difference, however, is one of degree. Some noninsurance transferees or indemnitors also accept transfers from two or more entities. Indeed, some noninsurance transferees may enter into more such agreements than some small insurers. This is rare. The number of transferees dealing with a single indemnitor tends to be much smaller than the number of insureds dealing with a single insurer. (An exception is a surety bonding company.)

Insureds Contribute to a Fund Another distinctive feature of insurance (which also applies in part to surety bonding) is that insureds contribute or promise to contribute to a fund out of which payments are made. Although most insureds pay a premium in advance for their protection, some promise to pay at least part of the cost later. The promised payment may be an extra premium based on the experience of the insured during the policy period or an assessment based on the total experience of the insurer. Under most noninsurance transfers, the indemnitor does not receive any money from the indemnitees specifically in return for the promise to indemnify. The indemnitor relies on his or her own resources to fulfill promises made under the contract. Like noninsurance transferees, insurers may either make cash payments or render services such as repairing broken glass or investigating and defending liability claims.

Insurance Contract Deals Solely with the Transfer Unlike most noninsurance transfers, an insurance contract is concerned exclusively with the transfer and does not deal with other matters. Noninsurance transfers are usually accomplished through clauses in contracts dealing primarily with other matters such as a sale of goods, lease of premises, or construction of a building.

Benefits Provided by the Insurance Technique

The insurance technique provides many important benefits. The benefits to society will be explored in Chapter 6. The discussion here will consider only the benefits that individual insureds can receive directly from the purchase of insurance.

The benefits to insureds can be categorized as:

(1) payment for losses,
(2) reduction of uncertainty, and
(3) various risk management services not dependent on the happening of the insured event.

Payment for Losses The most apparent benefit of insurance is the payment of dollar benefits or the rendering of certain services to or on behalf of insureds who suffer covered losses. Because insurance money or service is available, the insured may be able to achieve the post-loss objectives presented in Chapter 1.

- *Survival*—if the loss is catastrophic, insurance may make the difference between survival and nonsurvival.

- *Continuity of Operations*—insurance may provide funds that permit an insured to pay the extra costs of more rapid repairs or replacement, and of continuing operations with alternate facilities until damaged property is replaced or repaired. Thus, the insured may be able to continue operations at or close to the same rate as before the accident, with little delay.
- *Earnings Stability*—the cash provided by insurance may pay repair or replacement costs that would otherwise reduce earnings, defend and pay a liability claim that would otherwise be a charge against earnings, replace earnings lost because of an interruption in operations, or provide the funds that would otherwise come from earnings to train a replacement for a key employee who has died.
- *Continued Growth*—the above outcomes may contribute not only to a more efficient operation, but also to continued growth of the enterprise.
- *Social Responsibility*—the image of the firm in the community and its sense of public responsibility might also be enhanced by insurance proceeds that permit it to continue normal operations, not lay off workers, meet customer demands, accept business from suppliers, pay employees' medical expenses, and pay legitimate liability claims.

Reduction of Uncertainty To the insured, payment for losses reduces the cost of losses that *actually* occur. An even more important benefit of insurance is that it reduces the cost of losses that *might* occur (cited in Chapter 1). Only those who suffer insured losses benefit directly from loss payment, but all insureds experience a lessening of uncertainty concerning loss. Thus, insurance is an important tool for meeting the pre-loss objective of reduction in anxiety.

Although insurance reduces uncertainty about financial loss, it does not affect the cause of financial loss. The entity that purchases insurance is as uncertain as before concerning the loss-causing event itself. The insured also continues to be uncertain concerning losses that are not covered under the contract.

Services Provided by Insurers Insurers provide services that are often valuable even if an insured event does not occur. A part of the insurance premium pays for services that, at least in part, benefit the insured. If the exposure is retained, some of these services must either be forgone, purchased from outsiders, or handled with the entity's own resources.

Some valuable services are provided by insurance producers (agents and brokers). Others are provided directly by insurance companies.

Risk Management Services Provided by Insurance Producers. Producers have long provided risk management services, often including:

- loss exposure identification and measurement,
- suggestions on how these loss exposures might be handled,
- selection of an insurer and, where insurance is recommended, the best coverage and pricing method for those loss exposures,
- loss control services,
- claims adjustment services,
- assistance in meeting legal requirements, and
- management services.

Producers create a market for their services by identifying and measuring loss exposures. Because of their experience in dealing with many insureds, they can bring to this task an orientation and experience that the entity exposed to loss may not have or be able to command otherwise.

After identifying and measuring a client's loss exposures, the producer suggests which exposures should be insured. Many producers also suggest other appropriate risk management tools.

For those loss exposures that are to be insured, producers serving more than one insurer help the firm or family to select an insurer. Many are able to advise the prospect about various insurers' financial stability, service, and prices. Sometimes they must search diligently for an insurer willing to cover the loss exposure. All producers can help the insured select the most appropriate insurance contracts and pricing methods.

Some producers have loss control personnel or departments that advise firms and families how to prevent losses or reduce their severity. Depending upon their extent, these loss control services may be provided at no extra cost to the insured or as an extra service for which a charge is made.

Small losses frequently are adjusted by the producer on behalf of the insurer. Larger losses are usually adjusted by others, but insureds expect their producer to help them deal with the insurance company.

The government often requires evidence of insurance before it will grant or continue some privilege. For example, evidence of auto insurance may be required under a financial responsibility law or workers' compensation insurance under a workers' compensation law. Producers may provide this evidence. Some large agencies and brokerage firms provide a variety of services important in risk management, beyond those already mentioned. Property appraisal assistance, for example, is available from some agencies and brokerage firms, and a number of firms provide administrative services in managing retention programs for clients.

Risk Management Services Provided by Insurance Companies. Insurers themselves often provide some or all of the following risk management services:

- loss exposure identification and measurement,
- loss control services,
- claims adjustment services,
- assistance in meeting legal requirements, and
- management services.

Insurers provide loss exposure checklists that may be used by their marketing representatives or by risk managers themselves to identify and measure loss exposures. Insurers sometimes appraise properties for insurance purposes. These valuations can be useful in exposure measurement.

The contracts and pricing methods developed by insurers provide risk managers with the opportunity to choose among various combinations of coverage and price.

Many insurers have long offered extensive loss control services. They inspect insured locations and make loss control recommendations. Through trade associations, they conduct research, publish safety literature, educate the public, measure the dangers in products, and otherwise seek to prevent or reduce losses. Through their individual loss control departments, insurers have offered their insureds safety inspections, posters, literature, and advice. Through various rating procedures that recognize loss control efforts and loss experience, insurers have encouraged employer safety measures. More recently, insurers have formed subsidiaries to provide safety services beyond those normally provided.

Through a network of staff adjusters or agreements with independent contractors, insurers provide loss adjustment services. For some property losses such as glass breakage, insurers may arrange the necessary repairs. For liability losses, they provide experts to investigate and defend the claim. For some employees injured on the job, they may provide rehabilitation services.

Costs Imposed by the Insurance Technique

In deciding whether to purchase insurance, the insured must decide whether the benefits exceed the direct and indirect costs. The major cost items are:

(1) the premium,

(2) the time and effort spent negotiating with insurers,

(3) the lessening of incentives to control losses, and

(4) the exaggeration or false reporting of losses because of the existence of insurance.

Premium Costs The cost of insurance includes not only the dollar outlay for the premium, but also the loss of use of the premium paid in advance, that is, the opportunity costs. The premium includes three components:

(1) the *expected loss component,*

(2) the *expense component* to cover the expenses incurred by the insurer in paying benefits and rendering services, and

(3) an *allowance for profit and contingencies.*

Expected Loss Component. The expected loss component of the premium is the insurer's estimate of the dollar loss that will be sustained by the *average* insured among a large number of insureds with the same quantity and quality of exposure. If the insurer collects this amount from each of these insureds and the actual losses approximate the expected losses, the insurer will have a sufficient fund to meet its obligations.

Expense Component. The expense component of the premium is an additional cost. Part of the expenses go to provide important services for the insured that would otherwise have to be financed by the insured's own funds. This component varies widely among lines of insurance and insurers; furthermore, actual expenses may differ greatly over time. To illustrate the magnitude of the expense component and the diversity just noted, some information on actual expenses is presented in Exhibit 3-1 for four major lines of property and liability insurance: (1) commercial multi-peril insurance, (2) homeowners insurance, (3) auto liability insurance, and (4) workers' compensation insurance.

Profit and Contingency Allowance. This component of the premium is designed to provide the insurer with a reasonable allowance for underwriting profit and provide some margin for differences between expected and actual losses and expenses. In property and liability insurance, the typical profit and contingency allowance is 2.5 to 5 percent. Theoretically, one would expect the allowance to be higher the greater the insurer's uncertainty concerning the loss experience during the coming year. Exhibit 3-2 shows the actual stock insurer underwriting profit ratios on the same lines for which expense ratios were shown in Exhibit 3-1. Data are presented for the most recent ten years for which profit ratios are available. Particularly noteworthy is the

Exhibit 3-1
Expenses Incurred† by Stock Insurers for Four Major Lines
Expressed as a Percentage of Premiums Written—1970-1979*

Year	Commercial Multi-Peril Insurance			Homeowners Insurance			Automobile Liability Insurance			Workers' Compensation Insurance		
	Commissions	Other	Total	Commissions	Other	Total	Commissions	Other	Total	Commissions	Other	Total
1970	18.5	16.2	34.7	20.8	12.8	33.6	14.5	12.2	26.7	8.9	11.8	20.7
1971	18.8	14.8	33.6	20.6	12.9	33.5	14.2	12.1	26.3	8.5	12.1	20.6
1972	19.0	14.3	33.3	20.3	12.9	33.2	14.3	12.8	27.1	8.7	12.3	21.0
1973	19.0	14.6	33.6	20.1	13.2	33.3	14.2	13.5	27.7	8.5	12.3	20.8
1974	18.6	15.5	34.1	19.5	13.9	33.4	14.2	14.3	28.5	8.2	12.5	20.7
1975	18.4	15.6	34.0	19.2	13.3	32.5	13.9	13.5	27.4	7.9	12.0	19.9
1976	18.3	14.5	32.8	19.1	12.7	31.8	13.6	12.7	26.3	7.4	11.3	18.7
1977	18.2	14.4	32.6	19.1	12.5	31.5	13.3	12.6	25.9	7.1	10.9	18.0
1978	18.3	15.0	33.3	19.2	12.8	32.0	13.7	13.3	27.0	6.8	11.1	17.9
1979	18.3	15.8	34.1	18.7	12.6	31.3	13.6	13.7	27.3	6.6	11.6	18.2
Average	18.4	15.1	33.5	19.4	12.9	32.3	13.9	13.1	27.0	7.5	11.6	19.1

† Not including loss adjustment expenses.

*Adapted with permission from *Best's Aggregates and Averages, 1980* (Oldwick, NJ: A.M. Best Co., 1980), pp. 140, 141.

Exhibit 3-2
Underwriting Profits Earned by Stock Insurers in Four Major Lines
Expressed as a Percentage of Premiums Earned—1970-1979 *

Year	Commercial Multi-Peril Insurance	Homeowners Insurance	Auto Liability Insurance	Workers' Compensation Insurance
1970	6.3	—4.6	—6.5	7.0
1971	9.5	1.7	—1.5	2.0
1972	8.7	6.5	—1.3	—0.7
1973	6.7	4.4	—4.0	0.5
1974	—4.4	—7.0	—6.0	—2.9
1975	—0.4	—7.5	—13.5	—4.8
1976	3.8	0.4	—8.2	—8.2
1977	10.9	6.5	—2.6	—7.3
1978	13.2	5.8	—1.7	—3.3
1979	5.0	—1.5	—3.8	0.1
Average	6.4	0.9	—4.7	—2.6

* Adapted with permission from *Best's Aggregates and Averages* (Oldwick, NJ: A.M. Best Co., 1980), pp. 140, 141.

large variation in these profit ratios over time. The four lines sometimes move together and at other times move in quite different directions.

Ideally, insurers should be able to earn from all sources a reasonable rate of return on their net worth. Conceptually the underwriting profit on net worth should be the reasonable rate of return from both underwriting and investment activities less the investment profit. The 2.5 to 5 percent underwriting profit loadings currently used in property and liability insurance assume that insurers will earn some investment profits. For example, if insurers actually earn 2.5 percent underwriting profits on their premiums and they write about $2 in premiums per $1 in net worth, their underwriting profit as a percent of net worth would be only 5 percent. If they earn 5 percent underwriting profits on their premiums and they write about $2 in premiums per $1 in net worth, their underwriting profit would be 10 percent of net worth. Most observers would agree that, given the uncertainty faced by insurers in their operations, a reasonable total rate of return for insurers would be more than 10 percent. Authorities disagree, however, on exactly what the reasonable total rate of return should be, particularly for a given line of insurance, and the investment profits that should be subtracted from the total return to determine the reasonable underwriting rate of return. The point here is that the underwriting return would probably have to be higher if the insurer did not have investment profits. This observation tempers the comments to be made next with respect to opportunity costs of the premiums.

Opportunity Costs. Because all or a significant portion of the premium must usually be paid at the beginning of the policy period, the insured loses not only the premium but also the use of that money until, under retention, it would have been needed to pay losses and expenses. For example, the insured might have been able to invest an equivalent amount in short-term securities yielding 10 percent a year.

This yield that is forgone because of the payment of an insurance premium is a cost to the extent that it is not offset in the premium calculation by the insurer's anticipated investment earnings. For example, if the profit loading (and consequently the premium charge) is reduced by an amount that fully recognizes what the insured could earn with the money if the insured held the money, no "cost" in the sense of income forgone would be incurred by the insured. Such an exact offset is an unlikely result in actual practice.

The complexities of accurate opportunity cost calculations are beyond the scope of this section. Factors beyond those mentioned here are involved, such as taxes, accounting methods, and the timing of actual outlays for expenses and losses. Recognition of the opportunity cost concept is important. Because of high rates of return on investments and greater emphasis on financial management, current risk management practices increasingly recognize opportunity costs as a factor in the process of selecting among alternative methods of treating loss exposures.

Negotiating Time and Effort The implementation of a decision to insure takes time and effort.

- An insurer must be selected from among the many companies that write the type of insurance sought.
- The insured must cooperate with the insurer in its separate exposure analysis.
- The terms of the insurance contract and the price to be charged must be negotiated.
- The insured must cooperate with the insurer in the latter's loss control efforts.
- Following a loss, the insured will be expected to notify the insurer, file the necessary proofs of loss, and cooperate with the insurer in its investigation of the loss. If the loss is a liability claim against the insured, there may be court appearances, depositions, and so on.

Some of these expenses would be incurred even if the insured did not purchase insurance (for example, some of the loss control assistance and court appearances) but others would not (for example, selection of an insurer, contract and premium negotiations, and filing of the proof of loss). Only the *extra* steps create true costs of insurance.

Less Incentive for Loss Control One of the disadvantages commonly attributed to insurance is that it reduces the incentive for loss control. In other words, insurance creates morale hazards. Because the insurer will pay for at least part of the losses arising out of a covered event, many insureds reason that they gain little or nothing by loss prevention or loss reduction efforts. Others simply are less careful than they would be in the absence of insurance. To the extent that this is true, this attitude results in costs that are borne by insureds.

(1) If insured losses are higher because of this attitude, the insurer's expected loss estimate will rise, causing insurance premiums to rise.

(2) As demonstrated in the loss control discussion, insurance does not cover all the financial consequences of insured events. Laxity in controlling losses increases the financial impact of these uninsured financial consequences.

(3) A lax attitude toward control of insured loss exposures is likely to increase the incidence of noninsured losses as well. This may happen because the insured cannot distinguish accurately between insured and noninsured exposures or because a person who is careless with respect to insured events may develop the same tendency with respect to noninsured events.

Exaggeration or False Reporting of Insured Claims The presence of insurance may cause an insured or others to exaggerate insured claims or to report as an insured loss one that was not. In other words, insurance creates moral hazards. An insured who collects from the insurer on false or exaggerated claims personally benefits from this action. The benefit, however, may be short-lived, because subsequent premiums may rise or there may be difficulty renewing the insurance.

Exaggeration or false reporting of claims by an insured cannot be interpreted as a cost of insurance to that insured. Exaggeration by others, however, does hurt the insured because it increases the cost of insured losses. For example, if auto service stations or building contractors do more work than is necessary or charge more for their services when they know or suspect that the loss is covered by insurance, insured losses (and later premiums) will rise. If third parties collect larger settlements or court awards because of insurance, insured losses will also be higher than the losses would be under retention. Similarly, third parties can raise losses by collecting on claims that are unjustified.

Insurers try to combat the problem by carefully investigating doubtful claims, contesting claims they consider exaggerated or unjustified, prosecuting those guilty of illegal acts, and educating insureds and the general public on the adverse effects of exaggeration and false reporting.

Implementation

The implementation of a decision to purchase insurance involves several steps:

- An insurer must be selected to underwrite and service the insurance.
- The terms of the insurance agreement must be negotiated.
- A communications network dealing with insurance matters must be established within the firm.
- The risk manager must prepare for the adjustment of insured losses and dealing with the insurer when losses occur.
- The insurance costs may have to be allocated among various departments or divisions of the firm.

Selecting an Insurer Over 5,000 insurers write one or more types of property and liability insurance, life insurance, and health insurance. The risk manager must determine which insurer or insurers should cover the exposure to be insured. To make this decision, the risk manager should understand the various types of insurer. This subject will be described in detail in Chapter 6.

Four other factors also should be considered in selecting an individual insurer: (1) coverages provided, (2) financial strength, (3) service, and (4) cost. However, it often is difficult to obtain adequate information on each of these factors. Furthermore, even if the needed information can be obtained, the decision usually is not clear. One insurer may be superior to another in several respects and inferior in others. Consequently, the risk manager must determine the relative importance of these various factors. Some comments on each of these factors are presented below.

Coverages Provided. Obviously, it is necessary to select an insurer that is able to provide the types of insurance coverage that are needed. It is also important to evaluate the willingness of the insurer to provide the protection sought, and whether the insurer will accept and continue to insure all the exposures that the risk manager desires to insure.

Even if the insurer uses only standard printed policies, forms, and endorsements, the risk manager and insurer must agree on which combination of these printed documents will serve as the contract between the insurer and insured. The objective of the risk manager is to secure contract language that will provide or come closest to providing the desired protection and to maximize the protection that can be obtained from the insurer for a given price.

Insurers may vary in their willingness to provide protection. At one extreme, an insurer may be willing to accept a tailor-made contract drafted by the risk manager alone or in conjunction with representatives of the insurer. At the other extreme, which is more common, the insurer may offer the risk manager on a take-it-or-leave-it basis a contract drafted solely by the insurer. Other insurers may be willing to amend certain sections of a printed contract with endorsements tailor-made to the risk manager's needs. If the insurer is willing to tailor-make part or all of the contract to the insured's needs, the risk manager will play a much more active role in negotiating the contract language.

Another important consideration is whether the insurer will accept all the exposures that the risk manager wishes to insure—regardless of their quality and the insurer's standards for cancellation. Some insurers are quick to cancel a policy on which they have sustained a major loss or a succession of losses; others are much more inclined to wait for more evidence of the insured's overall loss experience.

Financial Strength. Of the remaining factors, financial strength is the most important. Unless the insurer is able to pay the insured's incurred losses, its promises are worthless. An insurer's financial strength depends on a number of characteristics, including:

(1) the net worth of the insurer relative to its liabilities and to its premium volume;
(2) its assets—their nature (stocks, bonds, mortgages, and real estate, for example) and how they are valued;
(3) its liabilities—their nature (mainly reserves for losses that have already occurred but not been paid and reserves for losses that will occur in the future under contracts that have been prepaid) and how they are valued;
(4) the lines of insurance written, some lines being much more stable than others;
(5) whether the insurer has the right to assess policyholders if its own funds prove inadequate;
(6) its future profit potential and the quality of its insureds;
(7) the experience and other qualifications of its management; and
(8) the arrangements it has made to share with a reinsurer large losses on single policies or, because of a catastrophe, large losses on multiple policies.

These characteristics are explored in more detail in CPCU 8. Various published sources such as *Best's Insurance Reports, Property and Casualty* present information on most of the points presented in the preceding list. In addition, *Best's Reports* rates insurers on the basis of their relative financial strength.

Services. The risk manager and the insurer must be able to agree on what services the insurer or its representative will be expected to provide and the nature and extent of these services. Exposure analysis, loss control, and loss adjustments are the three principal services to be considered.

(1) *Analysis of loss exposures.* Identifying these exposures and measuring their potential loss frequency and severity is a function usually performed by the producer. Thus, on this point, the selection of this individual is at least as important as the choice of the insurer itself. On the other hand, some insurers do encourage their representatives to do more exposure analysis than others. Some insurers provide technical aids such as exposure analysis forms for this purpose.

(2) *Loss control.* This service can reduce the insured's insurance premiums and noninsured losses. Insurers differ widely in the quantity and quality of the loss control services they provide. These services include inspections of the premises and recommendations on how they might be made safer for workers, customers, and visitors; educational materials and classes; assistance in securing certain types of safety equipment; salvage operations; and aid in complying with certain government regulations. In general, because the premiums paid by large insureds provide more dollars for such assistance, insurers are much more willing and able to provide loss control services for large firms than for small businesses.

(3) *Claims adjustment.* Criteria for evaluating this service include how promptly the insurer settles its claims, whether it adjusts these claims fairly, and how much of an administrative burden it places on the risk manager in the adjustment process. Often important is the insurer's ability to provide national or international claims services. For a firm with widespread operations or products that are widely distributed and could lead to liability claims in many locations, this criterion is especially important.

Information is not generally available on the quality of services rendered by insurers. Occasionally a consumer magazine rates selected insurers on the basis of how they have settled claims and handled renewals and cancellations. Some state insurance departments report how promptly workers' compensation insurers pay their claims and what proportion they contest. At least one state insurance department has also ranked auto insurers according to the number of complaints received by the department and settled in favor of the insured, relative to the premiums written. For most lines and for most insurers, however, there is no published information on the services they render. To evaluate insurers with respect to service, the risk manager must rely upon inquiries directed to the insurer and to acquaintances who have had experience with the insurer.

Cost. If the risk manager is satisfied with the coverage, financial strength, and services rendered by the insurer, the cost of its protection will probably determine whether it is to be favored over another insurer. For most families, the premium is not negotiable, but this is not always the case with businesses. If the firm is large enough to be rated at least in part on the basis of its past experience, the risk manager may be able to place a more favorable interpretation on that experience. Also, if the firm is a large one, the risk manager may have the opportunity to decide whether it will be rated in large part on the basis of the firm's experience during the policy period. Even if the firm is not large enough to be rated in part on the basis of its own experience, it may be able to negotiate a more favorable rate by checking whether the insurer has applied the most favorable rate available to its operations.

The cost of the insurance is the premiums less any dividends that may be paid or plus any assessments that may be levied at the end of the period plus the opportunity cost of paying the premiums in advance. Unless the insured is rated on the basis of its own loss experience during the policy period (retrospective rating), or the premium is based on a number of exposure units (such as $100 of payroll or sales) which is not known until the policy period expires, the premium can usually be determined in advance. Dividends and assessments, however, depend upon the insurer's aggregate underwriting and investment experience (though some insurers may have such a stable dividend policy that the insured can almost count on receiving the same return as in the past). The premium charged by one insurer may be less than that charged by other insurers because its underwriting experience is more favorable, its expenses are lower, or it is willing to accept a smaller underwriting profit and contingency allowance. The underwriting profit and contingency allowance that is acceptable may depend upon the insurer's investment opportunities, the stability of its underwriting experience, and its profit objectives. Some insurers make specific commitments to share investment earnings with their insureds.

Property and liability insurance cost information is not generally available. Property and liability insurance rates tend to depend on many variables including the location of the exposure. Nevertheless, more pricing information has become available in recent years. Several state insurance departments have issued "shoppers' guides" which permit consumers to compare the prices auto insurers and homeowners insurers operating in their states would charge some typical insureds located throughout the state.

Selection Procedures. Most risk managers select an insurer following individual negotiations with one or more insurers. The negotiations may be conducted through an independent agent or broker or directly with the insurer through a sales representative. Some risk managers, however, seek competitive bids. The risk manager may set rigid specifications and base the decision mainly on price or, more commonly, state the firm's needs broadly and select the best combination of recommended coverages, service, and cost from a financially stable insurer.

Communications Network Within Firm The risk manager is not the only person involved in an insurance arrangement. Others in the firm or family must be informed about the protection and services that have been secured from the insurer and the obligations that the firm or family has assumed under the agreement. For example, personnel throughout the firm should be alerted to changes in hazards that will affect the insurance, what loss control services the insurer will provide, what cooperation will be expected, and what records must be kept.

Preparation for Loss Adjustments In order to facilitate prompt, fair loss adjustments, the firm or family must be prepared to comply with the loss adjustment provisions in the insurance contract. Personnel throughout the firm should be made aware of their obligations in this regard. If a property insurance loss occurs, the insurer should be notified promptly, the property should be protected from further damage, the firm or family should assist the insurer in its investigation, and the necessary proof of loss should be submitted. Liability claims deserve special handling because of their tremendous potential. How the claim is settled may have important customer or public relations implications. Liability insurers must be notified whenever any accident occurs that *might* result in a liability claim. The insured must not voluntarily assume any obligation that would prejudice the insurer's ability to defend the claim. The insured must also cooperate with the insurer in investigating and defending the claim. Life and health insurers impose similar requirements on insureds.

Allocation of Insurance Costs In order to encourage loss control by each division and to determine more accurately the expenses contributed by each division, a firm may decide to allocate insurance costs as well as other risk management costs. Sometimes insurance costs can be allocated using the same rating characteristics as the insurer uses to establish its prices. For example, insurance priced on the basis of payroll can be easily segregated by division. In other cases, the allocation is more difficult.

Monitoring

Once an insurance decision has been implemented, the decision must be monitored to see whether it has been properly implemented and whether the decision itself needs to be modified. In either case, standards of performance must be set, actual performance must be measured against those standards, and changes made where appropriate.

Proper Implementation Controlling the implementation of the insurance decision involves checking the performance of the insurer and of the insured in carrying out their obligations under the insurance agreement.

Checking Insurer Performance. At the time the agreement was implemented, the risk manager had certain expectations concerning the insurer's performance. Perhaps the insurer was expected to provide the desired protection and suggest ways to improve the coverage; exposure analyses were to be updated periodically in a capable fashion together with suggestions for how to handle these exposures; the insurer's loss control program was expected to produce some measurable reduction in the frequency and severity of the firm's losses; losses should have been settled promptly and fairly; and the insurer's price should have remained competitive for the protection and services provided.

To evaluate the insurer's performance, information is needed on how the insurer did perform and the alternatives available. The insurer that seemed the best initially may no longer be the best available. To explore alternatives, the risk manager may query other risk managers, interview other insurers, or seek competitive bids. Before changing insurers, the advantages of selecting what appears to be the best possible insurer at the moment must be balanced against the uncertainty associated with any change and the value of a long-term relationship with the same insurer.

Checking Internal Performance. The risk manager should check on the effectiveness of the communications network within the firm; how the risk management department and other departments have cooperated with the insurer in its exposure analysis, loss control, and claims handling; and whether the risk management department itself is continually exploring ways to improve the insurance arrangements. The insured's losses, both insured and noninsured, should be analyzed to determine whether the coverage provided is consistent with the initial expectations. The coverage may, in fact, be inadequate if it did not cover some losses it should have covered or unnecessarily expensive in that it covers some losses the risk manager intended to retain.

Insurance Decision Itself The decision to use insurance in conjunction with or in place of some other treatment techniques was based on certain assumptions regarding the relative advantages of insurance. After the insurance decision has been implemented, the risk manager can test those assumptions against actual experience.

Because loss experience in the short run lacks credibility unless the insured has a very large number of exposure units, the risk manager must be careful not to assign too much weight to this experience. With the passage of time, however, it should be possible to assess whether the initial loss expectations should be revised. A change in the firm's or family's environment (the kind, quantity, and quality of its exposures) may suggest such a change even if the actual loss experience does not. Actual experience or new information may change the value assigned to insurer services and the cost of obtaining those services elsewhere.

Most important, the firm's or family's post-loss and pre-loss objectives may have changed causing insurance to become more or less attractive. For example, if a quiet night's sleep has become more important, the risk manager will worry about retaining losses and will tend to favor more insurance. If the insurance decision is to be revised, steps must be taken to implement the new decisions.

RETENTION

Retention is popularly known as "self-insurance." Although "self-insurance" is a misnomer, the term is so widely used and accepted that it is not likely to disappear. However, persons who claim to be informed about risk management and insurance should know why the term is a misnomer.

"Self-insurance" is a misnomer because "self-insurance" is *not* insurance. Insurance is a transfer device. Under "self-insurance" the firm or family retains the loss exposure.

Basic Characteristics

Two basic characteristics of retention are that it is (1) a financing technique, and (2) a residual method.

A Financing Technique Retention is concerned with financing losses that occur. If a firm decides to retain, say, its exposure to industrial injury losses under a workers' compensation act, it has elected to bear any financial losses out of its own resources (or out of borrowed funds that must be repaid). Alternative ways to arrange financing would be a transfer, which may or may not be insurance. Both financing techniques—retention and transfer—are often used with the same loss exposure. For example, a decision might be made to retain all losses per occurrence up to a certain dollar amount and to transfer the excess losses.

Retention differs from avoidance, loss control, combination, and noninsurance transfers of the control type. Unlike those techniques, retention does not seek to change the loss exposure itself. Retention, however, can be used in conjunction with all of these control techniques except avoidance. It can also be used with partial financial transfers. If the loss exposure is avoided or completely transferred, there is no exposure to retain. On the other hand, to reduce the frequency or severity of the potential losses, loss prevention or reduction can be used simultaneously with retention. Separation or combination used in conjunction with retention can make the retained losses more predictable. Part of an exposure can be transferred, the other retained.

A Residual Method Unless a loss exposure is handled *completely* through one or more of the other risk management techniques, the remaining exposure *must* be retained. For example, even when a building is insured for its full insurable value under the broadest policy available, the insurance transfer is incomplete and some exposures must be retained—such as the exposure to small losses within a deductible, the exposure to losses that exceed the policy limit because of rapid inflation, and the exposure to damage by uninsured perils such as war. In this sense, retention is residual in nature.

To avoid any misunderstandings, it is worth repeating that retention is *not* a method of last resort to be considered only after all other avenues have been attempted. Retention is often the *best* way to handle all or part of a loss exposure even when other techniques are readily available.

Types of Retention

Unplanned Retention Unplanned retention occurs when all or part of a loss exposure is retained without considering alternative risk management techniques. Unplanned retention is usually an unconscious act, but it need not be. The risk manager may be unaware of the exposure, or may know about it but postpone deciding how it should be handled. In either case, the retention is unplanned because alternatives were not considered.

Even though retention may be the best way to handle a given loss exposure, unplanned retention is undesirable. The best risk management technique or combination of techniques should be determined for each loss exposure.

Planned Retention Planned retention is always the result of a conscious decision. The risk manager is aware of the loss exposure and, after weighing the advantages and disadvantages of other techniques, decides that retention is the best way to handle part or all of that exposure. Planned retention may or may not be a wise decision. However, planned retention, in which alternatives are at least considered, is more likely to be a wise decision than unplanned retention.

Conditions Requiring or Favoring Use of Retention

Under what conditions must retention be used or at least receive careful consideration? There are three:

(1) no other technique is available;
(2) the worst loss that might occur is not too serious for the entity to handle; and
(3) the losses that will occur in the short run are fairly predictable.

No Other Technique Available Sometimes retention is the only loss financing method available. This may happen for several reasons:

● The risk manager may be able to alter the characteristics of the loss exposure through some control device but not eliminate all the potential losses.
● Insurers may not write insurance on the exposure in question, or if they do, the particular entity may be unable to obtain insurance for a variety of reasons.
● Noninsurance transfer possibilities may not exist.

Worst Loss Not Too Serious Retention deserves careful consideration when the worst loss that can occur is not so serious that the firm or family is unwilling or unable to bear the cost. What size loss the entity would consider serious depends upon its post-loss objectives and its present and prospective profitability and financial status. For example, if a business firm's only post-loss objective is survival, the amount the firm would be willing to retain would be much larger than if the goal were earnings stability. Similarly, a firm or family in a strong financial position is more able to sustain large losses than one on the verge of bankruptcy. Of course, the smaller the dollar value of the worst possible loss, the more likely it becomes that the exposure will be retained. Physical damage losses to autos are often retained for this reason.

Losses Fairly Predictable The third condition favoring the use of retention is a loss exposure with a small variation in potential losses. This circumstance involves actual losses that are fairly predictable because they tend to vary within a narrow range around the estimated average losses. This condition favors retention because, if the range is narrow enough, there will be few surprises. Enough money can be budgeted to cover the expected losses with a fair degree of confidence that the actual losses will not differ much from the budgeted amount. The narrower the range, the more attractive retention becomes.

Possible Advantages and Disadvantages of Retention

Compared with insurance, retention may produce certain loss savings, expense savings, service gains, or improvements to cash flow. However, there are also potential disadvantages in these same areas. This section discusses these *possible* advantages and disadvantages. The extent to which each is applicable in a particular situation would depend on the facts surrounding that case.

Potential Loss Savings It would not be correct to compare the entire loss costs under a retention program with the entire insurance premium under an insurance program, because some retained loss dollars might not be covered by insurance and because the insurance premium does more than cover loss costs. What can legitimately be compared is the portion of the premium intended to cover expected losses. The "expected loss component" can be compared with the retained losses that would be covered by insurance if the exposure were insured. Retention will result in savings when actual losses are less than the loss allowance in the premium. However, it may be difficult to properly measure this savings in the short run. Chance alone may produce a savings, particularly for smaller insureds and for exposures characterized by low loss frequency.

Actual short-run losses may also be greater than expected. In an extreme case, the short-run losses may be so large that they threaten economic survival. This could mean that there will be no opportunity to take advantage of better years when the losses will be less than the loss allowance. If the worst possible loss is within manageable limits, retention does deserve serious consideration. However, it remains true that losses may exceed the loss allowance in the premium.

In the long run and on the average, actual losses may produce fewer loss dollars than assumed in the insurance premium. Insurance pricing techniques are by no means infallible. For some insureds, the loss allowance in the premium exceeds the true expected losses; for others, the loss allowance is smaller than the true expected losses. When a firm or family's expected losses are less than the loss allowance in the premium, the firm or family is likely to save money in the long run by using retention rather than insurance.

This advantage may be more than offset by a disadvantage—retention involves the possibility of wide fluctuations in loss experience from year to year. Volatility may produce an unstable earnings pattern, which in itself may be undesirable.

In summary, retention may result in savings because, in the short run, actual losses are less than the loss allowance in the premium, or because, in the long run, actual losses average less than the loss allowance. On the other hand, retaining a loss exposure may expose a firm to volatility over time in its loss experience, potentially serious losses in the short run, and a long-run average loss that exceeds the loss allowance in the premium that is saved.

Potential Expense Savings Retention may permit expense savings if the services normally provided by the insurer can be provided by the firm or family at a cost lower than the expense and profit portion of the insurer's premium. As indicated earlier in this chapter, insurance premiums are intended to cover losses and also:

(1) loss adjustment expenses;
(2) loss control expenses;
(3) general administrative expenses;
(4) commissions, brokerage, and other acquisition expenses;
(5) taxes, licenses, and fees; and
(6) profits.

If the entity is willing to forgo all of the services provided by the insurer, it can save most of the expense and profit loading. (The possible exceptions are some state taxes, licenses, or fees that must be paid even if an exposure is retained. A few states levy a special assessment on "self-insurers" that is not paid by insurers. This special assessment is used to pay the expenses incurred in administering the "self-insurance" provisions of the act.)

The entity practicing retention may not be willing or able to forgo all the services provided by the insurer. It may decide to provide these services itself, or it may hire outsiders as servicing agents, or both.

Some of the services provided by the insurer have to be performed under a retention program. No choice exists concerning whether to have most claims services. On the other hand, not all insurer expenditures on loss adjustment activities benefit insureds. Some of these activities are designed to protect the insurer against claims it considers unjustified. Filing proofs of loss and meeting other requests of the insurer following a loss may result in some expenses that could be avoided through retention.

The loss control services provided by the insurer may be necessary or desirable to satisfy legal requirements. For example, a firm with steam boilers or elevators may be required to have them inspected periodically. If the firm purchases boiler and machinery insurance or liability insurance covering the maintenance, operation, or use of elevators, inspections by the insurer may satisfy the legal requirement. If the firm does not purchase insurance, it probably will hire some outsider to make these inspections. Further, while other loss control services provided by an insurer may not *have* to be replaced, it may be desirable to do so because these services have been effective in the past in reducing losses.

The exposure analysis services provided by the insurer may merely duplicate tasks regularly performed by the risk manager, in which case no expenses need be incurred to replace these services. On the other hand, if no careful analysis would have taken place otherwise, the insurer's analysis would most likely be replaced.

Instead of saving part of the expense and profit allowance in the premium by retaining a loss exposure, the firm or family may spend more on the services it decides to replace. Even if the quality of these services remains the same, it may be more expensive for internal staff or some outside agency to perform these services than to have the insurer do it. Insurers can spread the overhead cost of these services over many insureds. For example, if a business has a number of small operations at many locations, all of which require servicing, an insurer with a network of national loss control and loss adjustment offices would probably be able to provide those services much more efficiently than the business itself. Outside agencies may also lack the network of offices required to match this efficiency.

Some of the activities financed by the expense allowance in the premium benefit the insurer more than the insured. For example, the insurer probably engages in some pure selling activities designed to convince the insured to purchase insurance as an alternative to retention, or to purchase insurance from a particular insurer. To some extent, these activities help the insured to make a better decision. However, they benefit mainly the insurer.

By retaining the loss exposure, the firm or family also may save that part of the expense allowance allocated by the insurer to the underwriting process and other administrative functions. The insurer incurs certain expenses in selecting acceptable insureds from among the many applicants for insurance, arranging reinsurance that will protect the insurer from shock losses, establishing the premiums to be charged, calculating reserves that reflect the insurer's obligations under outstanding contracts, preparing contracts for distribution to policyholders, investing the monies not needed currently for losses or expenses, and performing general administrative tasks. Insureds also derive some benefits from these activities but the insurer is the main beneficiary. Finally, through retention the firm or family would save the amount included in the premium for the insurer's profit and contingency allowance.[2]

In summary, retention will result in a saving of the profit and contingency allowance and part of the expense allowance (the amount collected to cover selling expense, some administration costs, and taxes in most cases). How much more of the expense allowance will be saved will depend upon how many services such as loss control, loss adjustments, and exposure analysis will be forgone or obtained elsewhere at lesser cost.

Potential Service Gains By retaining an exposure and making alternative arrangements for the services that would otherwise be provided by the insurer, the entity *may* be able to improve the quality of those services. If the services are provided internally by employees or by family members, the quality may be improved because these persons are more familiar with the exposures than the insurer's representatives would be. Also, if the employees assigned responsibility for loss control and loss adjustment services know other employees personally, they may be better able to obtain the cooperation of these employees in rendering these services.

Internal staffing for service activities may use existing strengths effectively. Some of the money that would otherwise have been paid for insurer services may be used to increase the internal staff or otherwise improve its capability.

Use of internal staff also results in more control. In addition to setting policies concerning exposure analysis, loss control, and loss adjustment, the firm can check on how effectively and efficiently these policies are executed.

If some outside agency is used to provide these services, there is a loss of close knowledge of the exposures and personnel but a possible gain in expertise if the outsider specializes in these services. If the firm would have hired some outside supplementary services even if it purchased insurance, it can devote some of the expense savings to increasing these services or improving their quality. Thus, the possibility of building on existing strengths exists with outsiders as well as with insiders.

Retention may create the possibility of improved service; however, it may also reduce the quality of risk management services. Specifically, internal staff or outside agencies may not be able to provide the same expertise; the services may not be available at all locations; and, particularly in settling liability and workers' compensation claims, the advantage of a buffer between the firm and the claimant is lost.

Insurers have expertise gained by dealing with many insureds in a variety of situations that may be difficult or even impossible to match with internal staff. Outside agencies may be able to supply similar expertise but the risk manager should expect differences among outside agencies in this regard.

Similarly, insurers operating nationally or even internationally with a network of agencies and servicing centers can provide services at almost any location, a servicing spread that most large firms will probably not have using insiders for servicing. Moreover, few outside agencies have this potential for service.

Finally, in handling liability claims, it is often preferable not to deal directly with the claimant. Sometimes the negotiations are unpleasant or the settlement is considered unfair by the claimant. In such cases, it may be wise to have an insurer act as a buffer who absorbs any criticism for the handling of the claim. In addition, an insurer may be able to deal more effectively with employees regarding workers' compensation or nonoccupational disability claims because it assumes a more objective stance toward these claims.

Cash Flow   When insurance is purchased, the insured loses the use of prepaid premium dollars. By retaining the loss exposure, the firm or family can avoid paying out any money until it is needed to repair or replace property, investigate, defend, and settle liability claims, pay for loss control services, or handle other losses and expenses. Until the money is needed, it can be invested, thus earning an investment return. An advantage accrues to the firm or family to the extent that its investment return exceeds the reduction in premium by the insurer based on anticipated investment earnings by the insurer. Even if the retained losses and expenses equal the premium that would otherwise be paid to the insurer, this investment return would make retention attractive. The longer the time period over which the losses and expenses are paid the more important this advantage becomes. This feature of retention has become especially important in recent years as interest rates have risen and as businesses have become more skilled in financial management techniques.

Tax Implications

Retaining a property or liability loss exposure *may* mean higher taxes than if the exposure had been insured. To support this assertion, a brief summary of the relevant tax law is presented below. Both business and family tax implications will be discussed.

For a Business *If a business insures a property or liability exposure, it can deduct the insurance premium as a business expense. If it retains this exposure, it can deduct only actual losses.* This difference is important in at least three respects:

(1) Chance fluctuations in the firm's loss exposure affect premiums much less than they affect actual losses.
(2) On property losses, the permissible tax deduction with retention is limited to the book value of the property that is lost.
(3) For liability or workers' compensation losses, only amounts actually paid (or unequivocally payable in the future) are tax deductible with a retention program, according to current rulings.

Effect of Chance Fluctuations. The irregular deductions with a retention program may be less advantageous. Because of the progressive income tax, deducting a larger amount in some years than in others *may* lower the *average* tax bracket that applies to the deductions below the bracket that would apply to regular premium deductions. If so, the aftertax cost of a dollar spent to pay for a loss is greater than the aftertax cost of a dollar spent on insurance. In any single year, the tax bracket may be higher or lower depending on the loss experience relative to the premium.

Property Deductions Limited to Book Value. On retained property losses, the permissible tax deduction is limited to the book value of the property that is destroyed, is damaged, or disappears. To illustrate, assume that a firm purchased a building twelve years ago for $100,000 plus the land price. Because the firm chose to spread the cost of this building uniformly over the next twenty years, it assumed that the building depreciated $5,000 a year. Consequently, at the end of the twelfth year the book value of the building is the original cost of $100,000 less the accumulated depreciation of $60,000 (12 × $5,000), or $40,000. Assume that replacing this building today would cost $200,000; recognizing *physical* depreciation (wear and tear, not the *accounting* depreciation whose purpose was to spread the original cost uniformly over twenty years) would reduce the current value in its actual state to, say, $170,000. If the building were completely destroyed, the firm would lose $170,000; it could deduct only $40,000.

The situation with insurance is more complex. Assume that instead of retaining this exposure, the firm had insured it for $170,000. As noted above, the premium for this protection is a deductible business expense. If the property is destroyed, the insurer pays the firm $170,000, a "gain" of $130,000 over the book value of the property. The tax treatment of this gain is a complicated subject but usually one of two treatments is possible.[3] Under the first, the firm recognizes a gain from an involuntary conversion of property on which it pays a tax at a capital gains rate which is less than regular income tax rates. Under the second, if the involuntarily converted property is replaced by property having the same "functional use" as the destroyed property, the firm is permitted to ignore the gain for tax purposes. On the other hand, for tax purposes, the book value of the replacement property is the $40,000 book value of the converted property plus any amount in excess of $170,000 paid for the replacement property. This means that the annual deduction for depreciation expense will be less and future annual income taxes greater than if the book value of the replacement property were its actual cost. For example, if the new building cost $200,000, of which $170,000 was provided by the insurer, the original book value of the replacement property would be $40,000 (the book value of the converted property) plus $30,000 (the amount by which the $200,000 cost exceeded the $170,000 insurance proceeds). If the business decides to spread this original book value of $70,000 for the replacement property over a period of twenty years, the annual depreciation expense would be only $3,500, compared with $10,000 if the original book value were the actual cost of $200,000. Because of the lower deduction for depreciation expense, future taxable income and taxes will be higher when insurance proceeds are used to replace the property.

In summary, if the firm purchases property insurance, the premium is deductible. If insurance proceeds exceed the book value of a property loss, the excess is taxable in one of two ways:

(1) the excess is taxable immediately at capital gains rates, or
(2) the income tax will be higher in future years than if the replacement property were not purchased with insurance proceeds.

If the firm does not buy insurance, only the book value of a property loss is tax deductible; but, if the property is replaced, the book value of the replacement property is its actual cost and the income tax in future years will be less than if the property had been replaced, at least in part, by insurance proceeds that exceed the book value of the property loss.

The preceding discussion assumed complete destruction or disappearance of a property item. For partial losses that are retained, the tax deductible amount is the decrease in the fair market value of the property but no more than its book value.

Only Paid Losses Deductible. If retained loss is a liability or a workers' compensation claim, only amounts actually paid, or unequivocally payable in the future, are tax deductible. According to some current rulings, the firm is not even permitted to deduct reasonable estimates of money that is quite likely to be paid in the future because of events that have already occurred. For example, because a worker was totally and permanently disabled in an industrial accident, the firm may be obligated to pay him or her $200 a week for life. Because the continuation of these payments in future years depends upon how long the worker lives, only the amounts actually paid are tax deductible. Given a choice, most firms would prefer to deduct the "full" loss including the estimated future outlays because, in general, most would prefer to reduce taxes now rather than in the future.

Although they are operating contrary to current Internal Revenue Service rulings, many firms have deducted reserves established to cover estimated future costs of specific cases. Some have deducted reserves based on average costs. IRS has questioned many such deductions, but others have not been disallowed.

For a Family The portions of the tax codes applicable to individuals and families differ in several significant ways from those applicable to businesses:

(1) In determining its taxable income, a family cannot deduct its property and liability insurance premiums.
(2) Property losses are valued at the difference between the value of the property immediately before and immediately after the accident unless this difference exceeds the "adjusted cost" (usually the original cost, in which case the original cost is the allowable value). For example, assume a dwelling that cost $20,000 ten years ago is partially destroyed by a fire. The value immediately before the fire was $40,000; the value immediately after was $25,000. The $15,000 difference, which is less than the $20,000 original cost, is the allowable value for calculating income tax deductions.
(3) The first $100 of property losses is not tax deductible. Thus, in the dwelling example, the tax deductible amount was $14,900.
(4) The family can deduct payments on liability claims only if they were incurred in connection with business or professional pursuits. This provision strongly favors the purchase of liability insurance.

The tax implications of decisions to insure or to retain health and earning capacity exposures are discussed in CPCU 2.

Implementation

Once a decision has been made to retain a loss exposure, that decision must be implemented. Implementation includes:

(1) taking steps to meet any applicable legal responsibilities,
(2) evaluating and paying losses,
(3) controlling loss costs,
(4) arranging funding for retained losses, and
(5) allocating retention costs.

On each of these matters, a decision must be made as to whether the function will be performed internally or by outsiders.

Meeting Legal Responsibilities Some legal responsibilities may have to be satisfied before the retention program can commence or while it is operating. For example, if insurance is "compulsory" (as is workers' compensation insurance in all states and auto liability insurance in many), it is customary to permit retention under certain conditions. A firm or family that decides to retain these exposures must secure permission from some public agency or it will be violating the law. Furthermore, once the retention program begins to operate, it may be necessary to submit reports, set aside funds to meet outstanding losses, or satisfy other conditions imposed by the public agency. Finally, retention programs may have to meet some of the legal requirements imposed on insurers. For example, a state industrial commission or other agency usually must be kept informed on the progress and disposition of workers' compensation claims.

Evaluating and Paying Losses If property is destroyed, damaged, or disappears, an investigation should be conducted to determine the cause, amount, and other circumstances surrounding the loss. One reason for the investigation is to gather information that will be useful for loss control purposes. A second is to compile statistical information that will be needed to evaluate the decision to retain and possibly to obtain from insurers information on the availability and pricing of insurance. A third reason is that this information may help in deciding whether the property should be repaired or replaced. A final reason for investigation, at least in some losses, is to determine if someone else is legally liable for the damage or destruction. When insurance is purchased, the loss adjustment services of insurers are particularly important in handling liability claims. When changing to a retention program, they must be replaced. Because few firms are equipped to replace these services internally, it is customary to hire an insurer or an independent adjuster to provide these services.

Similarly, if employee benefit plans are not insured, disability income, medical expense, or death benefits claims must still be handled. Death claims are relatively easy to handle because the event is clearly defined and a stated amount is paid upon its occurrence. Disability income benefits are much more difficult to administer because the actual occurrence of the event involved—disability—is sometimes difficult to verify or refute. Medical expense benefits require an evaluation of the necessity for the treatment and the amount billed.

Loss Control Since any loss savings that result from loss control are recouped directly, the incentive for loss control is stronger under retention than under insurance. Under a retention program some tasks that would otherwise be an insurer's responsibility may also be assumed.

Funding Retained Losses One of the most important questions accompanying a decision to retain a loss exposure is how the losses, if any, will be funded. The possibilities include:

(1) current net income,
(2) earmarked retained earnings,
(3) earmarked assets,
(4) borrowing, and
(5) captive insurers.

For reasons to be explained shortly only the first and the fifth methods are important today.

Current Net Income. The simplest approach is to pay losses out of current net income when they occur, the losses being treated just like expenses incurred that year. If the loss involves payments over a period of years (for example, disability income payments until the person recovers from the disability), each year's payments would be met out of each year's net income. Because this method is so simple, it is inexpensive to administer. If net income is insufficient to meet the year's loss, accumulated assets must be tapped to meet the deficiency.

The major disadvantage of this approach is that losses may exceed the current net income and assets that can easily be liquidated. As a consequence, it may be necessary to convert nonliquid assets (furniture, fixtures, equipment, land) into cash at an inopportune time, receiving less than full value for the assets and thus increasing the real dollar loss sustained.

A second disadvantage is that even less serious losses may impair overall liquidity. Reduced liquidity may cause concern about the firm's future among lenders, investors, customers, suppliers, and employees.

A third disadvantage is that the net income picture for a given year is distorted by totally or largely uncontrollable events. An otherwise profitable year may be turned into a loss year by an unexpected fire, liability suit, or industrial accident. Some other year in which ordinary business operations were much less successful may report a higher net income because it was a "lucky" year in which there were fewer losses financed by retention.

Despite these disadvantages, paying losses out of current net income is the most common way to fund a retention program. The disadvantages are handled by (1) not retaining losses that are likely to cause serious liquidity problems or cause earnings to fluctuate greatly and (2) making advance arrangements to borrow funds to solve short-term liquidity problems following a loss.

Borrowing. This approach is a variation of the net income approach. Instead of financing losses with internally generated funds, the firm or family may borrow from some lender as the need arises. The loss is still charged against net income, but at least part of the losses are met out of borrowed funds rather than out of cash flow or the conversion of nonliquid assets. The advantages of borrowing are that the cash flow is not disturbed until repayments begin on the loan and nonliquid assets do not have to be converted at what may be inopportune times. On the other hand, interest must be paid on the amount borrowed. Furthermore, if the intent is to use borrowed funds, some prior arrangements are well-advised. Unless a prior commitment from a lending institution has been obtained, funds may not be available when they are needed. Borrowing to finance retained losses or obtaining prior commitments for such borrowing may also reduce opportunities to secure loans for other purposes. Finally, except for the fact that borrowing makes cash available to pay losses, the problems associated with the net income approach remain.

Earmarked Retained Earnings. In theory, one way to avoid fluctuations in annual earnings as a result of retaining unpredictable losses would be to include in the entity's balance sheet an item (earmarked retained earnings) to which there is added each year an estimate of annual expected losses and from which there is subtracted the actual losses that year. The expected loss estimate would be charged against the net income; the actual losses would not affect the net income. In the long run, if the expected loss estimates are correct, the aggregate actual losses will equal the aggregate expected losses.

For example, assume that a firm estimates its expected losses each year to be $10,000, and the actual losses over a period of ten years are as shown in Exhibit 3-3. If the annual net income over this period excluding the actual losses is $100,000, charging the actual losses against this income would have produced annual incomes ranging from $100,000 − $1,000, or $99,000, to $100,000 − $40,000, or $60,000.

Exhibit 3-3
Actual Loss Experience

Year	Actual Losses
1	$ 6,000
2	2,000
3	1,000
4	5,000
5	20,000
6	1,000
7	1,000
8	40,000
9	4,000
10	20,000

Exhibit 3-4
Earmarked Retained Earnings Account for Expected Losses

Year	Earmarked Retained Earnings at Beginning of Year	Credit Expected Losses	Charge Actual Losses	Earmarked Retained Earnings at End of Year
1	$ 0	$10,000	$ 6,000	$ 4,000
2	4,000	10,000	2,000	12,000
3	12,000	10,000	1,000	21,000
4	21,000	10,000	5,000	26,000
5	26,000	10,000	20,000	16,000
6	16,000	10,000	1,000	25,000
7	25,000	10,000	1,000	34,000
8	34,000	10,000	40,000	4,000
9	4,000	10,000	4,000	10,000
10	10,000	10,000	20,000	0

Charging an annual expected loss of $10,000 against these incomes would have produced a constant annual net income of $90,000.

The earmarked earnings item in the balance sheet would be changed each year as indicated in Exhibit 3-4. To trace this account, start at its inception at the beginning of the first year, note the increase of $10,000 and the charge decrease of $6,000 (actual losses for the year), leaving an end-of-year balance of $4,000. Carry that balance to the beginning of the second year, repeat the credit and charge process, and so on.

Charging (i.e., reducing) each year's net income with the annual expected losses, instead of the fluctuating actual annual losses, would smooth out the annual incomes. This "bookkeeping" approach to the leveling of losses, though perhaps useful for other reasons, is not an acceptable approach to determining income for income tax purposes. In other words, it might be desirable "financial accounting" for a firm but it is not permissible "tax accounting." As previously indicated, for tax purposes only actual losses are deductible in determining taxable income.

There are at least four major problems with this approach. First, it often is difficult to estimate the expected losses accurately enough for a charge against net income.

Second, the actual losses may differ greatly from the expected losses in the short run. Unlike the example presented above, the losses in the first few years may far exceed the amount in the earmarked retained earnings item—which cannot be reduced below zero. In this event, the excess would have to be charged against net income or past retained earnings. Because the expected loss is likely to be much less than possible losses, it may be several years before the earmarked retained earnings item reaches an amount that could accommodate a large loss or even a moderate loss.

Third, the retained earnings item does not guarantee that an equal amount of liquid assets will be available on the asset side of the balance sheet. For example, in the eighth year of the illustration presented above, the earmarked retained earnings item was sufficient to cover the $40,000 loss but there might not be $40,000 in liquid assets.

Fourth, the Financial Accounting Standards Board (FASB) has prohibited the use of this approach in financial statements presented to the public.[4] The FASB is authorized to establish accounting principles pursuant to Rule 203 of the Rules of Conduct of the American Institute of Certified Public Accountants. Their action means that if a business does earmark part of retained earnings for expected retained losses and smooths out its income accordingly, no CPA firm can certify that its annual or interim statements have been prepared in accordance with Generally Accepted Accounting Principles. Such statements would also not be acceptable to the Securities and Exchange Commission. In general terms, the position of the American Institute of Certified Public Accountants is based on the belief that financial statements using the practices discussed above could present a misleading picture of the stability of the firm's earnings over time.

Earmarked Assets. A third approach to financing retained losses would create an earmarked item, consisting of liquid assets, on the asset side of the balance sheet, that would equal the earmarked retained earnings item created in the manner described in the preceding section. Because this approach guarantees liquidity equal to the amount of the earmarked retained earnings item, it eliminates the third problem—no commitment of liquid assets to cover the potential loss— associated with the mere creation of an earmarked retained earnings item. The other three problems remain, however, and an additional problem is created. Keeping liquid assets that may not be needed until some future date may reduce the rate of return because these assets could be more productively employed elsewhere.

Captive Insurer. The fifth and final approach to be discussed here is the creation of a captive insurer. A captive insurer may be defined as "a wholly owned insurance subsidiary with a primary function of insuring the outstanding exposures of the parent organization."[5] Captive insurers are distinguished from other insurers in that they confine or largely limit their writings to exposures belonging to their owner (or owners).

Why might a firm establish a captive insurer?[6] To some extent, a captive insurer may be advantageous for accounting reasons, for tax reasons, because it improves access to the reinsurance market, or because there are special advantages for international operations. It will be noted that accounting restrictions and tax rulings have effectively eliminated the accounting and tax reasons at present.

ACCOUNTING REASONS. Until recent action by the Financial Accounting Standards Board, one objective might have been to stabilize net income over time by reducing the effect of chance losses on the net income reported in annual financial statements. In order to understand how a captive insurer might have helped a firm to accomplish this objective, one must consider the effect on the incomes of both the parent and the captive insurer.

If, instead of a captive insurer, the parent firm had used the net income approach to finance a retention program, it could have subtracted only its *actual losses* from its net income. Payments to be made in the future because of events that have already occurred could not be deducted unless the amount could be reasonably estimated. A premium paid to a captive insurer, however, could be deducted from net income, thus removing the effect on the parent of chance fluctuations in losses.

The captive insurer, on the other hand, was affected by chance fluctuations. To determine its underwriting profit for the year, the captive insurer subtracted from its earned premiums its *incurred losses* and expenses. The incurred loss figure recognized the amounts already paid on that year's losses plus the amounts still to be paid. Thus, when the financial statements of both parent company and captive insurer were combined, the premiums paid by the parent were offset by the premiums received by the captive, but the consolidated net income was affected by chance fluctuations in the captive insurer's *incurred* losses. The principal difference between this approach and the net income approach on the question of stability, therefore, was that the captive insurer was permitted to deduct some reserves on incurred but not paid losses that could not have been deducted by the parent under the net income approach. FASB action (Statement No. 5), however, eliminated even this possibility. It prohibits the parent corporation from deducting premiums paid to a captive insurer to the extent that the protection is not reinsured with an independent insurer. The FASB reasons that premiums paid to a captive insurer for nonreinsured protection are not the same as premiums paid for outside protection. Thus, the effect of the FASB statement is to prevent the parent from stabilizing its own net income by forming a captive insurer if it wants its financial statements certified as being in accordance with Generally Accepted Accounting Principles.

TAX REASONS. Closely related to the accounting reasons for forming a captive is a potential deferred tax advantage. To the extent that a captive insurer stabilizes net income for tax purposes, it stabilizes tax payments. If the parent and the captive insurer could file separate returns, the parent could deduct each year from its taxable income the premium paid the captive. The captive insurer's taxable income, however, would vary according to its incurred loss experience. If the parent and the captive file a consolidated return, the taxable income varies according to the captive's *incurred* loss experience, *including* reserves on outstanding losses. By permitting the business to subtract from its consolidated net income the reserve for loss payments to be made in the future because of events that have already occurred, the captive insurer arrangement could defer the taxes to be paid on that amount until the reserve is reduced by actual loss payments. The tax deferment would give the business the opportunity to invest the deferred amount until it is needed.

For several years the Internal Revenue Service has questioned this potential tax advantage, using reasoning similar to that of the FASB. In late 1978, the U.S. Tax Court agreed with the Internal Revenue Service that the Carnation Company could not deduct premiums paid to a captive insurer. This decision was affirmed early in 1981 by the 9th Circuit Court of Appeals. Some questions remain, however, on several aspects of the decision, and further appeals may take place.[7]

ACCESS TO REINSURANCE. A captive insurer offers the advantage of easier access to reinsurers, many of whom will deal only with insurers. Because reinsurers are more venturesome than primary insurers in the kinds of protection they are willing to write, the business may thus be able to obtain protection tailor-made to its needs (for example, some unusual deductible feature). Reinsurers are more venturesome in part because they are less constrained than primary insurers by legal requirements, in part because their customers (primary insurers) are sophisticated buyers demanding at times unusual coverages, and in part because this is their traditional method of operating.

INTERNATIONAL ADVANTAGES. Captives offer some special advantages for businesses with international operations.[8] For example, some countries require the business to insure local operations with local insurers. A captive insurer may be able to reinsure the locally admitted insurer which in turn may be willing to write broader insurance than would otherwise be the case. A captive insurer can also serve as a vehicle to move money through international markets. For example, it can lend money at high interest rates to affiliated operations in countries with high income taxes and at low interest rates to operations in countries with low income taxes.

COSTS ASSOCIATED WITH DOMESTIC CAPTIVES. Captive insurers impose some additional costs on the parent company. To establish a domestic insurer, the business must invest money and time satisfying the state's legal requirements and preparing itself to commence operations. For example, captive insurers must satisfy the minimum capital and surplus requirements established by the state of domicile. The business must also supply some funds or personnel to meet the operating needs of the captive. Captive insurers, like all insurers, must also pay some special taxes (such as state premium taxes) not paid by other businesses. The captive insurer may also be forced to accept its share of business written by pools created to handle insureds who cannot obtain insurance through regular channels—such as property owners whose buildings are insured under FAIR Plans or auto owners whose cars are insured under automobile insurance plans. To the extent that these pools experience underwriting losses, as has frequently been the case, the captive insurer shares in losses not associated with the parent's business. Finally, captive insurers may be required to participate in programs that have been established in most states to pay obligations of insolvent insurers.

OFFSHORE CAPTIVES. In order to increase the tax advantages and to avoid some of the disadvantages associated with captive insurers, many businesses with overseas subsidiaries have formed offshore captive insurance companies. The three most popular locations are Bermuda, the Bahamas, and the Cayman Islands.[9] The premiums paid the captive insurer by the overseas subsidiaries are an expense to the subsidiaries which reduces the tax they owe the countries where they are located. The captive insurer pays little or no tax to the country where it is located, this low tax rate being the major reason for selecting that site for the captive insurer. Until the captive insurer's income is repatriated to the United States, none of its income is subject to United States federal income tax. The captive insurer can insure some of the United States operations of the business as well as its overseas subsidiaries without losing this tax deferral. Specifically, the premiums derived from United States operations can be as much as 5 percent of the captive's total premiums.[10] Another advantage associated with offshore captives is minimal supervision by the country of origin, which permits the insurer to be more flexible in its coverages and its operations—rates and investments, for example. Furthermore, offshore captives are not required to participate in pools established to handle applicants who cannot obtain insurance through normal channels.

In 1972, the Colorado legislature enacted a Captive Insurance Company Bill which made it much more attractive to establish a domestic captive insurer in that state. Under this law, captive insurers domiciled in Colorado are excused from participating in the special pools established in that state. The cost of establishing and operating a captive insurer is also closer to that of offshore captives than of captives domiciled in other states. Tennessee and Virginia have also passed special laws to encourage the formation of captives in their states.

CURRENT STATUS. Over 1,000 captives currently exist. Many of these captives, however, are not pure captives. They serve a group of common owners or they sell insurance to outsiders. To the extent of the outside involvement, however, the arrangement is changed from retention to insurance. Many believe that it will also eliminate any doubt about the parent's premiums being tax deductible.

Allocating Retention Costs Allocating retention costs among the various divisions of a firm is designed to achieve the same objectives as the allocation of other risk management costs: (1) to obtain a more accurate reading of the profitability of each division, and (2) to encourage loss control. However, retention costs are the most difficult of all risk management costs to allocate. Except in unusual cases, it would be unfair and illogical to charge each division with its actual losses because these losses are largely determined by chance. A better approach would be to charge each division with its expected losses. If these expected losses cannot be estimated on the basis of division or firm experience, a common approach is to charge each division the premium it would have had to pay if it purchased insurance. These division premiums might also be adjusted upward or downward on the basis of how the firm's retention costs (losses and expenses) compare with its hypothetical insurance costs. Some divisions may have such extensive experience that some credibility should be assigned to that experience, the allocated cost being some weighted average of the actual experience and the hypothetical insurance premium.

Monitoring

Decisions to retain, like other risk management decisions, must be monitored to determine whether they have been most effectively and efficiently implemented and whether retention is in fact the most appropriate technique. Monitoring is a four-step procedure:

(1) establishing standards for judging the performance of the retention program,
(2) analyzing the losses that have been retained against these standards,
(3) reviewing the retention decision itself, and
(4) altering the retention decision or its implementation where this seems appropriate.

Establishing Performance Standards   Performance standards are determined in large part by the objectives of the particular risk management program and by the advantages and disadvantages originally considered in making the decision to retain. Performance standards should be established for

(1) the worst losses sustained,
(2) fluctuations in the annual losses,
(3) the average loss,
(4) the expenses incurred in servicing the plan, and
(5) the quality of those services.

Worst Losses Sustained and Fluctuations in Annual Losses.   The standards established for the worst losses sustained and for fluctuations in the annual losses will depend on whether the entity has set as its post-loss objective mere survival, continuity of operations, earnings stability, or continued growth.

If the goal is mere survival, some substantial losses and wide fluctuations in annual losses would be acceptable. On the other hand, if the goal is earnings stability, the worst loss should not be too large and the fluctuations in annual losses should be small. These standards will also depend upon how much importance is assigned to the reduction of anxiety. The more important it is to reduce the worry about what might happen, the tighter the standards are likely to be with respect to the worst losses and fluctuations in annual losses.

Average Losses. If complete retention is to be preferable to insurance in the long run, the average losses under the retention program should compare favorably with the allowance for losses in the insurance premium. Whether the standard for the average losses based on this reasoning should be above, equal to, or below that loss allowance depends on (1) how the expenses incurred in servicing the plan compare with the expense and profit allowance in the premium, and (2) whether some loss saving is on the average considered to be a necessary ingredient of the retention program. If the actual expenses equal the expense and profit allowance, the average losses must not exceed the loss allowance. If the expenses are higher, the average losses must be less than the loss allowance; if the expenses are lower, the average loss can be higher than the loss allowance without causing a loss of money in the long run.

On the other hand, as compensation for absorbing fluctuations in annual losses and for worrying that the worst possible loss might occur, the entity might demand that, regardless of the relationship between the expenses and the expense and profit allowance, the average losses be less than the loss allowance. In establishing an average loss standard it must be recognized that, unless there are a large number of exposure units, it will take many years before a credible average can be calculated. Indeed, if there are few exposure units the average may never be highly credible and it may be impossible to evaluate whether average losses compare favorably with the loss allowance in the premium.

Expense Standards. Expense standards should be established for each of the major classes of expenses and some subcategories. For example, standards might be set for exposure analysis expenses, loss control costs, and loss adjustment expenses. The actual expenses should be compared with the amount an insurer would charge for these services. The acceptable standard may be higher or lower depending on (1) how the average losses are expected to compare with the loss allowance, (2) the relative quality of the services rendered, and (3) how large is the desired saving on the average on losses and expenses.

Quality Standards. Quality standards must also be set for services rendered. For example, the exposure analysis might be expected to be "as thorough as that performed by an insurer or its representatives." Possible tests are a comparative evaluation of the time, effort, and skills brought to this task, whether or not any exposures have been identified following a loss that would have been identified earlier by an insurer. Conversely, the risk manager or some servicing agency may have discovered some exposures that would probably not have been identified by an insurer. Similarly, loss control efforts can be monitored using measures suggested in Chapter 2 and the services that might reasonably be expected from an insurer. Loss adjustment service standards might be set for such aspects as promptness, efficiency, accuracy, and customer relations, particularly with respect to liability and workers' compensation claims.

Analyzing Losses Against Standards As noted above, determining whether the actual loss experience under retention meets the standards established is difficult. Detailed development of this point must await the discussion of probability distributions in Chapters 4 and 5, but the point is so important that it deserves brief mention here. If a loss has already exceeded the worst acceptable loss, this experience may be enough to suggest a change in the retention program because this event was not supposed to happen. If, however, the standard had been phrased in terms of the worst *probable* event, the risk manager would have to recognize that it was *possible* that the standard would be exceeded. The question then becomes how likely it is that the event will happen in the future, a question that requires some sophisticated data and analysis. Similarly, if a standard is set for fluctuations in annual losses, the conclusion and need for further analysis differs depending upon whether losses outside that range are not acceptable, or are acceptable only if unlikely. Comparing average losses with the standard is not possible until one has sufficient experience to develop a reliable estimate of the true average in the long run.

Reviewing the Retention Decision Itself At the time the retention decision was made, the risk manager had certain perceptions concerning the probable loss experience, the servicing the plan would require and the amount it would cost, the premium that would have to be paid for insurance protection, and the firm's or family's post-loss and pre-loss objectives. With the passage of time, each of these factors is subject to change which may in turn make the retention decision more or less attractive. If less attractive, the risk manager must decide whether the retention decision should be altered.

Altering the Retention Decision or Its Implementation Where Appropriate If the monitoring process reveals that the retention decision should be altered, retention may be replaced in whole or in part by insurance or some other transfer device. Some possibilities for combining retention and insurance are discussed later in this chapter. Instead, however, the review may suggest that retention is the best approach but that its implementation should be improved. For example, the quality of the exposure analysis, loss control, and loss adjustment services might be improved or they might be performed at less cost. If an outside agency has been providing this service, more responsibility might be assigned to insiders, or vice versa. If the losses that occur are to be financed through borrowing, attempts might be made to reduce the interest rate or to secure other, more favorable terms.

Retention Combined with Insurance

In many instances, the firm may wish to retain only part of the exposure. In some cases, it is common to purchase insurance that will cover only those potential losses that the firm does not wish to retain. After discussing briefly some less formal formats for combining these financing techniques, this section will discuss some of the insurance products that can be combined with retention and the advantages and disadvantages of such combinations. An explanation of a common application of this concept in workers' compensation concludes this section.

Coverage Limitations Usually, insurance does not cover all of the events that might produce a loss. Thus, the firm usually retains part of the exposure whenever it purchases insurance. This point will be discussed in detail in Volume II of this text.

Inadequate Insurance One way to share the amount of the exposure is to purchase insurance that is less than the maximum possible loss. One such case is illustrated in Exhibit 3-5. The insured retains that portion of any loss that exceeds the policy limit.

This variety of partial retention may occur because the insurer refuses to issue higher limits. In such a case, the risk manager has no choice. Sometimes it occurs because the risk manager refuses to pay the premium for higher limits. Because it is usually impossible to determine the *maximum* possible liability loss, most liability insurance is, in this sense, "inadequate."

Deductible and Excess Insurance Another approach to retaining part of the amount of the exposure is to retain the first part of any loss, using deductible or excess insurance. The terms "deductible" and "excess" are sometimes used interchangeably. In this text, however, they denote two different approaches to combining retention with insurance.

- Under deductible insurance, the firm retains a relatively small part of the maximum possible loss, as shown in Exhibit 3-5.
- Under excess insurance, also illustrated in Exhibit 3-5, the insured retains a relatively large part of the maximum possible loss. For example, the retention level may be set at the maximum probable loss.

The services provided by insurers vary between deductible insur-

Exhibit 3-5
Ways of Combining Retention With Insurance

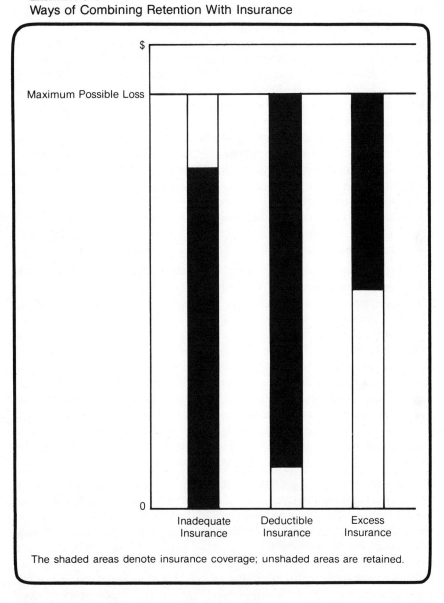

The shaded areas denote insurance coverage; unshaded areas are retained.

ance and excess insurance. The excess insurer does not usually provide
any exposure analysis or loss control services. Unless the loss exceeds
the retention level, the excess insurer does not usually participate in
loss adjustment.

With deductible insurance, unless the loss is clearly less than the deductible amount, the insurer usually adjusts the loss and subtracts the deductible amount from the insurance proceeds. The insurer also provides loss control services and other services.

Because liability losses are difficult to evaluate until they are settled, excess insurers often wish to become involved in claims at a lower level because of the chance that the loss ultimately will exceed the insured's retention. For the same reason, the insurer providing deductible insurance usually adjusts all liability losses—even those that seem likely to be settled within the deductible.

Insurance practice is more complicated than this brief discussion would suggest, with some types of insurance being a hybrid of deductible and excess insurance. Nevertheless, the distinction between deductible insurance and excess insurance is useful in indicating different retention concepts.

Whether the form is deductible or excess insurance, the portion of the exposure that is retained can be referred to as a "deductible." Deductibles are discussed in greater detail in Volume II of this text.

Advantages. Compared with complete retention, retention combined with insurance has the advantage of allowing the firm to purchase protection against losses in excess of the deductible amount. The risk manager's uncertainty is thereby reduced.

Many of the advantages of complete retention are also preserved. If the insurer's loss allowance is too low relative to the average insured losses in the long run, the long-run results will favor the insured. If the insurance is deductible insurance, the firm may also benefit if the insurer can provide more efficient or more effective services. The insurance premium is tax deductible and the insurance proceeds subject to the special tax treatment noted earlier. Furthermore, the premium dollars saved by purchasing deductible or excess insurance can be invested until they are needed to pay losses or expenses.

Disadvantages. Compared with complete retention, the retention-insurance combination may cost more in the short run because the actual losses retained under the combination plus the loss allowance in the premium for the deductible or excess insurance exceed the actual losses that would have been borne under full retention. If the insurer's loss allowance is too high, the loss cost will be higher in the long run. Services provided by the insurer may cost more or be of lower quality than those associated with complete retention. The opportunity to keep the premium dollars paid for insurance invested until they were needed would also be lost.

A Common Application: Workers' Compensation. Many large firms handle their workers' compensation exposure with some combination of retention and insurance. This exposure is a particularly suitable candidate for retention because (1) these firms have such a large number of exposure units that their experience is fairly predictable, (2) the exposure is particularly susceptible to loss control and (3) the claim arising out of an industrial injury or disease may be paid over a long period of time. On the other hand, the possibility exists that a single accident will cause many workers to be seriously injured or that there will be many serious accidents in a single year. Therefore, a combination retention-insurance program is the usual choice among those who do not completely insure this exposure. Some states require the purchase of excess insurance protection against substantial losses by those firms electing to retain workers' compensation losses.

An alternative approach, which is quite popular, is to hire a management service organization which in effect takes over the administration of the plan and arranges excess aggregate or "stop-loss" insurance that protects the employer against aggregate losses per year that exceed some specified amount. For example, under one typical arrangement, the employer pays the management organization an amount equal to about 25 percent of what the employer's normal annual insurance premium would be. The remaining 75 percent is retained by the employer as a claims fund for payment of losses if and when they occur. The 25 percent payment purchases (1) excess insurance from an outside insurer that covers annual losses in excess of the 75 percent claims fund, and (2) services performed by the management organization. These services include loss control, claims adjustments, dealing with regulatory agencies, accounting, data processing, auditing, and other general administration.

The Future

Retention programs are expected to become increasingly important. Three reasons account for most of the growing interest in retention:

(1) Because of inflation and other pressures on profits, business has become more aware of and more concerned about costs in general and risk management costs in particular. The rising cost of insurance and the growth of risk management functions have combined to cause businesses to carefully consider risk management techniques besides insurance.

(2) Because some businesses have been unable to secure adequate protection against certain exposures (such as products liability) or such insurance has been available only at what they consider exorbitant prices, they have chosen active retention as a way of handling these exposures.

(3) The cash flow advantage of retention has become more important with increasing attention to the time value of money.

Insurers have recognized the growing interest in retention. Many have actually encouraged increased use of retention. For example, some insurers will write only deductible or excess insurance in certain lines to avoid handling small losses or to encourage insureds to control losses. Many insurers have formed departments or subsidiaries that sell services to firms using retention programs.

CASH FLOW INSURANCE PLANS

Cash flow insurance plans are alternative methods for paying insurance premiums. They combine some advantages of prepaid insurance and of retention as techniques for financing loss exposures. Although the financial consequences of a loss exposure are transferred to an insurer, the insured does not forgo all the cash flow advantages of retention.

The cash flow *disadvantages* of insurance were mentioned earlier in this chapter. It was noted that the timing of payments can be an important risk management consideration, and that, by retaining a loss exposure, the firm or family can earn an investment return until the money is needed to pay for losses. With prepaid insurance, the use of funds is sacrificed when the premium is paid.

Many insurance costs are not incurred by the insurer at the beginning of the policy term, but are incurred as loss payments become necessary. Any premium payment plan that recognizes the deferred nature of these expenditures could be called a *cash flow plan.* During recent years, insurers have devised a variety of more sophisticated programs to share with policyholders the advantages of delayed payout of loss and expense. Two such plans are the compensating balances plan and the paid loss retro:

- *Compensating balances plan*—This plan requires full premium payment at policy inception. However, the portion remaining after the insurer's initial expenses are deducted is deposited in a bank at the policyholder's direction to support a line of credit. Therefore, funds previously tied up in "compensating balances" are freed for use by the firm, and thus earn generally higher returns on investment. Funds are returned to the compensating balance account only as losses and expenses are paid by the insurer.
- *Paid loss retro*—Essentially, this plan allows for the billing of insurance costs as they are actually paid by the insurer. Most

premiums are paid "retrospectively" (literally, "with hind-sight") based on the actual dollar cost of insured losses. The insured firm initially pays a relatively small portion of the premium to cover some early administrative and loss costs, while supplying the insurer with a promissory note or letter of credit for the balance. The policyholder is then billed as costs arise while maintaining control of and receiving investment income for these remaining funds.

Cash flow plans are *not* retention programs. They are merely alternative methods of paying insurance premiums. During periods of high investment returns, they enable policyholders to defer the payment of insurance premiums as long as possible, while maintaining the reduction in uncertainty available only through the use of an insurance transfer.

Chapter Notes

---

1. Robert I. Mehr and Bob A. Hedges, *Risk Management: Concepts and Applications* (Homewood, IL: Richard D. Irwin, 1974), pp. 148-149.
2. Saving the profit and contingency allowance, however, exposes the insured to the same uncertainties that face the insurer—that the losses will exceed the loss allowance and that the expenses will exceed the expense allowance. The discussion should not be interpreted to mean that the insurer earns, even on the average, the exact amount of the profit and contingency allowance. Only if the actual losses equal the expected losses and the actual expenses the expected expenses will this be true. This is an unlikely event for at least two reasons. First, because of chance fluctuations the actual losses during a year will probably differ from the true expected losses. Second, the insurer's expected loss and expense estimates may be inaccurate. Insurance pricing is by no means an accurate science—there are too many variables such as accident conditions and inflation that are subject to rapid changes.
3. For a more detailed treatment, see Appendix A, Summary of Selected Portions of the Internal Revenue Code Applicable to Insurable Introductory Conversions of Property in Michael L. Smith, "Selection of Deductibles in Property and Liability Insurance," unpublished doctoral dissertation, University of Minnesota, 1974. For a shorter but comprehensive and more readily accessible source see Robert I. Mehr and Bob A. Hedges, *Risk Management: Concepts and Applications* (Homewood, IL: Richard D. Irwin, 1974), pp. 45-49.
4. *AICPA Professional Standards, Volume 3, Accounting: Current Text, as of September 1, 1975*, pp. 9181-9219. For the arguments that the Risk and Insurance Management Society presented against the FASB position see R. J. Keintz and J. F. Lee, "Accounting for Future Losses: The Risk Management Problems," *Risk Management* (January 1975), pp. 6-14.
5. Frederick M. Reiss, "Corporations and the Captive Insurer," *Proceedings of the 12th Annual Insurance Conference*, The Ohio State University (1961), p. 15. Captive insurers are the subject of a monograph in CPCU 10.
6. For an extensive answer to this question, see Edward P. Lalley, *Self Assumption, Self Insurance, and the Captive Insurance Company Concept* (New York: Risk and Insurance Management Society, Inc., 1975), pp. 9-20.
7. "Tax Court Affirms IRS Veto of Captives in Carnation Co. Test Case," *Business Insurance*, 8 January 1979, pp. 1 and 86; Jerry Geisel and Kathryn J. McIntyre, "Carnation Co. Loses Tax Fight Over Captive," *Business Insurance*, 16 March 1981, pp. 1, 75.
8. For more details see Norman A. Baglini, *Risk Management in International Corporations* (New York: Risk Studies Foundation, 1976), pp. 97-101, 105-106.

9. The tax treatment of offshore captive insurers is complex and not easily determined without reference to specific Revenue Rulings and tax court decisions. Further information can be obtained from Revenue Rulings 77-316 and subsequent developments.

10. If instead of owning the offshore captive completely the parent owns 25 percent or less of the captive's stock, the 5 percent limitation on the premium derived from United States operations is raised to 75 percent. See Lalley, *Self Assumption, Self Insurance and the Captive Insurance Company Concept*, p. 15.

CHAPTER 4

Measuring Loss Exposures

INTRODUCTION

In Chapter 1, the risk management process was described as beginning with the identification and analysis of loss exposures. Analysis was defined as measuring potential loss frequency and severity. Chapters 4 and 5 deal with this analysis. The approaches to measuring loss exposures presented here can be of great assistance to the risk manager, particularly in the selection of the most appropriate techniques for dealing with loss exposures.

Chapter 4 will start with a discussion of the types of measurement the risk manager needs and why they are needed. Next, it will explain one risk manager's widely quoted approach to measuring loss exposures. Because a more rigorous approach requires some knowledge of probability and probability distributions, the rest of the chapter will explore these concepts. Chapter 5 will then show how the risk manager can use information obtained from a probability distribution to select the best techniques to deal with loss exposures. That chapter will also discuss how the risk manager might construct probability distributions from past experience and trends.

This text approaches probability and probability distributions from the perspective of the risk manager. However, these concepts are also related to the discussion of insurance pricing in CPCU 5. Furthermore, the concepts are applicable to the work of underwriters, producers, and others whose work involves analyzing loss exposures.

Regardless of who performs or assists in the measurement of loss exposures (employees of a firm with the loss exposure, a member of a family exposed to the loss, an insurance producer, or a consultant), the need for analytical skills and knowledge is the same. Familiarity with the basic techniques used to measure the dimensions of exposures to loss will also provide additional insight into how insurance works.

The type of material included in Chapters 4 and 5 requires a different reading style than that used in other chapters. Students are advised to read slowly and carefully, following closely the examples, computations, and exhibits. Special study guidelines are contained in the CPCU 1 Course Guide, along with review and discussion questions. In any study of mathematical materials, it is important for the student to tackle some problems. Working the problems in the review and discussion questions of the CPCU 1 Course Guide should be considered an indispensable part of this reading assignment.

WHAT SHOULD BE MEASURED AND WHY

The discussion begins with a listing of the measurements needed and an explanation of why these measurements are important. Before reading this section, it is helpful to review the following terms and concepts introduced in Chapter 1:

- *Possibility of loss*—the state of being exposed to loss.
- *Probability (or chance) of loss*—the relative likelihood that a loss will occur. Probability of loss varies between 0 and 1.
- *Variation in potential losses*—a concept relating to the range of possible outcomes and the degree of certainty that can be attached to a prediction of which outcome will result.
- *Uncertainty concerning loss*—doubt concerning ability to predict the future.

Measurements Needed

To analyze a given loss exposure, a risk manager needs to determine the following:

(1) the number of events (e.g., fires, thefts, liability claims) that are likely to occur within some time interval such as a year, a month, or a week (loss frequency);

(2) how serious these individual occurrences are likely to be (loss severity);

(3) how serious the total dollar losses are likely to be (the number of occurrences times the average dollar loss per occurrence, or frequency times severity); and

(4) how accurately the risk manager can predict the number of occurrences, the dollar losses per occurrence, and the total

dollar losses. In other words, what is the variation in potential losses?

Why Needed

This information is important to the risk manager for the following reasons:

(1) *It reduces uncertainty concerning loss.* For a loss exposure that has been measured, there is greater ability to predict the future than for an exposure of unknown dimensions.
(2) *It indicates which exposures should receive more immediate or concentrated attention.* When loss exposures have been measured, it becomes easier to identify those exposures that are most serious.
(3) *It helps the risk manager determine what risk management techniques would be most appropriate for the particular exposure.* By evaluating how different risk management techniques affect each measurement, the risk manager can test the effects of possible risk management techniques.

THE PROUTY APPROACH

Richard Prouty, a corporate risk manager, has suggested some measures of loss frequency and loss severity that provide useful approximations of the kind of information desired. Although much less precise than some other measurements, most risk managers can readily obtain and use the Prouty measures. Furthermore, these measures force risk managers to perform the risk management process carefully and systematically.

For each potential loss-cause combination identified by the risk manager—such as loss of a shipment by theft or a liability suit arising out of the manufacture of a defective product—Prouty suggests the risk manager should estimate:

(1) the likelihood of a loss,
(2) the severity of a loss, and
(3) the expected dollar loss.

Likelihood of a Loss

According to Prouty, the risk manager should estimate whether the likelihood of a loss during the coming year (or some other time period) is *almost nil, slight, moderate,* or *definite.* These four degrees of likelihood are defined as follows:

(1) *Almost nil*—although the exposure has not been avoided, in the opinion of the risk manager for all practical purposes, this loss-cause combination could not happen.

(2) *Slight*—this loss-cause combination could happen, but it never has in the past.

(3) *Moderate*—this loss-cause combination happens once in a while.

(4) *Definite*—this loss-cause combination happens regularly.

The likelihood that any loss-cause combination will occur depends not only on the likelihood that any single exposure will be affected, but also on the *number* of exposures involved. For example, if a business makes only a few shipments per year, none of these shipments may be stolen, because the firm is lucky. On the other hand, because the risk manager recognizes that a shipment *could* be stolen, the likelihood may be rated as *slight,* not *almost nil.*

Another business making thousands of shipments a year under essentially the same conditions loses several shipments a year. The likelihood of losing a single shipment might be the same as the smaller firm's likelihood of loss on a single shipment, but, because of the much larger number of exposure units, the larger firm is almost certain to lose at least one shipment. Consequently, for this business, the likelihood of this loss-cause combination is *definite.*

This dependence of the loss frequency measure on the number of exposure units means that, in order to interpret the stated degree of likelihood, one must know the number of units exposed. A *definite* likelihood of a loss when only one unit is exposed may mean a much higher probability of a loss per unit than a *definite* likelihood of a loss when many units are exposed. One would also expect a much larger number of *slight* and *moderate* likelihoods compared with *definite* likelihoods for a smaller business than for a larger business. It is possible to refine the Prouty technique to include two loss frequency measures: (1) the likelihood of loss *per unit,* and (2) the likelihood that *at least one unit* will suffer a loss when many units are exposed.

Severity of a Loss

For each loss-cause combination, Prouty also suggests two measures of the severity of *individual* occurrences: (1) the *maximum possible loss,* and (2) the *maximum probable loss.*[1] The maximum *possible* loss is the worst dollar loss that could possibly happen in the lifetime of the business or the family, such as the complete destruction of a building. The maximum *probable* loss is the worst dollar loss that is likely to happen. An actual loss *could* be greater than the maximum *probable* loss, but the risk manager believes the likelihood that it will be greater is so small that it can be ignored. The maximum probable loss measure, therefore, depends on the risk manager's estimate of the likelihood that losses of various sizes will occur and the likelihood that he or she is willing to ignore. Prouty suggests, as an example, ignoring losses in excess of an amount that is exceeded no more than once every forty years. A more conservative person would use a larger figure, such as 100 years. To illustrate, assume that a business has a building valued at $400,000. The risk manager estimates that a fire causing more than $300,000 damage to the building is so unlikely that such a fire would not occur more than once in 100 years, and he or she is willing to ignore events that happen so seldom. For this risk manager, the maximum probable loss is $300,000.

Expected Dollar Loss

A third measure of loss severity suggested by Prouty, *the annual* (or quarterly, monthly, or other time interval) *expected dollar loss*, is a composite indicator of loss frequency and loss severity. The annual expected dollar loss is the *average* annual loss that can be expected over a long period of time if the exposure and its environment remain unchanged. It reflects both loss frequency and loss severity because it is equal to the average number of loss occurrences per year times the average dollar loss per occurrence. For example, if one expects on the average thirty occurrences per year averaging $100 per occurrence, the annual expected dollar loss is $3,000.

As valuable as these Prouty measures may be, they provide only part of the information that is available to and needed by the risk manager. A more rigorous approach employs the probability and probability distribution concepts that will now be explained.

PROBABILITY

Probability applications can make dealing with uncertainty more rational and less dependent on intuition or hunches. Probability deals with the "chance" of events that may or may not occur. However, it addresses the subject with precision and objectivity. Probability theory provides information concerning uncertain events, and is thus ideally suited for risk management—which involves decision making in the face of uncertainty.

The *probability* of an event is a measurement of the "chance" that the event will occur within a given time period. Probability can be described as *a number that varies between 0 and 1.* If the probability is 0, the event cannot occur. If the probability is 1, the event is certain to occur. For other values, the closer the probability is to 1 the more likely the event becomes. For a firm with a warehouse exposed to fire, if the probability of fire damage next year is one chance in a thousand, or 1/1000, a fire is unlikely. If the probability of a fire is 1/2, the odds are 50-50; a fire is as likely as no fire.

How Determined

There are two possible approaches to determining the probability that a particular event will occur. The *a priori* approach is based on obvious propositions. Although this approach is suitable for determining such things as the probability of a head or tail on a coin toss, it is of little use to risk managers. Risk managers and insurers use the experience-based *a posteriori* approach, which bases probability estimates on past experience projected into the future.

A Priori *Method* The self-evident, or *a priori*, approach applies only when there are a known number of outcomes, each with a known probability or a probability that can be calculated precisely from known laws. This approach is applicable in games of chance. For example, the probability that a coin will land with the head up is 1/2 because:

(1) there are two equally likely outcomes—a head and a tail, and
(2) one of these two outcomes, or one-half, represents the event whose probability is being determined.

The probability that a card drawn from a well-shuffled deck will be an ace is 1/13 because:

(1) there are fifty-two equally likely outcomes—the fifty-two cards in the deck, and
(2) four of the outcomes—the ace of hearts, the ace of spades, the ace of diamonds, and the ace of clubs—would produce an ace.

Using similar reasoning, the probability of drawing a heart is 13/52, or 1/4; of drawing either an ace or a king 8/52, or 2/13; and of drawing either an ace of spades or a king of hearts 2/52, or 1/26.

Risk managers and insurers usually cannot use the *a priori* approach because very few, if any, of the events with which they are concerned can be analyzed in terms of outcomes with known probabilities. Fires at warehouses, theft of shipments, and products liability suits cannot be analyzed in this way. For example, a firm with fifty-two warehouses does not possess the irrefutable information that only four can burn. In contrast, a gambler *knows* (not thinks, hopes, or estimates) that exactly four cards in a fair deck of fifty-two are aces.

A Posteriori *Method* Risk managers and insurers may be able to estimate probabilities fairly accurately on the basis of past experience. The law of large numbers provides a basis for estimating probability when it is unknown.

If the probability is *known*, the probability specifies the proportion of times one would expect to experience losses out of a large number of exposure units. One cannot be certain that the actual proportion in the future will be equal or close to the known probability, but the larger the number of exposure units that went into estimating the probability, the more likely it becomes that the probability can be used reliably to predict what will happen.

If the probability is not known, observation can be used to estimate the probability. By observing the proportion of times the event has occurred in the past among a large number of exposure units, one can, with considerable confidence, assume that the probability derived from the observations is close to the true probability. This procedure is sometimes known as *a posteriori* or statistical probability because the true probability is estimated from the observed numbers of exposures and occurrences, rather than being calculated from known laws and causes as in *a priori* probability. For example, if a fast-food restaurant chain had 10,000 identical hamburger stands scattered throughout the country and 200 of them sustained fire damage in one year, the firm might well assume that the true probability of fire in one of their stands was 2/100, or 1/50.

The larger the number of exposure units observed, the more confidence can be placed in the experience-based *a posteriori* probability estimate. If the fast-food chain had only 100 stands (instead of 10,000) and 2 sustained loss, the calculated probability would be the same. However, the level of confidence that the calculated probability was close to the true (but unknown) probability would be much lower. The reason is that the proportion of stands that sustain losses will fluctuate much more widely from year to year if there are only 100 stands. This relationship between the number of exposures, the variation in the expected losses, and the accuracy of the estimates will be explored more precisely in Chapter 5.

Interpreting Probability

Probability can be interpreted as *the proportion of times the specified event will almost certainly occur out of a large number of trials*. This interpretation follows from the *law of large numbers,* which states that, as the number of independent trials increases, it becomes more and more likely that the actual number of trials in which the event occurs will not differ from the expected number of occurrences by more than a specified amount. As the number of units exposed independently to loss increases, it becomes more and more likely that the proportion of units that actually suffer losses will be close to the probability that each particular unit will suffer a loss. If the probability that a particular unit will suffer a loss during a year is, say, 1/5, on the average one would expect about one-fifth of a large number of similar units to suffer losses. If there are 1,000 similar units, approximately 200 will suffer a loss in a typical year.

Temporal and Spatial Interpretations of Probability Probability can be interpreted temporally or spatially.

- The temporal interpretation emphasizes the proportion of times a loss will occur to a given number of units in the long run.
- The spatial interpretation emphasizes the proportion of similar units that will suffer loss during a given time period.

Temporal Interpretation. Under the temporal definition, each "independent exposure unit" is some _time_ interval—such as a month, six months, or a year. The probability that a firm will suffer at least one loss next month, say, is the proportion of months in which losses are expected to occur over a long period of time. This definition assumes that the extent and quality of the exposure remain the same from month to month and that each month's exposure is independent of the other months' exposures. To illustrate, if the chance that a firm will suffer some losses during a month is 1/10 and it can be assumed that what happens in one month has no impact on what happens in other months (i.e., the units are independently exposed to loss), this means that, on the average over a long period of time, the firm will suffer losses in one month for each ten months of exposure.

Note that this proportion would occur on the average over a long period of time. No one knows what will happen next month or next year. If the probability of some losses is low, as is often the case in risk management problems, the experience is likely to be highly variable in the short run. For example, if the probability of some losses in the preceding example had been 1/100 instead of 1/10, this would mean that, on the average over a long period of time, the firm would suffer some losses in 1 out of each 100 months. With such a low probability, one would have to be exposed to losses many hundreds of months before one could expect the average proportion of months with actual losses to be 1/100. In the meantime, the loss environment may change, causing the probability of some losses next month to rise or fall. Even with a 1/10 probability it would typically take many years to actually experience an average proportion of precisely 1/10. Despite this limitation, this concept of probability provides a useful explanation of the meaning of a probability value.

Spatial Interpretation. Under the spatial interpretation of probability, each independent exposure unit is defined in terms of some item exposed during a given time period. For example, the exposure units might be:

- *each car* exposed next week,
- *each warehouse* exposed next year, or
- *each shipment* exposed next month.

Probability is the proportion of these independent exposure units that are expected to experience some losses during the specified time period assuming a very large number of such units. To illustrate, assume the chance that a firm will suffer some losses to a particular unit exposed during a given time period is 1/10. Also, assume that what happens to that unit does not affect what happens to other units. This means that, if the firm has many such units, on the average about one in ten will suffer some losses during that time period. As one CPCU course leader has observed, the temporal interpretation of probability states "how often" over a long period of time. The spatial definition states "how many" exposure units will suffer losses during a given time interval.

Note once again that this proportion will occur *on the average over many units.* No one knows what will happen to any particular unit. For example, if a firm makes many shipments per year, for each of which the probability that it will be stolen is 1/10, it can expect that about 10 percent of next year's shipments will be stolen. The risk manager would still not know which shipments will be stolen, but knowing that about 10 percent will be lost calls attention to the magnitude of the exposure. It also makes it possible to measure the benefit the firm would derive from transferring the exposure to some other party or from reducing the chance of loss to, say, 1/20.

For firms with many units, the spatial interpretation has obvious value because it indicates the proportion of units that are likely to experience losses during the stated time interval. Those with only a few units cannot confidently predict their experience in the short run, but the spatial interpretation still has value.

Assembling Experience to Determine Probability

Experience with a large number of exposure units can be assembled in various ways. Sometimes a firm has had a large number of exposed units during a fairly short period in the past. Otherwise, in order to increase the number of exposure units on which experience is available, it may be necessary to:

(1) increase the number of years, months, weeks, or other time interval,
(2) include the experience of other entities, or
(3) do both these things.

In making probability estimates, one must be careful to include only experience with exposure units that are independent and homogeneous. Perfect independence is usually impossible because a loss to one exposure unit usually has some effect, though possibly slight, upon the probability of loss to other units. For example, two adjacent warehouses clearly are not independently exposed to fire. Two warehouses located ten blocks apart are more nearly independent, but there remains a chance that a fire at one warehouse will spread to the other. Two warehouses located in different states are much more nearly independent. It is virtually impossible that the same fire will touch both warehouses. In practice, two warehouses located ten blocks apart or in different states would be considered to be exposed independently to fire losses. In general, if the chance that two exposure units will be involved in the same occurrence is fairly low, it is reasonable to assume that they are independently exposed.

Homogeneity is an even more difficult condition to satisfy. So many factors affect potential loss frequency and severity that it is usually impossible to assemble many exposure units of exactly the same quality. Even if all the exposures being observed belong to the entity making the estimate, it is likely that the probability of loss will not be the same for all the units. For practical purposes, however, it is sufficient if the exposures share approximately the same major characteristics. Because conditions may change over time, heterogeneity becomes a more important problem the longer the time interval. It also becomes more important when it is necessary to include the units of other firms and families.

SOME ELEMENTARY LAWS OF PROBABILITY AND THEIR APPLICATION

In addition to stating the probability that a single exposure unit will experience a loss, the risk manager may be interested in the probability that two or more units will experience various combinations of losses. To illustrate this point, assume that a hypothetical firm, the Scott Company, makes four shipments each month. When a shipment does not arrive, it is presumed to have been stolen. The probability of loss of each shipment next month is 1/4. How could Scott's risk manager determine:

(1) the probability that *exactly zero, one, two, three, or four* shipments will be stolen next month?
(2) the probability that *at least one* shipment will be stolen?
(3) the probability that *no more than a stated number* of shipments will be stolen?
(4) the probability that *more than a stated number* of shipments will be stolen?

These questions are based on a spatial interpretation of probability. It is obvious that the answers to these questions could help the risk manager analyze the Scott Company's loss exposures.

Two elementary laws of probability make it possible to calculate answers to these questions and many others. The laws can be applied to cases where the exposures are either independent or not independent, but this text will consider only situations in which the exposures are independent.

First Law of Probability—Compound or Joint Outcomes

The first law of probability states: *the probability that two or more independent exposure units will suffer a loss is equal to the product of the probabilities of loss for each of these units.* The four questions above will be used to illustrate the application of this law. Assume that the four shipments are made to the same four customers (A, B, C, and D) each month and that the probability of theft for each of the four shipments next month (and each succeeding month) is 1/4. According to the first law of probability, the probability that the shipments to A and B both will be stolen next month is the product of 1/4 times 1/4, and $(1/4)(1/4) = 1/16$. In contrast to this spatial view involving next month alone, one could rearrange the expression into a temporal view. Under the temporal view, 1/16 means that, in the months ahead, conditions remaining the same, one would expect theft of the shipments to both A and B once each 16 months, on the average in the long run.

Second Law of Probability—Mutually Exclusive Events

A second law of probability applies to mutually exclusive events: *Two or more events are mutually exclusive if they cannot occur at the same time.* For example, each month's shipment to A is either stolen or not stolen. Considering these two possibilities, theft or no theft, it is clear that *if one materializes the other cannot.* This second law states: *the probability that one of two or more mutually exclusive events will occur is equal to the sum of the probabilities for each separate event.* If the mutually exclusive events being considered include all of the possible mutually exclusive events, the sum of their probabilities must be 1. This exhaustive set will be illustrated first. Consider the shipments to A mentioned above. The probability that each monthly shipment will either be stolen or not stolen is equal to (a) the probability that they will be stolen plus (b) the probability that they will not be stolen. Because one of these two events must happen, the sum of (a) and (b) must be 1. Thus, the probability that each month's shipments to A will be stolen, which is 1/4, plus the probability that they will not be stolen, which is unknown, must equal 1. Therefore, the probability that each monthly shipment to A will not be stolen is $1 - 1/4$, or 3/4.

Applying the Laws of Probability

The following sections will explain how the two laws of probability can be used to answer the questions posed by Scott's risk manager. Recall that the risk manager wanted to determine, for the coming month:

(1) the probability that *exactly zero, one, two, three, or four* shipments will be stolen,
(2) the probability that *at least one* shipment will be stolen,
(3) the probability that *no more than a stated number* of shipments will be stolen, and
(4) the probability that *more than a stated number* of shipments will be stolen.

(1) Probability That Exactly Some Specified Number of Units Will Suffer a Loss These two laws can be used to calculate the probability that exactly any specified number of shipments will be stolen during the coming month.

Probability of Theft of Zero Shipments. To determine the probability that *none* of Scott's four shipments will be stolen, we need first the probability that each shipment will not be stolen. As we have just seen, according to the second law of probability, the probability of no theft of the shipments to A is 3/4. The same probability applies to each of the other three shipments. According to the first law of probability, the probability that none of the shipments will be stolen is the product of the probabilities that each of the shipments will not be stolen. The desired probability, therefore, is $(3/4)(3/4)(3/4)(3/4) = 81/256$.

This probability is fairly high. It indicates that, in the long run, on the average, the firm can expect to experience no losses about one month out of three (81/256 is close to 1/3).[2]

Exhibit 4-1
Scott Company Probability of Theft of Exactly One Shipment

Theft of Shipments To:	No Theft of Shipments To:	Probability	
A	B, C, D	(1/4)(3/4)(3/4)(3/4) =	27/256
B	A, C, D	(3/4)(1/4)(3/4)(3/4) =	27/256
C	A, B, D	(3/4)(3/4)(1/4)(3/4) =	27/256
D	A, B, C	(3/4)(3/4)(3/4)(1/4) =	27/256
Probability of theft of exactly one shipment			108/256

Probability of Theft of Exactly One Shipment. This calculation is more complicated. One way in which one and only one shipment will be stolen is for the shipment to A to be stolen but not the shipments to B, C, or D. What is the likelihood of this happening? The probability of theft of the shipment to A is 1/4; for each of the other three shipments, according to the second law of probability, the probability of no theft is 3/4. According to the first law of probability, the probability of theft of the shipment to A but not to the shipments to B, C, or D is $(1/4)(3/4)(3/4)(3/4) = 27/256$.

There are four ways in which only one of the four shipments can be stolen. The stolen shipment could be the shipment to either A, B, C, or D. For each of these mutually exclusive possibilities the probability can be calculated in the same way. The results are summarized in Exhibit 4-1.

By the second law of probability, the sum of these four probabilities is the probability that one of these mutually exclusive events will occur. This probability is 108/256, or almost once per two months on the average in the long run.

Probability of Theft of Exactly Two Shipments. To determine this probability, the risk manager must again use both laws of probability. One way that the firm could experience theft of two shipments during the next month is to have the shipments to A and B stolen, but not the shipments to C and D. The probability of theft of A's shipment is 1/4, and of B's shipment 1/4; not of C's shipment 3/4, and not of D's shipment 3/4. The probability that all four of these separate events will occur is $(1/4)(1/4)(3/4)(3/4) = 9/256$. Over a long period, on the average, one would expect theft of A's and B's shipments but not of C's and D's shipments 9 times for every 256 months. The likelihood of theft of only A's and B's shipments is clearly low.

Theft of exactly two shipments, however, can be experienced in

Exhibit 4-2
Scott Company Probability of Theft of Exactly Two Shipments

Theft of Shipments To:	No Theft of Shipments To:	Probability	
A, B	C, D	(1/4)(1/4)(3/4)(3/4) =	9/256
A, C	B, D	(1/4)(3/4)(1/4)(3/4) =	9/256
A, D	B, C	(1/4)(3/4)(3/4)(1/4) =	9/256
B, C	A, D	(3/4)(1/4)(1/4)(3/4) =	9/256
B, D	A, C	(3/4)(1/4)(3/4)(1/4) =	9/256
C, D	A, B	(3/4)(3/4)(1/4)(1/4) =	9/256
Probability of theft of exactly two shipments			54/256

other ways. A's and C's shipments may be stolen but not B's and D's shipments; A's and D's shipments may be stolen but not B's and C's; and so on. A complete list of the possibilities, together with their probability of occurrence, is shown in Exhibit 4-2. Because these six events are mutually exclusive ways in which exactly two shipments can be stolen, the sum of the six probabilities is the probability that exactly two shipments will be stolen. The probability is 54/256, about once every five months on the average in the long run.

Probability of Theft of Exactly Three Shipments. The reasoning here is the same as that used to determine the probability of exactly one stolen shipment and the probability of exactly two stolen shipments. The calculation of the probability for each of the four ways in which exactly three shipments can be stolen and the sum of these four probabilities are shown in Exhibit 4-3. This probability is only 12/256 or once every 21 months on the average in the long run. But it could happen next month.

Probability of Theft of Exactly Four Shipments. What is the probability that all four of Scott's shipments will be stolen next month? This could happen in only one way. Its probability is (1/4)(1/4)(1/4)(1/4) = 1/256. It is extremely unlikely that all four shipments would be stolen next month, but it could happen.

All possible outcomes have now been considered: theft of none of the shipments, of exactly one shipment, of exactly two shipments, of exactly three shipments, and of all four shipments. According to the second law of probability, the sum of the five possible outcomes must equal one. The result can thus be checked as shown in Exhibit 4-4.

Exhibit 4-3

Scott Company Probability of Theft of Exactly Three Shipments

Theft of Shipments To:	No Theft of Shipments To:	Probability	
A, B, C	D	(1/4)(1/4)(1/4)(3/4) =	3/256
A, B, D	C	(1/4)(1/4)(3/4)(1/4) =	3/256
A, C, D	B	(1/4)(3/4)(1/4)(1/4) =	3/256
B, C, D	A	(3/4)(1/4)(1/4)(1/4) =	3/256
Probability of theft of exactly three shipments			12/256

Exhibit 4-4

Scott Company Probability Distribution for Number of Stolen Shipments

Number of Stolen Shipments Next Month	Probability
None	81/256
One	108/256
Two	54/256
Three	12/256
All four	1/256
	256/256 = 1.0

(2) Probability That at Least One Shipment Will Be Stolen
The probability that at least one unit will be stolen in the coming month can be calculated in two ways. First, at least one unit will suffer a loss if the number of loss units is any number other than zero. Using the second law of probability, therefore, one can obtain the probability of this event by summing (a) the probability that one unit will suffer a loss, (b) the probability that two units will suffer a loss, (c) the probability that three units will suffer a loss, and (d) the probability that all the units exposed will suffer a loss. In Scott's case, the calculation would be as shown in Exhibit 4-5.

The second approach, which is usually easier to apply, relies on the principle that either there will be no loss or at least one unit will suffer a loss. Therefore, to obtain the probability of at least one loss, subtract from 1 (which is the same as 256/256) the probability that no units will

Exhibit 4-5
Scott Company Probability of Theft of One or More
Shipments Next Month

Number of Stolen Shipments	Probability
One	108/256
Two	54/256
Three	12/256
All four	1/256
One or more	175/256

suffer a loss. Thus, in Scott's case, the probability that at least one of the four shipments will be stolen can also be calculated as follows:

$$1-81/256 = 256/256-81/256 = 175/256$$

This equals approximately once per 1.5 months on the average in the long run.

Since $175/256 = 0.68$, there is a probability of about 2/3 that at least one shipment will be stolen next month. (This rounded-off figure will be used shortly.)

(3) Probability That No More Than a Stated Number of Shipments Will Be Stolen The probability that no more than a stated number of exposure units will suffer a loss can be calculated in two ways. Either method will develop the same answer. First, using the second law of probability, it is possible to sum the probabilities that (a) no units will suffer a loss, (b) one unit will suffer a loss, (c) two units will suffer a loss, and so on up to the stated number. To illustrate, in Scott's example, what is the probability that no more than two shipments will suffer a loss next month? The calculation is shown in Exhibit 4-6.

The second approach is to subtract from 1 the probability that each of the possible greater number of units will suffer a loss. In the shipments example:

$$1- \left(\begin{array}{c} \text{Probability that exactly} \\ \text{three shipments will be} \\ \text{stolen} \end{array} \right) - \left(\begin{array}{c} \text{Probability that all} \\ \text{four shipments will} \\ \text{be stolen} \end{array} \right)$$

$$=1-12/256-1/256=243/256$$

Which of these two approaches is easier to apply depends on

Exhibit 4-6
Scott Company Probability of Theft of No More Than
Two Shipments Next Month

Number of Stolen Shipments	Probability
None	81/256
One	108/256
Two	54/256
Two or Fewer	243/256

whether the stated "no more than" number is closer to no units or the maximum number of units. In the Scott Company example, to calculate the probability that no more than one unit will suffer a loss, the first approach should be used. To calculate the probability that no more than three units will experience losses, the second approach is easier.

(4) Probability That More Than a Stated Number of Shipments Will Be Stolen Subtracting from 1 the probability that no more than a stated number will suffer a loss produces the probability that the number of units suffering a loss will exceed that stated number. For example, what is the probability that the number of stolen shipments next month will exceed two? The answer is $1 - 243/256 = 13/256$. Alternatively, one can sum the probabilities that each greater number of units will suffer losses. In the Scott Company example, the desired probability is the sum of the probabilities of theft of exactly three shipments and exactly four shipments, or $12/256 + 1/256 = 13/256$.

Probabilities Using Temporal Interpretation

Three more questions could be considered by Scott's risk manager:

(5) What is the probability that at least one shipment will be stolen *in two, three, five, or some other number of months* out of the next twelve months?
(6) What is the probability that some theft will occur in *no more than a stated number* of these twelve months?
(7) What is the probability that some shipments will be stolen in *more than a stated number* of these twelve months?

In answering question (2), determining the probability that at least one shipment will be stolen, we determined that there is about a 2/3 probability that at least one shipment will be stolen next month. Thus, using this 2/3 probability figure, the above questions could also be answered, using the same approaches. With twelve months to consider, however, the computations are considerably more complex.

PROBABILITY DISTRIBUTIONS

To obtain the types of measurement suggested at the beginning of this chapter, it is necessary not only to know the probability that certain events will occur, but also to have complete probability distributions. The remainder of this chapter will define the term "probability distribution" and illustrate with three examples the information that can be obtained from a probability distribution.

Definition

A *probability distribution* is a table or graph that shows for each possible outcome the probability that that outcome will occur. One probability distribution has already been introduced in analyzing Scott Company's question (1). The probability distribution in Exhibit 4-4 showed the probability that the firm making four shipments each month will sustain loss next month of no shipments, exactly one shipment, exactly two shipments, exactly three shipments, and all four shipments. Because the outcomes are mutually exclusive and no other outcomes are possible, the sum of the probabilities in a probability distribution must equal 1.

Information That Can Be Obtained from Probability Distributions

The previous discussion of Scott Company's number of lost shipments has shown some of the information that can be obtained from a probability distribution. This section will review those measures and explain some other highly useful information that can be derived from probability distributions.

Probability of Ranges of Outcomes In addition to determining:

(1) the probability that exactly zero, one, two, three, or four shipments will be stolen next month,

the probability distribution presented in Exhibit 4-4 also made it possible to calculate:

(2) the probability that at least one shipment will be stolen,
(3) the probability that no more than a stated number of shipments will be stolen, and
(4) the probability that more than a stated number of shipments will be stolen.

These latter three probabilities illustrate a general category of probabilities—the probability that the outcomes will fall within a certain *range*. The ranges illustrated were:

(2) one to four shipments stolen (illustrated in Exhibit 4-5),
(3) zero to two shipments stolen (illustrated in Exhibit 4-6), and
(4) three to four shipments stolen (discussed in the narrative).

To simplify the calculation of the probability that the outcome will fall within a specified range (and to expedite other calculations described later), statisticians commonly construct a *cumulative probability distribution*. A cumulative probability distribution is a table or graph that shows for each possible outcome the probability that the actual outcome will be the stated outcome *or less*. In other words, the cumulative probability of a stated outcome is the probability of that outcome added to the probabilities for all smaller outcomes. For example, the cumulative probability for the loss of two shipments is the probability of losing two shipments added to the probability for zero losses and the probability for one loss; i.e., $54/256 + 108/256 + 81/256$, or $243/256$. The cumulative probability for the loss of three shipments is the probability of losing three shipments added to the probabilities for zero, one, and two losses; i.e., $12/256 + 54/256 + 108/256 + 81/256$, or $255/256$. (A simpler approach adds the probability of the specified outcome to the *cumulative* probability of the next lower outcome. For example, the cumulative probability for the loss of three shipments is the probability of losing three shipments added to the *cumulative* probability for the loss of two shipments; i.e., $12/256 + 243/256$, or $255/256$.) Exhibit 4-7 presents the complete cumulative probability distribution for the shipments lost and presumed stolen.

The probability that the number stolen will be a stated number or less can be taken directly from the cumulative probability distribution. For example, the probability of two or fewer losses is $243/256$. The probability that the actual number will fall in any other range can be obtained by subtracting from the cumulative probability for the number at the top of the range the cumulative probability for the number just below the bottom of the range. To illustrate, the probability that the number will exceed two is the cumulative probability for four stolen shipments (the top of the range) less the cumulative

Exhibit 4-7
Scott Company Cumulative Probability Distribution
for Number of Shipments Stolen

Number or Less	Cumulative Probability
0	81/256
1	189/256
2	243/256
3	255/256
4	256/256

probability for two shipments stolen (the number just below the bottom of the range); i.e., $256/256 - 243/256 = 13/256$.

The probability that the number of shipments stolen will be two or three is equal to the cumulative probability for three shipments less the cumulative probability for one shipment; i.e., $255/256 - 189/256$, or $66/256$.

Measures of Central Tendency Probability distributions can be analyzed to determine measures of central tendency. These measures are discussed below, using the probability distribution of theft of next month's shipments presented in Exhibit 4-4 to illustrate the calculation of these measures.

Measures of central tendency are the values around which the outcomes tend to cluster. In the context of risk management, the measures of central tendency can be used to estimate the number of losses or the dollar amount of those losses around which the yearly numbers or amounts tend to cluster. Three commonly used measures are:

(1) the arithmetic mean, hereafter referred to simply as the mean,
(2) the median, and
(3) the mode.

Of these three measures, the mean is especially important to risk managers.

Mean. The mean is the average outcome one would expect in the long run after being exposed many times to the chance situation represented by the probability distribution. Of course, the mean will be the average outcome only if the circumstances that cause a loss or control the seriousness of a loss remain constant. In the Scott Company example, the mean is the average number of shipments one would expect to be stolen per month over a period of many, many months. The mean also is known as the *expected value* or, in the Scott example, the number of shipments expected to be stolen per month. To calculate the mean, each possible outcome is multiplied by the probability of its occurrence and the products are summed. The calculation of the mean for the probability distribution of the number of shipments stolen is shown in Exhibit 4-8. The mean is 1.0, which means that the firm can expect on the average in the long run to have one shipment stolen every month.

Median. A second measure of central tendency is the median. The median is the "middle" value in a distribution, or the number that would represent a point midway between the two middle ones. The median can be found by examining the set of numbers and selecting the middle value. For example, in the following set of numbers:

4   9   10   18   23

the number 10 is the median. In the following set:

4   7   15   23

the median is the number midway between the two middle numbers 7 and 15. The number exactly midway between 7 and 15 is 11, and this is the median. In the set:

4   7   8   8   8   10

the median is 8. Note that, in this set, only one number is larger; two are smaller.

The median of any set of numbers can be determined by listing the numbers in order from the smallest to the largest (as was done in these simple examples) and counting to the middle of the distribution. If the middle of the distribution falls between two numbers, the average of these two numbers is used as the median.

If Scott Company's loss experience for 256 months matched the probability distribution in the center column of Exhibit 4-8, such a listing would begin with 0,0,0,0,0,0,0. . . . There would be 81 zeros, followed by 108 ones, 54 twos, 12 threes, and 1 four. The middle of this list of 256 numbers would fall between the 128th and the 129th number. Both numbers would be ones, so the median of this distribution would be 1.

There is an easier way to determine the median of a set of values when a cumulative probability distribution is provided. Because the median is the "middle" value, about as many values are likely to occur above the median as below the median. To be more exact, the probability is (1) at least 1/2 that the outcome will equal *or* exceed the median and (2) at least 1/2 that the outcome will equal *or* be less than

Exhibit 4-8
Scott Company Calculation of Mean: Probability Distribution—
Shipments Stolen Per Month

(1) Number	(2) Probability	(3) Number Times Probability
0	81/256	0
1	108/256	108/256
2	54/256	108/256
3	12/256	36/256
4	1/256	4/256
		Mean = 256/256, or 1.0

the median. In a cumulative distribution like the one that was shown in Exhibit 4-7, in which only integral values (0, 1, 2, 3, and 4, with no chance of fractional values) are possible, and no outcome has an exact cumulative probability of 128/256 or 1/2, the outcome for which the cumulative probability first exceeds 1/2 may be used as the median. In Exhibit 4-7, the median is 1 because the cumulative probability for 0 is less than 1/2 and for 1 more than 1/2.

If one outcome in a cumulative probability distribution has an exact cumulative probability of 1/2, the median has a value somewhere between that outcome and the next highest outcome. The half-way point between these two outcomes is generally considered to be the median.

Mode. A third measure of central tendency is the mode. The mode is the value with the highest probability—the outcome most likely to occur. For many exposures encountered by risk managers, the mode is 0 because the most likely outcome is to have no losses. In the Scott Company example, however, the mode is 1.

Comparison. Of the three measures of central tendency, the mean is the most useful because it measures the average loss in the long run. The median is useful because it indicates the outcome that has at least a 1/2 probability that it will be equaled or exceeded and at least a 1/2 chance that the actual outcome will be the same or less. The mode tells what outcome or outcomes is (are) most likely to occur. Knowing the median and the mode helps determine the skewness of the distribution, a characteristic to be discussed later.

Measures of Dispersion Measures of dispersion tell how closely the outcomes tend to cluster. The possible outcomes may be concentrated near one another or be widely dispersed. In risk management, measures of dispersion are used to evaluate the variation in potential losses. The less the variation the more predictable the future becomes. (Some would say there is less "risk" when variation is low.) Three measures of dispersion commonly used by statisticians are:

(1) the range,
(2) the standard deviation, and
(3) the coefficient of variation.

Range. The range states the smallest and the highest outcomes. For the Scott Company example, the range is 0 to 4 shipments stolen. The range is an interesting but incomplete measure of dispersion because it depends only on the two extreme outcomes. The range is sometimes stated as the difference between the two extreme values, 4 in the Scott Company example (4 − 0 = 4). Knowing "the range is 4" is even less useful than knowing the two end points, 0 and 4.

Standard Deviation. The most popular measure of dispersion is the standard deviation. The standard deviation measures the dispersion of the possible outcomes around the mean. The standard deviation is calculated as follows:

(1) Subtract the mean from the value of each possible outcome.
(2) Square the differences.
(3) Multiply each of these squared differences by the probability that the outcome will occur.
(4) Sum these products.
(5) Take the square root of the sum.[3]

Exhibit 4-9 shows the calculation of the standard deviation for the Scott Company probability distribution of the number of shipments stolen. For the numbers of shipments from 0 to 4, the squared differences times their respective probabilities of theft add up to 192/256 or 3/4. The standard deviation is the square root of 3/4, or $\sqrt{3/4} = 0.87$.

The standard deviation has no obvious meaning. Unlike probability, for example, the standard deviation does not vary between 0 and 1 nor does it represent the proportion of times some outcome will occur. The standard deviation does, however, provide a measure that can be useful in comparing dispersion in two or more distributions. In two distributions, the one with the higher standard deviation has the greater dispersion. The higher the standard deviation, the greater the dispersion or scattering of the possible outcomes around the mean and the less predictable the future outcomes. (In certain types of distribution— for example, the "normal" distribution—additional meaning can be assigned to the standard deviation, as will be explained in Chapter 5.)

The range and the standard deviation are *absolute measures* of

Exhibit 4-9
Scott Company Calculation of Standard Deviation: Probability
Distribution—Shipments Stolen Per Month

Number	Mean	Difference From Mean	Difference Squared	Probability	Difference Squared Times Probability
0	1	−1	1	81/256	81/256
1	1	0	0	108/256	0
2	1	1	1	54/256	54/256
3	1	2	4	12/256	48/256
4	1	3	9	1/256	9/256

Standard deviation = $\sqrt{192/256}$ = $\sqrt{3/4}$ = 0.87 $\overline{192/256}$

dispersion. Absolute measures have two disadvantages. First, *absolute measures do not take into account differences in the means,* as illustrated with this brief example. Assume you are comparing two probability distributions based on the following information:

	Standard Deviation	Mean	Mean + Standard Deviation
Distribution 1	0.87	5	5.87
Distribution 2	0.87	1	1.87

A standard deviation of 0.87 for a distribution with a mean of 5 indicates much less variability than a standard deviation of 0.87 relative to a mean of 1. In Distribution 1, an outcome that is one standard deviation above the mean is only about 17 percent greater than the mean (0.87/5 = 0.17). In Distribution 2, an outcome that is one standard deviation above the mean is about 87 percent greater than the mean (0.87/1 = 0.87). The risk manager may predict that the mean will occur (because the mean represents the outcome that will occur on the average in the long run). If the actual outcome is one standard deviation above the mean, the forecast will be off by only 17 percent if the standard deviation is 0.87 and the mean is 5. The prediction will be off by 87 percent if the standard deviation is 0.87 and the mean is 1.

A second disadvantage of absolute measures is that *they are stated in the same unit of measurement as the variable.* This characteristic makes it impossible to compare the variation in potential losses of probability distributions using two different units of measurement. For example, for the probability distribution of the number of Scott Company shipments stolen, the standard deviation is 0.87 shipments. For a probability distribution of, say, the number of warehouse fires that will occur, the standard deviation might also be 0.87 fires. Obviously, 0.87 fires is not the same as 0.87 shipments.

Coefficient of Variation. The way to overcome both disadvantages of the standard deviation is to use a relative measure of dispersion such as the coefficient of variation. The *coefficient of variation* is the standard deviation divided by the mean. In other words, it expresses the standard deviation as a fraction or percent of the mean. With a standard deviation of 0.87 and a mean of 1, the values calculated for the Scott Company probability distribution of the number of shipments stolen, the coefficient of variation is 0.87 divided by 1, or 87 percent. If the mean had been 5 instead of 1, the coefficient of variation would have been 0.87 divided by 5, or 17 percent, indicating a smaller relative dispersion. Because the coefficient of variation is expressed as a percent of the mean, comparisons can be made among distributions of variables stated in different units. For example, if a probability distribution of the number of warehouse fires also had a standard deviation of 0.87 and a mean of 1, this would imply that both distributions had about the same dispersion and that the risk manager would have about the same confidence in both cases in predicting the future.

Likewise, if loss exposure A has a coefficient of variation of 17 percent and loss exposure B has a coefficient of variation of 87 percent, there is clearly more uncertainty involved regarding exposure B, because there is a greater variation in potential losses relative to the expected loss.

Skewness The final dimension of a probability distribution to be discussed in this text is its skewness. As illustrated in Exhibit 4-10, a distribution that is symmetrical around the mean has no skewness. If a distribution is symmetrical, outcomes that are the same distance to the right and to the left of the mean have the same probability of occurrence. For example, if the mean is 5, the outcomes of 4 and 6 have the same probability of occurrence, 3 and 7 have the same probability of occurrence, and so forth. If a distribution is symmetrical and has only one mode, then the mean, the median, and the mode have the same value. Half of the outcomes will exceed the mean and half will be less; the mean is also the most likely outcome.

A probability distribution that is not symmetrical is called a *skewed distribution.* In a graphic display, if a distribution is not symmetrical, there are more possible outcomes to the right of the mean than to the left of the mean, or vice versa. If there are more possible outcomes to the right of the mean than to the left, the distribution will have a "tail" to the right and is said to be "positively skewed" or "skewed to the right." If there are more possible outcomes to the left of the mean than

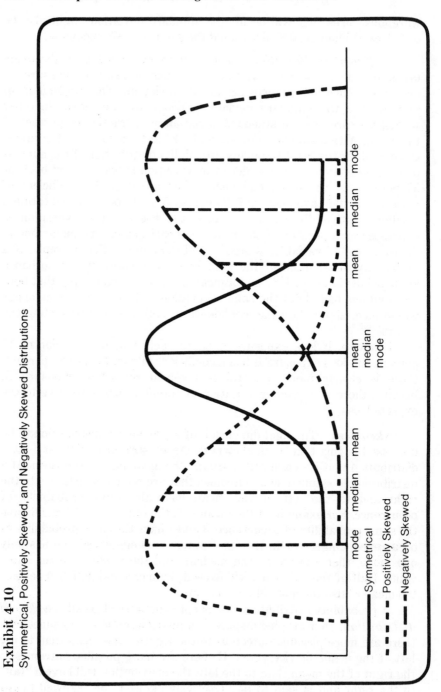

Exhibit 4-10
Symmetrical, Positively Skewed, and Negatively Skewed Distributions

to the right, the distribution will have a "tail" to the left and is said to be "negatively skewed" or "skewed to the left." Exhibit 4-10 shows a symmetrical distribution, a positively skewed distribution, and a negatively skewed distribution.

If a distribution is skewed to the right, the mean typically exceeds the median because the mean is pulled up by the large values in the right hand tail. If a distribution is skewed to the left, the mean is usually less than the median, the mean being pulled down by the small values in the left hand tail.

ILLUSTRATION

The discussion now turns to a more complex probability distribution and an analysis of that distribution. We will first analyze the number of shipments suffering a loss per month. Subsequently, we will evaluate total dollar losses per month.

Number of Shipments Damaged Per Month

Consider the Hemcher Corporation, a firm that makes 500 shipments a month, a considerably larger number than the Scott Company. The probability distribution to be analyzed for the Hemcher Corporation is the number of shipments that will be *stolen or damaged* next month. Exhibit 4-11 shows the distribution, which states the probabilities in *decimal*, not fractional, form. The true probability of theft or damage for each shipment is about 1/100, which is also considerably different from the 1/4 probability of theft assumed in the Scott Company case. With such a low probability and so many possible outcomes, the Hemcher Corporation probability distribution was not constructed using the two elementary laws of probability. How it was constructed will be discussed in Chapter 5. For the present, the reader should accept the distribution as given.

Although the maximum possible number of Hemcher's shipments that could be stolen or damaged is 500, Exhibit 4-11 lists only numbers up to fifteen. The reason for stopping at fifteen is that the probability of any larger number of losses per month is extremely small. Indeed, the probability that the number of shipments stolen or damaged will be greater than fifteen (> 15) is only 0.0001.

From this distribution, the risk manager can determine as in the Scott case:

(1) the probabilities of various outcomes,
(2) the probabilities of outcomes falling within specified ranges,
(3) measures of central tendency,

Exhibit 4-11
Hemcher Corporation
Probability Distribution— Shipments
Stolen or Damaged Per Month

Number	Probability
0	0.0067
1	0.0337
2	0.0842
3	0.1404
4	0.1755
5	0.1755
6	0.1462
7	0.1044
8	0.0653
9	0.0363
10	0.0181
11	0.0082
12	0.0034
13	0.0013
14	0.0005
15	0.0002
> 15	0.0001

(4) measures of dispersion, and
(5) skewness.

Probabilities of Various Outcomes On the average over a period of many months, we would expect zero shipments to be stolen or damaged less than 1 percent of the time, or more precisely, 0.67 percent. In other words, on the average, we would expect no losses about 1 month out of 149 (1/0.0067 = 149). Some loss(es), therefore, should be expected almost every month, 148 months out of 149 on the average. Using similar reasoning, on the average in the long run, the number of shipments stolen or damaged would be about:

1 once per 30 months
2 once per 12 months
3 once per 7 months
4 once per 6 months
5 once per 6 months
6 once per 7 months
7 once per 10 months
8 once per 15 months

9 once per 28 months
10 once per 55 months
11 once per 122 months
12 once per 294 months
13 once per 769 months
14 once per 2,000 months
15 once per 5,000 months

The extremely small likelihood of some of these outcomes is readily apparent.

Probabilities of Outcomes within Ranges In addition to being interested in the probability of single outcomes, the risk manager needs information on the probability that the outcome will fall within various ranges. The probability that the outcome will fall within a given range is equal to the sum of the probabilities of each individual outcome falling within that range, as illustrated:

- The probability that this firm will lose *either two, three, or four shipments* is the sum of the individual probabilities of losing two, three, and four shipments; i.e., 0.0842 + 0.1404 + 0.1755, or about 40 percent—once per two or three months.
- The probability that the firm will suffer *at least one* loss is most easily calculated by subtracting from 1 the probability that the firm will suffer no losses; i.e., 1 − 0.0067 = 0.9933 or 99.33 percent.
- The probability that the firm will suffer *no more than three* losses can be calculated by summing the probabilities of zero, one, two, and three losses. This probability, therefore, is 0.0067 + 0.0337 + 0.0842 + 0.1404, or 26.5 percent.
- The probability that the firm will incur *more than three* losses is 1 − 26.5 percent, or 73.5 percent.
- The probability that the firm will suffer *more than ten* losses is the sum of the probabilities of eleven, twelve, thirteen, fourteen, and fifteen losses plus the 0.0001 probability that the firm will lose sixteen or more shipments. This sum is 0.0082 + 0.0034 + 0.0013 + 0.0005 + 0.0002 + 0.0001, or 1.4 percent.

Exhibit 4-12 presents the *cumulative* probability distribution for the Hemcher Corporation example which, as already explained, can also be used to calculate the probability that an outcome will fall within a range of outcomes. For example:

- The probability that the number of shipments stolen or damaged will be *more than three* is the cumulative probability for 500 (the top of the range) less the cumulative probability for

Exhibit 4-12
Hemcher Corporation—Cumulative
Probability Distribution—Shipments
Stolen or Damaged Per Month

Number or Less	Probability
0	0.0067
1	0.0404
2	0.1246
3	0.2650
4	0.4405
5	0.6160
6	0.7622
7	0.8666
8	0.9319
9	0.9682
10	0.9863
11	0.9945
12	0.9979
13	0.9992
14	0.9997
15	0.9999
. . .	. . .
500	1.0000

three lost shipments (the number just below the bottom of the range); i.e., 1.0000 − 0.2650, or 73.5 percent.

• The probability that the number of shipments lost will be *in a range from two to four* is equal to the cumulative probability for four shipments less the cumulative probability for one shipment; i.e., 0.4405 − 0.0404, or about 40 percent.

Measure of Central Tendency The three measures of central tendency discussed in this text are the mean, the median, and the mode. The calculation of the mean for this distribution is shown in Table 4-13. The mean is more than 4.9988. If the table had been extended to include all other possible outcomes (16, 17, and so on, up to and including 500), as it should be for an accurate calculation, the mean would be 5.

The median has been described as the outcome for which the cumulative probability first exceeds 0.50. In this illustration the median is 5 because, in Exhibit 4-12, the cumulative probability for 4 is 0.4405 and for 5 it is 0.6160.

The mode is the most likely value. In this example, two adjacent

Exhibit 4-13
Hemcher Corporation—Calculation of Mean:
Probability Distribution—Shipments Stolen or
Damaged Per Month

(1)	(2)	(3) Number x
Number	Probability	Probability*
0	0.0067	0.0000
1	0.0337	0.0337
2	0.0842	0.1684
3	0.1404	0.4212
4	0.1755	0.7020
5	0.1755	0.8775
6	0.1462	0.8772
7	0.1044	0.7308
8	0.0653	0.5224
9	0.0363	0.3267
10	0.0181	0.1810
11	0.0082	0.0902
12	0.0034	0.0408
13	0.0013	0.0169
14	0.0005	0.0070
15	0.0002	0.0030
. . .	. . .	. . .
		4.9988+

*(3) = (1) x (2)

values, 4 and 5, are the mode because, as seen in Exhibit 4-11, they are equally likely (each has a probability of 0.1755) and no other outcomes are as likely.

Of the three measures of central tendency, the mean is the most useful because it measures the average loss in the long run. The median is useful because it indicates the outcome that has at least a 0.50 probability that it will be equaled or exceeded and at least a 0.50 chance that the actual outcome will be the same or less. The mode tells what outcome or outcomes is (are) most likely.

Measures of Dispersion The three measures of dispersion discussed in this text are the range, the standard deviation, and the coefficient of variation.

Exhibit 4-14
Hemcher Corporation—Calculation of Standard Deviation: Probability
Distribution—Shipments Stolen or Damaged Per Month

Number	Difference from mean	Difference squared	Probability	Difference squared times probability
0	−5	25	0.0067	0.1675
1	−4	16	0.0337	0.5392
2	−3	9	0.0842	0.7578
3	−2	4	0.1404	0.5616
4	−1	1	0.1755	0.1755
5	0	0	0.1755	0.0000
6	1	1	0.1462	0.1462
7	2	4	0.1044	0.4176
8	3	9	0.0653	0.5877
9	4	16	0.0363	0.5808
10	5	25	0.0181	0.4525
11	6	36	0.0082	0.2952
12	7	49	0.0034	0.1666
13	8	64	0.0013	0.0832
14	9	81	0.0005	0.0405
15	10	100	0.0002	0.0200
...	...	...	...	...
				5.0000

Standard deviation = $\sqrt{5}$ = 2.24

Range. For the Hemcher Corporation, the range is 0 to 500 shipments stolen or damaged.

Standard Deviation. Exhibit 4-14 shows the calculation of the standard deviation for the probability distribution of the number of shipments stolen or damaged. For the numbers of shipments from 0 to 15, the squared differences times their respective probabilities add up to only 4.9919. Adding the squared differences times their respective probabilities for numbers of shipments from 16 to 500 would increase this total to 5.0000. The standard deviation is the square root of 5, or 2.24.

Coefficient of Variation. The coefficient of variation is the standard deviation divided by the mean. With a standard deviation of 2.24 and a mean of 5, the values calculated for the Hemcher Corporation probability distribution of the number of shipments stolen or damaged, the coefficient of variation is 2.24 divided by 5, or 45 percent.

Skewness The probability distribution of the number of Hemcher's shipments that will be damaged or stolen is positively skewed, but this is not readily apparent based on information within the scope of this text.

Total Dollar Losses Per Month

The preceding discussion used the probability distribution of the number of losses per month. These concepts will now be reviewed using the probability distribution of the total after-tax dollars lost per month for the Hemcher Corporation.

The Probability Distribution Based on available data, Hemcher Corporation's dollar losses per shipment lost or damaged seem to cluster closely around a mean dollar loss of $45.50. The probability distribution of the total after-tax dollar losses per month is presented in Exhibits 4-15 and 4-16. Some of the possible outcomes have been omitted to simplify the discussion. For illustrative purposes, it has been assumed that the only possible losses are losses of exactly these dollar amounts.

Probabilities of Various Outcomes The probability of *no dollar losses* is the same as the probability that *no shipments* will be lost or damaged (once per 149 months). Over a period of many months, one would expect to suffer a loss of:

$ 40 once per 81 months
50 once per 30 months
80 once per 18 months
100 once per 12 months
150 once per 7 months
200 once per 5 months
250 once per 6 months
300 once per 8 months
350 once per 12 months
400 once per 20 months
450 once per 33 months
500 once per 71 months

Loss amounts in excess of $500 would occur less often than once per 100 months.

Probabilities of an Outcome Within a Range The cumulative probability distribution is shown in Exhibit 4-17.

Over a period of many months, the monthly dollar loss should be $100 or less 19 percent of the time; $200 or less, 53 percent; $300 or less, 81 percent; and $400 or less, 94 percent. The monthly dollar loss

Exhibit 4-15
Hemcher Corporation—Tabular
Probability Distribution—Monthly
After-Tax Dollar Losses on
Shipments Stolen or Damaged

Dollar Losses	Probability
$ 0	0.0067
40	0.0123
50	0.0335
80	0.0550
100	0.0860
150	0.1470
200	0.1885
250	0.1600
300	0.1200
350	0.0820
400	0.0510
450	0.0300
500	0.0140
550	0.0065
600	0.0035
650	0.0015
700	0.0004
750	0.0001
. . .	. . .
	1.0000

would exceed $100 in 81 percent of the months; $200 in 47 percent of the months; $300 in 19 percent of the months; and $500 in less than 2 percent of the months. The probability of monthly losses exceeding $150 but not exceeding $300 is 0.8090 − 0.3405, or almost 47 percent.

Measures of Central Tendency The mean is calculated by multiplying each possible outcome by its probability and summing the products, as shown in Exhibit 4-18. Over a period of many months, losses will average about $227.50 per month, because the average number of shipments stolen or damaged per month is five, and the average dollar loss per shipment stolen or damaged is $45.50. The median is $200, as is the mode.

Measures of Dispersion The range is $0 to $25,000. The calculation of the standard deviation, which is $113.95, is shown in Exhibit 4-19. The coefficient of variation is $113.95/$227.50, or about 50

Exhibit 4-16
Hemcher Corporation—Graphic Probability Distribution—Monthly
After-Tax Dollar Losses on Shipments Stolen or Damaged

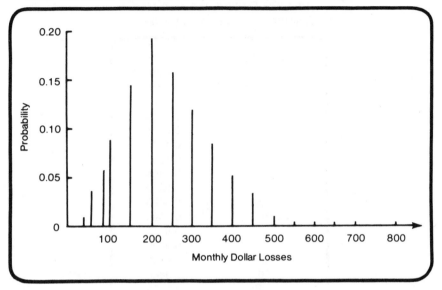

percent, which is just slightly larger than the coefficient of variation for the probability distribution of the *number* of shipments stolen or damaged.

Skewness Like the distribution of the number of shipments stolen or damaged, this probability distribution is skewed to the right. For this distribution, this is readily determined because the mean exceeds the median.

RELATIONSHIP OF PROBABILITY DISTRIBUTION INFORMATION TO THE PROUTY MEASURES

Earlier, this chapter presented some measures of loss frequency and loss severity suggested by risk manager Richard Prouty. For each loss-cause combination, Prouty suggested that the frequency of loss be stated as *almost nil, slight, moderate,* or *definite.* If the probability distribution of the number of occurrences is known, the frequency estimates can be sharpened substantially. In addition to having a more solid foundation for estimating the loss frequency, the risk manager can state these estimates more precisely. The chance of a warehouse fire next year can be stated as, say, 0.20, the chance of losing at least one shipment during the coming month as, say, 0.99, and the chance of

Exhibit 4-17

Hemcher Corporation—Cumulative
Probability Distribution—Monthly
After-Tax Dollar Losses on
Shipments Stolen or Damaged

Dollar Losses or Less	Cumulative Probability
$ 0	0.0067
40	0.0190
50	0.0525
80	0.1075
100	0.1935
150	0.3405
200	0.5290
250	0.6890
300	0.8090
350	0.8910
400	0.9420
450	0.9720
500	0.9860
550	0.9925
600	0.9960
650	0.9975
700	0.9979
750	0.9980
. . .	. . .
25,000	1.0000

being sued because of a defective product as 0.60. Prouty would probably classify the 0.20 probability as *moderate*, the 0.99 probability as *definite*, and the 0.60 probability as *moderate* or *definite*.

Prouty suggested the maximum possible loss per occurrence and the maximum probable loss per occurrence as measures of loss severity. The maximum possible loss is the worst loss that could possibly happen; in a probability distribution, the maximum possible loss is the largest loss among the possible outcomes. For a warehouse fire, if the firm has only one warehouse, the maximum possible loss is the value of that warehouse. If the firm has more than one warehouse and the warehouses are widely dispersed, the maximum possible loss is the value of the most valuable warehouse. For a shipment loss, the maximum possible loss per occurrence is the value of the most expensive shipment. For a products liability exposure, the maximum possible loss is unlimited.

Exhibit 4-18
Hemcher Corporation—Calculating the
Mean Monthly Dollar Losses

$ 0	×	0.0067	= $	0
40	×	0.0123	=	0.4920
50	×	0.0335	=	1.6750
80	×	0.0550	=	4.4000
100	×	0.0860	=	8.6000
150	×	0.1470	=	22.0500
200	×	0.1885	=	37.7000
250	×	0.1600	=	40.0000
300	×	0.1200	=	36.0000
350	×	0.0820	=	28.7000
400	×	0.0510	=	20.4000
450	×	0.0300	=	13.5000
500	×	0.0140	=	7.0000
550	×	0.0065	=	3.5750
600	×	0.0035	=	2.1000
650	×	0.0015	=	0.9750
700	×	0.0004	=	0.2800
750	×	0.0001	=	0.0750
...				...
				$227.50

Probability distributions do not provide any information that is useful in identifying maximum possible losses that cannot be obtained just by asking what is the worst thing that can happen. But, probability distributions do greatly improve estimates of the maximum probable loss. The maximum probable loss may be exceeded, but the probability of this happening is small. How small is a matter for the risk manager to decide. Once the decision has been made, one can obtain the maximum probable loss from a cumulative probability distribution of the dollar losses per occurrence. For example, if the risk manager is willing to ignore losses that happen only 5 percent of the time, the maximum probable loss is that outcome for which the cumulative probability is 0.95. If no outcome has an exact cumulative probability of 0.95, the maximum probable loss is the one for which the cumulative probability first exceeds 0.95.

As a joint measure of loss frequency and loss severity, Prouty suggested the annual expected losses, the mean. This measure can be calculated from a probability distribution of the total dollar losses per year. For example, we have already calculated the monthly expected losses to be approximately $227.50 for the probability distribution of the total dollar losses per month on shipments damaged or stolen.

Exhibit 4-19
Hemcher Corporation—Calculation of Standard Deviation—Monthly
After-Tax Dollar Losses on Shipments Stolen or Damaged

Dollar loss	Difference from mean	Difference squared	Probability	Difference squared times probability
$ 0	−227.5	51,756	0.0067	346.77
40	−187.5	35,156	0.0123	432.42
50	−177.5	31,506	0.0335	1,055.45
80	−147.5	21,756	0.0550	1,196.58
100	−127.5	16,256	0.0860	1,398.02
150	− 77.5	6,006	0.1470	882.88
200	− 27.5	756	0.1885	142.51
250	22.5	506	0.1600	80.96
300	72.5	5,256	0.1200	630.72
350	122.5	15,006	0.0820	1,230.49
400	172.5	29,756	0.0510	1,517.56
450	222.5	49,506	0.0300	1,485.18
500	272.5	74,256	0.0140	1,039.58
550	322.5	104,006	0.0065	676.04
600	372.5	138,756	0.0035	485.65
650	422.5	178,506	0.0015	267.76
700	472.5	223,256	0.0004	89.30
750	522.5	273,006	0.0001	27.30
				12,985.17

Standard deviation = $\sqrt{12,985.17}$ = $113.95

CONCLUSION

This chapter has described what should be measured and why. The Prouty method has been discussed as a useful but somewhat imprecise way of getting at the desired measurements. Various probability and statistical concepts have been introduced and carefully defined. Finally, it has been demonstrated how probability and statistical concepts provide measurements that are more definitive than the verbal Prouty measures.

At this point, much of the theory developed in Chapter 4 has not been applied to actual risk management decision making. However, the groundwork has been laid for further development in Chapter 5. In addition to illustrating how probability and statistical concepts can be used in making risk management decisions, Chapter 5 will explain how we arrived at some of the probability distributions you have been asked to accept on faith.

Chapter Notes

1. The maximum possible loss is sometimes called *possible maximum loss* or the *amount subject*. Many different definitions of these terms are found in insurance literature.
2. $81/256 = 0.316$. In every one out of 3.16 months, on the average, there will be no losses.
3. To square a number, multiply it times itself. For example, $3^2 = 9$, and $4^2 = 16$. The square root of "x" is that number which, if multiplied by itself, would produce "x." The square root of 4 is 2; the square root of 16 is 4. The square root of a number may be determined through an intricate mathematical procedure, but is most easily obtained using an electronic calculator with a square root key ($\sqrt{}$ or $\sqrt{x}$).

CHAPTER 5

Measuring Loss Exposures, Continued

INTRODUCTION

The first part of this chapter discusses how risk managers can use probability distributions to select the most appropriate techniques for handling loss exposures. In addition, the discussion will enable the reader to review these measures and their calculation.

The second part of the chapter will explain how a risk manager can construct a probability distribution by using only data from past experience or by combining such experience with some statistical theory.

The chapter will conclude with a discussion of how many exposure units a risk manager must observe to make a fairly accurate estimate of the true probability of loss. The same discussion will consider how many units a risk manager must have to be able to predict future loss experience with the intended degree of accuracy.

HOW PROBABILITY DISTRIBUTIONS CAN BE USED TO SELECT THE MOST APPROPRIATE RISK MANAGEMENT TECHNIQUES

Probability distributions can enable risk managers to make informed, systematic decisions concerning which risk management techniques should be used to handle a given loss exposure. By testing the effect that various risk management techniques will have on the probability distributions for each exposure, the risk manager can determine:

(1) whether each technique would produce more benefits than it would cost, and

(2) which of the techniques would be most appropriate.

Illustration—Evaluation of Alternatives

To illustrate this use, consider the 500 monthly shipments exposed to theft or damage in transit in the Hemcher Corporation example in Chapter 4. Assume that there are three risk management techniques under consideration as alternatives to complete retention:

(1) Better packaging, a loss control measure that will cost, after-tax, $40 monthly.

(2) Complete insurance for which the monthly after-tax premium is $300 (assuming no change in packaging or loss control activity).

(3) Insurance with a deductible that will cover monthly after-tax dollar losses in excess of $100, for which the after-tax premium is $180.

The method used to select among risk management techniques will be the *minimum expected loss method* introduced in Chapter 1. There, we explained that the minimum expected loss method is a method for identifying that technique or combination of techniques that will minimize the expected loss in the long run, that is, the long run average loss. We also stated that "loss" in this context includes:

(1) dollar losses borne by the entity, and

(2) costs incurred by the entity in treating loss exposures, and

(3) the cost of the worry or anxiety associated with any uncertainty that remains concerning the losses retained by the entity.

By building on additional information in Chapters 2, 3, and 4, it is now possible to examine this concept more closely by demonstrating how it might be used in the Hemcher Corporation case.

To simplify the analysis and to shorten the discussion, only the results of some mathematical analyses will be presented here. The verification of the calculations of the measures of central tendency, the standard deviation, and the coefficient of variation are left as an optional exercise for the reader. Also, the analysis will be limited to the effect of the three alternatives on only one probability distribution—the probability distribution of the total after-tax dollar losses per year.

Loss Control Better packaging is expected to reduce both the number of shipments that are damaged en route and the extent of the loss to those that are damaged. The composite effect of the packaging change on the probability distribution of the total dollar losses per year

Exhibit 5-1
Hemcher Corporation
Probability Distribution—Total After-Tax Dollar Losses on Shipments
Per Month Before and After Better Packaging

Dollar Losses	Probability Before Better Packaging	Probability After Better Packaging	Cumulative Probability After Better Packaging
$ 0	0.0067	0.0199	0.0199
40	0.0123	0.0300	0.0499
50	0.0335	0.0600	0.1099
80	0.0550	0.0900	0.1999
100	0.0860	0.1260	0.3259
150	0.1470	0.1600	0.4859
200	0.1885	0.1600	0.6459
250	0.1600	0.1300	0.7759
300	0.1200	0.1000	0.8759
350	0.0820	0.0700	0.9459
400	0.0510	0.0350	0.9809
450	0.0300	0.0100	0.9909
500	0.0140	0.0090	0.9999
550	0.0065		
600	0.0035		
650	0.0015		
700	0.0004		
750	0.0001		
...	...	...	
	1.0000	1.0000	

is assumed to be that shown in Exhibit 5-1. Because remaining losses
would be retained, this technique is actually not just loss control, but
retention with loss control.

Because better packaging would reduce the extent of loss to those
shipments that are damaged, the *relative* frequency of smaller losses
would actually increase, but overall loss frequency would decrease.
Better packaging would increase the probability of all loss amounts
from $0 to $150 and decrease the probability of the $200 and larger loss
amounts. The probability that losses would exceed $250 would drop
from about 31 percent to 22 percent.

In Chapter 4, we determined that Hemcher Corporation's average
(mean) monthly dollar loss has been $227.50. The packaging change
would reduce the average monthly loss in the long run from $227.50 to

$190. This reduction of $37.50 in itself would almost justify the $40 per month expenditure. In addition to reducing the average monthly loss and the probability of larger losses, better packaging would reduce the cost of adjusting customer claims, which almost certainly is worth $2.50 a month. The median would remain $200 while the single mode of $200 would be replaced by two adjacent values, $150 and $200.

Applying Minimum Expected Loss Method. This conclusion can be rephrased in terms of the minimum expected loss method as follows. In comparing loss control with retention, a decision must be made as to whether the firm is willing to incur a long-run average loss of $2.50 ($230 − $227.50) more than the expected loss of $227.50 to reduce (1) the probability of larger losses and (2) the cost of adjusting customer claims.

Complete Insurance If the Hemcher Corporation purchases complete insurance and does not change packaging, it will "lose" the $300 premium instead of facing the probability distribution before better packaging presented, in Exhibit 5-1. For this $300 insurance expenditure, the firm would transfer to the insurer the $227.50 loss Hemcher would otherwise retain in an average month in the long run. *In the long run,* if a firm assigns no value to the services such as loss control provided by the insurer, the firm will *always* save some money by retaining the exposure, unless the insurer has greatly underpriced the protection or the cost of insurer services.[1] The reason is that the premium always includes a profit and expense loading in addition to an expected loss allowance. If the firm does assign some value to these services or would incur some costs to replace these services, it will still save money in the long run through retention unless the value assigned to the services or the replacement costs equals or exceeds the allowance in the premium for profits and expenses. But, *next month* Hemcher's loss may be $500, $750, or some much larger amount—all of which would exceed the premium saved.

In this example, it is practically impossible for the loss next month to bankrupt the firm and negate the chance to save money in the long run. For many exposures, however, such as exposures to liability claims, the possible maximum loss is so great that insolvency is a distinct possibility if all exposures are retained. Hemcher's risk manager would not be concerned about bankruptcy because of a lost shipment, but he or she could, with justification, worry that over several months—or even over several years—the actual losses may exceed the saved premiums.

Applying Minimum Expected Loss Method. If the minimum expected loss method is used to evaluate the attractions of complete insurance, a decision must be made as to how much the firm is willing to pay in addition to the average loss:

(1) for reduction in uncertainty, and
(2) the services (such as loss control and claims services) rendered by the insurer.

The impact of insurer services on retention-versus-insurance decisions was explored in Chapter 3. For Hemcher Corporation, the question really is whether it is worth $72.50 ($300 − $227.50) more than the average loss of $227.50 to (1) reduce uncertainty and (2) obtain insurer services.

The decision is necessarily subjective. Two risk managers faced with the same set of facts may make different decisions. However, we would expect the decision to depend on the magnitude of the potential losses, what financial impact these losses would have upon the firm, and the weighting the firm assigns to its various post-loss and pre-loss objectives. For example, if Hemcher Corporation management places great emphasis on earnings stability and reduction in anxiety, the decision probably would be to insure the shipments. If, on the other hand, the risk manager is concerned solely with survival as a post-loss objective and is not by nature a worrier except about serious potential losses, the shipments exposure probably would be retained.

Insurance with a Deductible   For $180 a month, the Hemcher Corporation can obtain a policy under which the insurer will pay all monthly losses in excess of $100. Note that this deductible is cumulative, applying to aggregate losses per month. Exhibit 5-2 shows how this deductible insurance will change the probability distribution of the total dollar losses per month.

The probability of each outcome up to $80 is unchanged, but the new probability of a monthly loss of $100 is equal to the old probability of $100 *or higher* losses. When loss in any month exceeds $100, only $100 will be retained by Hemcher.

Retained losses will not exceed $100, which also becomes the median and the mode. The mean is $95.82; the standard deviation, $14.12; and the coefficient of variation relative to the average retained losses only is $14.12/$95.82, or 15 percent. Relative to these retained losses plus the $180 monthly premium for the deductible insurance, the coefficient drops to $14.12/$275.82, or 5 percent.

Applying Minimum Expected Loss Method.   Under the minimum expected loss method, in comparing deductible insurance with retention the question is whether the risk manager is willing to pay $48.32 ($180 + $95.82 − $227.50) more than the expected loss of $227.50 under retention:

Exhibit 5-2
Hemcher Corporation
Probability Distribution—Total After-Tax Dollar Losses on Shipments
Per Month Before and After Insurance with a $100 Deductible

Dollar Losses	Probability Before Insurance	Probability After Insurance	Cumulative Probability After Insurance
$ 0	0.0067	0.0067	0.0067
40	0.0123	0.0123	0.0190
50	0.0335	0.0335	0.0525
80	0.0550	0.0550	0.1075
100	0.0860	0.8925	1.0000
150	0.1470		
200	0.1885	1.0000	
250	0.1600		
300	0.1200		
350	0.0820		
400	0.0510		
450	0.0300		
500	0.0140		
550	0.0065		
600	0.0035		
650	0.0015		
700	0.0004		
750	0.0001		
	1.0000		

(1) to limit the maximum loss to $100, thus reducing uncertainty substantially, and

(2) to receive some insurer services.

Which Technique Is Best?

Of the four possible risk management techniques considered here—complete retention, loss control (plus retention), complete insurance, and deductible insurance (with partial retention)—which is best? Loss control, complete insurance, and deductible insurance have been compared with retention, but not with one another. The minimum expected loss method used to make these comparisons did not tell whether each of these techniques was superior to complete retention, but it did provide a systematic approach to making this decision. It also restated the decision in terms of how highly the risk manager valued:

(1) the reduction in uncertainty that would result from the alternative technique, and
(2) if the alternative is insurance, the services provided by the insurer.

The same method can be used to compare loss control, complete insurance, and deductible insurance with one another, as well as comparing each of them with retention.

The effects of these techniques on certain key features of the probability distribution are summarized in Exhibit 5-3. In that exhibit, the bottom-line "coefficient of variation relative to expected value of uncovered loss plus cost of applying technique" provides the best measure of the uncertainty associated with each technique. Ranking these techniques from "most uncertain" to "least uncertain," the list would be:

(1) retention (most uncertain),
(2) loss control,
(3) deductible insurance, and
(4) complete insurance (least uncertain).

The minimum expected loss method uses a process of elimination to narrow down the number of choices to one. The "most uncertain" alternative is selected or eliminated. If it is eliminated, the "next most uncertain" alternative is selected or eliminated and so forth until only one alternative remains. Because the minimum expected loss method emphasizes the dollar *value* the risk manager assigns to reduction in uncertainty, the comparative desirability of any two techniques depends on the risk manager's willingness to pay the additional cost, if any, of applying the technique that would reduce the firm's uncertainty. Each of the three alternatives to retention has already been compared with retention—the approach with the greatest uncertainty. If retention is favored over each of the three other alternatives, the risk manager has already selected the best technique. Otherwise, the next step is to compare two of these three alternatives with the one having the next most uncertainty—loss control. Finally, unless this alternative is preferred to the other two, the technique among those two with the least uncertainty is compared with the other.

Thus, in comparing the three risk management alternatives other than retention, Hemcher's risk manager will have to determine:

(1) which is preferred, complete insurance or loss control; and
(2) which is preferred, deductible insurance or loss control.

Exhibit 5-3
Hemcher Corporation
Effects of Risk Management Techniques on Key Features of the
Probability Distribution

Feature	Retention	Loss Control	Complete Insurance	Deductible Insurance
Probability that uninsured loss will exceed				
$100	0.81	0.67	0.00	0.00
300	0.19	0.12	0.00	0.00
500	0.01	0.00+	0.00	0.00
Expected value of uncovered loss	$228	$190	$0	$96
Cost of applying technique	$0	$40	$300	$180
Expected value of uncovered loss plus cost of applying technique	$228	$230	$300	$276
Standard deviation	$114	$107	$0	$14
Coefficient of variation relative to expected value of uncovered loss	0.50	0.56	0.00	0.15
Coefficient of variation relative to expected value of uncovered loss plus cost of applying technique	0.50	0.47	0.00	0.05

Then, if both types of insurance (complete or deductible) are preferred
over loss control, a choice must be made between complete insurance
and deductible insurance.

It is not always necessary to go through all these steps. A decision
has been made as soon as it is possible to conclude that one alternative
is clearly preferable to all other alternatives.

Complete Insurance or Loss Control   As shown in Exhibit 5-3,
the cost of full insurance is $300 per month, and the total cost of the
loss control option is $230 per month, consisting of $190 of expected
losses and $40 of loss control expense. Therefore, the choice between
them would hinge on the risk manager's willingness to pay the extra

$70 per month for full insurance in order to eliminate uncertainty and receive whatever other services the insurer might provide. A counter-consideration that favors loss control is the effect of better packaging on consumer satisfaction.

Deductible Insurance or Loss Control The comparison of deductible insurance and loss control follows a similar pattern. The total monthly cost of the deductible insurance is $276, composed of $180 of premium and $96 of expected retained losses. The total cost of the loss control option is $230, as indicated in the preceding paragraph. Again, the choice between these two options would depend on the risk manager's willingness to pay the extra monthly cost of $46 for the deductible insurance in order:

(1) to reduce uncertainty, and
(2) to receive the insurer's other services.

The effect of better packaging on consumer satisfaction must be considered, along with cost, reduction of uncertainty, and the availability of the insurer's services.

Complete Insurance or Deductible Insurance In comparing complete insurance with deductible insurance the question is whether the risk manager is willing to pay monthly the amount by which the average cost of complete insurance (the $300 premium) exceeds the average cost of deductible insurance (the $180 premium plus the average uninsured loss of $96) in order:

(1) to reduce uncertainty, and
(2) to receive the benefit of the insurer's claims adjusting service on claims of $100 or less.

Reducing uncertainty in this instance, however, is not an advantage because the worst loss that could happen, $100, would raise the cost of the deductible insurance approach to $180 + $100, which is still less than the $300 premium cost of complete insurance. The decision thus depends on the value the risk manager attaches to having the insurer adjust small losses. The uncertainty factor actually favors the deductible insurance, a most unusual situation. It occurs because 89 percent of the monthly losses under deductible insurance will be $100. The average uncovered loss plus the extra expenses that the insurer would have incurred, primarily to adjust these losses, exceeds the deductible amount. Usually this does not happen because the average uncovered loss is much less than the deductible amount.

Arriving at a Decision through Paired Comparisons Through these *paired comparisons*, each technique being compared with each other technique, the risk manager can select the preferred approach. To illustrate this, assume that Hemcher's risk manager answered the question raised in connection with each comparison with the following preferences:

(1) complete insurance preferred over retention,
(2) deductible insurance preferred over retention,
(3) loss control preferred over retention,
(4) complete insurance preferred over loss control,
(5) deductible insurance preferred over loss control, and
(6) deductible insurance preferred over complete insurance.

Because deductible insurance is preferred over complete insurance, which in turn is preferred over the other two methods, deductible insurance is the preferred technique.

Combining Techniques Suppose the risk manager introduced better packaging in addition to purchasing deductible insurance. By spending $40 per month on this loss control measure, the risk manager can reduce the average uninsured loss in the long run from $95.82 to $91.41. (The calculation of this amount is left as an optional exercise. Hint: Use as the probabilities of these losses occurring the probabilities under "After Better Packaging" in Exhibit 5-1.) This modest reduction in the average loss plus the larger chance that the loss will be less than $100 probably is not enough to justify the $40 expenditure on better packaging. However, this combination of techniques would be much more attractive if the insurer would reduce the premium charge because of the loss control. The decision would also depend upon the value assigned to the improvement in consumer satisfaction.

If this combination of techniques is selected, Hemcher Corporation will manage its shipping exposure by using one control technique and two financing techniques. Better packaging is a loss control measure that serves both to reduce and to prevent losses. Deductible insurance combines insurance transfers with partial retention.

HOW TO CONSTRUCT A PROBABILITY DISTRIBUTION

How can a risk manager construct or estimate the probability distributions that describe a particular exposure? Basically there are two approaches:

(1) from past experience of the individual firm or family or of others, or
(2) by combining limited past experience with some probability theory.

Exhibit 5-4
Hemcher Corporation
Frequency Distribution and Derived Probability
Distribution of Shipments Stolen or Damaged Per Month
Over a Ten-Year Period

Number of Shipments Stolen or Damaged	Number of Months	Derived Probability*
0	0	0.0000
1	4	0.0333
2	10	0.0833
3	17	0.1417
4	22	0.1833
5	22	0.1833
6	17	0.1417
7	12	0.1000
8	8	0.0667
9	4	0.0333
10	3	0.0250
11	1	0.0083
	120	1.0000

*Number of Months
120

Past Experience

One can confidently rely on past experience to predict the future only when one has had a very large number of units exposed to loss in the past under essentially the same conditions. The 500 shipments a month of the Hemcher Corporation comes close to having these characteristics. Enough units are exposed to keep the variation in losses from month to month fairly small and, assuming monthly data are available for the past ten years, the firm would have 120 months of observations. These observations can be used to construct a *frequency* distribution that shows the number of months each outcome occurs. Exhibit 5-4 shows how this distribution might look and how a frequency distribution can be converted into a probability distribution by dividing each frequency by the total number of observations.

Although this derived probability distribution is instructive and could be used to great advantage to make the types of decisions noted above, it has certain limitations because of the small number of observations on which it is based:

(1) The derived probability distribution says there will be no months of no losses, but the possibility of no losses cannot be dismissed completely, even though the probability of no losses may be very small.

(2) The derived probability distribution says the maximum number of losses is eleven but the actual number may be higher, even though that outcome is improbable.

(3) With only 120 observations, each probability is some multiple of 1/120 or 0.00833. For example, if a certain number of losses occurred four times, its derived probability is 4×0.00833, or 0.0333. Each month carries too much weight.

To correct these limitations, assume that the Hemcher Corporation can exchange data with nine other firms, each of which also makes about 500 shipments a month under essentially the same conditions. The mechanism for pooling this information could be a trade association, an insurance organization, or a government agency. Instead of 120 observations over a ten-year period, 1,200 observations would then be available. The frequency distribution of these 1,200 observations and the derived probability distribution are presented in Exhibit 5-5.

This distribution looks more reasonable. There is a small likelihood that no shipments will be lost or damaged. Each month carries less weight in determining the probability. The distribution is still unsatisfactory in that the maximum possible loss is fourteen, but it is possible to keep this limitation in mind. This more broadly based derived distribution, using data from a number of firms, closely resembles the distribution in Exhibit 4-11 (which you were asked to simply accept as given) in the detail and shape of the distribution. The reason for this will become apparent shortly.

Pooling of data by separate firms would seldom work out so well in practice. The firms are likely to make different numbers of monthly shipments and make them under different conditions. Nevertheless, such pooled information used intelligently by one who is aware of its limitations is much better than no information at all.

Similarly, probability distributions can be derived for the dollar losses per shipment stolen or damaged and for the total dollar losses per year. Deriving these distributions from empirical data is even more difficult than deriving probability distributions for the number of shipments stolen or damaged. In real life, the dollar amounts can be any multiple of $.01. Consequently there are many more possibilities than we have examined here.

Exhibit 5-5
Hemcher Corporation plus Nine Similar Firms
Frequency Distribution and Derived Probability
Distribution of Shipments Per Firm Stolen or Damaged
Per Month Over a Ten-Year Period

Number of Shipments Stolen or Damaged Per Firm	Number of Months	Derived Probability
0	8	0.0067
1	40	0.0333
2	101	0.0842
3	168	0.1400
4	211	0.1758
5	211	0.1758
6	175	0.1458
7	125	0.1042
8	78	0.0650
9	44	0.0367
10	22	0.0183
11	10	0.0083
12	4	0.0033
13	2	0.0017
14	1	0.0008
	1200	1.0000

Theoretical Probability Distributions

For those who cannot construct probability distributions solely by tabulating past experience, estimates of probability distributions can be developed mathematically. Such estimates are possible because (1) the outcomes in many practical situations tend to follow the same laws of nature as those determining many theoretical probability distributions, and (2) these theoretical probability distributions require only one or two measures that can be obtained from past experience. It is much easier to estimate one or two measures from past experience than it is to determine the probability of each possible outcome. For example, even though the probability distribution derived in Exhibit 5-4 had many limitations, the mean (5) and the standard deviation (2.24) of that distribution are close to the mean and the standard deviation of the more acceptable distribution in Exhibit 5-5.

Poisson Distribution A case in point! Years ago, the Prussian army lost the services of many soldiers who were kicked by their horses. A statistician determined that the probability that a specified number of injuries would occur in, say, the next year could be calculated by using the formula:

$$P(r) = \frac{m^r e^{-m}}{r!}$$

where r = the number of injuries, $P(r)$ = the probability of r injuries, m = the mean number of injuries per period in the long run (to be estimated from past experience), and e = a constant, 2.71828.... With the aid of this formula, a probability distribution of the number of injuries can be constructed. A distribution calculated with this formula is called a Poisson distribution, after the person who developed this formula in a different context.

At first sight, this formula appears complex, but actually it is easy to apply and is extremely useful. Only the mean, m, needs to be estimated. If no changes are expected and past experience is extensive enough to establish a sound estimate of the mean, the mean is the total number of injuries in the experience period divided by the number of months (or other intervals of time depending upon the time interval to which the probability distribution applies) included in that period. If changes in the conditions are expected, the risk manager's task is more difficult because he or she must estimate how these changes will affect the mean. Instead of calculating the e^{-m} in the formula, one can consult tables that give the value of e^{-m} for various values of m. For example:

m	e^{-m}	m	e^{-m}
0	1.00000	5	0.00674
0.5	0.60653	6	0.00248
1	0.36788	7	0.00092
2	0.13534	8	0.00034
3	0.04979	9	0.00012
4	0.01832	10	0.00004

Finally, $r!$ (or r factorial) is simply $r(r-1)(r-2)(r-3)...1$. For example, 3! = 3 × 2 × 1, and 5! = 5 × 4 × 3 × 2 × 1. By definition, 0! = 1.

An injury resulting from a Prussian soldier being kicked by a horse was an event to which there were a large number of independent exposures (each time a soldier went near a horse) and for which the probability was quite small that the event would happen at any given exposure. The same is true of many events that concern risk managers, such as:

- fires to warehouses (if each day, each hour, or some other time interval that each warehouse is exposed to loss can be considered a separate exposure)
- missing or damaged shipments out of a large number of shipments (each shipment being considered a separate exposure)
- products liability claims (most businesses being exposed daily to many such potential claims), and
- injuries to employees (each day, each hour, or some other time interval an employee works being considered such an exposure)

One limitation to the application of the Poisson probability distribution is that the probability that the event will occur should be the same during each exposure. However, if the probabilities during each exposure are not too different, the approximation is still useful. If they differ widely, statisticians would suggest another slightly more complex distribution that will not be considered here.

Another problem is that the exposures may not be independent; a fire loss to a warehouse today may change the probability of a fire loss to a different warehouse today or to the same warehouse next week; a loss to one shipment may change the probability of loss to another shipment; a products liability claim from one exposure may change the probability of a products liability claim from another exposure; and an injury to one employee today may change the probability of an injury to another employee today or to the same employee next month. Perfect independence almost never exists; in this discussion, enough independence will be assumed to permit the practical application of the formula.

Exhibit 5-6 shows the Poisson probability distributions that would apply if the means were 0.5, 1, 2, 3, 5, and 10, respectively.[2]

The reader is now asked to compare the distribution in Exhibit 5-6 for a mean of 5 with Exhibit 4-11. In constructing Exhibit 4-11, the authors assumed that this distribution provided a reasonable fit. In many cases, it will. Remember the conditions for using the Poisson distribution:

(1) many independent exposures, and
(2) a low (approximately 1/10 or less) probability that the event will happen at any given exposure.

When an exposure meets these criteria, the Poisson distribution may be used to construct a probability distribution that provides a fairly accurate projection of future loss experience (assuming conditions remain unchanged). All that is needed is one piece of information—the

Exhibit 5-6
Poisson Probability Distributions for Means of 0.5, 1, 2, 3, 5, and 10

Number of Occurrences	Means					
	0.5	1	2	3	5	10
0	0.6065	0.3679	0.1353	0.0498	0.0067	*
1	0.3033	0.3679	0.2707	0.1494	0.0337	0.0005
2	0.0758	0.1839	0.2707	0.2240	0.0842	0.0023
3	0.0126	0.0613	0.1804	0.2240	0.1404	0.0076
4	0.0016	0.0153	0.0902	0.1680	0.1755	0.0189
5	0.0002	0.0031	0.0361	0.1008	0.1755	0.0378
6	*	0.0005	0.0120	0.0504	0.1462	0.0631
7	*	*	0.0034	0.0216	0.1044	0.0901
8	*	*	0.0009	0.0081	0.0653	0.1126
9	*	*	0.0002	0.0027	0.0363	0.1251
10	*	*	*	0.0008	0.0181	0.1251
11	*	*	*	0.0002	0.0082	0.1137
12	*	*	*	*	0.0034	0.0948
13	*	*	*	*	0.0013	0.0729
14	*	*	*	*	0.0005	0.0521
15	*	*	*	*	0.0002	0.0347
16	*	*	*	*	*	0.0217
17	*	*	*	*	*	0.0128
18	*	*	*	*	*	0.0071
19	*	*	*	*	*	0.0037
20	*	*	*	*	*	0.0019
...	*	*	*	*	*	*

*Less than 0.0001

mean number of events per year (or other time period) that have been experienced in the past.

Normal Distribution Hemcher Corporation's expected total dollar losses per month with retention have been estimated at $228 (rounding upwards to the nearest dollar). What is the probability that total dollar losses next month will be some other figure—such as $300, or $100, or $10,000? The probability distribution of total dollar losses per year or month is difficult to approximate with a theoretical probability distribution. Occasionally, however, the distribution can be approximated by a "normal" distribution—the best known of all the theoretical distributions. This distribution has been used successfully to describe such varied phenomena as the probability distribution of neck sizes of men's shirts and the annual message use of telephone subscribers. To determine the normal distribution applicable to a given situation, two measures from past experience or other information must be estimated: (1) the mean and (2) the standard deviation. The distribution can then be constructed from tables contained in introductory statistics textbooks. The principal concern here is not with how this distribution can be constructed, but how the resulting distribution might be used. As will be shown, the standard deviation has a unique meaning when outcomes are distributed "normally." This gives the normal distribution a special appeal.

The normal distribution differs from the others discussed up to this point in several ways:

(1) It assumes the losses can assume all values from minus infinity to plus infinity.
(2) The distribution can be used to determine only the probability that certain ranges or classes of losses occur, not the probability that specific dollar losses will occur.
(3) The distribution assumes that the losses can assume all values (such as $100, $.50, and $.000004) *continuously* from minus infinity to plus infinity. This assumption is unrealistic (how can a loss be negative? how can a loss be $.003 or some other fraction of a cent?) but, as will be demonstrated, this feature poses no great problem.
(4) The vertical distances in a graph of the normal probability distribution do not show the probabilities that the corresponding losses occur. Instead the *area* under the curve is considered to equal 1 and the *portion of the area* lying within any range of losses is the probability that losses will fall within that range. For example, if one-tenth of the area is within the range $500.01-$1,000, the probability is 10 percent that the losses will fall between $500.01 and $1,000.

Exhibit 5-7
Hemcher Corporation
Total After-Tax Dollar Losses Per Month Assuming Normal Distribution—Mean of $228 and Standard Deviation of $114

Dollar Losses Per Month	Probability	Corresponding Probabilities from Table
Under $100	0.1308	0.1075
$100 or more but under $200	0.2720	0.2330
$200 or more but under $300	0.3335	0.3485
$300 or more but under $400	0.1969	0.2020
$400 or more but under $500	0.0586	0.0810
$500 or more but under $600	0.0076	0.0205
$600 or more but under $700	0.0004	0.0050
$700 or more but under $800	0.0001	0.0005
$800 or more	*	*

*Less than 0.0001

Exhibits 5-7 and 5-8 show the normal probability distribution that would correspond to a mean of $228 and a standard deviation of $114, two values that are close to those derived from Exhibit 4-15 and the assumed probability distribution of the total after-tax dollar losses caused by the theft of or damage to Hemcher Corporation's shipments.

It is clear that the symmetrical bell-shaped normal distribution does not apply to distributions for which one of the most likely outcomes is no losses. The normal distribution is, however, appropriate when the distribution is bell-shaped (symmetrical with a single peak at the center) and meets some other tests not within the scope of this text.

The special appeal of the normal distribution is that, given only the mean and the standard deviation, one can obtain from tables in introductory statistics texts the probability that the losses will fall within a range extending from the mean to a specified number of standard deviations above (or below because the distribution is symmetrical) the mean. For example, according to these exhibits, the probability that the losses will fall between the mean, $228, and the mean plus one standard deviation, $228 + $114 = $342 (or between $228 and $228 − $114 = $114), is 0.3413. Exhibit 5-9 shows how the probabilities change as the number of standard deviations above (or below) the mean increases.

The probability of falling within a specified number of deviations

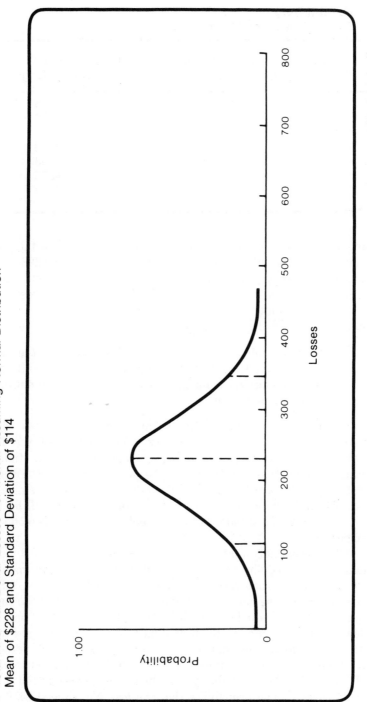

Exhibit 5-8
Hemcher Corporation
Total After-Tax Dollar Losses Per Month Assuming Normal Distribution
Mean of $228 and Standard Deviation of $114

Exhibit 5-9
Probabilities of the Normal Distribution

Number of Standard Deviations Above (or Below) Mean	Probability of Falling Within Range
0.5	0.1915
1.0	0.3413
1.5	0.4332
2.0	0.4772
2.5	0.4938
3.0	0.4986
3.5	0.4998

above *or* below the mean is twice these numbers. Thus the probability that the losses will fall between $228 + $114 and $228 − $114, is 2(0.3413), or 68 percent. The probability that the losses will fall between $228 + 2 ($114) and $228 − 2 ($114) is 2(0.4772), or 95 percent.

The probability that losses will not exceed the mean by more than some specified multiple of the standard deviation is equal to the sum of:

(1) the probability that the losses will be less than the mean, plus
(2) the probability that the losses will equal or exceed the mean but will not exceed the mean by more than the given multiple of the standard deviation.

In the normal distribution, the probability that the losses will be less than the mean is always 50 percent. The second of the foregoing probabilities depends, of course, on the selected multiple of the standard deviation. For example, the probability that the loss will be less than $342 (which is one standard deviation above the mean) is 0.50 + 0.34, or 84 percent. The probability that the loss will be less than $114, which is one standard deviation below the mean, is 0.50 − 0.34, or 16 percent.

The probability that the loss will exceed any specified value is 1.0 minus the probability that the loss will be less than that amount. Thus, the probability that the loss will exceed $342 is 1.0 − 0.84, or 16 percent. Since the normal distribution is symmetrical, the probability that the losses will be less than $114 (the mean less one standard deviation) is the same as the probability that the losses will exceed $342 (the mean plus one standard deviation), namely 16 percent. This relationship is shown graphically in Exhibit 5-10, which is an adaptation of Exhibit 5-8. The probability that the loss will exceed $114 is 1 − 0.16, or 84 percent. The probability that the loss will exceed $456 (which is two standard deviations above the mean) is about $1 - (0.50 + 0.48)$, or 2 percent.

Because of this special property of the standard deviation in a normal distribution, one need not actually construct the normal distribution to obtain the needed measurements. Indeed it is easier to obtain these measurements than it would be if some other distribution were a better approximation. For this reason, it is tempting to assume normality when it does not exist. This temptation must be resisted, but when the normal distribution does seem to be a reasonable fit, the preceding description of this distribution should be helpful.

Many other theoretical probability distributions might be mentioned, but the preceding is enough to indicate their usage. Researchers are improving our knowledge of theoretical probability distributions and their uses in risk management. In the future, their application should become increasingly precise and useful.

HOW LARGE IS LARGE?

Probability was defined in Chapter 4 as "the proportion of times the specified event will almost certainly occur out of a *large* number of trials." How large is "large"? The answer to this question is extremely important to both risk managers and insurers.

The Law of Large Numbers

According to the law of large numbers, as it is applied to exposures to accidental loss, as the number of units independently exposed to loss increases, it becomes more and more likely that the *actual* proportion of units that suffer losses will not differ by more than a specified amount from the estimated probability that each unit will suffer a loss. To illustrate, assume that the Cosby Company makes many shipments per month and the probability of losing each shipment is 0.02. As the number of shipments per month increases, it becomes more and more likely that the proportion of shipments lost each month will not differ from 0.02 by more than some specified amount, say 0.002.

This law is useful in two ways. First, if the probability of each unit suffering a loss is known and if the number of exposure units is "large," the risk manager or an insurer can predict with a high degree of confidence that the proportion of units sustaining a loss will be close to the probability of loss to each unit. For example, if the risk manager of a firm knows that the probability of losing each shipment is 0.02 and that the firm makes a "large" number of shipments each month, he or she can predict with confidence that each month the firm will lose about

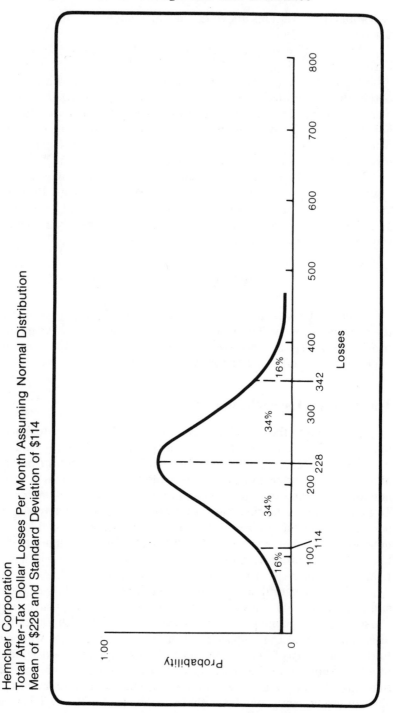

Exhibit 5-10
Hemcher Corporation
Total After-Tax Dollar Losses Per Month Assuming Normal Distribution
Mean of $228 and Standard Deviation of $114

2 percent of its shipments. Second, if the probability that a firm will suffer a loss to each exposure unit is not known, the risk manager can estimate this probability by calculating the proportion of exposure units that have sustained a loss in the past. For example, if the risk manager of the Cosby Company did not know that the probability of losing each shipment was 0.02, he or she could observe what proportion of shipments had sustained losses during past months. If the number of shipments observed is "large," it is quite likely that the observed proportion with losses would be *close* to the true proportion 0.02.

How Likely? How Close?

What is a "large" number of exposure units depends on two criteria:

(1) What is the maximum acceptable difference between the proportion of units that will suffer losses and the true probability of loss? In other words, within what range are results being predicted?

(2) What is the minimum acceptable probability that the actual proportion will differ from the true probability of loss by no more than the maximum difference set under the first criterion? In other words, what degree of confidence is needed that actual results will fall within the range mentioned above? How reliable must the prediction be?

The smaller the range set under the first criterion and the greater the required confidence set under the second criterion, the larger the number of units must be. Cosby's criteria might be established as illustrated in the following examples. In each case, the example deals with the number of shipments (exposure units) required to achieve the goal spelled out in the example:

(1) Probability that at least 95 percent of the time the proportion of shipments lost during each month will not vary from 0.02 by more than 0.002.

(2) Probability that at least 68 percent of the time the proportion will not vary from 0.02 by more than 0.002.

(3) Probability that at least 95 percent of the time the proportion will not vary from 0.02 by more than 0.006.

(4) Probability that at least 68 percent of the time the proportion will not vary from 0.02 by more than 0.006.

Number Required to Satisfy Criteria

To calculate the number of units required to satisfy any set of criteria, it is often assumed that a normal distribution accurately describes how the proportion of units suffering losses varies around the probability of loss. The method of calculating the required number of units under this assumption will be illustrated by reference to the first of the four sets of criteria in the preceding section: probability at least 95 percent that the proportion of shipments lost during each month will not vary from 0.02 by more than 0.002, *a maximum difference criterion* of 10 percent. The calculation involves three steps:

(1) Determine the number of standard deviations within which results must fall to satisfy the 95 percent probability criterion. If the probability distribution is assumed to be normal, this number, as explained earlier, is two standard deviations above and below the mean.

(2) Set the maximum acceptable difference equal to this probability range. In this case set:

$$0.002 = 2 \ standard \ deviations$$

This permits us to restate the question as follows: If the true proportion of shipments lost is 0.02 (two out of every hundred shipments), we wish to know how many observations are necessary—how many shipments must be made each month—to satisfy Cosby's criterion that the actual proportion of lost shipments will be between 0.018 and 0.022 (within two standard deviations of the true proportion) 95 percent of the time. The answer to this question is obtained in step 3.

(3) Solve for n, using the following formula:

$$n = \frac{(x)^2 p(1-p)}{a^2}$$

where n is the number of observations required, x is the number of standard deviations corresponding to the probability criterion, p is the true probability, and a is the maximum acceptable difference. In this case,

$$n = \frac{(2)^2(.02)(1-.02)}{(.002)^2} = 19,600$$

To be 95 percent certain that the proportion of shipments lost during each month will not differ from 0.02 by more than 0.002, the firm must make 19,600 shipments per month, an extremely large number.

Shipments lost would range from 353 to 431 at least 95 percent of the time. [$19,600 \times (0.02 - 0.002) = 353$, and $19,600 \times (0.02 + 0.002) = 431$.]

Using the same approach, the number of shipments required to achieve Cosby's other criteria can also be calculated:

(2) 4,900 shipments are required for there to be a probability that at least 68 percent of the time the proportion will not vary from 0.02 by more than 0.002. Shipments lost would range from 88 to 108 at least 68 percent of the time.

(3) 2,178 shipments are required for there to be a probability that at least 95 percent of the time the proportion will not vary from 0.02 by more than 0.002. Shipments lost would range from 30 to 57 at least 95 percent of the time.

(4) 544 shipments are required for there to be a probability that at least 68 percent of the time the proportion will not vary from 0.02 by more than 0.006. Shipments lost would range from 8 to 14 at least 68 percent of the time.

Many firms do not make enough shipments per month to have these required numbers of exposure units. If the exposure units had been warehouses exposed to fire, cars exposed to physical damage, or workers exposed to industrial injuries instead of shipments, still fewer firms would have this many exposure units.

One reason the required numbers are so large is that the Cosby Company standards are rather severe. If the risk manager estimates the probability of loss to be 0.02 and the actual proportion lies in the range from 0.00 to 0.04 (a maximum difference of 0.02 or 100 percent), this deviation might not be considered too great. To achieve this result, or a maximum difference of 0.02 (as opposed to a maximum difference of 0.002) with a 95 percent probability would require a much smaller number of exposure units—196, to be exact. With 196 exposure units, losses would range from 0 to 8 at least 95 percent of the time.

A summary of the calculations up to this point and those for some other combinations are presented in Exhibit 5-11. Analysis of this exhibit will help the reader see the relationships among these factors that determine "how large is large?"

These numerical illustrations demonstrate a fundamental fact about loss exposures: when the probability of loss is small, a larger number of exposure units is needed than is commonly believed in order to achieve a desired level of confidence in the prediction. Increasing the number of homogeneous exposure units allows an insurance company—or any firm retaining its loss exposures—to have greater confidence that its experience will not differ greatly from what is anticipated according to the loss distribution. Understanding the

Exhibit 5-11

Number of Exposure Units Required for a Given Probability and Level of Accuracy

Probability of Loss (p)	Probability Criterion	Maximum Difference Criterion	Number Required (n)
0.02	95%	10%	19,600
		30	2,178
		50	784
		100	196
	68	10	4,900
		30	544
		50	196
		100	49
0.05	95	10	7,600
		30	844
		50	304
		100	76
	68	10	1,900
		30	211
		50	76
0.20	95	10	1,600
		30	178
		50	64
	68	10	400
		30	44
0.25	95	10	1,200
		30	133
		50	48
	68	10	300
		30	33
0.30	95	10	933
		30	104
		50	37
	68	10	233
		30	26

interactions between the number of exposure units, the probability of loss, the maximum difference criterion, and the desired confidence level is essential in reaching sound risk management decisions.

A CONCLUDING NOTE

The materials presented in Chapters 4 and 5 can be useful in at least two ways. First, because risk management decision making is becoming more quantitative, a risk manager must be prepared to meet the more sophisticated demands of the future. Second, even if most current risk management decisions are made on a far less quantitative basis, an understanding of the reasoning presented in Chapters 4 and 5 should enable one better to understand how insurance works, why retention is attractive to firms with many exposure units, and why other consumers purchase insurance.

Chapter Notes

---

1. This is true even of a million dollar liability loss. However, the "long run" in such a case might require thousands of years.
2. Some samples of the calculations used to develop Exhibit 5-6 are presented below:

$$m = 0.5$$

$$P(1) = \frac{(0.5)^1 \, e^{-0.5}}{1!} = 0.5(e^{-0.5}) = 0.5(0.60653) = 0.3033$$

$$P(3) = \frac{(0.5)^3 \, e^{-0.5}}{3!} = \frac{0.125(e^{-0.5})}{3 \times 2 \times 1} = \frac{0.125(0.60653)}{6} = 0.0126$$

$$m = 5$$

$$P(5) = \frac{(5)^5 \, e^{-5}}{5!} = \frac{3,125(e^{-5})}{5 \times 4 \times 3 \times 2 \times 1} = \frac{3,125(0.00674)}{120} = 0.1775$$

$$P(10) = \frac{(5)^{10} \, e^{-5}}{10!} = \frac{9,756,625(e^{-5})}{10 \times 9 \times 8 \times 7 \times 6 \times 5 \times 4 \times 3 \times 2 \times 1}$$

$$= \frac{9,765,625(0.00674)}{3,628,800} = 0.0181$$

CHAPTER 6

Insurance and Society

INTRODUCTION

The first five chapters of this text have examined principles of risk management. Chapters 6 through 15 are devoted to principles of insurance. While insurance has been analyzed as one type of loss financing technique used by risk managers, the remainder of this text focuses almost exclusively on insurance as a business and on a business framework for insurance coverage analysis. Chapters 6 and 7 examine insurance primarily from the viewpoint of society, rather than from the viewpoint of the risk manager.

Chapter 6 starts with an attempt to define insurance. Deciding which loss exposures are insurable occupies another important portion of this chapter. The many different types of insurer that operate in the United States are classified and discussed. The analysis in this chapter also examines the benefits and costs of insurance, from the viewpoint of society. Attention will be given to various social problems for which insurance has been advanced as a partial solution and what insurance can and cannot contribute to the solution of those problems. The concluding section of Chapter 6 outlines the size and economic significance of the insurance business.

"WHAT IS INSURANCE" REVISITED

Definition in This Text

Unfortunately, perhaps, there is no universally accepted definition of "insurance." Many definitions have been proposed by the American

Risk and Insurance Association, the courts, Congress, state legislatures, state insurance commissioners, and a variety of authors. However, no one definition has come close to universal acceptance. Strengths and flaws can be found in all definitions of the term.

This section reexamines the definitions of insurance offered earlier in this text and discusses other definitions.

Chapter 3 presented two definitions of insurance:

(1) From the viewpoint of a risk manager, insurance was defined as *a technique that makes it possible to transfer the financial consequences of potential accidental losses from the insured entity, family, or individual to an insurer.*

(2) As a mechanism, insurance was defined as *a social device under which two or more (generally many more than two) entities make or promise to make contributions to a fund from which the insurer promises to make certain cash payments or render certain services to those contributors who suffer accidental losses.* Insurance was said to differ from most noninsurance transfers in that:

- The insurer pools or combines many loss exposures,
- The insureds contribute to a fund out of which cash payments or services are provided, and
- The insurance contract deals solely with the transfer.

The first definition of insurance as a transfer technique is widely accepted. However, many disagree with the above characteristics attributed to insurance as a mechanism or social device.

Some Other Conceptual Definitions

Various definitions of insurance are found in risk management and insurance literature. The following analysis of some of these other definitions should improve the reader's understanding of the nature of insurance.

Pfeffer According to Pfeffer, "Insurance is a device for the reduction of uncertainty of one party, called the insured, through the transfer of particular risks to another party, called the insurer, who offers a restoration, at least in part, of economic losses suffered by the insured."[1] In his opinion, this definition contains the minimum necessary and sufficient conditions for the existence of the device. On the other hand, for the business or institution of insurance to be safe, equitable, or both, Pfeffer observes that certain additional elements are required. He agrees that ideally the insurer would be able to rely on the law of large numbers in setting rates and, through insuring a large number of exposure units, to reduce fluctuations in the annual loss experience. However, he observes that no line of insurance fulfills all of the conditions that must be present for the law of large numbers to apply perfectly. (This point will be demonstrated in more detail later in this chapter.) Hence, though these conditions may be desirable, they are not essential to the concept or practice of insurance. To the extent that these conditions are not satisfied, however, the financial capacity of the insurer to bear the unexpected becomes a more important consideration.

Pfeffer constructed his "generic" definition following an extensive analysis of definitions used by the courts, historians, economists, government "insurance" organizations, and insurance authors. A generic definition defines a word by naming the class of which it is a member ("insurance is a *device*") and identifying the traits that distinguish that word from other members of the same class. Pfeffer's analysis of other definitions suggested that they were not generic definitions. Most, especially the legal definitions, were ostensive-type definitions that indicated examples of the class to which the word applied but did not provide a basis for identifying all the examples to which the word applied. In other words, such definitions provide some illustrations of what the word means, though many other illustrations may exist. Other definitions, he observed, require more of insurance than is necessary to differentiate it from other members of the same class. To illustrate, he argues that:

(1) Insurance need not *eliminate* uncertainty, as is claimed in some definitions; it *reduces the degree* of uncertainty of the insured. Some uncertainty remains concerning whether the contract will cover the loss and whether the insurer will remain solvent.
(2) The law of large numbers need not apply. The insurer may rely on some principle such as specialized experience and judgment or financial power to feel less uncertain about the consequences of the potential losses.
(3) The event need not be accidental. What is required is that the insured hazard (to use Pfeffer's term) cause uncertainty on the part of the insured. In an extreme case, the event may already have occurred, unknown to either the insured or the insurer.

To develop his definition, Pfeffer started with a broad set of terms which he then narrowed in a search for a generic definition. He noted that (1) out of a large number of terms *associated with uncertainty* (for example, anticipation, avoidance, bet, expectation, guarantee, hedge, insurance, prediction, risk, risk reduction, risk transfer [which to Pfeffer meant the transfer of the exposure itself to someone else], and speculation), (2) only a subset are *uncertainty-reducing devices* (for example, guarantee, hedge, insurance, risk reduction, and risk transfer). Of these devices a still smaller number (for example, guarantee, hedge, insurance, and risk transfer) (3) *involve the transfer of risk* to another party, and of *these* devices only two (guarantee and insurance) are (4) devices that *promise to restore the economic consequences of a loss.* Finally, insurance can be distinguished from guarantees in that an insurance contract (5) *involves only two parties.* Guarantees (such as surety bonds) involve three parties. Pfeffer's definition includes these five characteristics. Under this definition, most of the noninsurance transfers described in Chapter 2 would appear to be insurance.

The definitions of insurance presented in introductory insurance or risk management texts tend to be more restrictive, with a large number of exposure units being a necessary, not just a desirable, characteristic. Some illustrations are presented below. Like Pfeffer's, all of these definitions use the word "risk," which this text has tried to avoid. "Risk" can be interpreted in these definitions as either the variation in potential losses faced by the insured or the insured's exposure to loss.

Athearn　According to Athearn, insurance "is a social device which combines the risks of individuals into a group, using funds contributed by members of the group to pay for losses." The funds may be accumulated in advance or through assessments following a loss.[2] The definition implies that there is a group of insureds, with each person transferring his or her "risk" to the whole group.

Bickelhaupt　Bickelhaupt defines insurance as a method that "reduces risk by a transfer and combination (or 'pooling') of uncertainty in regard to financial loss." From the insured's point of view, however, he states that only a transfer, not a combination, is necessary to have an insurance plan. Indeed, if "self-insurance" is considered insurance, only combination may be necessary, but usually insurance involves both transfer and combination.[3] In CPCU texts "self-insurance" is considered to be retention, not insurance.

Denenberg, et al.　Insurance is defined by Denenberg, et al., as the business of transferring risk by means of a contract. In explaining their definition, these authors pointed out that the term "business" distinguishes insurance from the casual transfer of risk. Indeed, serving as a transferee of risk is the primary economic function performed by the insurer, not an incidental activity as is the case in, say, hold-harmless agreements. The term "business" also implies that the insurer accepts a large number of insureds on a continuing basis. Consequently, with only a few exceptions, the insurer can and does use the pooling technique.[4]

Greene   The most detailed definition of insurance has been suggested by Greene. According to Greene:

> *Insurance* is an economic institution that reduces risk by combining under one management a group of objects so situated that the aggregate accidental losses to which the group is subject become predictable within narrow limits. Insurance is usually effected by, and can be said to include, certain legal contracts under which the insurer, for consideration, promises to reimburse the insured or render services in case of certain described accidental losses suffered during the term of the agreement.

Although the first part of this definition suggests that combination is a necessary part of insurance, Greene observes that the definition includes an arrangement under which risk is simply transferred to an insurer by means of a legal contract. Although the basis of commercial insurance operations is pooling or combination, Greene notes that (1) insurers sometimes act merely as transferees with respect to *some* of their contracts (for example, a Lloyd's of London contract covering the hands of a famous pianist or other unique exposure); and (2) some insurers have too few insured exposure units in the aggregate to predict their loss experience with much confidence. The second part of the definition acknowledges that insurance can be effected without a contract but that this is not *usually* the case.[5]

MacDonald   MacDonald does not define insurance but he does state that the "ability of an insurance company to protect a concern against financial harm rests upon its pooling of the concern's risks with the risks of many others." Pooling, therefore, is viewed as an essential condition of insurance.[6]

Mehr and Cammack   According to Mehr and Cammack, insurance "may be defined as a social device for reducing risk by combining a sufficient number of exposure units to make their individual losses collectively predictable. The predictable loss is then shared proportionately by all those in the combination." Uncertainty is reduced *and* losses are shared through this device. However, Mehr and Cammack state specifically that insurance need not involve a transfer of the risk to someone else. Self-insurance, mentioned above in connection with the Bickelhaupt text, satisfies the necessary conditions for insurance if the self-insurer has many units and makes regular deposits to a self-insurance fund.[7]

Mehr and Hedges   In their first text on risk management, Mehr and Hedges developed in more detail the definition advanced by Mehr and Cammack.[8] Their later text does not define insurance or use the term self-insurance. Insurance is viewed as a loss transfer technique.[9]

Williams and Heins These authors define insurance as "a device by means of which the risks of two or more persons or firms are combined through actual or promised contributions to a fund out of which claimants are paid." Like the earlier definitions, this one stresses transfer by the insured and combination by the insurer but it would accept as insurance a combination of as few as two units. Thus, this definition does not require that losses be "collectively predictable," a requirement imposed by some of the earlier definitions.[10] It is observed elsewhere in the Williams and Heins text that many units should be insured to achieve this objective. The number of units required to make the experience predictable depends upon the criteria selected and the nature of the exposure units. Williams and Heins accept two units as sufficient in their desire to make the definition more precise. If more than two units are required, it is impossible to find agreement on what that number should be.

Conclusions Contemporary insurance and risk management authors, like most of their predecessors, would add some combination or pooling of exposure units to Pfeffer's list of necessary and sufficient conditions. Some authors recognize that insurers may, as part of their business, occasionally enter into unique agreements to which the ability to predict losses through combination is not applicable. If written by an insurer, these agreements are properly considered insurance. These ingredients are consistent with the conceptual definition of insurance suggested in this text.

Legal Definitions

Importance of Legal Definitions Legal definitions of insurance are important because they explain what activities are subject to some special statutes, regulations, and common-law principles applicable to "insurance." Whether or not an activity is legally regarded as "insurance" can affect (1) who regulates the activity, (2) the tax status of the purported insurer, and (3) the enforceability of the contract.

Regulation. State insurance departments are charged by state laws with the regulation of insurers. These departments, among other things:

- certify that newly formed insurers comply with special statutes governing organization;
- license out-of-state insurers who meet certain requirements to operate in their state;
- require the filing of detailed annual statements showing the insurer's assets, liabilities, income, losses, and expenses; and
- supervise the general conduct of insurers.

In more than half the states, property and liability insurers must file most proposed premium rate changes with the state insurance department for approval before they can use them. In performing their various functions, state insurance departments often issue regulations with which insurers must comply.

Tax Status. Special federal income tax laws, generally considered more favorable than those applying to other corporations, apply to life insurers. On the other hand, states levy premium taxes on insurers. These taxes may impose an unfavorable cost burden on insurance relative to competing products or services.

Enforceability of the Contract. In interpreting insurance contracts, courts usually find that they are *contracts of adhesion* and, with some types of insurance, *contracts uberrimae fidei* (of the utmost good faith).

If a contract of adhesion is ambiguous, the ambiguity is interpreted in favor of the person (the insured) who was asked to adhere to the contract drafted by another (the insurer).

Contracts uberrimae fidei require both parties to the transaction to disclose all relevant facts. Neither the buyer nor the seller should have to be wary of the other in negotiating their agreement. If, for example, an insured innocently but incorrectly answers a factual question posed by the insurer, the insurer might later be able to deny a claim if the correct answer would have caused the insurer to refuse to issue the insurance. Special rulings also apply to such matters as when an insurance contract goes into effect and under what conditions an insured may have rights that are at variance with policy provisions.

Legal Definitions Examined Denenberg has isolated some of the common threads running through judicial and administrative decisions involving the legal definition of insurance. He concluded that "the line between insurance and non-insurance may be more fluid than many dare imagine."[11] He also concluded that "the problem of separating insurance and non-insurance will continue to grow more complex in nature, operation, and purposes."[12]

According to Denenberg, the most important definitions follow the definitions of four states: Kentucky, California, Massachusetts, and New York.[13] These four definitions, all of which define insurance as a contract rather than a mechanism, are as follows:

Kentucky: Insurance is a contract whereby one undertakes to indemnify another or pay a specified amount upon determinable contingencies.

California: Insurance is a contract whereby one undertakes to indemnify another against loss, damage, or liability arising from a contingent or unknown event.

Massachusetts: A contract of insurance is an agreement by which one party for a consideration promises to pay money or its equivalent, or to do an act valuable to the insured, upon the destruction, loss, or injury of something in which the other party has an interest.

New York: The term "insurance contract"...shall...be deemed to include any agreement or other transaction whereby one party, herein called the insurer, is obligated to confer benefits of pecuniary value upon another party, herein called the insured or the beneficiary, dependent upon the happening of a fortuitous event in which the insured has, or is expected to have at the time of such happening, a material interest which will be adversely affected by the happening of such event. A fortuitous event is any occurrence or failure to occur which is, or is assumed by the parties to be, to a substantial extent beyond the control of either party.

A contract of guarantee or suretyship is an insurance contract... only if made by a guarantor or surety who or which, as such, is doing an insurance business. (To meet this requirement the surety must be engaged in suretyship as a vocation and not as merely incidental to any other legitimate business or activity.)

None of these definitions requires that the insurer combine exposures. All, except possibly Masachusetts, require that the covered event be fortuitous. They differ on whether an insurance contract must be an indemnity contract; i.e., the insured should not benefit from the happening of the event insured against.

Factors Considered in Court Decisions Courts sometimes use these statutory definitions, but it is not unusual to find cases in which they refer to earlier judicial decisions and the writings of insurance experts. Denenberg found that the following factors are sometimes considered in determining whether a transaction is insurance or an entity is engaged in insurance:

1. Nature and operation of the insuring entity:
   - *Need for regulation.* The case for characterizing a transaction or series of transactions as insurance is weakened if the court or other legal agency is not convinced that there is a need to impose insurance regulation. On the other hand, some contracts seem to have been characterized as insurance largely because they required insurance-like regulation.
   - *Ability to comply with regulations.* Although much less important than the perceived need for regulation, some agencies apparently consider whether the proposed insurance regulation would be feasible.
   - *Whether the organization solicits business from the general public.* If the activity is a personal venture, not a business, or limited to insureds tied together by some

other bond (e.g., members of a mercantile association), it may not be considered insurance.

• *Whether the insurance is employed only as an advertising stunt or as a service to stimulate sales.* If the activity is incidental to some other legitimate business activity, it may not be considered insurance.

• *Whether insureds are graded or classified according to the quality of their exposures.* This requirement is not common but it has been important in some cases.

• *Whether there is a scheme to distribute actual losses among a large group of persons.* This pooling or combination requirement is common, but a single isolated transaction could apparently qualify. Some statutory definitions include this characteristic.

• *Whether the contract provides any guarantees for the insureds as a group.* If the insureds bear all the uncertainty concerning the loss, expense, and investment experience, this issue is raised but it seldom prevails. Usually the reasoning is that a mechanism that makes it possible for persons to share losses even if there is no guarantee from others *is* insurance.

2. Nature of the benefit:

• *Whether the contract is merely one to provide services or an insurance contract.* The question is not whether the contract provides services—many insurance contracts do, but whether the insurance promise is significant. This test becomes important in judging service contracts that provide auto repairs, television services, plate glass repairs, and the like.

• *Whether the investment element (cash value) part of a life insurance or annuity contract should be considered separate from the protection element.*

3. Nature of the exposure:

• *Whether the contract covers an exposure to potential loss.* Although the question has arisen occasionally, no legal importance has been attached as to whether the exposure is pure or speculative or whether the exposure is commercially insurable.

4. Name of the transaction:

• *Whether or not it calls itself insurance.* A contract that has insurance features is insurance regardless of the name it bears. Some states have forbidden certain transactions from being advertised as insurance when they are not legally insurance.

5. Nature of the premium:

- *Whether the premium must be separately stated if the insurance is provided as part of a transaction involving additional costs.* It is generally agreed the premium need not be earmarked in such cases.

Denenberg appears to accept as most meaningful—or the most important in practice—the need for regulation, the underlying scheme to distribute the actual losses among a group, the relative importance and significance of service and indemnity in contracts that provide both, and whether the contract covers an exposure to potential loss.

The application of these tests is by no means consistent. Clearly there is no single legal definition of insurance.

The listing of contracts in Exhibit 6-1 that have been found to be insurance or not insurance illustrates the varied legal definitions and interpretations that exist in practice.

WHAT EXPOSURES ARE COMMERCIALLY INSURABLE?

"Private insurers" are organizations under private sponsorship and control that engage in insurance transactions as their principal business. Insurance written by private insurers is called "commercial insurance," to distinguish it from the "governmental insurance" issued by "public insurers" such as the federal government. The following discussion identifies factors that are considered in determining whether a given type of exposure is commercially insurable. Subsequently, several perils are examined in the light of these factors.

Factors to Be Considered in Appraising Commercial Insurability

In determining whether to insure a particular type of exposure, the insurer has two major objectives. First, the insurer wishes to avoid financial "ruin" or serious financial reverses in any single year. Second, the insurer wishes to make a reasonable profit, or avoid a loss, on the average in the long run. To achieve these objectives, the insurer will

Exhibit 6-1
Contracts Found to Be Insurance or Not Insurance *

Insurance	Not Insurance
Watch company promise to provide a new watch if old watch is lost or stolen	Agreement to service and repair burned out and defective parts of fluorescent fixtures
Promise to replace plate glass if broken during the period of contract	Agreement by a bicycle association to clean and repair a member's bicycle and to replace it if stolen
Agreement to reimburse attorneys' fees incurred in defending traffic violation charges	Agreement to defend malpractice suits brought against physicians but not to pay judgments
Undertakings to defend malpractice suits brought against physicians and to pay judgments if any	Guaranty to an employee for services on goods damaged or destroyed by fire
Contracts guaranteeing the value of corporate stock upon a certain date	Written warranty that provides for an adjustment if an article fails from faulty construction or materials
Comprehensive guarantee of auto tires except losses by fire or theft	but expressly excludes happenings not connected with imperfections in the articles themselves
	Promise by a lessor to restore or replace a chattel injured by fire

* Adapted with permission from American Jurisprudence (2nd Ed.) *Insurance*, Secs. 7-15, Vol. 43, pp. 71-79.

ideally provide insurance on pure loss exposures with the following characteristics:

(1) many persons exposed independently to the loss will purchase the insurance;
(2) the exposures will not be too heterogeneous;
(3) the losses will be definite as to cause, time, place, and amount;
(4) the expected loss for each insured during the policy period will be calculable; and
(5) the loss will be accidental from the viewpoint of the insured.

No exposure, however, is ideal in terms of possessing these characteristics. Practical approximations are sufficient. In some instances, insurers are willing to accept substantial departures from ideal conditions because they believe that conditions will improve, they feel the coverage is important to the sale of other coverages that are clearly commercially insurable, they wish to meet an important public need, or they want to make public insurance unnecessary.

Many Insureds Exposed Independently to Loss By our definition in this text, insurance involves the combination of at least two (and usually many more) loss exposures. Assume for the present that an insurer is considering writing insurance on fire damage to dwellings. If that exposure is to be insurable, *many* dwelling owners must be exposed to the loss and the potential loss must be serious enough, relative to the premium that the insurer will have to charge, that many of these owners will purchase insurance. Furthermore, the exposures must be *independent* so that one insured's loss, or the event that causes it, has no effect on the probability of loss to other insureds or on the severity of those losses that do occur.

These conditions are necessary if the law of large numbers is to operate effectively. As indicated in Chapter 5, this law states that, as the number of independent exposure units in, say, a year increases, the annual loss experience tends to approach the expected or long-run average experience. To be more exact, as the number of units increases, it becomes less likely that the annual loss experience will differ from the expected or long-run average experience by more than a specified percentage.

The same principle applies whether the loss experience is expressed in terms of (1) the number of occurrences, or (2) the total dollar losses. To illustrate, assume that Insurer A with 1,000 insured dwelling units expects in an average year to lose twenty dwellings and pay $100,000 in losses. Insurer B with 100,000 insured dwelling units expects in an average year to lose 2,000 dwellings and to pay $10 million in losses. Actually, neither insurer expects to lose *exactly* $100,000 or $10 million. Based on the principles discussed in Chapter 5, it is readily apparent that actual results next year are much more likely to equal the expectations, plus or minus 5 percent, of Insurer B than of Insurer A.

Using the Law of Large Numbers. Insurers can use the law of large numbers in two ways.

First, the insurer can use the law of large numbers to determine the expected dollar loss in the future by observing the past experience of a large number of exposure units. Because the actual loss experience tends to approximate the expected loss experience as the number of exposure units increases, the actual loss experience can serve as a good estimate of the expected loss that will be experienced during the period under observation. Whether this estimate will hold in the future depends upon whether the underlying conditions in the future will differ from those during the experience period. In property and liability insurance, they frequently do.

Second, the insurer may use the law of large numbers in setting a contingency allowance. Assuming the insurer knows the expected dollar loss per period in the long run, by insuring a large number of units the insurer can be fairly certain that the actual experience will be close to the expected experience. The chance that the insurer will have financial problems because of a substantial difference between revenues and expenditures is greatly reduced. Knowing this chance is small, the insurer can also include a smaller allowance in its premiums for unexpected contingencies if it wishes to do so.

One important difference between the two uses of this characteristic is that the contingency allowance use requires that the insurer itself have many insured exposure units. For prediction use, the insurer may rely on units insured in the past by one or more insurers, assuming that these units are of the same type and quality as those it intends to insure. For example, auto insurers frequently base premiums on the data gathered from many insurers by rating bureaus and insurance statistical agencies. Indeed, the insurer may study the experience of *noninsured* units compiled by the government, trade associations, or some other noninsurance organization *if* the type and quality of these units are the same as those the insurer seeks to insure.

How Many Units? To be commercially insurable, "many" insureds must be independently exposed to loss. How many? The number of units an insurer needs to satisfy the law of large numbers was discussed under the heading of "How Large Is Large?" in Chapter 5. Briefly, two issues are involved:

(1) How broad a range between actual loss experience and expected loss experience is the insurer willing to tolerate?
(2) How high a probability does the insurer demand that the actual loss experience will fall within the range the insurer is willing to tolerate?

The narrower the range and the higher the probability demanded, the larger the number of exposure units must be to satisfy this requirement.

Spread Among Different Types of Insurance. To set premiums using past experience, the insurer needs data on the experience of many exposure units. Insurers, however, may be willing to set premiums for some unique exposure on the basis of very little statistical information.

To this point, we have assumed that an insurer is considering writing insurance against only the type of exposure (e.g., dwelling fire) whose insurability is being assessed. If the insurer does or intends to write more than one type of insurance, the requirement of large numbers (but not of independence) can be relaxed for any one type of exposure. Although the insurer would prefer to be able to accurately predict its loss experience next year with respect to each type of exposure, it can operate safely as long as it can predict fairly well its *composite* loss experience. The law of large numbers works in the same way for this composite exposure as it does for each type of exposure. Hence the insurer need not have a large number of exposure units of just one type to satisfy the law of large numbers. It is sufficient if it has a large number of independent exposure units included among all its insureds. Indeed an insurer may for this reason consider a certain type of exposure to be insurable even if it expects to insure only one unit. On the other hand, the smaller the number of exposure units of a given type the insurer covers, the less able it will be to judge how well it is underwriting that type of exposure.

Summary. An insurer intending to insure only one type of exposure should consider whether there will be a sufficient number of independent insured exposure units for its loss experience to be reasonably stable. If it intends to write many different types of exposure, there must be a sufficient number of independent insured exposure units of all types combined. In either case, there must be a sufficient body of experience on past exposures if the premiums are to be statistically based. Of course the premiums need not be based entirely on past experience, but the type of exposure becomes more attractive to an insurer the stronger the statistical base. If the past experience is too limited to be useful for rate-making purposes and unlikely to improve, the expected loss allowance in the premium is subject to considerable error.

Exposure Units That Are Not Too Heterogeneous To be insurable, the many independent exposure units insured should not be too heterogeneous. They should face about the same probability of an occurrence and the same potential loss severity. This condition holds whether the insurer intends to insure only one type of exposure or several different types. The greater the variation among exposure units in the probabilities of an occurrence and the magnitudes of the potential dollar losses, the more exposure units the insurer must have to achieve a certain degree of accuracy in predicting its future loss experience. For example, if an insurer insures 100 dwellings, 90 of which are worth $50,000 and 10 of which are worth $200,000, the relative variation in the potential losses will be greater than if the insurer insures 100 dwellings, all of which are worth $65,000, even though the total insured values are the same ($6.5 million) in each case.

The problem would be even more evident if 99 of the dwellings were worth $10,000 and one were worth $5.51 million instead of 100 being worth $65,000 each. The loss of the $5.51 million dwelling would be equivalent to losing 551 $10,000 dwellings.

Losses Definite as to Cause, Time, Place, and Amount The losses that are insured should be fairly definite as to cause, time, place, and amount. This minimizes loss adjustment problems and leads to accurate loss prediction. When a loss occurs, a claims adjuster must determine whether the event is insured under the insurance contract and, if so, how much the insurer should pay. In determining whether an event is insured the adjuster determines:

(1) whether the property or activity involved was covered;
(2) whether the cause of the loss was covered;
(3) whether the consequences of the particular loss (property damage, interruption in gross earnings, investigation expenses, defense of liability claims) were covered;
(4) whether the event involved covered circumstances; and
(5) whether the event occurred during a covered time period.

Chapter 10 contains a detailed study of "insured events."

The less doubt there is as to what caused the loss and when and where the event occurred, the less controversial the settlement process will be. Further, the more question there is as to the *amount of recovery* provided for in the contract, the more controversy, dissatisfaction, and expense that will be incurred in adjusting claims. Therefore, to be insurable, the amount of the insured loss should be definite or subject to relatively precise determination. How this is accomplished will be discussed in Chapters 11, 12, and 13.

Expected Loss During the Policy Period Calculable If an insurer decides to insure a particular type of exposure, it must be able to establish premiums that will pay losses and expenses and also provide a reasonable profit. To establish such premiums, the insurer must estimate the expected losses during the next policy period for each group to be charged a different premium. To meet this criterion, the underlying conditions must be essentially the same during the policy period as in the past, or the insurer must be able to predict the change in the underlying conditions and in the expected losses. Thus, this condition favors an exposure where changes occur slowly and in predictable ways or not at all.

Loss Accidental from Point of View of Insured The final condition for an exposure to be insurable is that the loss must be accidental from the viewpoint of the insured. The law of large numbers requires that the loss be accidental. This condition simply means that the loss is not an intended result of the insured's activities and, from a statistical viewpoint, is a random occurrence. Otherwise, the law of large numbers is not operative.

Institutional Constraints

Even though an insurer may decide that a particular type of exposure is commercially insurable, it may be unable to write that type of insurance because of several institutional constraints.[14]

Regulatory Constraints Most state laws prohibit the writing of life insurance by property and liability insurers and vice versa. This constraint can be bypassed in various ways—e.g., by writing the other type of insurance through a subsidiary. Before the passage of multiple line legislation, a much more serious constraint existed. Property and liability insurers were compartmentalized into (1) fire and marine insurers, and (2) casualty insurers. Fire and marine insurers could not write casualty insurance and casualty insurers could not write fire and marine insurance. Even this constraint, however, could be avoided by such devices as joint ownership and control or the formation of a subsidiary.

Many state laws also list the kinds of insurance that can be written by any insurer. If the insurance under investigation is not on the list, it cannot be written. Many lists include "any line approved by the state insurance commissioner," in which case lines not specifically mentioned may be approved—but only after a process that may not be worth the effort. This limitation was more serious in the past.

State laws prescribe the minimum capital and surplus a domestic stock insurer must have to transact business. Similarly these laws prescribe minimum surplus requirements for domestic mutual insurers. These minimum requirements vary with the kinds of insurance the insurer intends to write. Some requirements may be so high that an insurer will forgo writing a line it would otherwise prefer to include in its portfolio.

Another factor that may deter entry into a new line is how state insurance departments regulate rates for the field the insurer is about to enter. Certain lines sometimes require substantial red tape, making entrance into those lines much less attractive. The effect of regulation on the profitability of insurers in that line must also be considered.

Other Constraints An insurer may wish to enter a certain line but may conclude that its present *personnel*—such as actuaries, underwriters, and claims adjusters—are not capable of writing and servicing this new line at a profit. Hiring new personnel may not be easy, and the reactions of existing personnel to new people, especially if they command higher salaries, may cause some serious problems.

Reinsurance facilities for the new line may also be needed. The interest of the insurer in writing the new exposure may be conditional on its ability to protect itself against catastrophe losses (which may occur even among exposures that for practical purposes are independent) and against substantial losses on single exposures.

Financing may also be a problem. To write more insurance at what the insurer considers an acceptable premium-to-net-worth ratio may require the insurer to seek more funds from its stockholders or to generate more surplus from internal operations.

Custom and tradition cannot be ignored. Most insurers hesitate to pioneer in areas that have not been successfully tested by other insurers. Despite the fact that the exposure under consideration appears to meet all the requirements established for a commercially insurable exposure, there may be a natural reluctance to enter a new area.

Finally, a line of insurance may confront the insurer with great *potential variation in underwriting results.* In the face of severe pricing difficulties, an insurer may choose not to enter into the line at all rather than expose its net worth to severe depletion.

Other Factors Affecting Insurability   Insurers often insure exposures that fail to satisfy the ideal conditions listed above. Insurers may differ in their assessment of the seriousness of the problems involved in writing a particular type of insurance.

Some exposures may not satisfy insurability conditions when they are first written, but are expected to do so with the passage of time. For example, the insurance may have to be written for several years before the insurer can base its rates on experience. Other exposures are different from what an insurer seeks ideally, but it may still issue such insurance for some other compelling reason. For example, the insurer's sense of public responsibility to meet an important need may be persuasive. An insurer also may include an unprofitable line in its portfolio to facilitate the sale of profitable lines of insurance. Finally, insurers may write an otherwise unattractive line because of concern about the government entering the field if private insurers do not meet the need. Illustrations of each of these factors are provided later in this chapter.

Publicly Insurable Exposures

Insurers sponsored and controlled by a government may be able to write insurance on exposures that private insurers reject as uninsurable. Governments have an advantage over private insurers, because governments can (1) require the purchase of insurance and (2) subsidize losses from insurance operations.

Compulsory Insurance   If the insurance provided by the public insurer is compulsory, the insurer will have a large number of insured exposure units regardless of the premium that must be charged. Furthermore, the insurer need not be able to estimate the expected losses of the insured in the short run. If the program is compulsory, the insurer can raise the premiums next year to make up for losses this year without fear of losing some of its insureds, particularly those who might find the costs high relative to the benefits.

If the plan is compulsory, the public insurer may set premiums at a level that will enable it to meet its expected losses over a period of years instead of in the short run. Compulsion also permits the insurer to reduce the number of rating classes to as few as one, thus requiring some insureds to subsidize others to a greater extent than would occur in a more refined classification system.

Government Subsidies   Even if the program is not compulsory, a public insurer may be willing to write insurance on an exposure that is not commercially insurable because it is financially able to absorb a bad year that would cripple a commercial insurer. Furthermore, as a matter of public policy, a public insurer might choose to subsidize insurance it provides in order to maintain affordability.

Evaluation of Certain Exposures

In this section, characteristics of seven exposures are matched against the characteristics suggested for ideally insurable exposures. These exposures involve losses from (1) fire, (2) windstorm, (3) flood, (4) premature death, (5) sickness, (6) unemployment, and (7) war. In most cases, the "exposure" is narrowed to make the analysis most relevant. For example, "fire" is discussed in terms of fire damage to dwellings.

Fire   For over 300 years, fire insurance on dwellings has been commercially available. The exposure is obviously insurable, but it is helpful to review how the exposure meets the criteria established for commercial insurability.

Many Independent Insureds.   Many dwellings exist and each is exposed to loss by fire. Most dwelling owners will probably purchase insurance because the maximum probable loss is serious and the expected loss is low enough to make the premium attractive.

The exposure units are not entirely independent because a fire that starts in one part of a state could conceivably spread to another. The chance for such a catastrophe is so small that for practical purposes it can be ignored. On the other hand, the chance that a fire at one end of a city block will spread throughout the block is too high to ignore, especially if the block contains many dwellings close to one another. Insurers can handle this situation in at least two ways. They can refuse to insure more than one dwelling in a city block. Alternatively, they can insure two or more units exposed to common fire losses but arrange to transfer part of the combined exposure to a reinsurer. Thus, for practical purposes, this criterion can be satisfied.

Homogeneity. Dwellings are not homogeneous exposure units. Their expected losses vary according to such factors as the value of the dwelling, its construction (brick, frame, or fire resistive), the number of families in the dwelling, and the fire protection available. Dwellings are not so heterogeneous, however, that an insurer cannot predict fairly accurately the combined loss experience of a large number of various types. Some rating classes contain few dwellings and their loss experience during the recent past is so sparse that it generates an inadequate statistical base for estimating future losses. Nevertheless, insurers have been willing to establish rates for such classes on the basis of limited data and informed judgment. Although their actuarial foundation is weak, insurers have found these rates acceptable.

Definite Loss. Fire losses to dwellings are fairly definite as to cause, time, place, and amount. In some cases, it is difficult to distinguish fire damage from damage caused by other perils, such as lightning or explosion. This seldom presents a problem because property insurance policies usually also cover such related perils. The time may also be questioned if the fire occurs at a time or place where no one can determine when it started. However, an hour or so usually makes no difference as to whether there is coverage. Place may be questioned if property is insured only at a specific location or within a specified area. Valuation of the loss is the major loss adjustment problem in fire insurance. If the insured has replacement cost coverage, the insurer and the insured must agree on the cost of a new item. If he or she has actual cash value coverage, the insured and insurer must agree on the amount to be deducted from the replacement cost for depreciation. Although these problems cannot be ignored, insurers have found them to be manageable.

Calculable. As noted earlier, the requirement that expected losses be calculable in the short run is affected by the number of independent exposure units to be insured, the availability of statistical data on past losses, and the heterogeneity of the exposure units. The question here is whether the underlying conditions are sufficiently stable or change so slowly or predictably that recent experience is representative of what will happen in the near future. Usually these conditions are satisfied by dwellings exposed to fire losses, but inflation has posed serious difficulties in adjusting fire insurance rates. Arson trends are also upward. Insurers worry about these developments but they do not believe they make the exposure commercially uninsurable.

Accidental. The insured may cause the fire intentionally. Insurers, however, satisfy the requirement that the loss be accidental from the viewpoint of the insured by not paying insureds who intentionally burn their properties. Although the standard fire insurance policy does not exclude such losses, insurers clearly do not intend to pay them and courts have upheld this position. Still, the danger remains that some insureds will be able to conceal their intent and collect when they should not. Through careful loss adjustment, exchange of information concerning suspicious fires, and prosecution of arsonist-insureds, insurers seek to minimize this problem.

Conclusions. For practical purposes the exposure of dwellings to fire losses is commercially insurable. However, insurers may have to engage in selective underwriting, purchase reinsurance, combine in the same rating class some heterogeneous exposures, accept subjective elements in loss adjustments (especially property loss valuations), include inflation trend factors in their rates, and discourage insureds from intentionally causing losses. Among the various lines of insurance, fire insurance on dwellings is considered one of the safest in which to engage.

Windstorm Although windstorm insurance on dwellings was not written until the latter half of the nineteenth century, it is readily available today.

Many Independent Insureds. The exposure of dwellings to windstorm losses does meet the requirement that there are many such exposure units, most of which can be expected to be interested in insurance. Whether these units are independently exposed to losses is more questionable than in the case of fire. Windstorms, notably tornadoes and hurricanes, tend to affect many buildings at the same time. Hurricanes may enter the United States from the Gulf of Mexico, travel northward to the Middle Atlantic and New England states, and exit into the North Atlantic, leaving a long, wide band of destruction. As with fire insurance, insurers can take into account this feature of windstorm insurance through selective underwriting, reinsurance, and marketing over a wide geograhical area. The task, however, is more difficult and requires somewhat different solutions (such as catastrophe reinsurance with much higher limits). Furthermore, insurers who restrict their activities to a few counties or a single state may well

Exhibit 6-2
Tornado Losses in Selected States, 1975-1979 *

State	Tornadoes	Deaths	Injuries
Alabama	131	25	427
Alaska	0	0	0
California	29	0	5
District of Columbia	0	0	0
Kentucky	30	2	85
Mississippi	116	21	608
Oklahoma	188	16	340
Oregon	4	0	0
Rhode Island	0	0	0
Texas	712	68	2,019
Countrywide Total	4,245	284	7,517

* Adapted with permission from *Insurance Facts*, 1980-81 Edition (New York: Insurance Information Institute), p. 52.

decide not to write (or even be prohibited by law from writing) windstorm insurance.

Homogeneity. Windstorm exposures are not homogeneous. As was true for fire insurance, the units exposed to loss vary greatly in value. Insurers combat this problem by limiting the amount of insurance written and by purchasing appropriate reinsurance.

A more serious problem is the diversity among geographical areas in the frequency and severity of windstorms. For example, during the five-year period 1975-1979, there were 4,247 tornadoes in the United States, causing 284 deaths. The number of tornadoes in some selected states is shown in Exhibit 6-2. Windstorm insurance premiums reflect this diversity by varying rates among geographical areas. Also, windstorm insurance is sold as part of a broader package of perils so that the variation in windstorm exposure among geographical areas might be averaged in with the variation of other perils. An example is the perils combined under "extended coverage." This packaging approach has also extended the sale of windstorm insurance to insureds who might otherwise reason that their exposure to windstorm is too small to justify the purchase of protection against that peril, thus reducing the problem of adverse selection.

Definite Loss. As with fire losses, windstorm losses are fairly definite as to cause, time, place, and amount. The problems that exist are similar to those presented in the analysis of fire exposures.

Calculable. Except for the effects of inflation, which have been noted in connection with fire insurance, expected windstorm losses in the short run are much more calculable on a national basis than on a state level. Therefore, as noted above, windstorm insurance is frequently combined with other types of insurance to improve predictability. Also, insurers can include in their premium a catastrophe loading which, when added to the normal windstorm loss component, will produce enough premium to cover losses in the short run and should in the longer run cover both normal and catastrophe losses in individual states.

Accidental. Windstorm exposures do satisfy the requirement that the losses be accidental from the viewpoint of the insured. Insureds cannot create a windstorm. They can, however, claim that windstorm caused a loss that it did not, or that the damage was more extensive than it actually was.

Flood Buildings and most personal property at fixed locations are generally regarded as commercially uninsurable against loss from flood. (Insurance is available, but the National Flood Insurance Program is not *commercial* insurance. This program is described in Chapter 7.) Why is this the case?

Many Independent Insureds. There is a large number of units exposed to flood losses and the loss is serious enough to create a strong interest in insurance. The independence criterion, however, is not satisfied because typically a flood affects many units at the same time. Because buildings are not movable, the lack of independence is more a problem in insuring buildings than in insuring personal property. Thus, certain types of personal property—such as autos, boats, jewelry and coin collections, property in transit, and contractors' equipment—can be insured against flood loss as part of a coverage package that includes many perils. However, broad classes of personal property—such as household contents and business inventories, fixtures, and machinery—that essentially remain in one place are subject to the same lack of independence as buildings. This analysis relates to buildings and the contents normally situated therein.

Homogeneity. The units exposed to flood losses are not homogeneous. The differences in value could be handled through selective underwriting and reinsurance as they are in other types of property insurance. The difference in the quality of the exposure, some areas being much more flood-prone than others, could be handled through differential pricing. However, the statistical base becomes weaker as the number of rating classes increases.

Definite Loss. Flood losses are fairly definite as to cause, time, place, and amount. The problems are those common to many property lines.

Calculable. Aggregate national expected flood losses to personal property and to buildings are somewhat predictable in the short run, but not for each geographical area. Insurers would have to be satisfied with predicting their losses in local areas over a longer period of time than they would prefer. The major problem is that the premium on properties in flood-prone areas would be much greater than prospective insureds would be willing to pay. Consequently, the criterion of *many insureds* would probably be violated. Despite the seriousness of the potential loss, few persons would be willing to pay the high premiums commercial flood insurers would impose. Because there would be few insureds, predicting their expected losses would be almost impossible.

Accidental. Flood losses are generally accidental from the viewpoint of the insured; but an insured, alerted to an impending flood, may ignore the warning intentionally, and not take steps to minimize the damage. The occurrence of loss, however, is beyond the insured's control.

Premature Death Exposure to premature death is clearly a commercially insurable exposure. In early Greece and Rome, societies developed that furnished burial insurance and cash funds for beneficiaries. The commercial insuring of lives has been traced back to the sixteenth century. Yet, even this well established line does not perfectly meet all criteria.

Many Independent Insureds. The potential economic loss from premature death is so great that, given a reasonable premium, one would expect many to seek life insurance. While a single event such as a plane crash or an epidemic may cause the death of numerous persons—thus threatening the independence criterion—catastrophe possibilities cause little concern in the writing of life insurance.

Homogeneity. Exposures to death are heterogeneous, the major factors affecting the chance of death being the age, gender, activities and physical condition of the individual. Heterogeneity does not cause serious problems because enough data exists to establish a number of rating classes. The heterogeneity among insured units in each class is not so great as to make the combined loss experience unacceptably volatile.

Definite Loss. Exposure to premature death rates high on the criterion that the loss be definite as to cause, time, and place. A few relatively minor problems do exist. For example, is a missing person dead? Did a person die before a term insurance policy expired? On the other hand, the magnitude of the financial loss is not definite. Estimates that can be made of the loss of future earning power (the major loss to families caused by death) are too imprecise to serve as a basis for adjusting life insurance losses. Funeral expenses are more tangible but the insurer would have to prescribe the type of services to be covered. To resolve these problems, life insurers promise to pay a stated dollar amount when death occurs. The actual financial loss is not a basis for payment. Life insurance underwriters try, however, to keep the amount of life insurance written in a reasonable relationship to the prospective income loss of the new insured.

Calculable. Expected life insurance losses are calculable in the short run. Indeed, no other exposure comes closer to meeting this criterion than the exposure to death. Because the insurer delivers a stated amount when death occurs during the policy period, inflation does not cause the problems noted earlier for property insurance rates. Furthermore, the probability of death at a given age changes very slowly over time. Predictions based on standard mortality tables are quite accurate. On the other hand, life insurance prices are set and typically apply over much longer periods than property and liability insurance prices. If an insurer issues a straight life insurance policy, it must set a premium to be paid for the rest of the insured's life. Even so, conditions are usually stable enough to permit acceptable premiums.

Accidental. Although a person may intentionally cause a loss by committing suicide, state laws require the insurer to pay the face amount unless the suicide occurs within one or two years (depending on the state) after the policy was put in force. The suicide possibility conflicts with the requirement that losses be accidental from the viewpoint of the insured. However, the one- or two-year period during which the insurer can successfully deny suicide claims reduces the chance that a person will purchase insurance with suicide in mind. Insurers may be unable to prove some suicides during the first year or two. This resembles the problems involved with proving arson, but there is a much greater natural reluctance to commit suicide than to burn a building. For these reasons, suicide claims are not considered a major barrier to writing life insurance.

Sickness The sickness exposure is insured in conjunction with health insurance. Despite the commercial importance of sickness insurance, it poses serious problems for insurers.

Many Independent Insureds. All persons are exposed to sickness, and the potential income loss and medical expenses are usually serious enough to prompt individuals to seek insurance. Independence, however, is a problem because some diseases are easily transmitted from one person to another and tend to affect many persons at the same time. Even so, this is a relatively minor difficulty.

Homogeneity. In this regard, the sickness exposure closely resembles the premature death exposure previously discussed.

Definite Loss. The principal difficulty in writing insurance for illness is that it may be almost impossible to determine whether a person is sick. Sickness is a matter of degree and the line between it and normal health is sometimes difficult to define. One individual may claim to be ill while another under the same circumstances goes on about normal activities. There is seldom a single type of easy-to-isolate event that can be identified as the cause of loss as there is in the case of death or accidental injury. The sickness exposure, in the opinion of many insurers, is not definite as to cause, time, and place.

Sickness disability income losses are made definite in amount by providing specified dollar benefits. Medical expenses are usually related to actual expenses incurred. For practical purposes, therefore, the sickness exposure meets the test that the potential losses be definite as to amount.

Calculable. Sickness losses are difficult to forecast. Varying definitions of "sickness" are used, but rates should be based on the same definitions of sickness and disability that the insurer expects to use in the future. In practice, this is difficult to achieve. Epidemics or other unusual events may cause claims frequency or severity to fluctuate but this is usually within tolerable limits. Inflation is also troublesome in pricing sickness insurance covering medical expenses.

Accidental. An insured can cause himself or herself to become sick but few persons go to this extreme. On the other hand, some insureds feign illness successfully and collect benefits. Through surveillance and requiring independent medical evaluation, insurers can usually keep this problem under control.

Conclusions. Because of the difficulties associated with the sickness exposure some insurers do not write sickness insurance even though they provide accidental injury insurance. Sickness insurance is, however, a major private insurance line and is the major line for many insurers. They do not consider it to be more troublesome than many other lines they might have entered. Others, perhaps the majority, write sickness insurance but do not consider the exposure to be an attractive one from an insurability viewpoint. They may feel that the availability of the coverage is important to the sale of other life insurance or accidental injury insurance products they sell. The availability of sickness insurance also helps to maintain the private insurance market by providing a socially needed service.

Unemployment The financial loss to individuals from unemployment is considered commercially uninsurable.

Many Independent Insureds. All workers face the possibility of unemployment. However, although large numbers of workers are exposed to loss, the exposure as a whole does not sufficiently meet the test of independence. An economic recession affects many workers at the same time, causing national unemployment rates to rise. "Structural" conditions such as the decline of an industry or the movement of most firms in an industry from one area of the country to another may cause unemployment rates in an industry or an area to rise. This lack of independence means that an insurer might suffer catastrophic losses because many of its insureds could be unemployed at the same time.

Homogeneity. Unemployment exposures are highly heterogeneous and the establishment of equitable rating would be made difficult by fluctuations in regional or industry losses (even though national unemployment rates might be both low and stable over the same period).

Definite Loss. The unemployment exposure is fairly definite as to the cause and timing of losses. It should be a relatively simple matter to determine whether a person has lost a job and when that loss occurred. On the other hand, an insurer probably would not want to pay benefits to those discharged for good cause and certainly not to those terminating voluntarily. Defining these causes and determining whether they were in fact the reason for the discharge creates considerable uncertainty in the ability to agree that a covered loss has occurred.

The amount of the loss could be difficult to determine. If the objective is to pay the unemployed person a certain percentage of his or her lost wage, this amount can be estimated fairly accurately in the short run by using the most recent wage as a base. However, wage loss becomes more difficult to estimate the longer unemployment continues. Would the person's wages have risen or fallen in the absence of unemployment? Has the person done everything that might reasonably be expected to find another job? Otherwise, the duration of the benefit may be longer than the insurer intended. Finally, if the person had not been discharged, would he or she have left the job voluntarily during the period unemployment benefits are paid? All of these problems, while solvable, would require considerable care and special attention and would result in relatively high administrative costs.

Calculable. A major difficulty with the unemployment exposure is that expected losses in the short run are almost impossible to predict. Economic conditions are constantly changing, causing variations in "expected" or average unemployment rates for the nation, industries, and areas, as well as for individual employers. Witness the wide range of predictions when economists forecast next year's unemployment rates. Over longer intervals, the expected losses become more predictable but are still subject to considerable error in prediction.

Accidental. In many cases it is difficult to determine whether a person resigns or is voluntarily discharged. Unemployment insurance could create a moral hazard that would increase this problem.

Conclusions. On balance, private insurers have found the unemployment exposure not to be commercially insurable for two principle reasons: (1) individual units are highly interdependent, creating significant potential for catastrophic loss, and (2) expected losses are extremely difficult to predict, particularly in the short run. Private insurers have sometimes reconsidered this position but to date unemployment insurance has been written only under very special circumstances and only then in conjunction with other types of insurance. For example, one insurer did promise to continue mortgage payments, subject to some maximum amount, for home buyers who died, became disabled, or became unemployed.

On the other hand, unemployment insurance is one of the most important forms of public insurance. Each of the fifty states plus the District of Columbia has an unemployment insurance program. Special programs also exist at the federal level. Government insurers have the great advantage that they can require certain employers (the premium payors) to participate and remain in the program no matter how much contribution rates might be increased to cover future expected losses and deficiencies in past contributions. The government insurer may also be able to operate at a loss for a period of time. Consequently, it need not be as concerned about fluctuations in short-term unemployment. Catastrophic losses also pose less of a problem.

Private supplemental unemployment plans exist in certain industries, such as the auto and glass industries. These plans provide additional benefits to workers receiving public unemployment insurance benefits. Financed by annual contributions by employers, these plans encountered serious problems during recent periods of recession.

War War losses are excluded under most property and liability insurance contracts because the exposure is not considered insurable. The major exception is "war risk" insurance sold by marine insurers on ships and their cargoes. Even this insurance typically becomes unavailable or available only from government insurers after hostilities are imminent or actually start.

Many Independent Insureds. Although many units are exposed to war losses, the exposures are not independent. Many, many units can be affected at the same time, resulting in aggregate losses far beyond the ability of the private insurance sector to absorb. Furthermore, during wartime the cost may be so high that few persons could afford or wish to purchase war insurance. War insurance is available commercially on hulls and their cargoes because these movable, separated items are much less subject to catastrophic losses than are buildings and their contents.

Homogeneity. The heterogeneity of the exposure is also a problem, the likelihood of war losses varying greatly among units.

Definite Loss. War exposures meet as well as most property exposures the condition that the losses be definite as to cause, time, place, and amount.

Calculable. Expected losses from war are almost impossible to predict over any time interval, thereby creating severe pricing difficulties. Government insurers writing this coverage usually must be prepared to absorb annual fluctuations and, for public policy reasons, are willing to subsidize the cost of the coverage to insureds.

Accidental. On this criterion, the war exposure fares well. The typical insured is not likely to bring about a war.

Summary No exposure is commercially insurable in an ideal sense. Some exposures meet the stated conditions better than others, and insurers differ in their assessments of a particular exposure's characteristics. Institutional restraints (such as the minimum capital and surplus required to write certain lines or the type of government rate regulation) may influence the decision. Even if an insurer decides that a certain exposure does not meet one or more of the conditions prescribed for a commercially insurable exposure, it may still decide to insure the exposure if it expects conditions to improve, believes insurance against the exposure to be socially desirable, believes it would improve the sales of other lines of insurance, or wishes to avert government entry into this field. Exposures that are not insurable commercially may be insured by public insurers who can make the insurance compulsory and who may elect to subsidize the operation with public funds.

Seven exposures have been analyzed to determine the extent to which they are commercially insurable. Of those examined, the two that best satisfy the established criteria were dwellings exposed to fire and persons exposed to death. Even these exposures, however, pose certain problems that insurers deem minor enough to accept or capable of being handled through special techniques such as reinsurance.

At the opposite extreme are buildings and their contents exposed to flood damage, persons exposed to unemployment, and property exposed to war damage, all of which private insurers have considered uninsurable. Flood insurance on buildings and their contents is provided under a subsidized public insurance program. War damage insurance and unemployment insurance are also underwritten by public insurers. Of the other two exposures, windstorm is generally considered commercially insurable but it poses more problems than fire insurance. Opinions differ widely on whether the sickness exposure should be considered commercially insurable. Much sickness insurance is written, however, by insurers who do so willingly and even eagerly, and by others who do not regard the exposure highly but write it for other reasons.

TYPES OF PRIVATE INSURER

Most insurers are private; some are public. Private insurers are owned and managed by private citizens, public insurers by the government. This section describes seven ways of classifying private insurers. Public insurers will be discussed in Chapter 7.

Private insurers can be classified according to various criteria including but not limited to (1) legal form of organization, (2) domicile, (3) admission status, (4) types of insurance written, (5) types of customers served, (6) marketing system, and (7) pricing system.

Legal Form of Organization

Private insurers may be organized as (1) proprietary or (2) cooperative insurers.

Proprietary Insurers Proprietary insurers are owned and controlled by some person or persons who need not be, and usually are not, insured by the insurer. These owners receive the profits and bear the losses. Proprietary insurers are either (1) stock insurers or (2) Lloyds associations, such as Lloyd's of London.

Stock Insurers. Stock insurers are corporations engaged in the insurance business and owned by stockholders. The stockholders elect the board of directors that appoints the executive officers, who in turn hire the other employees. Although ultimate control rests in the hands of the stockholders, most stock insurers are effectively controlled by the board of directors, which usually includes some of the executive officers. The stockholders share the gains or losses from operations through stock dividends declared by the board of directors and through increases or declines in the market value of their shares of stock.

Stock insurers write almost three-fourths of the property and liability insurance premiums written by United States private insurers. Stock property and liability insurers range from small insurers writing only one line of insurance to large insurers writing practically all kinds of insurance.

Stock life insurance companies account for slightly more than one-half of the total life insurance in force. The vast majority of life insurance companies formed during the last quarter century have been organized as stockholder-owned corporations, bringing the current proportion of stockholder-owned life insurance companies to more than 90 percent.

Lloyd's of London. Lloyd's of London is not an insurance company or a corporation in the American sense of the word. Lloyd's is an association of private underwriters, each of whom backs insurance contracts on a basis of personal and unlimited liability. Lloyd's underwriting members are grouped into over 450 syndicates varying in size from a handful to over a thousand names. Each syndicate is managed by an "agent" who is responsible for appointing the appropriate underwriting specialist to accept insureds at Lloyd's on behalf of the syndicate members.

Although for practical purposes a Lloyd's syndicate operates as a single unit, its liabilities, expenses, profits, and losses are distributed in a predetermined proportion among all syndicate members. Lloyd's syndicates provide a market for worldwide insurance that is placed with them by representatives of brokerage houses accredited by the Society.

The Society (known as the Corporation of Lloyd's since it was incorporated by Act of the United Kingdom Parliament in 1871), is a nonprofit organization that provides the facilities for its members to do business. These facilities include the premises—principally the desks (or "boxes") in the large marble-lined hall known as the Underwriting Room—and a variety of central services such as the gathering and dissemination of information, policy signing, and data processing. In addition, the Society, through its management committee, lays down stringent requirements for the financial standing of underwriting members and the conduct of their business at Lloyd's.

The name "Lloyd's" derives from a seventeenth century London coffee house owned by one Edward Lloyd, who encouraged a clientele made up mainly of merchants, shipowners, and sea captains. In an age of poor communications and scanty newspapers, the coffee houses provided an excellent rendezvous to hear the latest news, exchange useful gossip, and do business. Three hundred years ago, the insurance of ships and cargoes was done by wealthy individuals very much as a profitable sideline to their main business. The broker with an insurance contract to place would take it around the coffee houses for subscription by men of substance who could be relied on to meet their share of a claim, if necessary to the full extent of their personal means.

During the eighteenth century, marine underwriting centered more and more on Lloyd's Coffee House, until, in 1771, the leading merchants who gathered there elected a committee to find and manage more exclusive premises. In 1774 they moved into the Royal Exchange and Lloyd's left the coffee-house era for good.

Since then, the Committee of Lloyd's has assumed increasing responsibility for maintaining the security of a Lloyd's policy and ensuring that those doing business there are of impeccable financial standing. As of 1980, there were some 18,500 Lloyd's underwriting members from 59 countries. Seventeen thousand are British, Commonwealth, or European Economic Community nationals, and nearly 1,200 are United States citizens.

Lloyd's members are men and women from many walks of life and professions. The majority are "external names" and take no active part in the Lloyd's day-to-day operations. About 17 percent of the membership actually works at Lloyd's either for underwriting syndicates or brokerage firms, and of these "working names" about 250 are "active" underwriters responsible for the acceptance of insurance on behalf of their syndicate members. The active underwriter may also be an underwriting agent and in any event will often be closely involved in the conduct of an underwriting agency.

Assuming he or she is not an active underwriter or one of an underwriter's deputies, the syndicate name agrees to leave the day-to-day conduct of his or her underwriting affairs in the hands of an agent.

Membership in Lloyd's provides a unique opportunity for the private individual to participate in insurance transfers, allowing the member's personal assets to be used as security against his or her underwriting liabilities. In return, however, his or her entire personal fortune is pledged to meet underwriting commitments. For this reason the member's assets must be substantial and must be in part deposited with the Society. This deposit is in cash, approved securities, or a letter of credit and is held by Lloyd's Corporation for the duration of membership. It is returned only after all a member's underwriting commitments have been met.

The member's deposit is one of several links in the chain of security behind a Lloyd's policy. Others include a rigorous yearly scrutiny of syndicate accounts and a central fund (to which all members contribute) for the protection of policyholders should a member's resources prove inadequate. A candidate for underwriting membership has to be sponsored by an existing member and the candidate's admission is at the discretion of a Lloyd's Committee. In this respect membership is rather like that of a private club.

On election, a member usually joins syndicates specializing in each of Lloyd's four main insurance categories: marine, aviation, United Kingdom, or automobile and nonmarine (i.e., property/casualty, property-liability). Some syndicates are acknowledged market leaders whose active underwriters are expert in assessing a particular type of exposure; others are content to follow a good lead. Lead underwriters usually dictate the rate, terms, and conditions of the contract. Competition for the lead among Lloyd's syndicates, and between Lloyd's and the insurance company market in London, is strong.

Lloyd's underwriters have a reputation for flexibility and being able to tailor coverage to the needs of their insureds. The great concentration of insurance expertise in the Room at Lloyd's makes it certain that, if an exposure is insurable, it will be placed in a very short time. Brokers can let their clients know the rate, terms, and conditions of most insurance contracts in the Lloyd's market more quickly than anywhere in the world.

Lloyd's is licensed for all lines in only a small number of the United States. In the other states they function only as excess or surplus lines underwriters. (Excess or surplus lines refer to types or amounts of insurance not available from companies licensed to do business in a state.) Nonetheless, the United States accounts for about 60 percent of Lloyd's premiums. United States insurers are among the principal buyers of reinsurance from Lloyd's.

All placements of insurance at Lloyd's must be made through a Lloyd's broker. These brokers vary greatly in size, some operating worldwide. The bulk of the United States business is handled by about thirty of these brokers.

Domestic Lloyds Associations. Lloyds associations domiciled in the United States resemble Lloyd's of London in their basic approach but they differ greatly from Lloyd's of London in many operating characteristics and in importance. The number of individual underwriters is much smaller, their liability is often limited, and their personal net worth is generally much less than that of Lloyd's of London underwriters. Lloyds associations do not operate through syndicates; instead, one attorney-in-fact speaks for all the underwriters. Only about thirty Lloyds associations exist. The insurance written by about half these associations is completely reinsured by some other insurer. Most specialize in fire insurance, auto physical damage insurance, or liability insurance other than auto liability insurance.

Cooperative Insurers Cooperative insurers are owned and ultimately controlled by their insureds. The two major types of cooperative insurers are (1) mutuals and (2) reciprocal exchanges. In addition, several other cooperative insurance organizations that have developed in the United States will be discussed briefly in this section.

Mutual Insurers. Mutual insurers are corporations owned by their insureds. Insureds elect the board of directors who appoint the executive officers. The latter hire the other employees. In practice few insureds exercise their right to vote, leaving effective control of the insurer in the hands of the board of directors. The board usually includes some executive officers.

Mutual insurers can be subdivided according to how their insureds share in the operating results of the insurer. *Assessment mutuals* may make a charge to insureds for losses and expenses *after* they have been incurred.

The most important class of mutuals is the *advance premium mutuals*. These mutuals have no legal right to assess their policy-holders. Because state regulators will not permit mutuals to issue nonassessable policies unless their policyholders' surplus (the difference between their assets and their liabilities) exceeds a certain amount, advance premium mutuals tend to be larger and more financially secure (except for the safety valve provided by the right to assess) than the assessment mutuals.

Advance premium mutuals may in turn be divided into two subclasses. What until recently was the dominant form of advance premium mutuals pays dividends with some regularity, but at the discretion of the board of directors. Indeed, most of these insurers charge more than they expect they will need; consequently they plan to return some of the excess premium as dividends on a regular basis. The other advance premium mutuals, whose number and importance have been increasing in property and liability insurance, pay policyholder dividends only under exceptional circumstances. Instead they set a price that is close to their expected needs and the "dividend" takes the form of a lower initial premium.

Advance premium mutuals write about one-quarter of the property and liability insurance in force and almost one-half of the life insurance in force. Many of the nation's largest insurers are advance premium mutuals.

Reciprocal Exchanges. Reciprocal exchanges are a type of coop-erative insurer that developed in the United States in the late 1800s. Unlike mutuals, reciprocal exchanges are not corporations. Instead they are unincorpoated associations that, like Lloyd's associations, involve individuals writing insurance as individuals, not jointly. They differ from Lloyd's associations in that the individual members (often called "subscribers") insure one another, not outsiders. Basically each member agrees to insure individually all of the other members in the exchange and is in turn insured by each of the other members. In other words, there is a "reciprocal exchange" of insurance promises. Instead of writing a separate contract for each promise, the reciprocal exchange issues one contract to each subscriber which states the nature of the operation.

The reciprocal is managed by an *attorney-in-fact*. The attorney-in-fact may be a corporation. For the larger reciprocals, this is most often the case. As far as insureds and the public are concerned, the attorney-in-fact appears to be the insurer. Typically, the attorney-in-fact is authorized as an agent of subscribers to "sell" insurance by seeking new subscribers, to contract with persons to represent the exchange, to collect premiums, pay losses, underwrite new and renewal business, buy and accept reinsurance, invest exchange funds, and the like. In return for administrative services, the attorney-in-fact receives a percentage of the gross premiums paid by subscribers. For example, the subscriber's agreement may allow the attorney-in-fact to retain up to 25 percent of the premium deposits received and investment earnings of the exchange for the year. Nonetheless, it is the assets of the exchange as an unincorporated association that provide the financial security for subscribers. While the management of these assets, and indeed all association affairs, rests with the attorney-in-fact, the latter is not the insurer—the association is.

In their purest form, reciprocals keep separate accounts for each subscriber. The balance in each account is the amount by which the subscriber's premiums and share of the investment income have exceeded the subscriber's share of the reciprocal's expenses and losses suffered by subscribers. Subscribers can be assessed, usually up to some maximum amount, if their balances are not sufficient to cover their obligations. If their balances are sufficiently large, they may receive a dividend. If a subscriber terminates membership in the association, he or she is entitled to the balance in his or her separate account.

In their modified forms, reciprocals more closely resemble advance premium mutuals. Individual surplus accounts are supplemented or replaced by undivided surplus accounts. If there are no individual accounts, terminating subscribers do not receive any refunds. If there are sufficient undivided surplus funds, the reciprocal may be permitted to and prefer to issue nonassessable contracts.

Although more numerous than Lloyds associations, reciprocals still number less than sixty and account for only a small fraction of the property and liability insurance premiums written. They write no life insurance. Many reciprocals specialize in one line, usually auto insurance, but a few are large multiple-line insurers. Some are affiliated with a trade association or an auto association and write insurance only for members of the association.

Other Cooperative Insurers. In addition to the mutual and reciprocal insurers discussed above, there are several other cooperative insurance organizations. Not all of these insurers differ in their legal form of organization from the insurers already discussed, but they are distinguished by their unique operating characteristics.

Fraternal Benefit Societies. During the late nineteenth and early twentieth centuries, a number of lodges and fraternal societies organized welfare plans that provided benefits to members and their families in the event of accident, sickness, or death. Over the years, many of these welfare plans developed formal insurance operations very similar to commercial insurance companies. Today, fraternal benefit societies are authorized under special sections of state insurance codes to conduct the business of insurance within the guidelines set forth by the code. These organizations usually are incorporated but have no capital stock. Only members of the society, order, or voluntary association are able to purchase insurance from the fraternal. Membership requires compliance with specified provisions of the organization's charter, bylaws, and related amendments.

Fraternal insurers generally offer only life and health insurance contracts. Although a few societies continue to operate on an assessment basis, most fraternals have adopted the level premium and legal reserve system used by commercial life insurers. Fraternal contracts often contain unique provisions; for example, eligible beneficiaries may be limited to specified classes of the members' dependents or designated relatives. In recognition of their charitable and benevolent character, fraternals are exempt from federal income taxes and from many state and municipal taxes. Although the volume of fraternal insurance is relatively small when compared to total life and health insurance in force, several of these insurers are large national and international organizations with aggressive marketing systems.

Savings Bank Life Insurance. Three states—Connecticut, Massachusetts, and New York—permit mutual savings banks to establish life insurance departments and sell life insurance to residents or workers in the state. Persons purchasing the life insurance need not be depositors of the mutual savings bank. The usual types of participating life insurance are sold but the amount that can be purchased by an individual is limited by state law. Insurance is purchased over-the-counter at the bank in order to minimize expenses. There is better persistency (fewer lapses) of savings bank life insurance than is true in the life insurance industry as a whole. These factors help keep the net cost of savings bank life insurance remarkably low. Still, life insurance in force with savings banks represents less than 0.4 percent of the legal reserve life insurance in force in the United States.

Blue Cross-Blue Shield. The first organizations to provide health expense benefits on a widespread basis in the United States were the Blue Cross and Blue Shield plans. The "Blues" are tax exempt, nonprofit associations organized in accordance with provisions of special "enabling legislation" enacted in the several states.

Blue Cross plans first developed in the 1930s as a means of financing hospital costs. The Blue Shield plans that developed somewhat later provide for prepayment of physician services. Although Blue Cross and Blue Shield plans are legally separate entities, they commonly work jointly within a state or local area. The plans have been established by local hospital and physician associations and fostered by the American Hospital Association and the American Medical Association. About seventy-five Blue Cross plans and a similar number of Blue Shield plans operate autonomously within defined territories. Although the Blues are local in orientation, benefits are made available nationwide through inter-plan agreements and the coordination services of the Blue Cross Association and the National Association of Blue Shield Plans. Control of local plans resides in a board of directors made up of hospital and medical personnel and public representatives. Persons covered by the plans, called "subscribers," are not owners and do not exercise control over plan operations.

Blue Cross traditionally has emphasized basic hospital services provided through employer group coverages. Blue Cross provides most benefits on a service basis by specifying that a subscriber is entitled to a maximum number of days of hospitalization in a particular type of accommodation. Similarly, Blue Shield contracts for surgical and other physician's services with members of the local medical profession. Medical services benefits may be specified by use of a fee schedule or the contract may provide for payment of the usual, reasonable and customary charges for covered services.

The Blues compete vigorously with commercial insurance companies and other health care financing plans for health insurance business. Nationally, over 40 percent of the private hospital, surgical, regular medical, and major medical expense benefit payments made annually come from Blue Cross and Blue Shield associations.

Health Maintenance Organizations (HMOs). A nontraditional form of health expense plan, known as a health maintenance organization (HMO), has become important in health care financing. Unlike commercial insurance and the Blues, HMOs emphasize preventive care, early diagnosis, and ambulatory treatment. An HMO has been defined as an organization that provides for a wide range of health care services for a specified group at a fixed periodic payment. This broad definition includes a wide range of health care financing and delivery systems. HMO sponsors include governmental units, medical schools, hospitals, employers, labor unions, consumer groups, insurance companies, hospital-medical plans, and private individuals and organizations specializing in HMO operation. Within the range of organizations encompassed by the term HMO, four characteristics are common:

(1) Plan members enroll voluntarily.
(2) Fees are not charged for most health care services when provided. Instead, members pay a fixed, level, periodic premium (capitation payment) that entitles them to the health care services provided by the HMO without limitation as to the number of physician's office visits, and so on.
(3) The HMO offers a comprehensive package of health care services and benefits.
(4) Health care is provided by HMO physicians or other medical personnel through designated facilities.

Unlike other health expense plans, HMOs finance *and* deliver health care services. Delivery is provided by a *prepaid group practice prepayment* arrangement or by an *individual practice association.* The group(s) of physicians practicing together as a team under the prepaid group practice arrangement serve exclusively the needs of the plan's enrolled population. An individual practice association is an HMO organized around a "panel" of participating physicians who agree to serve plan members while continuing their own private, fee-for-service practices.

Even though the fundamental concept underlying HMOs is not new, the growth of HMOs had been extremely slow until recent years. The relatively recent interest in HMOs and their resulting growth can be attributed to two major factors: (1) increased interest in and support of HMOs by employers and unions concerned about the relentless rate of inflation in health care costs experienced in recent years; and (2) the Health Maintenance Organization Act of 1973 (Public Law 93-202) and the subsequent amendment to that act passed in 1976 (Public Law 94-460). Among other things, this Act provided for HMO planning and development and required employers of twenty-five or more workers to offer their employees an HMO option if there is a certified HMO in the area that has not closed its enrollment. Both commercial insurers and the Blues have founded their own HMOs or developed working relationships with other HMOs.

Domicile

Classified according to domicile, insurers may be domestic, foreign, or alien. *Domestic* insurers are domiciled in the state for which the status is being determined, *foreign* insurers in some other state, and *alien* insurers outside the United States.

Admission Status

Insurers may also be classified as *admitted* or *nonadmitted* to conduct an insurance business within a particular state. Domestic insurers are by definition admitted insurers because the state insurance commissioner must approve their formation. Foreign and alien insurers must be licensed in each state in which they wish to be admitted. This admission status is important because otherwise the insurer cannot have any representation in the state except possibly excess or surplus lines brokers. Excess or surplus lines brokers may be licensed to obtain insurance from nonadmitted insurers if they can demonstrate that the insurance sought is not available from admitted insurers.

Types of Insurance Written

Insurers can be classified in two ways according to the types of insurance written. First, according to the lines of insurance written, insurers are either (1) life insurers who can write either life insurance or health insurance, or (2) nonlife insurers who may write any line other than life insurance. Nonlife insurers may write only one line of insurance such as fire insurance or auto insurance, several lines, or most kinds of property and liability insurance plus health insurance.

Second, insurers can be classified as (1) originating, primary, or direct insurers; or (2) reinsurers. *Direct insurers* are primarily engaged in insuring individuals, families, or businesses other than insurers. *Reinsurers* insure the direct insurers; they assume responsibility for that portion of the business written directly that the direct insurers do not wish to keep. Direct insurers may also be engaged in reinsurance through agreements with other direct insurers, membership in reinsurance pools, or through reinsurance departments that actively solicit customers. They may also own reinsurance subsidiaries. Their primary target, however, is the general public.

Types of Customers Served

Insurers may service the general public or specialized clientele. Examples of specialized clientele are members of an auto association, college teachers, churches, present and past military officers, and senior citizens.

Marketing System

There are four different types of marketing systems used by property and liability insurers in the United States: (1) the independent agency system, (2) the exclusive agency system, (3) the direct writer system, and (4) the mail order system. Some insurers use more than one of these distribution systems. For example, one large primarily direct writer also uses some independent agents. Some primarily independent agency insurers sell some insurance by direct mail. Marketing systems are dealt with thoroughly in CPCU 5. The subject is discussed briefly at this point as another aid in classifying insurers.

Independent Agents   Independent agents are independent business persons who enter into marketing agreements with more than one insurer. Under these agreements, the agent agrees to place some of the business he or she writes with the named insurer who in turn promises to pay the agent a commission for business placed with the insurer. The agreement also spells out the duties of each party (for example, who prepares the contract, who sends out renewal notices, and so on) with respect to the transactions covered under the contract.

An important provision in the agreement gives the agent ownership of the business written by the agent. This characteristic is sometimes referred to as *ownership of expirations.* If the agent or the insurer terminates the agency agreement, the insurer cannot give information on the insureds placed with the company by the former agent to a new agent. The agent thus has the opportunity without interference from the insurer or its new agent to explain to these insureds what has happened and to encourage them to continue their insurance with the same agency but with another insurer.

Independent agents claim that they can give the prospective insured a choice among the insurers they represent. They also claim that if a dispute arises between the insurer and the insured their ownership of the insured's account gives them some extra clout in representing the insured's interests.

Until recently, most insurers using this system—known as the American Agency System—were not well known to the general public even though many were giant insurers. The insured had few direct contacts with the insurer. The agent sold the insurance, issued the contract, received premiums, sent out renewal notices, and adjusted small losses. Unless the insured read the contract, he or she might not even know the name of the insurer. Indeed, the agent might transfer the account from one insurer to another without the insured being aware of the change. Today, insureds purchasing insurance from independent agents are much more likely to know the name of the insurer. The insurer commonly has more contacts with the insured and directs much more of its advertising toward the ultimate consumer.

Insurers operating through independent agents write roughly two-thirds of the property and liability insurance written. (Independent agency insurers write more than two-thirds of the premiums paid by businesses, but *less* than two-thirds of the premiums paid by families.) Life and health insurers, particularly those with property and liability insurance affiliates, also do some of their marketing through independent agents but usually this is not their primary marketing effort. Independent agency insurers emphasizing property and liability insurance include both stock and mutual companies but this distribution system is more popular with stock insurers.

Exclusive Agents   Instead of reaching consumers through independent agents or brokers (see below) many insurers market their products through exclusive agents. Exclusive agents agree to represent only one insurer. Technically, they are not employees of the insurer but are independent contractors paid commissions for the business they produce. In many cases, exclusive agents have no ownership of expirations; in other cases limited ownership exists. The home offices or regional offices of these insurers have more direct contacts with their insureds than independent agency insurers. These offices typically prepare and mail contracts, request renewal information, send out premium notices, and handle most claims. Businesses and families insured by companies using exclusive agents will likely know the name of the insurer.

Exclusive agents cannot give their insureds a choice among insurers. Because they do not own the business they have written, these agents have as a rule less bargaining strength than independent agents. Also, because this approach tends to be a less expensive way to market insurance, companies using it tend to charge lower premiums.

Companies marketing through exclusive agents or the direct writer system, explained next, account for about one-third of the property and liability insurance premiums written. They dominate the life and health insurance field.

Most property and liability insurers marketing in this fashion are mutual companies. Some are stock insurers, however. Life and health insurers usually market in this fashion whether they are stock or mutual insurers.

Direct Writer System   The direct writer system bears a striking resemblance to the exclusive agency system. The only essential difference is the nature of the relationship between the producer, called a sales representative, and the insurer. The direct writer producer is an employee of the insurer, not an independent contractor. In the direct writer system, the ownership of expirations usually is vested solely in the insurer. The producer usually does not have any ownership rights in expirations even during the effective period of the employment.

There is wide variation in the compensation plans in the direct writer system. Some producers receive only a salary; others receive a salary plus a bonus or commissions; still others receive only commissions. The direct writer producers frequently are restricted to performing the sales function, with all other functions performed by the insurer.

Mail Order System   The mail order marketing system, sometimes called direct mail system or the direct response system, differs from the other three systems in that no producers are involved. The insurer's sales message is communicated to the prospective purchaser either through the mail or through the mass media, such as newspapers, magazines, radio, or television. The prospective purchaser is expected to contact the office of the insurer directly by mail, or sometimes by telephone.

Brokers   Brokers are legally representatives of the insured who in effect do the insured's insurance shopping. They have no agency relationship with the insurer. Insurers who accept business from brokers may require that the business be placed through one of their agents or sales representatives. Brokers receive part or all of the commission that would ordinarily be paid to the agent.

Independent agency insurers deal with brokers much more than do companies marketing through exclusive agents or sales representatives.

Brokers are also much more likely to specialize in property and liability insurance than in life and health insurance. However, property and liability insurance brokers write a considerable amount of life and health insurance in connection with employee benefit plans.

Agents often act as brokers in placing business outside their regular channels. Likewise, sometimes brokers will operate under agency agreements. In other words, the same person may legally be an agent for some transactions and a broker for others, and it is often difficult to analyze in which capacity he or she is functioning in a particular instance. Some states do not permit the separate licensing of brokers. In those states the marketing intermediaries who would prefer to be brokers must be licensed as agents for transaction. Such brokers are often called broker-agents.

Pricing System

The final classifications to be considered divide insurers according to how they price their product.

Participating or Nonparticipating Insurers The first classification asks whether policyholders participate in the insurer's underwriting and investment experience through dividends. From the earlier discussion of mutual insurers it is clear that many but not all mutual property and liability insurers are participating insurers. Life insurance mutuals are almost always participating insurers. Stock property and liability insurers do not pay dividends to policyholders in general. However, some stock property and liability insurers pay dividends (if results so warrant) to policyholders in certain lines of insurance, particularly workers' compensation insurance. About one-sixth of the life insurance written by stock life insurers is participating insurance, most of it by insurers who sell both participating and nonparticipating insurance.

Bureau or Independent Insurers An insurer may establish its own rates or join with others to use rates developed by a rating bureau from the pooled experience of numerous insurers. Some insurers modify bureau rates but still use bureau rates as a point of departure. For example, they may "deviate" from bureau rates by reducing them 10 percent.

Many property and liability insurers are bureau insurers, but in recent years there has been a trend toward independent pricing. Many insurers use bureau rates for some lines but their own rates for others. For example, in most states all insurers use the worker's compensation insurance rates developed by a rating bureau. An insurer may set its own prices except in that line. In the personal lines of property and liability insurance, particularly private passenger automobile, most of the large insurers base rates upon their own experience. Because there are no rating bureaus in life or health insurance, all insurers establish their own rates in those lines.

BENEFITS TO SOCIETY

Chapter 3 described how *individual businesses and families* can benefit from the purchase of insurance. These benefits are (1) payment for losses, (2) reduction of uncertainty, and (3) various services provided by insurers. Insurers pay dollar benefits or render certain services to those insureds who incur covered losses. Because insureds can anticipate these benefits or services, their uncertainty about the financial consequences of these covered losses is reduced. Finally insurers provide certain services such as exposure analysis and assistance in controlling losses.

To the extent that individual members of society benefit without hurting other members, society benefits. *Society as a whole* also receives additional benefits from the existence of insurance. These benefits are (1) payment for loss, (2) a reduction of the uncertainty in society, (3) improved loss control activity, and (4) a source of long-term investment capital.

Payment for Loss

When an insured business or family is paid following a loss, other members of society may also benefit. For example, the survival of a business that might otherwise have been forced to shut its doors may benefit employees who keep their jobs, suppliers who value the orders they receive, customers who continue to receive the products and services produced, and the community whose tax base is not reduced. Because a family is not disrupted, its members may be more productive members of society. Without insurance it might have been forced to seek public assistance, causing welfare costs to rise. The benefits are not only economic. Social and political stability is enhanced by indemnifying those victimized by sudden financial misfortune.

Reduction of Uncertainty

For the individual insured, uncertainty regarding consequences of covered financial losses is virtually eliminated (assuming the insurer will honor its obligations under the contract). For society as a whole, uncertainty is reduced but not eliminated. Insurers face some uncertainty because there is never total assurance that actual losses will precisely match expected losses.

The most important reason insurers still face some uncertainty is that the environment or underlying conditions are never the same from year to year. For example, the expected loss experience of auto insurance may be changed by such diverse factors as inflation; how autos are designed and manufactured; the attitudes of claimants, judges, and juries; legal doctrines and statutes; highway construction; traffic density; and state licensing practices. Consequently, in order to estimate its expected losses next year, an insurer must modify the estimate based on past experience to reflect its judgment on projected changes in underlying conditions. This is so regardless of how extensive that experience may be.

Insurers have more units than their insureds, thus permitting them to make much more effective use of the law of large numbers. The uncertainty they face because of changing conditions would affect the insureds themselves if there were no insurers. Indeed, because of their skills and attitudes insurers should be much better able than their insureds to cope with this uncertainty. On balance, the uncertainty in society is substantially reduced by the existence of insurance. This reduction in uncertainty leads to more efficient use of resources, social stability, better price structures, and enhanced competition.

More Efficient Use of Resources When they are less uncertain about the future, businesses and families make more efficient use of existing capital and labor. Society benefits from this greater efficiency through increased production and lower prices. If insurance were not available, certain industries, firms, products or methods of production and distribution would be avoided or receive too little attention even though society might otherwise benefit from applying more resources to these uses. This fact has been illustrated dramatically on several occasions. For example, as a consequence of the riots in several urban core areas in the late sixties, many small businesses and families in those areas were unable to secure insurance. This insurance shortage was so undesirable that Congress and state legislatures took steps to improve the availability of insurance.

The reduction of uncertainty does more than make the utilization of existing capital more efficient. It also encourages the accumulation of new capital and its more efficient allocation. Persons and institutions are more likely to make additional commitments of capital and labor and these commitments are more likely to be long term. Credit is easier to obtain, or it is available on more liberal terms, or both. Also, by reducing the effect of differences in the potential impact of pure loss exposures among industries, firms, and methods of production and distribution, insurance enables investors of capital and labor to concentrate on what would otherwise be the most efficient use of these resources.

Social Stability Society is more stable, socially and politically, because the reduction in uncertainty lessens tensions, physical stress, and concern about the future.

Better Price Structure If it were not for insurance, each business would have to include in the prices for its products or services an allowance for its uncertainty concerning loss. Because they have limited experience and expertise in measuring expected losses, many businesses make only rough estimates of their expected losses. The extra amount they would add for their uncertainty would be highly subjective and open to considerable error. When a business purchases insurance, it can substitute the insurance premium for its expected loss estimate and uncertainty allowance. As a consequence, the prices in society are more accurate and more equitable.

Enhanced Competition Insurance contributes further to increased production, lower prices, and a more equitable price structure by improving the ability of smaller firms to compete with larger businesses. If insurance were not available, small firms would face greater uncertainty because they have so few exposure units. Some would decide to avoid certain operations because of this uncertainty; others would feel compelled to charge high prices, thus damaging their competitive position. Large businesses, with their larger number of exposure units, could predict their loss experience with greater confidence and accuracy. This greater ability to predict the future would give these large businesses a great competitive advantage over smaller firms. Accidental losses would pose less of a threat to their continued survival and their prices would on the average include smaller allowances for uncertainty.

Insurance is a leveler because it provides certainty for businesses of all sizes. Small businesses that might otherwise not exist, are able to survive and can price their products and services more effectively.

Loss Control

The loss control services and incentives individual insurers directly provide their insureds have been described in Chapter 3. Other members of society also gain from these activities and from the research efforts of some insurers.

For example, if an insurer can help a business reduce the number of collisions between autos in its fleet and other autos, the owners of these other autos gain as well as the business. If an insurer can help a business reduce the number of defective products it produces, it helps the business prevent a products liability suit and damage to the persons or property of customers.

The research findings of insurers on such matters as air bags, industrial noise, and rehabilitation have been shared with the public. Insurers actively support trade associations and independent bodies whose principal activity is loss control. Examples are

- Underwriters Laboratories, which test building materials, appliances, electrical wiring, and other products to determine that fire and other safety standards are being met;
- the Insurance Institute for Highway Safety, which conducts research projects and educational programs in matters related to traffic safety;

- the National Fire Protection Association, which sets fire safety standards and serves as a clearing house of information about fire loss control;
- the National Automobile Theft Bureau, which attempts to prevent automobile thefts and recover stolen vehicles; and
- the National Safety Council, which publishes safety materials of all kinds and conducts extensive public information and publicity programs.

Long-Term Investments

Insurers are a major source of funds for long-term investments. An insurer generally collects a premium from the insured at the beginning of each insured's policy period, pays some expenses immediately, and pays the losses (if any) and the other expenses during or after the policy period. Because premiums are written throughout the year, the insurer always has on hand some money for which it does not have any immediate use. Instead of allowing this money to lie idle, insurers invest it in bonds, mortgages, stocks, and other investments. The income from these investments permits insurers to increase the return to their owners, to lower the premiums paid by policyholders, or to do both. Society gains because the money is put to productive uses. Exhibit 6-3 shows that insurance companies and pension funds supplied about one-third of the investment funds raised in recent years. Only thrift institutions, principally savings and loan associations, provided as large a share. Except for mortgages, insurers are the most important source of long-term funds. They provided a market for 96 percent of the corporate bonds issued, 93 percent of the gross new issues of corporate stocks, only 11 percent of the private funds raised by the U.S. government and its agencies, and 49 percent of the private funds raised by state and local governments.

COSTS TO SOCIETY

Insurance imposes certain costs on society. These are (1) resources employed in the insuring activity, (2) moral hazard losses, and (3) morale hazard losses.

Resources

The conduct of an insurance business requires human and material resources. Human resources include producers, claims adjusters, underwriters, investment analysts, actuaries, and other personnel.

Exhibit 6-3

Investment Funds Raised and Supplied—
1976-1979 (Billions of Dollars)*

	1976	1977	1978	1979	Total Amount	Percent
Funds Raised						
Corporate bonds	29.9	30.0	28.2	28.7	116.8	14
Corporate stocks	11.1	3.6	4.1	4.4	23.2	3
State and local securities	17.7	23.9	26.8	22.2	90.6	11
Real estate mortgages	87.1	134.0	149.0	160.0	530.1	64
Foreign securities	9.1	5.5	3.5	4.3	22.4	3
Term loans	-0.7	5.7	16.1	22.5	43.6	5
Total	154.1	202.7	227.6	242.1	826.5	100
Funds Supplied						
Insurers and pension plans						
Life insurers	23.6	26.2	27.6	27.8	105.2	13
Private noninsured pension plans	11.3	13.5	15.2	18.3	58.3	7
State and local retirement plans	9.6	10.2	9.5	11.6	40.9	5
Property and liability insurers	9.0	15.7	18.3	17.0	60.0	7
Subtotal	53.5	65.6	70.7	74.7	264.5	32
Thrift institutions	58.2	73.9	66.3	55.7	254.1	31
Investment companies	1.9	2.2	0.9	2.5	7.5	1
Other financial intermediaries	-1.1	1.4	2.0	2.1	4.4	1
Commercial banks	16.4	43.8	61.6	67.0	188.8	23
Business corporations	-1.1	—	0.2	0.3	-0.6	—
Government	8.3	6.9	17.8	24.9	57.9	7
Foreign investors	3.1	3.5	2.8	0.7	10.1	1
Individuals and others	14.9	5.3	5.3	14.2	39.7	5
Total	154.1	202.7	227.6	242.1	826.5	100

*Reprinted with permission from *Credit and Capital Markets 1980* (New York: Bankers Trust Company, 1980), p. T2.

Material resources include buildings, computers, paper, autos, and other physical items. If these resources were not employed in the insurance business, they could be used to produce other goods and services.

To reduce the human and material resources used in the insurance industry, insurers have sought more efficient ways to conduct their business—such as package policies, direct billing, group insurance, and improved cash management.

Moral Hazards

A *moral hazard* has been defined as a condition that exists when a person may try to cause a loss, or may exaggerate a loss that has occurred. Insurance creates moral hazards. Some persons intentionally cause losses in order to collect or gain from the payment of insurance proceeds. One of the major causes of fires in recent years has been arson, much of which was committed in order to collect insurance proceeds.

Persons whose losses are accidental often exaggerate the loss amount in order to make a profit on the event. For example, insureds may claim that a building or a piece of equipment destroyed by a windstorm was in much better condition than was actually the case or that the number of cartons destroyed by a fire was much greater than the actual number. Liability insurance claimants may allege that their bodily injuries or property losses are much greater than is the case. Some auto repair shops, doctors, contractors, and others charge higher amounts for their services when insurance is available to pay for the loss because they believe that insurance reduces the insured's resistance to such charges and they have less concern about overcharging insurers, with whom they have no personal dealings.

To the extent that insurance produces incentives for persons either to cause or exaggerate losses, it has created moral hazards. Insurers combat moral hazards by careful underwriting and by investigating suspicious claims and prosecuting persons guilty of fraudulent or exaggerated claims.

Morale Hazards

A *morale hazard* is a condition that exists when a person is less careful than he or she should be because of the existence of insurance. Unlike moral hazards, morale hazards are not associated with intentionally caused or exaggerated losses. Instead, morale hazards are conditions short of intent that increase the chance or severity of loss because of the existence of insurance. An insured may exert a lesser degree of care over an exposure because he or she knows that if there is a loss the insurer will bear it. For example, a firm may not be as careful as it should be about protecting itself against fire losses, in part because it reasons that if there is a loss it will be indemnified by its insurer. A family may leave a car unlocked partly because an insurer protects the family against theft losses. Another example of a morale hazard is the tendency of juries to award higher verdicts if the defendant is insured, not because they would gain personally but because they have less sympathy for an impersonal insurer than for the insured and because they know that the insurer has more assets.

Insurers attack morale hazards by educational campaigns that indicate how higher insured losses mean higher premiums for insureds, how insurance does not usually cover all the losses arising out of an insured accident, and how insurance does not stop the loss of important human and material resources.

SOCIAL PROBLEMS OF INSURANCE— AVAILABILITY AND AFFORDABILITY

The benefits of being insured are increasingly recognized and appreciated. With increasing recognition, however, have come pressures on insurers to increase the availability and affordability of insurance. To improve availability, insurers are required to provide insurance to applicants they would ordinarily reject. To improve affordability, various methods are used to have some lower-hazard insureds subsidize the cost of insurance for some higher-hazard insureds. Availability and, increasingly, affordability of insurance have become key objectives of social policy.

Chapter 7 will describe in detail some of the mechanisms that have been developed to meet these pressures. Insurance pricing is not an exact science, and reasonable persons will always disagree on some of the issues involved. The discussion here is limited to those situations in which the relationship of certain characteristics and loss potential is admitted but, for broader social purposes, these differences are to be ignored. The purpose of this section is to emphasize that government action, including a subsidy, is sometimes considered necessary to achieve social objectives not consistent with competitive pricing.

Common Rate Approach

Opinions on the obligation and ability of insurers to provide insurance on affordable terms depend in part on opinions regarding the insurance mechanism. At one extreme, it could be suggested that an insurer should charge all its insureds the same premium rate regardless of their individual loss and expense potential. Persons who hold this view argue that the purpose of insurance is to share losses among all insureds and that ignoring differences in loss potential is part of the sharing.

If an insurer is forced to provide protection to insureds it would ordinarily reject, if these insureds do in fact cost more to insure, and if the insurer charges everyone the same rate, this common rate must be higher than would be the case if the insurer had freedom of choice (unless the insurer is willing or forced to accept a reduced underwriting profit or greater underwriting loss). If the rate does rise, the insureds who would ordinarily be accepted are subsidizing those who would usually be rejected.

Under this pricing system, because of the common rate, the higher quality insureds among those who are acceptable would already be subsidizing lower quality insureds. If the common rate is to be set at a level that all insureds can "afford" to pay, the rate may not cover the expected losses and expenses. The lower insureds' income levels, the lower the "affordable" premium and the more likely the rate will be deficient.

Only a monopoly insurer can charge all insureds the same rate. If the insurer has any competitors who do not use a one-price system, those competitors will attract many of the higher quality insureds by charging them a lower rate. The one-price insurer would then be left with an inadequate rate for the lower quality insureds who remain because its insured group would be of a lower overall quality than was originally contemplated.

Even if there are no competitors, unless the insurance is compulsory, some of the higher quality insureds may find the common rate so high that they decide not to purchase insurance. Consequently, if social policy dictates that all insureds should pay the same price, insurance must be compulsory and provided by a single insurer or by several insurers charging the same price. If the price is to be affordable by everyone, a government subsidy would probably be necessary.

Individual Rating

If the common rate approach is rejected, it might be suggested that each insured should pay a different premium rate, because no two insureds have exactly the same loss and expense potentials. In practice, such an extreme approach is impossible for most lines of insurance because of the expense of administering such a system and the impossibility of assessing individual loss and expense potentials so precisely. Instead, insureds are often grouped into classes with others having approximately the same loss and expense potential. The smaller the number of classes, the closer this practice moves to the common rate approach.

Class Rating

Grouping insureds into rating classes also requires those with a lower loss potential to subsidize those with a higher loss potential—

particularly when an insurer charges different rates to groups of insureds that include some broad heterogeneous classes. If applicants who would otherwise be rejected must be insured within the regular class rate structure, the extra cost of insuring these persons will cause the rates for the other insureds to rise (unless the insurer absorbs the loss). Furthermore, within each heterogeneous class some of the insureds would be subsidizing the others. If class rates are set at an affordable level for some members of the class, the other insureds or the insurer must make up any differences between the affordable level and an adequate level.

Only a monopoly insurer, private or public, could survive with such broad classes. Otherwise, competitors could attract the higher quality insureds by dividing each heterogeneous class into two or more subclasses and by creating a separate higher-rated class for those insureds it was forced to insure. If the state prohibits separate higher rates for the forced acceptances, all insurers must either absorb the extra cost of insuring these persons or spread this cost among all other insureds.

This point is illustrated in a ruling by a state insurance commissioner that forced an insurer to combine two rating classes into one. An auto insurer was prohibited from charging different physical damage rates for autos garaged overnight and those not garaged overnight. His reasoning was that in certain neighborhoods people have no garages. Assuming that the loss potential depends in part on whether the auto is garaged, those with garages are now subsidizing those in the same rating class who do not have garages.

Government Subsidies

A monopoly insurer can use its price structure to favor some insureds over others. Its position is stronger if the protection is compulsory. In a competitive environment, it is possible to insure some people for less than their expected losses and expenses by requiring insurers to take the losses or having the government provide a subsidy. Another possibility is to require all insurers to use the same rating structure, in which case some insureds would be subsidizing others.

In real life, the subsidy of those paying less than their fair share is most likely to be borne in part by other insureds and in part by the insurer. If the private subsidy is large, the government may have to provide a public subsidy if the insurer is to continue writing insurance.

Illustrations

These principles can be illustrated with a few examples.

Flood Insurance   Flood insurance on real property was virtually unattainable until recently because the best prospects were those with high loss potential. Few of those persons could afford to pay an adequate premium. Under the National Flood Insurance Act of 1968 the federal government now subsidizes insurance sold at bargain rates.

Auto Shared Market Plans   To provide auto insurance for consumers who cannot purchase this protection through normal channels, most states require that insurers establish some facility that will accept most, if not all, these applicants. For example, there may be an underwriting pool serviced by a few insurers and reinsured by all auto insurers in the state. The rates charged by the pool exceed those charged in the voluntary market except by insurers specializing in substandard applicants. Even so, these pools have frequently incurred underwriting losses which have caused the member insurers to absorb a loss or charge their other insureds more.

FAIR Plans   In about half the states no owner of property in an "urban area" can be denied insurance merely because of environmental hazards such as a high vandalism rate or riot potential. Furthermore, in their pricing, insurers must ignore these environmental hazards. If applicants cannot obtain insurance through the usual channels and the property would be insurable except for these environmental hazards, it must be written by a FAIR Plan, which is usually serviced by a few insurers and reinsured by all property insurers operating in the state. Because environmental hazards must be ignored in underwriting and pricing, the cost of these hazards must be borne by the insurers or distributed among other insureds.

SIZE, GROWTH, COMPOSITION, AND ECONOMIC SIGNIFICANCE

The preceding discussion has indicated the many benefits that society derives on balance from the existence of public and private insurers. This section sheds more light on the size, growth, composition, and economic significance of the public and private insurance sector. Three measures will be used to tell the story: (1) premiums, (2) assets, and (3) employment. In order to indicate how the sector has grown over time and how its composition has been altered, data are presented for 1960, 1970, and 1979, the most recent year for which data are available. The data are not meant to be exhaustive but they do encompass all of the major private and public insurance operations.

Exhibit 6-4
Private and Public Insurance Premiums—
1960, 1970, and 1979 (Billions of Dollars)

Insurer	1960	1970	1979	Percent of Increase 1960-1979	Percent of Increase 1970-1979
Private Insurers					
Property and liability					
Insurance	$13.6	$ 31.0	$ 86.9	538%	181%
Life insurance	13.3	25.4	57.0	327	124
Health insurance	7.5	20.0	62.2	731	211
Total	$34.4	$ 76.3	$206.2	499%	170%
Major Public Insurers					
Old Age, Survivors, Disability, and Health Insurance	$11.9	$ 40.8	$126.7	967%	211%
Railroad Retirement Board	0.6	1.0	2.3	286	138
State unemployment compensation funds	2.3	2.5	12.4	440	391
Total	$14.8	$ 44.3	$141.4	858%	219%
All Insurers Combined	$49.2	$120.6	$347.6	606%	188%

Premiums

According to Exhibit 6-4, total insurance premiums written in 1979 were $347.6 billion, a 188 percent increase over 1970 and a 606 percent increase over 1960. One way to assess the economic significance of insurance is to relate those premiums to the gross national product, which measures the annual flow of goods and services in an economy. More specifically, GNP is the sum of (1) personal consumption expenditures on all goods and services, (2) government expenditures on all goods and services, and (3) gross investment expenditure on all new machines and construction. In 1979 insurance premiums were 14.4 percent of GNP. In 1970 the proportion was 12.4 percent, in 1960, 9.8 percent.

Private insurance premiums accounted for about 59 percent of the 1979 total, compared with 63 percent in 1970 and 69 percent in 1960. The rapid growth of Old Age, Survivors, Disability, and Health Insurance is the major reason for the increasing proportion of premiums written by public insurers.

Of the private insurance premiums written in 1979, property and liability insurance premiums were 42 percent. The 1970 proportion was 41 percent, the 1960 proportion 40 percent. Exhibit 6-4 does not break down the property and liability insurance premiums by line but the

Exhibit 6-5
Private and Public Insurer Assets—
1960, 1970, and 1979 (Billions of Dollars)

Insurer	1960	1970	1979
Private Insurers			
Property and liability insurers	$ 30.1	$ 58.6	$187.4
Life and health insurers	119.6	207.3	432.3
Total	$149.7	$265.9	$619.7
Major Public Insurers			
Old Age, Survivors, Disability, and Health Insurance	$ 22.6	$ 41.5	$ 48.4
Railroad Retirement Board	3.7	4.8	2.7
State unemployment compensation funds	6.6	11.9	8.3 [a]
Total	$ 32.9	$ 58.2	$ 59.4
All Insurers Combined	$182.6	$324.1	$679.1

a. 1978 data, 1979 not available.

major components are automobile insurance (35 percent), multiple peril homeowners and commercial insurance (20 percent), workers' compensation insurance (15 percent), liability insurance (11 percent), and fire and allied lines insurance (7 percent).

Assets

Exhibit 6-5 shows the assets of private and public insurers. Total insurer assets were $679.1 billion in 1979, 110 percent more than in 1970 and 272 percent more than in 1960. These assets place insurers among the major financial institutions in the United States. The importance of insurers as a supplier of investment funds has already been noted earlier in this chapter.

Private insurers owned 91 percent of the total insurer assets in 1979, up from 82 percent in 1970 and 82 percent in 1960. Despite the rapid premium growth of public insurers, their asset growth has been modest. The main reason is that Old Age, Survivors, Disability, and Health Insurance currently operates with much smaller trust funds relative to the OASDHI premium volume than was the case in the earlier years.

Life insurers are the principal asset holders among private insurers. Their share of the total private assets was 64 percent in 1979, 78 percent in 1970, and 80 percent in 1960. Unlike property and liability insurers who sell pure protection, the principal products of life insurers are long-term contracts combining pure protection with an increasing savings or investment element. About 80 percent of the assets of life insurers are related to these policyholder savings.

Employment

The final measure to be considered is the number of persons employed in the private insurance industry. Comparable data are not available on public insurer employees. In 1979 the annual average number of persons employed by private insurers was 1.8 million, 26 percent more than in 1970 and 66 percent more than in 1960. Private insurance employees were 1.8 percent of the total civilian labor force in 1979, 1.8 percent in 1970, and 1.6 percent in 1960.

According to a special survey in 1967, about 57 percent did work related to life insurance or both life and nonlife insurance. The remainder worked in nonlife insurance only.

Chapter Notes

1. Irving Pfeffer, *Insurance and Economic Theory* (Homewood, IL: Richard D. Irwin, 1956), p. 53.
2. James L. Athearn, *Risk and Insurance* (New York: Appleton-Century-Crofts, 1969), 2nd ed., pp. 29-30.
3. David L. Bickelhaupt, *General Insurance* (Homewood, IL: Richard D. Irwin, 1979), 10th ed., pp. 27-28.
4. Herbert S. Denenberg, et al., *Risk and Insurance* (Englewood Cliffs, NJ: Prentice-Hall, 1974), 2nd ed., p. 149.
5. Mark R. Greene, *Risk and Insurance* (Cincinnati: South-Western Publishing Company, 1977), 4th ed., p. 49.
6. Donald L. MacDonald, *Corporate Risk Control* (New York: Ronald Press Company, 1966), p. 59.
7. Robert I. Mehr and Emerson Cammack, *Principles of Insurance*, 5th ed. (Homewood, IL: Richard D. Irwin, Inc., 1972), pp. 27, 32, 578-580.
8. Robert I. Mehr and Bob A. Hedges, *Risk Management in the Business Enterprise* (Homewood, IL: Richard D. Irwin, 1963), pp. 143-144.
9. Robert I. Mehr and Bob A. Hedges, *Risk Management: Concepts and Applications* (Homewood, IL: Richard D. Irwin, 1974), Chapter 6.
10. C. Arthur Williams, Jr. and Richard M. Heins, *Risk Management and Insurance*, 4th ed. (New York: McGraw-Hill Book Co., 1981), p. 210.
11. Herbert S. Denenberg, "The Legal Definition of Insurance," *The Journal of Insurance*, vol. 30, September 1963, p. 323.
12. Denenberg, "The Legal Definition of Insurance," p. 323.
13. Denenberg, "The Legal Definition of Insurance," p. 328.
14. Mehr and Hedges, *Risk Management: Concepts and Applications*, pp. 172-181.

CHAPTER 7

Insurance and the Government

INTRODUCTION

This chapter examines reasons why insurance is regulated more extensively than most other industries; the objectives, nature, and scope of regulation; and the operations of public insurers. The respective roles of the federal and state governments are described as well as the roles of the legislative, administrative, and judicial branches of government. To illustrate the nature and extent of government regulation of insurance, three areas will be discussed in detail—the regulation of contract design and interpretation, the formation and licensing of insurers, and insurance producer licensing and trade practices.

Public insurers are becoming increasingly important. This chapter explores the reasons for this and describes the operations of some prominent public insurers. Some public insurers write lines not written by private insurers, others duplicate private insurance coverage, and many cooperate with private insurers in providing insurance.

WHY REGULATE INSURANCE?

In 1914 the United States Supreme Court designated insurance as a "business affected with a public interest."[1] Such businesses are subject to much more extensive regulation than those not placed in this category. Contributing to the need for strong insurance regulation were a number of abuses perpetrated around the turn of the century. Although much time has passed since 1914, current public attitudes still seem to favor strong insurance regulation.

Insurance—Public-Interest Business

Two reasons for classifying insurance as a public-interest business are: (1) insurers sell complex promises, not immediate performance, and (2) the insurance business has considerable potential for abuses against consumers.

A Complex Promise, Not Immediate Performance Insurers sell a promise to indemnify or render services for the insured upon the happening of an event which may or may not occur. The ability of the insurer to perform on this promise is extremely important, subject to change, and difficult to judge. Most persons consider the insurance promise to be complex and difficult to understand. They believe the government should review the contracts sold, how they are sold, how they are underwritten, and how they are priced. Moreover, the public depends on the government to monitor the financial condition of the insurer so that contractual promises can be honored when they are due.

Potential for Abuse Abuses actually perpetrated around the turn of the century may be largely responsible for the insurance industry's being labeled a public-interest industry. Many insurers became insolvent, allegedly because of destructive competition; many insurers earned excess profits; rating bureaus dominated property and liability insurance pricing; and many insurers favored some insureds over others in underwriting and pricing. Legislatures and courts responded with tighter regulation to reduce the potential for abuse.

Current Public Attitudes Toward Insurance Regulation

According to a 1977 public attitude survey by the Insurance Information Institute:

> ... while the public will accept rate-making through competition in the marketplace, it wants at the same time the guardian hand of government to provide that prices will not get out of control. ... Many people feel they are being overcharged for many of the things they buy today—including auto insurance—and that tighter controls should be imposed. People generally feel that regulation is in their best interest.[2]

A 1979 survey showed that, although public sentiment is apparently moving toward less government regulation of business, over half of those interviewed think the government should regulate the prices charged by auto insurers.[3] The public still apparently favors strong government control. Periods of rapid inflation during the seventies and early eighties have contributed toward this attitude.

Auto insurance pricing is not the only issue involved. The public has also expressed concern regarding the availability of insurance, using terms like "redlining" to depict arbitrary territorial underwriting restrictions.

GOALS OF INSURANCE REGULATION[4]

Professor Spencer Kimball, a leading student of insurance regulation, has divided the goals of insurance regulation into two groups—internal and external. Another approach, taken by Richard L. Stewart, states the general objective as simply "helping people get the most insurance for their money."

Internal Goals

The internal goals of insurance regulation relate directly to the operation of the insurance business:

(1) *Solidity.* Unless an insured can be sure that the insurer has sufficient financial strength to pay claims, considerable uncertainty and concern about the future will remain. The most important contribution of insurance to individuals and society would be lost.

(2) *Equity and fairness.* Insurance rates should not be so high that insurers earn exorbitant profits. Furthermore, the rate paid by one insured compared to another should be "fair." Policy language should be clear and dealings with the insured made in good faith.

External Goals

The external goals of insurance regulation may not relate exclusively to the insurance business but to other sectors of society as well. These goals include, but are not limited to, the following:

(1) *Freedom from governmental restraint.* This leads to constitutional, statutory, and common-law limitations on regulation. Regulation should help maximize the benefits that flow from the normal workings of free markets. The social benefits of regulation, broadly speaking, should outweigh the social costs.

(2) *Local protectionism.* Discriminatory tax structures have been established in some states to protect local (domestic) insurers. Countersignature laws for agents also are intended to protect the interests of producers domiciled in a state.

(3) *Dispersion of decision-making power.* This might be attained through state level regulation rather than by one central government and is consistent with our structure of federalism.

(4) *Socialization of loss costs.* This external goal has special meaning for the insurance business. Chapter 6 referred to the fact that, in terms of insurance costs, insurers sometimes have been required to favor some insureds over others to achieve some social objective. For example, the cost of environmental hazards (loss producing characteristics of the area in which a property is located) affecting urban core properties may be spread among all insured property owners instead of being borne only by those exposed to these hazards. The purpose of spreading cost more widely is to lower premiums for the owners of urban core properties, thus making insurance more affordable and encouraging the maintenance and development of urban core areas.

(5) *Freedom of access to the market.* This is consistent with providing opportunities to new enterprises and with increasing the number of competitors.

(6) *Capital accumulation.* This is an external goal intended to achieve certain social objectives such as providing more public housing, strengthening the bond market, or developing more industries within the state.

Choosing Among These Goals

Some of the goals listed above do or may conflict with one another. Moreover, the capacity of regulators to achieve some goals may be limited. To be properly evaluated, benefits should be compared with costs.

Conflict Among Goals Some goals *may* conflict with others, and some goals *always* conflict with others. The solidity goal *may* conflict with equity and fairness. Making certain that an insurer is financially strong *may* not be consistent with keeping its rates at a reasonable level. The goal of financial strength may favor high projections of loss frequency or severity which, in turn, would support future rates that are higher than necessary. The solidity goal *may* be inconsistent with freedom of access to the market. Permitting new insurers to enter the market without restrictions *may* result in many incompetent or financially unstable insurers. Socialization of loss costs *is* by definition inconsistent with equity because socialization implies that some classes of insureds pay more and others pay less than their expected losses and expenses.

Insurance regulators may also be inconsistent in selecting the goals they emphasize when a conflict exists. For example, for most lines of insurance, regulators stress equity in rate regulation. They feel that prices charged insureds should vary according to differences in hazards involved. But, in some instances (such as the prohibition against considering environmental hazards in pricing property insurance in urban areas), regulators have stated that equity must give way to socialization. What usually results is a compromise among conflicting goals rather than a total acceptance of one goal and rejection of the other(s).

Regulatory Capacity The goals stressed may also depend on the capacity of the regulators to achieve them. For example, perfect equity is impossible. It is impossible to measure each individual's expected losses and expenses. Solidity is more achievable. Consequently, it makes sense to devote more resources to achieving solidity than to striving for perfect equity.

Benefit-Cost Considerations Even if it is possible and practical for insurance regulators to achieve certain goals, the benefits may not be attractive relative to the cost. Given limited regulatory resources, it is not enough that the activity produces some benefit or even that the benefits exceed the costs. Instead, the limited resources must be allocated so as to maximize total benefits.

Measuring costs and benefits is difficult. The weight assigned to various goals and the contribution made by any activity to the attainment of that goal significantly affect the benefit-cost relationship. For example, consider the cost-benefit relationship of regulators conducting three-year examinations of an insurer's financial condition. Consideration must be given to the importance of financial strength, the contribution of examinations to achieving financial strength and to the timely detection of financial weakness, and the cost of the examinations.

In evaluating prior approval of auto insurance rates as a way of achieving rate equity, consideration must be given to the importance of equity, the contribution of prior approval toward achieving that objective, and the cost of comparing rate relativities prior to their use.

If a choice must be made between financial examinations and evaluating auto rates, the decision clearly depends upon (1) subjective factors as well as the facts, and (2) the nature and effectiveness of the activity as well as the goal. In this example, equity in rates might be considered as important as financial strength, but prior approval may be considered to be much less effective in achieving equity than in-house examinations are in achieving financial strength.

A General Goal

Richard L. Stewart, a former New York state insurance commissioner, has described the goal of insurance regulation as "helping people get the most insurance for their money."[5] This means:

(1) *Most people should be able to obtain the insurance they want.*

> Generally, government can be expected to act to strengthen or replace the private insurance mechanism when the shortage of insurance is serious enough and the social cost of not acting—that is, of leaving the individual to take his chances alone—is too high. When government decides it must act [by forcing private insurers to provide coverage or by forming a public insurer] it can anticipate strong support from the public, for the public encourages government to look beyond insurance as a private contract to insurance as a public function.[6]

(2) *The insurance product should be of high quality and reliability.*[7] Policy provisions should be clear and fair, the insurer should be financially sound, and the insurer's performance on its contractual promises should be fair and consistent with the buyer's reasonable expectations.

(3) *The pricing system should help people receive the most for their money.* The best system is "one that yields prices as low as possible; stable prices not subject to large and sudden changes; and prices that are fair among other policyholders. The buyer also gains if the chosen system of rate regulation . . . increases rather than decreases the likelihood that insurance will be available and reliable."[8]

Government regulation, then, as Commissioner Stewart stated in a different address:

> . . . is no longer simply the application of countervailing power against a dominant economic group that might otherwise abuse its own power. Today government has an additional responsibility to encourage and guide and to require the regulated industry to respond to the current needs of society at large where it is important and necessary. To do this, government has to exercise an informed judgment as to what the evolving public needs are, and should develop its own position early enough and on a sufficient scale.[9]

REGULATORY JURISDICTION

Insurance regulation in the United States dates back to 1794 when the Pennsylvania Legislature granted a charter establishing the Insurance Company of North America. Since that time, regulation has increased greatly. All three branches of both federal and state governments have been involved in insurance regulation.

Historical Development

Around 1800, some regulatory provisions were found in the charters granted directly by state legislatures to insurers. Insurers typically had to (1) satisfy certain capital requirements, (2) limit investments to certain assets of high quality, and (3) submit reports to a designated state official. Deposits with a state official were frequently required, as was the periodic publication of ˉreports of financial condition.

Insurers next attracted attention as a source of revenue for the state. New York State was the first to act when, in 1824, it imposed a 10 percent tax on the premiums received in New York by fire insurers domiciled in other states. Many states soon thereafter taxed the stock of domestic (in-state) insurers or collected fees from insurance agents, who had to be licensed. To determine these taxes, the states needed periodic reports from insurers. The reports also provided information on their financial condition.

From Direct Charters to General Incorporation Statutes Around the middle of the nineteenth century several states stopped granting direct charters from legislatures to corporations, including insurers. Instead, general incorporation statutes were enacted. These statutes stated the mechanics involved, the minimum capital and surplus, and other special requirements. No administrator was charged with regulating insurers formed under these statutes, but the state treasurer or some other official had authority to examine the insurers' reports.

The Beginning of State Insurance Departments In 1851, New Hampshire established an ex-officio board to examine insurer reports and, if possible, prevent insolvencies. ˉA few other states followed. Because the board members usually had major responsibilities elsewhere, the boards were relatively ineffective.

In 1859, New York became the first state to establish a state insurance department headed by a single superintendent. In 1868, Massachusetts replaced its board with two full-time salaried commissioners, George Sargent and Elizur Wright, who remained in office eight years and were extremely active. Wright, who dominated the commission, is generally regarded as one of the most able and effective commissioners ever to have held office. A mathematics professor and abolitionist, Wright argued successfully for a nonforfeiture law (which required life insurers to grant surrender values to insureds who discontinued premium payments on contracts other than short-term insurance policies). His knowledge of mathematics enabled him to explain why there should be a surrender value and how to calculate the amount. Wright approached insurance regulation with the zeal he previously had applied in the antislavery movement. He is credited with numerous fundamental regulatory innovations that were instrumental in establishing life insurance in the United States on a sound actuarial basis. Although Elizur Wright is considered the founding father of state insurance regulation, he unsuccessfully advocated federal regulation of life insurance.

Other states followed Massachusetts and New York in establishing administrative bodies charged with the full-time regulation of insurance.

Paul v. Virginia State regulation of insurance was strengthened by an 1869 decision of the U.S. Supreme Court upholding the constitutionality of state regulation of foreign (out-of-state) insurers operating within their boundaries.[10] By the end of the Civil War, some insurers were already arguing that a uniform federal regulatory statute would be superior to the diversified state regulations that had been enacted or were being discussed by state legislatures.[11] To test the authority of states to regulate foreign insurers, a number of fire insurers decided to challenge a Virginia statute they found burdensome. They argued that one of their agents, a Mr. Paul, should not have to procure a license from the state of Virginia. They contended the Virginia statute was unconstitutional in two respects: (1) a corporation is a person and the federal Constitution gives the persons of each state all the privileges and immunities of citizens in the several states, and (2) only Congress has the power to regulate interstate commerce. The Court upheld the Virginia statute and rejected both of the insurers' contentions. It held that corporations were not persons within the meaning of the section of the Constitution assuring all privileges and immunities for all. Most important, it stated that an insurance policy was not an article of commerce. It was a contract of indemnity. *Because insurance was not even commerce, it could not be interstate commerce. Congress, therefore, did not have the authority to regulate insurance.*

National Association of Insurance Commissioners As more states established insurance departments, a need arose for them to exchange information and views. In 1871, to facilitate such exchanges, these state officials formed the National Convention (now Association) of Insurance Commissioners (NAIC). The organization has met at least annually since that time and has developed *model laws* covering many aspects of insurance regulation. For example, it developed model legislation establishing a statutory fire insurance policy, a model property and liability insurance rating law, and a model bill regulating mail order insurers. Although these model laws are merely advisory and have no legal status, the legislatures of the various states are influenced by the NAIC model laws; sometimes they enact the model laws verbatim. The NAIC has also secured uniformity in the financial statements insurers must file with state insurance departments, in how securities are to be valued, and in various other matters. Through formal and informal discussions with other commissioners, each insurance commissioner is influenced to varying degrees by what appears to be the consensus among the group on various issues.

Further Challenge to State Regulation   State regulation did not remain unchallenged.[12] The Supreme Court was asked to reconsider its decision in 1870, 1886, 1894, 1896, 1899, and 1901. The most serious attack came in 1913 in a case involving an assessment under a Montana premium tax law. The Court did more than uphold Paul v. Virginia; it extended the reasoning by stating that the way an insurer conducted its business (in this case through assessments) did not change the fact that an insurance policy is not an article of commerce.

On six occasions from 1868 to 1933, legislation was proposed that would have replaced state regulation with federal regulation.[13] State insurance regulation was specifically critiqued and criticized by a congressional committee that conducted extensive hearings on a variety of topics during 1939-40. No congressional action followed, however.

U.S. v. South-Eastern Underwriters Association   In 1942 Attorney General McKittrick of Missouri became frustrated in his attempt to prosecute a group of stock fire insurers for violations of the Missouri antitrust laws.[14] In his view, the interstate nature of the insurance business made it impossible for individual states to prevent the abuses that were developing. He urged United States Attorney General Biddle to take action under the federal antitrust laws. Biddle reasoned that although Paul v. Virginia and subsequent cases affirmed the authority of the states to regulate insurance, they did not deny the authority of Congress to also regulate this industry. Accordingly, in a test case in Georgia he charged the South-Eastern Underwriters Association and 198 member companies with the following violations of the Sherman Antitrust Act:

(1) conspiring to fix fire insurance rates in the Southeast,
(2) conspiring to monopolize the fire insurance business in those states,
(3) conspiring to fix commissions, and
(4) conspiring to boycott nonmembers of the association.

The lower court disagreed that the federal antitrust laws applied, citing Paul v. Virginia. On June 5, 1944, however, the U.S. Supreme Court, acting on an appeal by the federal government, held that *insurance was interstate commerce and subject to the federal antitrust laws.* The vote was 4-3 with two justices abstaining.[15]

McCarran-Ferguson Act The South-Eastern Underwriters decision shocked the insurance industry, state regulators, and many parts of the federal government itself. On March 9, 1945, Congress passed *Public Law 15* (technically Public Law 79:15 because it was Public Law 15 enacted by the 79th Congress), also known as the *McCarran-Ferguson Act.* This stated that *continued regulation of insurance by the states was in the public interest.* No act of Congress was to be "construed to invalidate, impair, and supersede any law enacted by any state for the purpose of regulating the business of insurance, or which imposes a fee or tax upon such business."[16] After June 30, 1948, however, the federal antitrust laws would apply to insurance but only to the extent that state regulation was not effective. In cases involving boycott, coercion, or intimidation, the Sherman Act would always apply.

The Present State regulation remains the dominant form of regulation, but the federal government has shown increasing concern over the adequacy of state regulation. Moreover, the federal government's direct involvement in several areas of insurance regulation has grown substantially since 1945.

One recent proposal that received considerable attention proposed a dual regulatory system. A bill introduced by Senator Edward Brooke of Massachusetts would have created a Federal Insurance Guaranty Fund to supplement state guaranty funds designed to pay obligations of insolvent insurers. Of even greater significance was a provision that would have allowed insurers, at their option, to obtain either a federal or state charter. Insurers who chose a federal charter would have been exempt from state regulation on some but not all aspects of their operations. For example, rates, reserves, and investments were to be subject to federal standards, with contract provisions continuing under state regulation. A Federal Insurance Commission was proposed to administer the new guaranty program and the chartering function. Under the bill, insurers would occupy a position analogous to that of banks (which can be chartered either as federal or state institutions).

Supporters of federal chartering argued that the dual system would provide an opportunity to improve the quality of insurance regulation without placing the industry under a single regulatory czar. They cited the advantages of federal regulation over state regulation that are presented later in this chapter. Opponents argued that insurers and banks were not as similar as the bill's supporters believed, that the present bank regulatory system had been severely criticized, and that dual regulation would be more expensive and more cumbersome than the present system. They also denied that federal regulation was superior to state regulation.

The Brooke Bill was not passed. However, in 1979 President Carter's National Commission for Review of the Antitrust Laws recommended repeal of Public Law 15. In its place, they argued, Congress should enact legislation affirming the lawfulness of a limited number of cooperative activities. They recommended that (1) states place maximum reliance on competition in pursuing their regulatory activities and (2) Congress or a special Presidential Commission should study the economic regulation of insurance with emphasis on equity and discrimination, availability and affordability, and the appropriate role of the federal government.

In 1980, Congress considered a bill introduced by Senator Metzenbaum that would delete the section of the McCarran-Ferguson Act that exempts insurance from the federal antitrust laws. Senator Metzenbaum was chairman of the Senate Subcommittee on Antitrust and Monopoly whose activities will be discussed later. This bill would also mandate federal standards for state insurance regulation pertaining to auto insurance and homeowners insurance. One standard would prohibit the use of certain rating factors such as sex, marital status, and occupation.

Federal Regulation The federal government already regulates insurance to some extent under powers it still possesses under Public Law 15. For example, the Attorney General has acted under P.L. 15 in several cases involving boycott, coercion, or intimidation. The Department of Justice has investigated cases in which a lending institution has allegedly required that the borrower purchase insurance from agents or insurers designated by the lender.[17] It has stopped some local organizations of stock company insurance agents from prohibiting their membership from representing any insurers who also engage in direct-writing or insurers not organized as stock companies.[18]

The first federal agency to test the adequacy of state regulation was the Federal Trade Commission, which in 1954 and 1955 questioned misleading advertising by health insurers and developed some rules it intended to apply to all these insurers. It withdrew these rules, however, following two important decisions by the United States Supreme Court dealing with the adequacy of state regulation.[19] The Court held in effect that it was sufficient for a state to have a law (in this instance an unfair trade practices law) regulating activities that would be affected by federal action even though the administration of that state law may be incomplete. The question was whether there were any jurisdictional gaps. On the other hand, the Court did uphold the right of the FTC to regulate mail order insurers not licensed to write insurance in all the states in which they operate.[20] Accordingly, in 1964 the FTC issued a "Guide for the Mail Order Insurance Industry." More recently, the FTC has issued several reports on the insurance industry including a highly controversial report on the possible rates of return on the savings element in certain types of life insurance contracts. It also financed a study on the economics of insurance discrimination. In 1980 Congress enacted a law that permits the FTC to make studies of the insurance industry only when requested by a majority vote of either the Senate or House Commerce Committees.

The Securities and Exchange Commission (SEC) is an active federal regulator of insurance in limited areas. Its authority is derived from a 1959 Supreme Court decision that variable annuities sold by life insurers are not insurance contracts.[21] Under a variable annuity a life insurer promises to pay the insured a lifetime income, the amount depending upon the performance of the insurer's common stock portfolio in which the premiums are invested. Because variable annuities resemble mutual funds in some ways (but mutual funds do not make the insurance promise of a lifetime income), the Court concluded that variable annuities should be subject to many of the same federal laws and regulations as mutual funds. The insurance aspects continue to be regulated by the states. The SEC also has responsibility for regulating the sale of insurance company securities that are subject to its jurisdiction.

The Department of Justice has successfully challenged the acquisition of some insurers by another insurer or by a noninsurer on the ground that the merger would discourage actual or potential competition. Its right to take this action has been upheld on the ground that the states do not have effective legislation comparable to Section 7 of the Clayton Act prescribing acquisition of the stock of another corporation.[22]

Congress has not passed significant regulation directed specifically at insurance, but recently it has conducted numerous investigations and considered several bills that would have had far-reaching effects on the insurance industry. The most active Congressional body has been the Subcommittee on Antitrust and Monopoly of the United States Senate Committee on the Judiciary. Under a number of strong leaders, it has since 1958 investigated and issued extensive reports on such varied matters as the nature and structure of rate regulation, ocean marine insurance, aviation insurance, alien insurers, substandard auto insurance, how to measure the cost of life insurance, and the use of age, sex, marital status, and territories in pricing auto insurance. Two other pending proposals indicate the growing interest of Congress in insurance and would, if enacted, have significant implications for private insurers. The proposed laws would (1) establish a model no-fault auto insurance statute that would replace state no-fault statutes not meeting the standards set by the federal law and (2) establish a similar model workers' compensation law.

The Employee Retirement Income Security Act (ERISA), passed by Congress in 1974, is the most important insurance-related act passed by Congress since P.L. 15. This act imposed on private pensions requirements that affect nearly all interested parties. For example, the act prescribes the minimum standards for the "vesting" of those pension benefits financed by employer contributions. A fully vested benefit is one to which the employee is entitled at retirement even though he or she left the employer *before* retirement. The act also prescribes the minimum time after which the pension plan is to have accumulated enough funds to meet all outstanding promises, and the disclosure of certain information concerning the plan's operations to participants and regulatory officials. The act is administered by the Department of Labor and the Treasury Department.

State Regulation   The U.S. Supreme Court decision in the South-Eastern Underwriters Association case created tremendous uncertainty as to the future of state insurance regulation. The most important immediate regulatory response to P.L. 15 was the development of a model rate regulatory law in the late forties by the National Association of Insurance Commissioners. Laws patterned after the NAIC model permitted insurers to agree to use the rates developed by rating bureaus. To counter the charge that pricing in concert would constitute a violation of the Sherman Act, the laws required prior approval of all rates. Insurers had to file their rates with the state insurance department. The department had a specified time such as twenty or thirty days to approve or disapprove the proposed rates. Price competition was possible because bureau insurers were permitted to request deviations from the bureau rates, insurers were not required to belong to the bureau, and all insurers, bureau or not, could pay dividends that would reduce the initial premiums.

Most states adopted the model law or a closely related law. Only California adopted an open-competition law applicable to most property and liability insurance lines other than workers' compensation.[23] It prohibited agreements to adhere to bureau rates and, in the spirit of the Sherman Act, relied more on competition to regulate rates. Today nineteen states have California-type laws; the rest permit agreements to adhere to bureau rates, which are usually coupled with model-law type prior approval requirements. In 1968 the NAIC in a short statement of principles switched its support from the model law to the open-competition approach favored by the federal government.[24] In December, 1980, the NAIC approved a model rating law that would eliminate all rate filing requirements except for personal lines, require insurers to file rates for personal lines but to use them prior to the filing deadlines, prohibit agreements to adhere to bureau rates, and permit rating bureaus to provide trended loss data for all lines but not expense or profit data. This model law was recommended as an alternative to, not a replacement for, prior approval laws for those states favoring the open competition approach.

Other state actions include the passage by most states of an Unfair Trade Practices Act for Insurance and an Unauthorized Insurers Process Act. The first prohibits unfair methods of competition and unfair and deceptive acts or practices such as misrepresentation and false advertising, boycott, coercion or intimidation, and filing of false financial statements. The second designates the state insurance official as the attorney-in-fact upon whom legal process-may be served in cases involving an unauthorized and unlicensed insurer. The budgets of state insurance departments, though still extremely small relative to their responsibilities, have increased, and the average caliber of state insurance departments appears to be improving. Wisconsin for several years has been developing what many consider to be a model insurance code based on research and extensive hearings. The NAIC has established a central research office which has already produced some excellent studies.

Federal and State Regulation Compared Which is better, federal or state regulation? The debate continues with essentially the the same arguments. However, the persuasiveness of these arguments changes as events seem to support or refute specific arguments and as the prevailing political philosophy regarding states rights and the importance of government regulation shifts. The prospects for more federal regulation seem stronger now than in the past, but most observers expect state regulation to dominate for some time.

Arguments Favoring Federal Regulation. The principal argument in favor of federal regulation is that most major insurers operate in two or more states and uniform regulation is desirable for an interstate business. When states regulate insurance, differences are almost certain to occur in state statutes, administrative rules and actions, and court decisions. These differences mean that insureds in one state may be treated differently from those in another state. Insurers are less efficient and their expenses higher because they have to comply with different regulations. For example, they may have to print more than one form of the same contract because wording acceptable in one state is not acceptable in another.

Federal regulation is also claimed to be more efficient merely because insurers would have to deal with only one agency. The argument rests not on the desirability of uniformity but on the belief that one stop means generally less time spent preparing for and conducting negotiations with regulators.

Another major argument advanced in favor of federal regulation is that the federal government could attract a more talented, capable staff of regulators than most states. These federal regulators would be less subject to pressures from insurance industry representatives. Because, it is argued, the federal regulatory agency would have considerable authority, prestige, and status—and because the federal government could probably afford to pay higher salaries than most states—it should be able to attract a high-quality staff. Because of their ability, higher salaries, and national viewpoint, these regulators would be more likely to resist pressures from the insurance industry, especially those reflecting local interests.

A final argument is that some federal regulation exists and, because of the interstate character of some insurance activities, state regulation will never be adequate. Exclusive federal regulation would remove the disadvantages of dual regulation.

Arguments Favoring State Regulation. Conditions vary among the states and a regulation that makes sense in one state may not be appropriate in another state. State regulation permits these differences to be recognized. Desirable uniformity among states is achieved through the National Association of Insurance Commissioners. The uniformity that is claimed for federal regulation would probably not be achieved because the federal administrator charged with this function would most likely establish regional offices whose interpretations would differ.[25]

State regulation, it is also claimed, permits comparisons of different regulatory approaches. For example, some states use the model law-prior approval approach to rate regulation; others have open competition laws. By comparing the profitability to insurers, availability of insurance, expense ratios, and other measures in these states, it may be possible to judge whether one approach is superior. If the evidence clearly favors one approach, the states would probably move in that direction. If not, a diversified approach may be acceptable or even desirable if it reflects local conditions. Because regulation must adapt to changes in the environment, constant experimentation with new approaches should be encouraged.

If one state should enact a statute or impose some regulation which turns out to have been ill-advised or ill-timed, only that state would be affected. If the federal government made the same mistake, the impact would be much greater. In addition to reducing the impact of such mistakes, this characteristic of state regulation reduces the barriers to experimentation.

Many states, it is claimed, have strong insurance departments with personnel as talented as those who would serve in a federal regulatory agency. Fortunately, these states influence the operations of insurers beyond their boundaries. In addition, regulations in other states tend to duplicate the approaches used in the better-staffed states. The staff in most states, it is argued, is responsive but not subservient to local insurance industry pressures. Indeed an insurance lobby might be more effective if it could concentrate its resources on the national body.

Decentralization and dispersion of political power is a desirable goal in itself. To centralize excessive power in one government agency, one business, one union, or any one group is inconsistent with the federal system.

State regulation already exists. It is a known commodity. The pluses and minuses of state regulation are a fact. The complete consequences of a shift to federal regulation are unknown.

Legislative, Administrative, and Judicial Controls

All three branches of government participate in the regulation of insurance at both the state and federal levels.

Legislative Controls The legislature enacts laws that govern various aspects of insurer operations. These laws may deal with organizational procedures, investment of funds, establishment of reserves, filing and approval of rates, mandatory offerings of certain coverages in some lines of insurance, and a variety of other matters. State insurance statutes also authorize regulation by the executive branch of government.

Administrative Controls The executive branch enforces the law. Because laws generally grant the administration considerable discretionary authority, the executive branch does much more than mechanically apply the statutes. Like the legislature, it may lay down some general rules telling insurers what they can and cannot do. These rules give substance to statutes by relating them to specific matters that thereby are made subject to regulation. The executive branch also establishes a form of case law by its daily dealings with insureds and insurers. For example, an insurance department may render a ruling on a complaint filed by an insured. Unless appealed to the appropriate court, that decision governs the resolution of the case.

Judicial Controls   The courts interpret the law and determine its constitutionality. Courts also resolve disagreements among insureds and insurers that cannot be settled out of court. The next three sections deal with three important tasks of insurance regulation and illustrate the important role of each of these branches.

CONTRACT REGULATION[26]

Contract regulation is one of the most important parts of insurance regulation. Many statutes and regulations govern what contracts may be issued and what wording they must contain. Three characteristics of insurance contracts may justify regulatory interest in the field:

(1) Contracts are usually complex. Nearly everyone finds the typical insurance contract difficult to understand and interpret.
(2) The contract is almost always drafted completely by the insurer who presents the contract to the insureds on a take-it-or-leave-it basis. It is this feature of insurance contracts that makes them *contracts of adhesion.*
(3) In exchange for a premium payment by the insured, the insurer promises only to perform in the future if an event covered by the contract occurs. In most cases the insurer need only issue a contract stating its promise; but if the accidental event does occur, particularly if it causes large dollar losses, it is extremely important to the insured and to society that the insurer perform promptly and equitably.

The insurance industry has generally favored contract regulation to the extent that it forces the practices of the more reputable insurers upon the entire industry. The public benefits from this upgrading of contracts that might otherwise be misleading or excessively restrictive. The better insurers are protected against unfair competition from a minority of insurers who might otherwise increase their share of the market unfairly by marketing contracts that appear to be worth more than is actually the case. On the other hand, insurers have tended to oppose contract regulation they consider unwarranted interference with contractual freedom.

Consumer groups have expressed even stronger interest in contract regulation than insurers, but they, too, oppose excessive interference with freedom of contract. Representatives of large businesses prefer more flexibility in contract negotiations than individual insureds. Large businesses have more bargaining power than the typical consumer and are much more likely to participate in drafting the insurance contracts they purchase.

Legislative Control

Contract regulation starts with the legislature. Legislative intervention in contract *formation* may take many forms. The legislature may:

(1) create binding rules of law that override the conflicting terms of the contracts,
(2) dictate the exact terms parties must insert in contracts,
(3) prescribe the substance of terms, or
(4) provide terms or legal rules effective only if the parties do not stipulate otherwise.

It may also empower an administrative agency to intervene in like manner.[27]

Historical Development[28]   Legislative controls over insurance contracts date back to provisions in some early corporate charters. For example, one charter issued in the early 1800s forbade a life insurer from paying if the insured was killed by the police or in a duel or if the insured committed suicide. Insurance statutes were later enacted dealing with other problems, particularly in life insurance.

Fire Insurance.   After the Civil War, legislatures began to exert more control over fire insurance policies. Legislatures singled out fire insurance for close attention earlier than life insurance. Fire insurance contracts contained more limitations on coverage than life insurance contracts. Many properties were insured by two or more insurers. Insurers and insureds encountered difficulties in settling claims because the contracts were not uniform. Also, fire insurance was much more established than life insurance at that time.

Fire insurers ultimately were required to use a standard policy whose terms were specified by statute. Contract uniformity replaced diversity. Connecticut passed such a law in 1867, but the law was repealed in 1868 before any standard policies had been issued. Massachusetts and Michigan took similar action in the next two decades. The 1886 standard policy law of New York State is usually cited as the beginning of this type of strong contract regulation, probably because most other states eventually copied it.

Some voluntary action preceded the enactment of the New York law. As early as 1867 the National Board of Fire Underwriters, a trade association of stock insurers, became interested in uniformity. The New York Board of Fire Underwriters, a local organization of insurers, actually produced a standard policy that was adopted by many of its member insurers. The insurance industry then pressed unsuccessfully for a New York standard policy law. Shortly thereafter two large fires gave two New York state senators, one as owner and one as legal counsel, personal experience with the diversity that existed among insurance contracts. The bill they introduced as a result of their experiences was opposed by the industry because it would have given the Superintendent of Insurance the authority to draft a standard policy. A compromise evolved giving the Superintendent this authority unless the New York Board of Fire Underwriters filed one within a limited period. Within six months the Board produced the 1886 New York Standard Policy. Nearly all state standard policies drafted after this date were closely related to the New York form.

The 1886 New York policy was not popular with insureds because of its highly technical and restrictive provisions. In 1913 the New York legislature told the New York Superintendent to request that the National Convention (later renamed Association) of Insurance Commissioners adopt a model standard policy that would replace the 1886 form. In 1914, following a cooperative effort by state insurance departments and insurer representatives, the NCIC recommended a form that was less technical and more liberal than the 1886 form, though still unreasonable by today's standards. New York and Wisconsin were the first states to adopt the revised policy, their laws becoming effective in 1918.

In 1943 the National Association of Insurance Commissioners revised the 1918 form making it more generous to insureds and easier to read. The 1943 version of the New York policy is the one used in most states today. How this standard policy affects the writing of fire insurance and allied lines will be discussed in more detail later in this chapter. The policy will be analyzed in detail in Chapter 15.

Life Insurance. Life insurance was the next line to be standardized by statute, but in a different way. Around the start of the twentieth century abuses in the life insurance industry prompted one of the most famous investigations of the insurance business—the Armstrong Investigation of 1905 conducted by a committee of the New York State Legislature. The investigation resulted in many new requirements for life insurers. One requirement was that all domestic insurers in New York use certain standard policies adopted by the legislature unless they received special permission to do otherwise. Foreign (out-of-state) insurers, not being subject to this requirement, soon had a competitive advantage over domestic insurers. For this reason and because of basic dissatisfaction with the rigidity of a standard policy, New York replaced the standard policy forms in 1909 with a law requiring all insurers *operating in* the state to include certain provisions in their policies. The law also prohibited certain other contract provisions. Freedom of contract was still possible to a considerable degree.

Health Insurance. A 1910-11 investigation of health insurance by the National Convention of Insurance Commissioners revealed some practices that were considered "shocking in the extreme."[29] The investigation also resulted in the enactment by most states of a uniform law requiring that health insurers include certain standard provisions in their policies.[30] In 1950 the NAIC adopted a revised Uniform Individual Accident and Sickness Policy Provisions Law that has been adopted by most states. During the sixties and seventies the NAIC recommended and several states adopted laws placing still more restrictions on insurers. The earlier uniform provisions law dealt primarily with post-loss matters, but the newer laws require health insurers to include certain minimum benefits in their contracts or restrict their cancellation rights.

Auto Insurance. Despite their great importance, auto insurance contracts have not been standardized by law. In 1920 the NCIC recommended a statutory auto policy, but no state enacted such a law. In 1934 West Virginia adopted a statutory auto policy hoping it would be used nationwide. Instead, voluntary standard policies were developed by intercompany agreement, and for many years these accounted for most of the auto insurance in force.

Some states have required insurers to rewrite some of their policies to make them more readable by policyholders. The statutes sometimes prescribe specific tests of readability such as the Flesch test. Both the format and the type style may be questioned as well. The policies most affected to date are auto policies and homeowners policies. One indication of more widespread interest in such statutes is the existence of an NAIC committee studying this matter.

Approaches to Standardization Compared Two approaches to statutory standardization were described in the preceding section—a statutory standard policy and statutory standard provisions. This section describes these approaches in more detail and discusses the advantages and disadvantages of each.

Advantages and Disadvantages of Statutory Standard Policy. Fire insurance is the only line with a statutory standard policy. In some states, a statute prescribes word for word the policy that must be included by insurers writing fire insurance in that state. In other states a directive from the state insurance department, operating under authority delegated from the legislature, achieves the same uniformity.

ADVANTAGES. The advantages of such uniformity are:

(1) Consumers do not have to compare differences in policy language among different insurers.

(2) No policy can provide fewer benefits than those prescribed by the standard policy.

(3) In losses involving two or more insurers, there are fewer claim settlement complications.

(4) Courts can develop a more consistent, comprehensive set of interpretations when the same policy is present in each case.

(5) Explanation of the insurance policy and dissemination of this explanation are facilitated when there is only one policy to explain.

(6) Because all insurers use the same policy, their comparable claims experience facilitates the use of pooled experience for rate making.

(7) State insurance departments would find it impossible to review carefully the multitude of policy provisions that would otherwise be developed.

DISADVANTAGES. On the other hand, some disadvantages are associated with uniformity:

(1) Statutory policies are difficult to change. A legislature must be convinced that change is necessary and desirable. Pressed by demands for action in so many areas, legislatures have tended to leave statutory policies unchanged for decades.

(2) Statutory policies, like most laws, are a compromise developed to satisfy competing interests. Legislators of various political persuasions, insurers who often disagree among themselves, and consumers with diverse interests may all influence the final product.

(3) Statutory policies are necessarily designed for the average insured but may not meet the needs of all insureds.

(4) The advantages of experimentation and competition are lost.

EVALUATION. The preceding advantages and disadvantages are both overstated. The standardized fire insurance policy is not the entire contract. The contract is always a combination of the statutory policy and at least one form that varies with the type of property insured and the extent of protection desired. For example, the contract may include the statutory policy plus a general property form (covering business properties against specified perils).

Although the fire policy is standardized, the attached form is not unless, as is seldom the case, there is a state directive calling for complete standardization. This lack of a standardized form gives rise to several possibilities:

(1) Consumers may have to choose among different contracts.
(2) Different contracts may be involved in the same loss (though this is not as likely).
(3) Courts may be faced with different contract language.
(4) There may be more than one contract that must be explained to consumers and insurance personnel.
(5) The experience of two insurers may not always be comparable because their contracts differ.
(6) State insurance departments must review various submissions.

Nevertheless, the differences among contracts are less than they would be without the statutory policy.

The fire insurance contract can be changed readily because changes can be effected through the form. Even if the state insurance department prescribes the form, these directives are more responsive to change than are statutes. The insured usually has a choice of more than one form. The contract can be adapted by combining forms and endorsements that meet various needs. Unless all insurers are required to use the same form, there can be some experimentation and response to competitive initiatives.

In recent years, insurers have developed many new policies that, like the standard fire policy, involve coverage of fixed-location property against the peril of fire. Though including the fixed-location fire exposure, these documents have been approved for use in some states without the complete incorporation of the terms of the standard fire policy. The desire for simplicity and improved readability has been an important factor in motivating this relaxation, which is much easier to accomplish in states where standardization was based on regulation rather than statute.

Advantages and Disadvantages of Statutory Standard Provisions. The most common approach to uniformity is through statutory prescription of standard provisions to be included in certain insurance contracts. This approach is used in life, health, liability, and workers' compensation insurance. At one time many states required the exact wording of these standard provisions to be included in the contract. Today the dominant practice is to permit different language so long as it is not less favorable to the insured. These laws may also prohibit certain types of provisions and permit others on an optional basis if the language is at least as liberal as the standard.

Standard provisions are more flexible than a statutory policy because (1) they are only part of the contract and (2) the provisions need not be uniform. Consumers are still protected against standard provision language that is less liberal than the statutory language.

Explanation of the insurance contract is facilitated because part of the contract is subject to minimum standards.

Statutory standard provisions are not easily changed, but it is much easier to change one or more of these provisions than to revise a statutory policy. Insurers and insureds gain from experimentation and competition related to the parts of the contract not covered by the standard provisions.

Policy Approval To ensure compliance with statutory policy laws and standard provisions and to reduce the possibility of misleading language, legislatures generally require insurers to file new contracts with the state insurance department for review. With a *prior approval* law, found in most states, the contract can be used only after department approval. If a specified period elapses without the contract being disapproved, the contract is "deemed" to have been approved. Some of these states permit the state insurance department to extend this *deemer period*. The purpose of the deemer clause is to encourage a prompt review, but it may also cause the review to be perfunctory. Most prior approval laws also give the insurance commissioner the authority to disapprove contracts at some later date, but in practice this is unlikely.

In states with a *file and use* law, the insurer can use the new contracts immediately. However, the contract is subject to subsequent disapproval.

Administrative Control

Administrative control includes:

(1) promulgation of general rules that may not be included in policies,
(2) enforcement of general rules developed by the legislature or the state insurance department, and
(3) action on individual cases.

General Rules The promulgation of general rules has become an increasingly important part of administrative control. These rules may be stated in (1) regulations communicated by the department, (2) informal circulars or bulletins, or (3) case law developed out of the approval process. Through some rules, state insurance departments carry out specific directives from the legislature; through others, they implement the general authority they have for contract control.

For example, the legislature specifically may give the state insurance department authority to prescribe standard language for the forms or endorsements to be added to the statutory fire policy. Through regulations, the department may prescribe the actual forms to be used. Through informal circulars, the department may use its general authority to inform insurers that certain provisions will be disapproved.

Promulgating a regulation is usually a more formal and lengthy process than issuing an informal circular or bulletin. Before a regulation is issued, it is common to hold a hearing at which affected parties may present their views.

Rule Enforcement The most characteristic, time-consuming type of administrative control is the enforcement of laws enacted by the legislature or rules generated by the insurance department. States vary greatly in the resources devoted to this effort and the formality of the process.

According to Kimball and Pfennigstorf, in reviewing contracts filed by an insurer:

> ...[a] first comparison is usually made of the submitted form with the statute and with applicable regulations to see whether formal requirements are met, whether the policies contain the required standard provisions, and whether they contain any prohibited provisions.... Rules and statutes now quite generally provide that the commissioner shall inform the insurer of his objections and that the insurer shall be entitled to a formal hearing ... this is also sometimes done even when the statute does not specifically require it.[31]

The formal review is often preceded by informal preliminary discussions about whether certain clauses are admissible.

The basic principles underlying the approval process are usually not stated explicitly. If a basic principle is stated, the statements may not be in writing, and, if in writing, they may be discernible only by reviewing thousands of files. Nevertheless, Kimball and Pfennigstorf have suggested some common criteria, three of which are described below:

(1) Insurance departments are inclined to encourage enlargement of coverage and to discourage its restriction. For example, departments tend to disapprove clauses that exclude coverage that would otherwise be provided under the general insuring clause.

(2) Some public policy principles mentioned explicitly in contexts other than contract approval are considered in reviewing contracts. Illustrations are reasonableness in the relationship of premiums to benefits and the financial solvency of the insurer.

(3) Except in their enforcement of the statutory standard fire policy and standard provisions laws, the elimination of diversity has *not* been an important objective.[32]

In reviewing contracts the commissioner has more discretion in fact than in law. The discretion granted by statutes varies among states and among lines. For example, commissioners have the least discretion with respect to the statutory fire policy, more with respect to statutory standard provisions which permit language at least as favorable, and most with respect to contract provisions subject only to general standards. Discretion in practice exceeds discretion in law because insurers have been reluctant to challenge the commissioner in court.

Complaint Function   State insurance departments frequently intervene in disputes between insurers and insureds concerning the interpretation of insurance contracts. The main focus of this activity is the settlement of losses, but the department also develops information relevant to its contract approval function. For example, it may discover that a previously approved contract contains some misleading language and should be disapproved. It also learns more about what language is likely to be misleading—information that is useful in its prior review function.

Judicial Control

Judicial contract regulation differs from legislative control and administrative control in that it depends upon the accidents of litigation. The only contracts reviewed are those brought to the attention of the courts. The litigation may involve laws by the legislature, regulations or rules promulgated by the state insurance department, rule enforcements by the department, and contracts issued by insurers.

One objective of judicial control is to determine whether laws are constitutional—whether state insurance department directives are constitutional and in compliance with authority delegated by the legislature, whether department rule enforcements are consistent with state laws and department directives, and whether contracts issued by insurers are consistent with the body of laws and directives applicable to them. A second objective is to interpret laws, state insurance department directives, and insurance contracts. Though unplanned, judicial control is thus far-reaching.

In exercising judicial control, courts sometimes cite public policy considerations. For example, courts require that property insurance contracts protect persons only to the extent to which they have a financial interest in the loss. Contracts that do not require insureds to have an insurable interest are contrary to public policy and void because they would permit some insureds to gain from a loss. Courts seldom face public policy questions, however, because insurers are anxious to draft and issue contracts that avoid these issues.[33]

Courts exercise significant control over the terms of insurance policies through being called upon to resolve disputes over their meaning. A major force in this process is the *contra proferentem* rule, which results in ambiguities being interpreted against the drafting party. Because insurers so often draft insurance contracts on a take-it-or-leave-it basis, those contracts are considered contracts of adhesion and thus subject to the *contra proferentem* rule. When the legislature drafts the contract, or the policyholder or the policyholder's representative plays a more active role, courts tend to follow the same rule, but the rationale must differ. With respect to statutory policies or standard provisions, it can be argued that the insurance industry probably exerted considerable influence during the drafting process. With respect to contracts drafted partly by legislatures or policyholders, it can be argued that ambiguities should still be resolved in favor of insureds so that insurance might continue to reduce uncertainty.

FORMATION AND LICENSING OF INSURERS

To transact business in a given state as an admitted insurer, the insurer must be licensed by the state insurance department. Only admitted insurers are permitted to have agents or sales representatives in the state and market types of insurance that are available from other admitted insurers. As will be discussed later, nonadmitted insurers can legally operate only through the mails or by marketing only insurance that cannot be obtained from admitted insurers. Nonadmitted insurers that attempt to sell through personal contacts insurance that is available on an admitted basis may subject themselves and their agents to civil or even criminal penalties.

A license declares that the insurer has complied with the state's insurance laws and regulations and is thus authorized to write specified kinds of insurance in the state. The issuance of the license indicates that, in the opinion of the state, the insurer meets minimum standards of financial strength, competence, and integrity. If this evaluation later changes, the license can be revoked. The legislature enacts the laws governing formation and licensing, the state insurance comissioner enforces them, and the courts rule on their constitutionality, their interpretation, and the legality of the department's enforcement actions.

Domestic Insurers

For domestic insurers, licensing is a two-step process. First, the insurer must be organized. Second, the insurer must be licensed or authorized to transact insurance in its home state. It must also secure a license in the other states where it operates as a foreign insurer. The license secured as a domestic insurer generally has no expiration date. The license secured by a foreign or alien (out-of-country) insurer generally has to be renewed each year. Attention in this section will be focused on the formation and licensing of domestic insurers.

Domestic insurers are almost always organized under general incorporation statutes. The organizers must meet the conditions imposed on corporations engaged in noninsurance activities plus some special conditions imposed on insurers. The organizers file an application for a charter which states, among other things, the names and addresses of the incorporators, the name of the proposed corporation, the territories and lines of insurance in which it plans to operate, the total authorized capital stock (if any), and its surplus. Whereas applications to incorporate other businesses are typically forwarded to the secretary of state, applications to form an insurer are typically sent to the state insurance commissioner who reviews the application to see whether the proposed insurer also meets the state's special licensing requirements.

Tests of Financial Strength A major concern of the state is that the insurer be financially strong. Because of this concern, state laws require that domestic *stock* insurers satisfy certain minimum capital and surplus requirements before the commissioner can grant them a license. For example, the minimum capital required may be $500,000 with a paid-in surplus equal to 50 percent of the capital amount. These requirements vary widely among the states as to their amounts and as to how they are affected by the lines of insurance written.

Breslin and Troxel have distinguished between the purpose of the capital requirement and the surplus requirement as follows:

> Capital and surplus in a stock insurance company serve distinctly separate functions. If the company fails, capital acts as a guarantee fund to protect policyholders from loss. Minimum capital therefore must be maintained at all times; an impairment renders the company technically insolvent even though admitted assets may substantially exceed liabilities. Paid-in surplus does not remain whole after the company is formed. It provides funds to pay for organizational fees, development expenses, establishment of an agency force, and to meet loss settlement fluctuations.[34]

Some states do not recognize this distinction. They require that the insurer *maintain* capital and surplus equal to the minimum initial requirements after it commences operations.

In most states the initial capital and surplus requirement does not depend on the premium volume the insurer intends to write. The requirement does vary, however, according to the lines of insurance the insurer will offer to the public. For example, to write fire insurance, an insurer might be required to have a specific minimum capital and surplus. For each additional kind of insurance listed in the statute that the insurer intends to write, the dollar requirement is increased. For a multiple-line insurer planning to write all kinds of insurance except life insurance, most states impose a lower capital and surplus requirement than the sum of the requirements for the separate lines.

Critics of present statutes object to (1) how the minimum requirements vary among the states, (2) what they consider to be very low minimum requirements in many states, (3) the failure of most states to relate these requirements to the premium volume to be written, and (4) the need for a more logical relationship between the amounts required and the mix of insurance lines in the underwriting portfolio. They also argue that (5) economic conditions change the adequacy of a fixed dollar requirement. For example, Hammond, Shapiro, and Shilling have shown that the "safe" maximum ratio of premiums to capital and surplus varies depending upon the size of the insurer, the lines of insurance written, and economic conditions. They favor a statute that permits the commissioner to use more judgment and consider many factors in establishing the minimum capital and surplus requirements.[35]

Because a *mutual* insurer has no capital, the minimum requirement applies only to paid-in surplus. Most states require that mutuals have an initial surplus equal to the minimum capital and surplus requirement for stock insurers writing the same line(s) of business. Some, however, set a minimum surplus requirement for mutuals that is lower than the capital and surplus requirements for stock insurers. Furthermore, while the stock insurer must often maintain in the future both its initial capital and surplus, some states require mutual insurers to maintain only a fraction, such as two-thirds, of the initial amount required. In most of these states, however, if the mutual insurer wishes to issue nonassessable policies, it must satisfy the requirements for stock insurers.

To organize a mutual, in many states, it is also necessary to have applications from more than a stated number of persons on more than a stated number of separate exposures with aggregate premiums in excess of a certain amount. The purpose of this requirement is to provide the insurer with a minimum book of business and hence more stability the day it opens its doors. The numbers and dollar amounts required, however, tend to be small.

Mutual insurers are more difficult to organize than stock insurers because (1) sponsors are reluctant to provide the initial surplus (which they can lose with no profit possibility as an offset) and (2) it is difficult for an insurer that has not commenced operations to sell policies. Consequently, some persons interested in forming a mutual insurer organize instead a stock insurer and minimize the profit objective. Later they may convert the stock insurer to a mutual.

Other Requirements. In addition to establishing tests of financial strength, states often have other formation or licensing requirements. For example, the proposed name for a mutual insurer must include the word "mutual." The proposed name of any new insurer must not be so similar to that of any existing insurer that it would be misleading. The commissioner may have the authority to refuse a license if he or she believes the incorporators or directors of the insurer are untrustworthy. Some states even permit the commissioner to deny a license to an otherwise worthy applicant if he or she believes that there is no need for additional insurers in the state. Once the license is issued it can be revoked if the insurer operates in a manner that is clearly detrimental to the welfare of its policyholders (for example, consistent failure to pay legitimate claims or fraudulent business conduct).

Foreign and Alien Insurers

To be licensed in a particular state, foreign insurers must demonstrate first that they have satisfied the requirements imposed on them by the state in which they are domiciled. Second, they must generally satisfy the minimum capital and surplus and other requirements imposed on domestic insurers by the state in which they wish to transact business.

Alien (non-U.S.) insurers must also satisfy the requirements imposed on domestic insurers by the state in which they desire to be licensed. In addition they must usually establish a branch office in some state and have funds on deposit in the United States equal to the minimum capital and surplus required.

Acceptable Nonadmitted Insurers

Under surplus lines laws a nonadmitted insurer may be permitted to transact business through agents or brokers if (1) the insurance cannot be obtained after a diligent search has been made to secure the protection from admitted insurers, (2) the nonadmitted insurer is "acceptable," and (3) the agent or broker has a special license authorizing him or her to place such insurance. Usually the surplus lines agent or broker must be a resident of the state.

Generally an "acceptable" nonadmitted insurer must file a financial statement that the commissioner finds satisfactory, appoint the commissioner as agent to receive service of process in the state, obtain a certificate of compliance from its home state or country, and, if an alien insurer, maintain a trust fund in the United States. Some states leave the determination of acceptability to the agent or broker. A few permit brokers or agents to use other nonadmitted insurers if the desired insurance cannot be obtained from either admitted or what the state has deemed "acceptable" nonadmitted insurers.

LICENSING OF AGENTS AND BROKERS

Agents and brokers must be licensed in each state in which they transact business. Agents or brokers who operate in the state without a license are subject to civil and sometimes criminal penalties. Most states issue both agents' licenses and brokers' licenses; the others issue only agents' licenses—in which case brokers become agents of the particular insurer involved in each transaction.

Until recently, some states simply required that an insurer sponsor persons seeking an agents' license. This approach assumed that insurers would not sponsor anyone who was not competent or trustworthy enough to become an agent. Today, all states require applicants to pass an examination administered by the department or, in several states, sponsored by the department but administered by Educational Testing Service.[36] The exams differ as to their degree of difficulty and as to how many different exams a candidate must pass to market all types of insurance. Some states require that before taking the license examination the applicant complete some classroom training. Currently, twenty-four states excuse applicants from the department exam if they have completed the CPCU Program. Applicants may also be excused if they have taken an exam similar to the department exam after completing an approved course. Some states have reciprocal agreements whereby the exam is waived for agents or brokers who have met the requirements in other states. A model licensing bill adopted by the NAIC in 1973 requires a written examination but excuses CPCUs from all parts of the property and liability insurance examinations except those dealing with the rules, regulations, and laws of the particular state.

Licenses generally have a term of one year but they are usually renewed automatically upon the payment of a fee. A few states, however, have introduced continuing education or, less commonly, reexamination requirements which agents and brokers must satisfy if they want their licenses renewed. For example, the Washington state insurance department has issued a regulation that requires thirty-six hours of continuing education annually for the first five years, twenty-four hours during each of the next five years, and twelve hours a year thereafter. In 1978 the NAIC adopted a model regulation establishing continuing education requirements. The Model Bill specifically includes CPCU courses as qualifying for these continuing education requirements, as does the Washington regulation.

Some states license only residents. All but a few states have *countersignature* laws which require that all policies covering subjects of insurance within a state be signed by a resident agent licensed in the state. Some require that the resident agent be paid some fraction (usually 25 to 50 percent) of the total commission. These laws currently are facing strong challenges.

Under an *unfair trade practices act* (found in all states) the commissioner may revoke or suspend an agent's license because of dishonesty or fraud, misrepresentation (including twisting), or unfair discrimination (including rebating). Instead of revoking the license or in addition to this revocation the commissioner may impose a fine for these misdeeds. *Dishonesty* or *fraud* may cheat the insurer or the insured. (For example, a dishonest agent may embezzle some of the premiums paid by policyholders or keep for himself or herself some of the money that the insurer had supplied for small loss payments to policyholders.) *Misrepresentation* of the losses that would be covered by an insurance contract may induce an insured to purchase that contract under false pretenses. *Twisting* is a special form of misrepresentation in which the agent or broker induces a policyholder through misrepresentation to replace one contract with another to the detriment of the insured. *Unfair discrimination* is any act that favors one insured unfairly over others.

Rebating can take many forms, but a good example is refunding by the agent to insureds of part of the agent's commission. Rebating was the first form of unfair discrimination to be prohibited by law—in an 1886 Louisiana statute. It is specifically listed among the unfair trade practices in the more recent unfair trade practices acts. If an agent were to rebate part of his or her commission to one policyholder but not to another, that act would be considered unfair discrimination. If the agent were to rebate the same percent of his or her commission to all policyholders, that act would not be unfairly discriminatory but it would still be considered illegal. The reasoning behind such laws is that they prohibit unfair discrimination, protect small agencies against large agencies, and protect career agents against noncareer agents. Rebating laws, however, have proved difficult to enforce. They also have not prevented the negotiation of the fees and commissions to be paid agents and brokers under rating plans designed for large-premium insureds.

States that issue separate brokers' licenses may use a set of examinations different from the agent licensing examinations to test the competence of candidates, or higher standards may be imposed on candidates for the broker's license. The reason for these tougher exams is that an applicant for a broker's license does not have a sponsoring insurer who is broadly responsible for his or her conduct. Some states prohibit persons from taking the brokers' examination until they have been a licensed agent for a specified period, such as two years.

Surplus-line agents or brokers must previously have been licensed as an agent or broker. In most states, the only additional requirement is the payment of a fee and the posting of a surety bond which guarantees, among other things, that they will pay the state premium tax on the nonadmitted insurance. Some states administer a special examination program for surplus-line agents or brokers.

GOVERNMENT INSURERS

The extreme form of government regulation is to substitute a public operation for private enterprise. The government has taken action in this direction in insurance at the federal, state, and local government levels. This section will examine the reasons for government insurance, indicate the degree to which private insurers are involved in government insurance operations, and describe in detail those government operations with particular relevance to property and liability insurance.

Reasons for Establishing Government Insurers

Government insurers fall into two classes: (1) those who write insurance on exposures not considered commercially insurable and (2) those who write lines also written by private insurers.

Exposures Not Commercially Insurable The discussion of commercially insurable exposures in Chapter 6 indicated that public insurers can safely write some exposures that private insurers would wisely reject. Three examples were buildings and personal property exposed to flood damage, persons exposed to unemployment, and property exposed to war damage. All three exposures could cause serious losses, making some type of protection highly desirable. If private insurance is not available, public insurance should receive

widespread acceptance (assuming it is soundly designed and administered).

Other important exposures generally considered commercially
uninsurable but covered under government programs include depositors with accounts exposed to bank failures, savings and loan association failures, or credit union failures; pension plan failures; exports
exposed to potential losses such as inconvertibility of foreign curren-
cies; business properties abroad exposed to expropriation or other
political losses; and investors exposed to brokerage house insolvencies.

Flood. Buildings and most personal property exposed to flood
damage were considered not commercially insurable principally because (1) the exposures are not independent; (2) the premiums required
in flood-prone areas would be much higher than most, if not all,
prospective insureds would be willing and able to pay; and (3) only
persons with exposures with an above-average likelihood of flood
damage would seek insurance. Despite these problems, subsidized flood
insurance is now readily available from a public insurer. More details
on this important government program which involved private insurers
until 1978, appear later in this chapter. Because the government pays a
substantial part of the cost, the premiums are affordable to many
persons in flood-prone areas, and this increases the number of insureds.
The federal government also requires the purchase of flood insurance
by persons living in a participating community who seek financial
assistance from a federal office or agency or a federally regulated or
insured institution for acquiring or constructing property in flood-prone
areas. This compulsion and some inducements increase the number of
insureds and reduce adverse selection.

Unemployment. Unemployment exposures were considered not
commercially insurable mainly because (1) the exposures are not
independent and (2) their expected losses are almost impossible to
predict in the short run. However, public unemployment insurers exist
in each of the fifty states plus the District of Columbia. Public insurers
can write unemployment insurance primarily because the insurance is
compulsory. Compulsion ensures a substantial number of insureds
regardless of the premiums charged. If the premiums charged one year
are too low, the insurer can raise the premiums later to compensate for
the earlier excess losses. Alternatively, it can set the premiums at a
level that will be adequate on the average even though they may be too
high some years and too low other times.

War. War exposures are not commercially insurable during
wartime because (1) the exposures are not independent, (2) the cost
would be very high, and (3) the expected losses are difficult to predict in

the long run or the short run. During wartime this insurance has been available only from government insurers.

Depositors' Accounts. Depositors in most commercial or mutual savings banks are protected against losses from bank failure by the Federal Deposit Insurance Corporation (FDIC). If one of these banks fails, the FDIC either pays the depositors or attempts to rehabilitate the bank or arrange a merger with another financial institution. The maximum coverage on single accounts is currently $100,000 per depositor. Each depositor's interest in joint accounts is also insured separately up to $100,000. The exposure is commercially uninsurable because the exposures are not independent and adverse economic conditions that cause one bank to fail may cause many other banks to fail at the same time. The principal problem, however, is that expected losses are too difficult to predict. The FDIC has the great advantage over private insurers that its coverage is compulsory for most banks. They must purchase the insurance for the benefit of depositors. This results in pricing flexibility.

The Federal Savings and Loan Insurance Corporation and the National Credit Union Administration provide similar protection for depositors in savings and loan associations and in credit unions. Private insurers do not insure these depositors for the same reasons they do not insure bank depositors.

Pension Plans. The Pension Benefit Guaranty Corporation guarantees participants in private pension plans that, if their plan is terminated with insufficient assets, they will receive at retirement, up to specified limits, the vested pension benefits they had earned up to the termination date.

Exports. The Export-Import Bank issues policies that protect United States exporters against losses incurred in extending credit to foreign buyers because of potential actions by foreign nations causing war, revolution, insurrection, confiscation, or inconvertibility (the inability of the foreign buyer to change its local currency into U.S. dollars). The Export-Import Bank is a federal agency. Private insurers have not been willing to insure this exposure because of its lack of independence and the inability to predict expected losses. Because the Export-Import Bank's program is voluntary, it cannot depend on insureds remaining in the program if it raises premiums. Nevertheless, the operation has proved feasible, perhaps because the insurance is not written alone. Instead, the exporter must purchase from the Foreign Credit Insurance Association a contract that also covers regular commercial credit exposures such as customer insolvencies. The Foreign Credit Insurance Association is an organization including about fifty private insurers. This combination policy has proved attractive to exporters.

Business Properties Abroad. Business properties abroad exposed to expropriation or other political losses have been considered commercially uninsurable because they are not independently exposed and because it is extremely difficult to predict the expected losses. Protection against such losses is provided by another federal agency, the Overseas Private Investment Corporation (OPIC), if the property is located in a less-developed country and it contributes to that country's economic development.

In addition to insuring buildings and their equipment, OPIC insures other properties such as patents, management services, and loan guarantees made to foreign banks. The insurance may be extended under certain conditions to cover all perils not specifically excluded, not just political perils. The insurance is voluntary, but the potential losses are so great and frequent that even without a subsidy the insurance has proved attractive to many investors.

Following some adverse experience which required government subsidies, Congress decided in 1974 that OPIC should become a self-sustaining operation and that by 1980 it should become only a reinsurer of potential losses above a certain amount with private insurers providing the base coverage. Toward this end, OPIC has involved a partnership of private insurers, the Overseas Investment Insurance Group, in some of its writings. In 1978 Congress reversed its privatization mandate. Private insurers now write reinsurance only, the Overseas Investment Insurance Group being replaced by the Overseas Investment Reinsurance Group, a consortium of private United States and foreign insurers.

Investors Exposed to Brokerage Insolvencies. Investors exposed to losses due to brokerage house insolvencies may be protected by the Securities Investor Protection Corporation (SIPC), a federal agency which became effective at the end of 1970, following the insolvency of some large investment firms holding securities and deposits belonging to their customers.[37]

Exposures That Are Commercially Insurable

Public insurers do not limit their writings to exposures that are not commercially insurable. Indeed, the bulk of the premiums written by public insurers cover exposures also written by private insurers. Some public and private programs are very similar while some are very different.

OASDHI. Old Age, Survivors, Disability, and Health Insurance is an example of government insurance that is quite different from its private sector counterpart—the private life and health insurance business. Both cover persons exposed to death, old age, and poor health. OASDHI, however, is also designed to achieve certain social objectives.

The OASDHI benefit structure deliberately favors low-income workers over high-income workers and workers with dependents over those with no dependents. Private insurers' cost-benefit relationships consider only actuarial variables such as interest rates and the probability of death. Private insurers stress actuarial or private equity among individuals while OASDHI balances private equity and social adequacy or socialization of exposures through a compulsory program. High-income workers and those with no dependents must participate even though the contributions made by them and their employers are used in part to pay benefits to low-income workers and those with dependents.

Compulsion also enables the program to shift costs among generations. Early participants received benefits that on the average far exceeded the actuarial value of their contributions and those of their employers; present participants and their employers will probably pay more *on the average* than the actuarial value of their benefits.[38] If the program were voluntary, some participants (such as high-income workers with no dependents) might choose not to join. Costs were shifted from earlier to later generations for a variety of reasons including (1) the desire when the program started to provide reasonable benefits as soon as possible for those approaching retirement, and (2) concern about the fiscal impact of increasing contribution rates to the level indicated by actuarial calculations.

Compulsion also forces citizens with ample financial resources to purchase protection against important losses that they could insure voluntarily but which many would leave uncovered. In short, the perils covered by OASDHI are commercially insurable, but voluntary private insurance could not achieve some of the social objectives of the government program.

Workers' Compensation. State workers' compensation insurance funds illustrate public insurers whose operations usually resemble those of private workers' compensation insurers. Six states plus Puerto Rico have exclusive (monopolistic) state funds; no private insurers write workers' compensation insurance in those states.[39] Twelve states have *competitive state funds* that compete with private insurers for the workers' compensation premiums in those states.[40] The terms of the competition (i.e., whether the rules are such that they favor public or private insurers), the nature of the public operation (e.g., the quantity and quality of the servicing facilities), and the proportion of the business written by the state fund vary greatly among the states. In a few states, such as Colorado and Utah, their current market share exceeds 50 percent. In others, such as Michigan and Pennsylvania, their share is less than 20 percent.

Supporters of exclusive state funds argue that:

(1) because workers' compensation is compulsory social insurance, private profit-oriented enterprises should not be involved; and

(2) because exclusive state funds have no selling costs and should experience economies of scale, they should have lower expense ratios than either competitive state funds or private insurers.

Exclusive state funds were established because these arguments were compelling or because of circumstances peculiar to a particular state. Those circumstances sometimes included a politician or organizations with considerable influence who philosophically favored the exclusive fund approach, widely scattered and hazardous exposures in which private insurers had not expressed much interest, and a workers' compensation law patterned after the German precedent (which was associated with a state fund) rather than the English precedent (which involved private insurers). Recent attempts to allow competition from private insurers in states with exclusive funds have not been successful. This is due in part to difficulties encountered in placing workers' compensation coverage in the private market.

Competitive state funds have been supported as an alternative to private insurers on the grounds that:

(1) employers who could not secure compulsory protection from private insurers should have an alternative source,

(2) a low-cost, nonprofit public insurance option should exist in a social insurance program, and

(3) a competitive state fund provides a useful yardstick for measuring the performance of private insurers. They have been preferred over exclusive state funds on the assumption that competition with private insurers produces a more efficient public operation.

Nonoccupational Disability.   Five states and Puerto Rico require that most employers make certain nonoccupational disability income benefits available to their employees. One state requires that employers purchase this insurance from an exclusive state fund, three states and Puerto Rico have competitive state funds, and the fifth state requires that benefits be provided through the purchase of private insurance or authorized retention.[41]

The arguments favoring these state funds are the same as those advanced in connection with workers' compensation insurance funds with one addition. In all five states a state fund is responsible for payments to unemployed workers formerly employed by a covered employer, a function that is closely related to that of state unemployment insurance funds.

FAIR Plans. In order to assure that no property owner is denied basic property insurance without a fair evaluation of the individual exposure, Fair Access to Insurance Requirements (FAIR) Plans are operative in twenty-six states, the District of Columbia, and Puerto Rico. These plans, briefly described later in this chapter, are pools of private insurers established by law to guarantee that persons with properties in urban core areas will not be denied insurance because of environmental hazards such as high riot potential. Although technically not a public insurer, the statutory requirement that private insurers participate in pools creates a quasi-public operation. In this instance, the general exposure of properties to fire and related perils is commercially insurable, but some particular exposures which society believes should be insurable are not.

Federal Crime Insurance. A federal crime insurance program, also explained in more detail later in this chapter, makes crime insurance available in states deemed to have a critical availability problem. A critical availability problem exists in a state if the Federal Insurance Administration (FIA) determines that crime insurance is not available from private insurers at an *affordable* price. Because of lower operating expenses and some special loss control requirements, the federal program rates are generally less than those of private insurers. Congress has agreed that, if losses and expenses exceed premiums, it will subsidize the program.

Nuclear Exposures. Despite the fact that the property and liability exposures associated with the operation of nuclear reactors pose many problems, they can be insured by some pools of private insurers. To protect themselves against the catastrophic loss potential and inadequate experience for accurate rate making, nuclear pools have limited the amount of insurance they will sell. The exposure is spread among hundreds of individual insurers.

Because the federal government requires operators of nuclear reactors to have liability insurance protection considerably in excess of the private insurance limits available, the Nuclear Regulatory Commission sells insurance up to the required amount. Congress granted this protection to encourage the development of nuclear reactors for peaceful uses and to protect innocent persons exposed to property losses or bodily injuries. Under a 1975 amendment to the Price-Anderson Act, the federal government's role as an indemnitor is supposed to be gradually phased out. In the event of a nuclear incident, each operator can be assessed up to $5 million for each facility owned to cover losses in excess of the private insurance. The federal insurance will cover losses that exceed the private protection and those assessments up to the $560 million maximum responsibility established by Congress for each operator in 1957. As the number of facilities and the potential assessments increase, the government indemnity will diminish. When the private protection plus the assessments equal $560 million, it will disappear. The $560 million limit on the operators' responsibility will increase beyond that point. This $560 million limit has been criticized as being too low, especially since the Three Mile Island incident in Pennsylvania in 1979.

Parcel Post and Registered Mail. The exposure of parcel post and registered mail shipments to losses in transit is commercially insurable, but similar protection is provided by the Postal Service. The Postal Service is acting like private truckers and other carriers who, in exchange for an extra fee, increase the amount of loss for which they will be responsible on property they transport above the minimum limits that would otherwise apply. Unlike other carriers, however, the Postal Service does not provide any protection with the basic charge.

Private parcel post insurance has proved an attractive alternative to government insurance for many businesses making frequent shipments because it is not necessary to make separate insurance arrangements for each shipment. In many instances the private insurance costs less.

Private registered mail insurance is more attractive to many fiduciary institutions for the same reasons and because the Postal Service limits its maximum liability per package to $10,000. The Postal Service protection, on the other hand, is less expensive and more convenient for shippers who make only a few shipments per year.

Crop Damage. Physical damage to crops is commercially insurable, but until recently the usual form of private insurance was limited to a few perils such as wind and hail or, for fruit and vegetable crops, frost or freezing temperatures.

The Federal Crop Insurance Corporation was originally established to insure cotton and wheat against all natural hazards at a time when such comprehensive insurance was not available privately. Later some private insurers wrote much broader crop insurance than was available at the time FCIC was formed, but even this broad coverage was more limited and was not available to as many farmers as the federal program. (The federal program itself was not available throughout the United States.) Furthermore, the FCIC program was subsidized, with the federal government paying most of the operating and administrative expenses.

The Federal Crop Insurance Act of 1980 has changed this situation dramatically. The objectives of this Act are to make crop insurance the primary form of disaster protection for farmers, to encourage to the maximum extent possible the sale of federal crop insurance through licensed private agents and brokers, to have private insurers become eventually the primary writers of "all-risks" crop insurance, and for the Federal Crop Insurance Corporation to reinsure to the maximum extent practicable private insurers writing "all-risks" crop insurance. To illustrate, farmers may elect to buy "all-risks" crop insurance from private insurers or from the FCIC. In either case, if they do not participate in federal disaster programs, they will receive a 30 percent premium subsidy. Also private insurers will be reimbursed for their marketing costs in order to enable them to price their policies competitively.

Title Insurance. The exposure to loss from a defective title is commercially insured by a large number of insurers. However, in many states, an alternative form of title insurance is underwritten by a state or county insurer. Private insurance indemnifies the insured against financial losses sustained because of a defective title. Public programs, operating within the *Torrens System,* guarantee the title, and indemnify a person who, without negligence on his or her part, sustains loss or damage in consequence of any error, mistake, or misdescription in any certificate of title issued under the system.

Life Insurance. Finally, the State Life Insurance Fund of Wisconsin sells insurance to Wisconsin residents. It was established as a low-cost alternative to private life insurance. Insurance is voluntary, and the maximum amount on any one life is limited.

Summary Public insurers (or quasi-public insurers) write exposures that are commercially insurable for one or more of the following reasons:

(1) to service a compulsory social insurance program for which private profit-oriented insurance is considered inappropriate,
(2) to favor some insureds over others in the pricing or benefit structure,
(3) to provide lower cost insurance through lower operating expenses,
(4) to insure applicants who cannot obtain or would experience difficulty obtaining insurance through normal private channels,
(5) to force citizens to protect themselves against serious potential losses,
(6) to provide insurance at affordable premiums,
(7) to supplement the amount of protection available from private insurers,

(8) to guarantee the service or product of some government agency, and/or

(9) to serve as a yardstick for judging the operations of competing private insurers.

Private Insurer Involvement

Private insurers are involved in a variety of ways in the operations of public insurers. Quasi-public operations, as the term is used in this text, by definition includes private insurers at some phase in the operation. Private insurers may be involved (1) as the primary insurer with the government acting only as a reinsurer or (2) as a servicing agent with the government performing the true insuring function.

Private insurers were until 1978 the basic insurers under the national flood insurance program with a federal agency serving as reinsurer. The government encouraged the purchase of private insurance through subsidized premiums and some compulsion. Generally, however, private insurers have not been involved in the insuring of exposures considered not commercially insurable.[42] Flood insurance on fixed-location property had been written by private insurers on a very limited scale prior to the establishment of the public program. This previous experience plus the many similarities between flood insurance and other forms of private property insurance qualified private insurance companies for an active role in the new government program. Why they are no longer active will be explained later. Private insurance producers still market the product.

With respect to the public insuring of commercially insurable exposures, private insurers often play an active role because of their expertise and widespread service facilities. To develop the necessary expertise and organize a servicing network independently might be difficult and costly for a public insurer. Private insurers are not involved in the old age, death, or disability portions of OASDHI. Private insurers do service the Medicare programs. They adjust claims on behalf of the government and receive a fee based on reasonable administrative costs. State workers' compensation insurance funds have not involved private insurers, but the Michigan competitive fund markets its product through private insurance producers. Private insurers perform a true insurance function in FAIR Plans and the special pooling arrangements for persons unable to secure insurance elsewhere in auto insurance, workers' compensation insurance, and professional liability insurance. The federal crime insurance program uses private insurers to market and service the insurance it alone underwrites. Private insurers are not involved in the programs of the Nuclear Regulatory Commission (except as the suppliers of the first layer of protection), the Postal Service, the Federal Crop Insurance Corporation, Torrens title funds, or the State Life Insurance Fund of Wisconsin.

THREE IMPORTANT PROPERTY
AND LIABILITY INSURANCE PROGRAMS[43]

Three programs overseen by the Federal Insurance Administration will now be examined in detail: (1) FAIR Plans and riot reinsurance, (2) flood insurance, and (3) crime insurance. These three programs were selected because of their importance, their recent formation, the large degree to which the private insurance sector is or has been involved, and the variety of approaches they represent. Emphasis here is on how these public insurance programs operate to meet social needs. Coverages available in these programs are discussed in CPCU 2 and CPCU 3.

FAIR Plans and Riot Reinsurance

Properties in urban areas may be unattractive to private insurers because of either physical or environmental hazards. Environmental hazards are (1) deficiencies in surrounding buildings such as poor construction, hazardous occupancies, poor housekeeping, or congestion; or (2) conditions that make riot, vandalism, theft, or some other human peril more likely. Private insurers have long been reluctant to insure such properties voluntarily. The situation worsened during 1965-67 when many of the nation's cities experienced serious riots and civil disorders. Insurers suffered substantial losses and became even more concerned about environmental hazards and the possibility of catastrophic losses. Businesses and families with properties in riot-prone areas found it increasingly difficult to secure insurance.

The riots also drew attention to the number of uninsured properties and the adverse effects of this lack of insurance. The federal government and many state governments became increasingly worried that the unavailability of insurance would cause many owners to close their business and leave the area. This would cause the inner cities to decline further, increasing the potential for more riots and social deterioration. If riots were to be prevented in the future, it seemed imperative to take steps to increase the availability of insurance in urban core areas.

In July 1967 President Johnson appointed a National Advisory Commission on Civil Disorders to study why the riots occurred and to suggest how they might be avoided in the future. Because the

Commission realized the importance of insurance in its investigation, it appointed a National Panel on Insurance in Riot-Affected Areas.

Voluntary urban-area insurance plans were already in operation in about one-fourth of the states. Under these plans, if fire and extended coverage insurance could not be obtained at standard rates, the property owner could request the local rating bureau to inspect the property. The owner designated an insurer to receive the inspection report. After examining the report, the insurer could (1) insure the property at standard or above standard rates, (2) insure the property only if the owner agreed to make certain changes in the property, or (3) decline to insure the property. Participation was voluntary, but state insurance departments monitored the plans to assess their performance. In its January 1968 report, the Panel suggested a five-part program, two parts of which were based heavily upon these voluntary plans. The Panel:

(1) recommended that urban-area plans should be extended to cover more types of properties, more areas, and additional lines of insurance. The revised plans were to be called FAIR (Fair Access to Insurance Requirements) Plans.
(2) urged the creation of state pools or some other facility for insuring under the FAIR Plans properties declined by individual insurers.
(3) recommended the establishment of a National Insurance Development Corporation to reinsure insurers participating in FAIR Plans against losses resulting from riots that would exceed a specified dollar amount per year.
(4) suggested deferring federal income taxes on amounts insurers set aside in special reserves to meet extraordinary riot losses.
(5) recommended several miscellaneous steps such as more refined premium and loss statistics, better handling of consumer complaints, more economical marketing methods, and recruitment and training programs that would make more inner-city residents a part of the insurance business.

Congress incorporated many of the Panel's recommendations in the August 1968 Urban Property Protection and Reinsurance Act (Title XII of the Housing and Urban Development Act). A National Insurance Development Fund was established to sell private insurers riot reinsurance against catastrophe losses. The Fund is administered by the Federal Insurance Administration, which at that time was part of the Department of Housing and Urban Development. As a result of a recent reorganization, FIA is now part of the separate Federal Emergency Management Agency. The federal riot reinsurance, however, is available only with respect to properties located in states that

(1) require all property insurers operating in the state to belong to an approved FAIR Plan and (2) agree to provide a "financial backup" for the Fund as explained below.

State FAIR Plans By 1980, twenty-six states, Puerto Rico, and the District of Columbia had FAIR Plans. Many of these Plans, however, no longer are approved by the Federal Insurance Administration because they do not meet a new requirement imposed in 1978. The federal statute now requires that the FAIR Plan rates for standard insureds be no higher than standard rates in the voluntary market.

The Plans cover both family and business property. Most provide protection only against the perils required under the federal statute— fire, the extended coverage perils, and vandalism and malicious mischief. Package policies such as homeowners contracts and the special multi-peril policy are offered in only a few states.

FAIR Plans typically provide that any person with an interest in real property or in tangible personal property located in an "urban area" may apply for insurance protection to an Insurance Placement Facility composed of all property insurers operating in the state. The applicant need not have experienced difficulty in securing insurance through normal channels, but those who have not are unlikely to apply because of the limited coverage offered by most FAIR Plans and the less attractive pricing structure. In some Plans "urban area" includes the entire state, but usually it means only the larger communities that are likely to have riots and civil disorders.

The Insurance Placement Facility can take many forms. Usually it is a joint reinsurance association administered by a few servicing insurers. The association shares its experience among all the property insurers operating in the state in proportion to their total writings of the kinds of coverage provided by the Plan. Some state facilities, however, write and service the business directly with a staff hired specifically by the Facility. Again, all property insurers operating in the state finance the Facility and share in its results on a proportionate basis.

If the Facility refuses to insure the applicant at regular rates, the property owner can request that the property be inspected by an inspection agency, typically the local rating bureau. The inspector looks at the building structure, its occupancy, and the condition of adjacent property. As with earlier urban-area plans, the Facility can take one of three actions:

(1) insure the property at regular or surcharged rates,
(2) indicate its willingness to insure the property if the owner makes certain specified improvements, or
(3) deny insurance for reasons noted in the action report.

The federal law that sets standards for Plan approval specifically prohibits the denial of insurance because of the neighborhood in which the property is located or any environmental hazard beyond the control of the property owner. Insurers are permitted to deny insurance because of conditions internal to the property such as faulty construction or defective wiring. Otherwise the program would make insurance available to insureds who should instead be forced to improve their properties.

Depending on the inspection report, the person whose application is accepted may pay either standard or substandard rates. Standard rates may be higher than normal rates outside the Plan because experience has shown that FAIR Plan insureds tend to have higher loss potential than other insureds. As noted above, however, to be approved by the Federal Insurance Administration (thus entitling participating insurers to purchase riot reinsurance), the FAIR Plan must charge standard rates that are no higher than those in the voluntary market. If the property is rated substandard, the extra charge or after charges are determined in the same way as in the voluntary channels. Physical conditions in adjacent properties, but not environmental hazards, affect these extra charges.

FAIR Plans have, since their inception, experienced losses and expenses exceeding their premium income. Many feel that arson has been a significant contributing factor because of the temptation created when value for loss adjustment purposes exceeds market value. This frequently is the case with properties in urban core areas. It may be that environmental hazards do in fact increase the loss potential but these increased exposures are not sufficiently recognized even in the higher standard rates. Another possibility is that the properties contain internal hazards that are not fully recognized. Some argue that the FAIR Plans are dumping grounds for undesirable exposures such as bars and bowling alleys that would tend to be unattractive regardless of their location. In recent years the number of policies issued by FAIR Plans has increased substantially, indicating a continuing shrinkage of the voluntary market's interest in urban participation.

Federal Riot Reinsurance   Insurers can purchase riot reinsurance from the National Insurance Development Fund on properties located in states with approved FAIR Plans. (As noted earlier, at present many FAIR Plans are not approved. Consequently, federal riot reinsurance is not available on properties located in these unapproved states.) Participation in approved FAIR Plan states is optional, but if an insurer elects to participate, it must purchase protection on all of the following lines: fire and extended coverage insurance, vandalism and malicious mischief insurance, allied fire insurance lines, theft insurance, and those portions of package policies covering the same perils. Some other lines may be included if the insurer so desires.

Reinsurance applies separately to each state. Under the standard reinsurance contract developed by the Federal Insurance Administration, each insurer retains the total reinsured riot-related losses it sustains in the state during the current calendar year up to a specified percent of the premiums it earned in the state on all reinsured lines combined, subject to a minimum retention of $1,000. Depending on the premium volume developed, the insurer's retention may be either a large or a small amount. If the insurer's riot-related losses exceed this retention limit, the federal reinsurer pays at least 90 percent of the excess.

The federal reinsurer can obtain the funds needed to pay losses from three sources. First, it uses the reinsurance premiums collected on properties located in that state during the current year or remaining from past years. Second, if the premiums do not supply enough money to pay the reinsurer's losses, the reinsurer can ask the state to contribute funds up to 5 percent of the aggregate property insurance premiums earned on reinsured lines in that state by all insurers, whether they participate or not. Most states have indicated they will obtain the funds for this backup through assessments or other charges on insurers. At least one state will call on general revenues. Third, if the reinsurance premiums and the state financial backup do not provide enough money, the reinsurer can borrow additional funds from the U.S. Treasury. However, the federal government does not subsidize the reinsurance operation; loans from the U.S. Treasury are to be repaid out of future reinsurance premiums.

Fortunately, until the Miami riot in 1980, riot losses since the middle sixties had been less than many persons expected. The federal reinsurer has paid some losses, all of which have been covered by reinsurance premiums paid by insurers. No assessments have been levied, and states have not been asked to provide any monies under the backup provisions. The Miami riot will not affect the program because Florida does not have a FAIR Plan.

The reinsurance program redistributes the reinsured losses among the insurers and, in turn, the insureds in a particular state. Unless the reinsurer is forced to use the second layer of protection, only participating insurers and their insureds share the losses. However, to finance its backup promise, the state may assess all property insurers. Some authorities have argued that the reinsurance program would be more useful if it redistributed losses on a national basis instead of statewide.[44] Others think the program should be disbanded because it is less needed than before and could be replaced by a private reinsurer. Congress, however, keeps extending the lifetime of the program.

National Flood Insurance

In addition to federal riot reinsurance, the Housing and Urban Development Act of 1968 created a national flood insurance program. Title XIII of that Act, called the National Flood Insurance Act, established a private-public venture in which the federal government was from the beginning much more deeply involved than in the riot reinsurance program.

The need for federal flood insurance had been discussed for many years prior to 1968. For reasons noted earlier, private flood insurance on real property was almost unobtainable. Following an extensive study of floods and flood damage in 1952, a major association of private insurers concluded that private flood insurance on real estate was not feasible and that the federal government should simply subsidize unfortunate victims following the loss.[45] Interest in national flood insurance rose dramatically in the middle fifties when serious floods caused substantial property losses, injuries, and deaths in the northeastern sector of the United States. Congress reacted by creating a federal flood indemnity corporation to provide protection at subsidized rates. No insurance was ever written, however, because Congress never appropriated the funds to operate the program and it was disbanded in 1957. Periodically, as serious floods hit various parts of the country, Congress considered establishing similar programs but did not act. In 1966, however, Congress asked the U.S. Department of Housing and Urban Development (HUD) to conduct a flood insurance program feasibility study which subsequently determined that, within limits, such a program was feasible.

The present program was established in 1968. An "emergency" flood program was added shortly thereafter. In 1973 the maximum coverage limits were increased substantially, and many property owners were forced to purchase the insurance. In 1977 the maximum coverage limits were again greatly increased. That year HUD also elected to federalize the program effective in 1978, thus eliminating private insurers as participants. As a result of a reorganization, HUD's role has been assumed by the Federal Emergency Management Agency (FEMA).

Program Details Prior to January 1, 1978, the flood insurance program was underwritten and managed by the National Flood Insurers Association, an organization including over 100 private insurers as members, in accordance with policies established by the Federal Insurance Administration.

During 1977, the Department of Housing and Urban Development proposed regulations that would give HUD management and operational authority over the program. NFIA charged that HUD was violating its contract with the participating insurers and that the new regulations would change the relationship between the Federal Insurance Administration and NFIA from a cooperative venture to one that would reduce the industry pool to a subordinate, mechanical entity. HUD responded that because the purchase of flood insurance is not really voluntary any longer in many cases, the program should not be left in the control of private insurers. NFIA notified HUD that it was terminating its contract as of December 31, 1977; HUD then announced that it was seeking a new administrative agent and invited bids from interested parties.

As a result, in 1978, by authority granted to HUD under the National Flood Insurance Act, national flood insurance became a program in which FEMA purchases administrative services only from a private contractor. The National Flood Insurance Fund, run by the FIA, is now the insurer. EDS Federal Corporation, a subsidiary of Dallas-based Electronic Data Systems, is the administrative services vendor. It is the vendor's responsibility to maintain all policyholder records and funds. Marketing of flood insurance is still performed by local agents in communities enrolled in the program. The vendor appoints local adjusting firms to assist in loss settlements involving flood damage. Financial and statistical reports on the program's performance are prepared by the contractor and submitted to the FIA.

In the debates that preceded the enactment of the flood insurance legislation, it was argued that flood insurance might encourage the unwise utilization of land in flood-prone areas. Consequently, Congress required that before flood insurance could be marketed in any community, its officials had to indicate a need for flood insurance and the willingness and ability to comply with certain requirements. In their application, these officials must (1) cite their legal authority to regulate land use, (2) summarize measures such as codes, ordinances, or regulations that the jurisdiction has already taken to reduce property damage from floods, (3) furnish any reports available on the community's flood problems, and (4) commit the community to enact and maintain in force for areas having "special" flood hazards (an area having at least 1 percent annual chance of flooding) land-use control measures designed to reduce exposure to these hazards. For example, the community must show, usually through a building permit system and subdivision regulations, that in locating, designing, and constructing new structures, flood hazards will be recognized and minimized.

In 1972 and 1973 major floods struck Rapid City, South Dakota, and a large portion of Pennsylvania. Unfortunately, only a small fraction of the loss was covered by flood insurance. In order to induce more communities and more persons to participate, Congress made the program compulsory under certain conditions.

An attempt was first made to provide coverage in more communities. Until 1977 communities with one or more special flood-prone areas had to participate in the flood insurance program or be denied financial assistance from any federal officer or agency or federally regulated financial institution on any acquisition or construction in those areas. In 1977 the program was amended to permit federally regulated financial institutions (but not federal officers or agencies including VA and FHA loans) to make such loans in nonparticipating communities. The lender, however, must explain (1) the flood loss potential to persons purchasing such property and (2) their ineligibility for any disaster relief on the property for a future flood. The law was also amended to permit federal officers or agents to grant federal assistance in those communities if there is a nonflood-related natural disaster. Second, to encourage property owners in participating communities to purchase flood insurance, no federal officer, agency, or federally regulated or insured financial institution can approve financial assistance for acquiring or constructing property in flood areas if the property is not insured.

The purchase of flood insurance is also encouraged by a provision that one year following the date the flood insurance becomes available in any community, property owners will not be eligible for any federal disaster assistance on losses they could have insured. The HUD Secretary, however, can excuse low-income persons from this provision.

The program now covers losses resulting from the inundation of normally dry land areas from (1) overflow of inland or tidal water, (2) the unusual and rapid accumulation or runoff of surface waters from any source, (3) mudslides that are caused by accumulations of water on or under the ground, and (4) erosion losses caused by abnormal water levels. The program originally covered only the first two categories.

Almost any structure and its contents can be insured. Originally the coverage was limited to family dwellings and buildings occupied by small businesses.

Maximum coverage and rates depend on whether the community qualifies for the regular flood insurance program or the so-called emergency program. Only communities for which the Federal Insurance Administration has determined actuarially adequate premium rates are eligible for the regular program.

People who live in communities for which the FIA has not determined actuarial rates but which have adequate land-use and control measures can obtain insurance under an emergency program. The insurance, however, is limited to the amounts for which subsidized protection is available. Moreover, new construction in special flood hazard areas cannot be insured at all.

The National Flood Insurance Program had over 1.8 million policyholders in approximately 20,000 communities at the middle of 1980. Total insurance in force was then $80 billion.

Federal Crime Insurance

Federal crime insurance is sold only in states where the administering agency, again the Federal Insurance Administration, finds that crime insurance is not sufficiently available at affordable rates. Private insurers market and service this insurance, but the federal government underwrites the exposure.

The same Housing and Urban Development Act of 1968 that established the federal riot reinsurance and flood insurance programs directed the Federal Insurance Administration to prepare a report on the availability of crime insurance and, if the findings were unsatisfactory, to suggest how this insurance might be made more generally available. To make crime insurance available in many areas at affordable rates, the FIA concluded that either (1) the government would have to establish a subsidized program or (2) one set of insureds would have to subsidize another set. The FIA favored the first alternative—subsidized programs established by each state. Instead, Title VI of the Housing and Urban Development Act of 1970 gave the states a few months to develop programs that would have made federal action unnecessary. Only New Jersey, Michigan, and California had acted by the August 1, 1971, deadline. After that date the FIA was authorized to provide crime insurance directly in areas where residents and businesses were having difficulty obtaining affordable crime insurance from other sources including a state program where one existed. The decision to sell directly through a federal agency a form of property insurance that is generally available from private sources was precedent breaking.

The concept of an "affordable" rate was also new. If this concept were interpreted literally, the test would be whether everyone who wanted crime insurance could obtain it at a price they could "afford" to pay. What they could afford to pay would depend upon their income, net assets, and the other demands on their income and assets. The affordable rates would probably be substantially less than the actuarial cost of providing the benefits. Determining affordable rates under this interpretation would be extremely complex and highly subjective. It might involve a determination that a family or business could afford to pay the actuarial value of crime insurance if they spend less on some "less important" item such as a vacation or new desks. Instead, the law defines an affordable rate as the rate the HUD Secretary determines would permit a reasonably prudent person in similar circumstances to purchase protection with due regard to the costs and benefits involved.[46] In another section, the law states that rates are not affordable if the insurance is available only at a prohibitive cost. Finally, in establishing affordable rates the law directs the Secretary to consult with appropriate state authorities and other knowledgeable persons and authorizes consideration of the following factors:

(1) nature and likelihood of the peril involved,
(2) protective devices employed,
(3) anticipated losses,
(4) prevailing rates for similar private insurance,
(5) economic importance of the particular coverage,
(6) type of property involved, and
(7) the "relative abilities of the particular classes and types of insureds to pay the full estimated costs of such coverages."

In other words, ability to pay is to be considered in determining affordable rates, but so is the cost of providing the protection. Furthermore, in determining ability to pay, the standard is that of a reasonably prudent person.

Program Details By mid-1980, persons living in twenty-five states, Puerto Rico, and the District of Columbia were eligible for the federal program. To determine whether crime insurance is available at affordable rates, the FIA has had to establish such rates. For businesses, the FIA calculates the rate a medium-sized business with about $100,000 in gross receipts and located in an average crime area would have to pay to produce the same total premium dollars nationally as the rates private insurers charge businesses with these characteristics. Using this rate as a base, the FIA then prepares a rate structure that varies the rates among businesses according to their type, gross receipts, and location (classified as a low, average, or high crime area). In establishing these rates, the FIA considers what a reasonably prudent person would be willing to pay for the policy, given some understanding of the cost of providing the policy benefits. By establishing lower rates for businesses with lower gross receipts, the FIA acknowledged a lesser ability to pay by small businesses. For some insureds these rates are lower than those charged by private insurers, and for other insureds they are higher.

In the states judged to have a problem with the availability of crime insurance, property owners can obtain an application for this insurance from any insurance agent or broker in the state or from the servicing company, almost always a private insurer. The FIA selects the servicing company through a competitive bidding procedure. Producers and the servicing company receive fees for their services.

No person is denied crime insurance or canceled because of loss frequency or amount. All insureds are required to protect their premises by means that are more demanding than those imposed by most private insurers. For example, for a residential property to be eligible for crime insurance, its exterior doors, other than sliding doors, must be equipped with either a dead bolt or a self-locking deadlatch. All sliding doors and windows opening onto stairways, porches, platforms, or similar areas must also be equipped with some type of locking device. For a business property to qualify, its doorways and accessible openings must be adequately protected during nonbusiness hours. The exact requirements, which are too extensive to detail here, vary according to the type of business.

The FIA believes the program should eventually be self-supporting, but Congress has agreed to subsidize the National Insurance Development Fund if the program's losses and expenses exceed the premiums. In fact, it was recently reported that between $90 million and $100 million has been "drawn down" from the National Insurance Development Fund since 1968 to pay net crime insurance losses.[47]

The act specifically exempts the crime insurance program from any form of federal or state regulation or taxation. The exemption applies to the private agents, brokers, and insurers servicing the program as well as to the federal agency itself. The act thus removed from state regulation some operations of private insurers and their representatives.

CONCLUSION

This chapter has dealt with two important aspects of public policy toward insurance—regulation and government insurance activities. While the processes are evolving continuously, the fundamental purposes of insurance regulation are relatively constant. The ongoing debate of whether a state, federal, or dual regulatory system can best achieve these purposes currently seems to be increasing in intensity.

As a "business affected with a public interest," the insurance industry probably is regulated more extensively than many other businesses. At the extreme, regulation may involve governmental units preempting private insurers. Government insurance can take many forms, ranging from government-owned corporations to government-mandated coverages provided through private insurers.

Three important government insurance programs were described in detail in this chapter. One plan of particular interest introduces the concept that the government should provide insurance at subsidized prices if coverage is not available from private insurers at rates defined by a government agency to be "affordable." It remains to be seen whether affordability will become the euphemism for government-mandated socialization of loss costs with the concomitant shift from individual price equity to publicly defined benefit adequacy. Private insurers have a high public responsibility to provide coverage efficiently in as many markets as possible. Recent history indicates that government intervention quickly fills insurance needs that are not effectively satisfied by private insurers.

Chapter Notes

1. German Alliance Insurance Co. v. Lewis, 233 U.S. 389 (1914).
2. Quotation from "Poll: Owners Want Competition Curbs," *The National Underwriter*, 23 July 1977, pp. 1, 28. The Insurance Information Institute is a public relations organization of the property-liability insurance industry.
3. Martin Zuger, "What Is the Public *Really* Telling Us?" *The Journal of Insurance*, May/June 1980, p. 35.
4. This section draws heavily upon Spencer L. Kimball, "The Regulation of Insurance," a paper reproduced in S. L. Kimball and H. S. Denenberg, eds., *Insurance, Government, and Social Policy* (Homewood, IL: Richard D. Irwin, 1969), pp. 3-16.
5. Richard E. Stewart, "Ritual and Reality in Insurance Regulation," an address reproduced in Kimball and Denenberg, p. 24.
6. Stewart, "Ritual and Reality...," pp. 25-26.
7. Stewart, "Ritual and Reality...," p. 26.
8. Stewart, "Ritual and Reality...," p. 30.
9. Richard E. Stewart, "The Social Responsibility of Insurance Regulation," an address reproduced in Kimball and Denenberg, p. 35.
10. 75 U.S. (8 Wall.) 168 (1869).
11. Glendon E. Johnson, "The Direct and Indirect Effect of Federal Programs and Regulations on Insurance Operations and Markets," in Kimball and Denenberg, p. 367.
12. Johnson, pp. 367-368.
13. C. A. Williams, Jr., and R. M. Heins, *Risk Management and Insurance*, 4th ed. (New York: McGraw-Hill Book Company, 1981), p. 678.
14. Johnson, "The Direct and Indirect Effects of Federal Programs and Regulations..." in Kimball and Denenberg, pp. 368-369.
15. U.S. v. South-Eastern Underwriters Association, 322 U.S. 533 (1944), rehearing denied, 323 U.S. 811 (1944).
16. 15 U.S.C. secs. 1011 et seq.
17. In one leading case, Investors Diversified Services was required by a consent decree to tell all loan applicants that they can choose any agent or insurer meeting reasonable standards. U.S. v. Investors Diversified Services, 102 F. Supp. 645 (1951).
18. The leading cases are United States v. Insurance Board of Cleveland, 144 F. Supp. 684 (1955); 188 F. Supp. 949 (1960) and United States v. New Orleans Insurance Exchange, 148 F. Supp. 915 (1957), affirmed, per curiam, 355 U.S. 22 (1957).
19. FTC v. National Casualty Co. and FTC v. American Hospital and Life Insurance Company, 357 U.S. 560 (1958).
20. Travelers Health Association v. FTC, 298 F. 2d 820 (8th Cir., 1962).

21. S.E.C. v. Variable Annuity Life Insurance Co. of America et al., 359 U.S. 65 (1959).

22. U.S. v. Chicago Title and Trust Co. et al., 242 F. Supp. 56 (N.D. Ill., 1965).

23. Some other states such as Idaho and Montana adopted open-competition laws applicable to some property and liability insurance lines and more restrictive laws for other lines.

24. "Report of Rates and Rating Organizations Subcommittee (F1), *Proceedings of the National Association of Insurance Commissioners*, Vol. 1, 1969.

25. Spencer L. Kimball, "The Case for State Regulation of Insurance" in Kimball and Denenberg, p. 420.

26. This section on product regulation relies heavily on two articles by Spencer L. Kimball and Werner Pfennigstorf. The first is "Legislative and Judicial Control of the Terms of Insurance Contracts: A Comparative Study of American and European Practice," *Indiana Law Journal*, Vol. 39, No. 4 (Summer 1964), pp. 675-731. The second is "Administrative Control of the Terms of Insurance Contracts: A Comparative Study," *Indiana Law Journal*, Vol. 40, No. 2 (Winter 1965), pp. 143-231.

27. Kimball and Pfennigstorf, "Legislative and Judicial Control. . .," p. 677.

28. For a more complete discussion see Thomas L. Wenck, "The Historical Development of Standard Policies," *Journal of Risk and Insurance*, Vol. 35, No. 4 (December 1968), pp. 537-550.

29. Presidential Address of F. W. Potter, *Proceedings of the National Convention of Insurance Commissioners*, Vol. 1, 1914, p. 14.

30. Kimball and Pfennigstorf, "Legislative and Judicial Control. . .," p. 684, ftn. 25.

31. Kimball and Pfennigstorf, "Administrative Control. . .," p. 157.

32. Kimball and Pfennigstorf, "Administrative Control. . .," pp. 158-167.

33. The statutory fire policy does not explicitly exclude fires intentionally set by the insured. To require insurers to pay such claims is so contrary to public policy that no insured could expect to recover such losses.

34. Cormick L. Breslin and Terrie E. Troxel, *Property-Liability Insurance Accounting and Finance*, (Malvern, PA: American Institute for Property and Liability Underwriters, Inc., 1978), p. 281.

35. J. D. Hammond, Arnold F. Shapiro, and N. Shilling, *The Regulation of Insurer Solidity Through Capital and Surplus Requirements*, Summary Report NSF Grant APR75-16550 (University Park, PA: The Pennsylvania State University, April 1978).

36. Educational Testing Service is a nonprofit organization devoted to measurement and research in education.

37. Harold C. Krogh, "The Securities Investor Protection Corporation: Financial Stringency in Securities Firms," *CPCU Annals*, Vol. 30, No. 1 (March 1977), pp. 78-85.

38. The benefits may exceed the contributions in their actuarial value if Congress improves the benefits or if consumer prices rise rapidly enough to produce sizable benefit increases.

39. Nevada, North Dakota, Ohio, Washington, West Virginia, and Wyoming.

40. Arizona, California, Colorado, Idaho, Maryland, Michigan, Montana, New York, Oklahoma, Oregon, Pennsylvania, and Utah.

41. Rhode Island; California, New Jersey, and New York; and Hawaii.

42. The joint export credit insurance operation of the Foreign Credit Insurance Association and the Export-Import Bank is a possible exception, but only Eximbank writes the portion of the exposure that is not commercially insurable. A clearer exception is the involvement of private United States insurers and Lloyd's of London in the operations of the Overseas Private Investor Corporation.

43. This section relies heavily upon the discussion in R. Riegel, J. S. Miller, and C. A. Williams, Jr., *Insurance Principles and Practices: Property and Liability* (Englewood Cliffs, NJ: Prentice-Hall, Inc., 1976), Chapter 23.

44. J. R. Lewis, "A Critical Review of the Federal Riot Reinsurance System," *Journal of Risk and Insurance*, Vol. 38, No. 1 (March 1971), pp. 29-42.

45. Insurance Executives Association, *Report on Floods and Flood Damage*, p. 15.

46. *United States Statutes at Large*, 1970-71, Part 2, pp. 1788-1790.

47. "View on Crime, Riot Cover Sought," *The National Underwriter, Property and Casualty Insurance Edition*, 6 March 1981, p. 1.

Index

I

M